M000251662

Mike Gould and Marilyn Rankin

Cambridge International AS and A Level
English Language

CAMBRIDGE
UNIVERSITY PRESS

CAMBRIDGE
UNIVERSITY PRESS

University Printing House, Cambridge CB2 8BS, United Kingdom

Cambridge University Press is part of the University of Cambridge.

It furthers the University's mission by disseminating knowledge in the pursuit of education, learning and research at the highest international levels of excellence.

Information on this title: education.cambridge.org

© Cambridge University Press 2014

First published 2014
3rd printing 2015

Typeset and project managed by Cambridge Publishing Management Limited

Printed by Multivista Global Ltd, India

A catalogue record for this publication is available from the British Library

ISBN 978-1-107-66227-8 Paperback

Additional resources for this publication at www.cambridge.org

Contents

Unit 5: Spoken language and social groups

Unit 6: English as a global language

Unit 7: Child language acquisition

Part 2: Practice and self-evaluation

Introduction

The core aim of this book is to help you to develop and apply the key skills in reading and writing you need to succeed in your AS and A level English Language course; it is particularly designed for those working towards the Cambridge International Examinations syllabus 9093. The book covers a wide range of reading skills, such as decoding questions, drawing out important words and phrases, and understanding aspects of style, voice and tone. It addresses the conventions of certain kinds of written and spoken language, from scripted speeches to travel articles, from memoirs to letters, and looks at how you can capture these conventions and writers' techniques in your own work. In writing, you will learn how to plan and structure shorter and extended responses, either for specified audiences or for a more general readership. You will learn how to adapt content from one text for a new purpose or context, and to write with originality and flair where appropriate. Most importantly, you will read model or sample responses which will help you evaluate your own work.

The **AS Level section** of the book is divided into three units:

- In **Unit 1** you will focus on responding to non-fiction texts as a reader, developing skills such as locating evidence and developing commentary. In particular, you will look at personal, descriptive and persuasive writing.
- In **Unit 2** the focus shifts to writing non-fiction with a strong emphasis on planning responses and on the range of text types you will need to master, for example letters, diaries, promotional texts, biography and character portraits.
- In **Unit 3** you will focus on imaginative writing with attention given to key areas such as characterisation, voice, setting, symbols, imagery and related linguistic techniques.

The **A Level section** of the book builds on the reading and writing skills you have learned at AS Level and applies them to significant areas of English language study.

The features of spoken language underpin much of the A Level course and you will focus on the conventions we use in our discourse with others. You will link these spoken language studies to an examination of the historical and cultural influences which have influenced the style of spoken and written English and which continue to do so today. You will find out about the variations of English along with people's attitudes to how the language is used, for example in relation to gender differences and political correctness. You will examine the many different varieties of English as a global language and, in the final unit, learn about the processes and theories of child language acquisition.

These are all very broad topics which lend themselves to further research beyond the core material covered in this book. You will therefore have many opportunities to research information as it applies to your own region.

A Level studies require extended essay writing using informed, clearly validated viewpoints and case studies. You will find examples and commentaries to help you develop an analytical framework.

There are a number of features in the book to help you in your study:

LINK – This suggests related sections or pages from the book which will help you make connections between skills or texts.

LINK

There is a follow-up task in the section on **Planning directed writing responses** on page 71.

TIP – This provides focused advice to help your study and revision.

TIP

An unusual or older character – often a relative – can be represented in memoirs or autobiographies by the writer creating a sense of mystery and offering no real **narrative**.

KEY TERMS – This defines important words that you need to understand or use in your studies.

KEY TERMS

assert state something as a fact with no real support or proof

FURTHER RESEARCH/READING – These suggest additional guidance or supporting material that can be accessed elsewhere, for example on the web.

FURTHER RESEARCH

You can usefully practise your understanding of *audience* by looking at four or five types of magazine (either online or in a shop) and trying to work out what their target readership is.

FURTHER READING

For more examples of war diaries visit **http://www.firstworldwar. com/diaries/index.htm**

Throughout the book, you will be given the chance to build and develop skills in small steps or stages, as well as writing extended, full responses to examination-style tasks and questions. Many of the texts you will encounter are challenging, but they come from a wide range of cultures, contexts and times. All have been included to engage and enrich your reading and writing experience and we hope that you will take the chance to explore some of them more fully.

In conclusion, we believe this book will provide a rich, enjoyable and useful course of study that will enable you to succeed in AS and A Level English Language.

Mike Gould
Marilyn Rankin

Part 1:
AS Level

Unit 1: Reading non-fiction

Reading is a core skill which underpins both AS and A2 English Language. It helps you to understand a range of different types of writing and also helps you to shape your own written responses in the light of the effects and techniques that you encounter.

In this unit you will explore different forms and genres of non-fiction writing. You will have opportunities to:

- analyse and interpret texts in a range of ways
- explore the techniques writers use and the effects they create
- plan and develop the skills needed to write your own extended commentaries on language and style
- link what you have learned to the requirements of the 'Writing non-fiction' aspect of the course.

READING AND WRITING SKILLS
Types of question, language and style

In this section you will:

- consider what *non-fiction* is and the sorts of texts you might encounter
- look at a range of commentary-style questions
- explore what *language* and *style* are.

What is non-fiction?

When we talk about non-fiction, we generally mean writing which is rooted in real experiences and which draws on factual information for its core content. Fiction generally refers to writing that is largely imaginative or invented. Yet non-fiction writing can share many of the same features as fiction writing, for example a description of a real-life trip to a vibrant city might share many of the same vivid style features as the depiction of an imagined city in a novel.

However, most of the extracts you are likely to encounter for examination would be largely categorised as 'non-fiction' though they will be drawn from a wide range of sources.

LINK

The techniques, effects and forms of writing you will meet in this unit will inform and help you with your own writing in **Unit 2: Writing non-fiction**.

TIP

Look for the common features that fiction and non-fiction writing share; the division between them may be less wide than you think.

ACTIVITY 1.1

With a partner, look at the diagram opposite.

1 Which of these would you generally consider to be 'non-fiction' – that is, largely based on real-life events, people or places?

2 Which of the non-fiction texts you have identified do you think would be *closest* in style to fictional writing? Why?

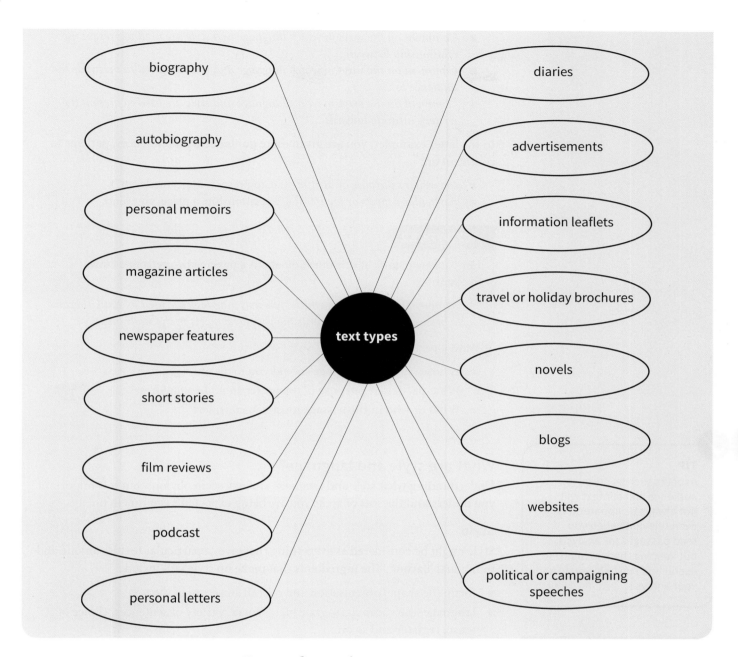

Types of question

This section of the book deals mainly with your understanding of and commentary on non-fiction passages you read, but bear in mind that what you take from these passages will also inform your 'Directed writing' tasks. More importantly, though, you need to understand what it is you are being asked to do.

Passage-based questions may ask you to:

Comment on the style and language of the set extract.

In this case, the questions are fairly open and would expect you to range widely in your response, covering a number of factors.

Or these questions may go further and ask you to address your analysis towards a particular angle, for example:

- *Comment on the ways in which language and style are used to present the relationship between …*
- *Comment on the ways in which language and style are used to persuade the audience to …*
- *Comment on the ways in which language and style are used to present the writer's attitude towards …*

In the latter examples, you are given more guidance with references, perhaps to comment on:

- *the writer's purpose or attitude* (i.e. to present, to persuade, etc.)
- *particular aspects or focuses* (i.e. a relationship, a place, an event).

ACTIVITY 1.2

On your own, look at this question about a passage taken from a travel account:

Comment on the ways in which style and language are used by Paul Theroux to present his attitude towards the people he meets in the stadium.

With a partner discuss:

- **Whose** style and language should you focus on?
- **What** particular **purpose** of the writer should you address?
- **What** or **who** in the passage must you consider?

What are style and language?

Understanding what *style* and *language* are may seem obvious, but it is important you understand the sort of areas you are being expected to comment on.

Style

Style might be considered as everything that gives a particular text its unique and individual 'flavour'. The ingredients that make up style will include:

- **form:** the shape, organisation and overall structure of the text
- **language:** the vocabulary, grammar, syntax, variety of sentences, choice of tense, **register** and so on.

To understand the particular style and language of a text, or that a writer employs, it is also helpful for you to explore:

- the **purpose** of texts (which may be explicit or implied), for example to persuade, inform, or describe
- the **audience** or reader at whom the text is aimed (which can be specific or general)
- the **context** of the text, for example when, where and how it was produced.

To get yourself thinking about style and language, begin by reading these three different paragraphs from texts.

TIP

Aspects such as purpose, audience and context will not always be apparent, or even relevant, when you read passages for analysis, but keeping them in mind is useful and can help you focus your analysis.

KEY TERMS

register the type of language used for a particular purpose, or in a particular setting

context the background, setting, form or culture in which the text was written or is set

4

A   I had never felt so alone. The wide sweep of the Andes stretched in front of me, a seemingly infinite expanse of ice and rock. The air cut into my cheeks, and blinded me, as I stood unsteadily looking down on the valley below. Then, for a moment, the skies cleared above me, and I saw a single, solitary condor rise on the breeze, effortless and free. I would be that condor. I would rise above my despair.

B   Do not be put off by the noise and smell of the city as you arrive. This is one of its charms, and just part of the heady brew that makes it such a wonderful and magical place to visit. The narrow streets, the Old City with its minarets, the street-vendors who shout out their wares – these simply add to the intoxicating recipe. You will soon be hooked!

C   All I can say is that the décor was more tasteful than the food ... and more colourful. My starter was brown paté on brown toast ... the effect was, how shall I put it ... er, brown and, if it is possible for a colour to be a taste, it tasted brown, or perhaps beige, which is even less powerful. The starter's lack of taste was only beaten by the gloopy slop that came with my steak. The menu said 'Celeriac purée', my plate said, 'Wallpaper paste'.

KEY TERMS

voice the distinctive tone and perspective of the writer

tone the 'feel', mood or emotion present in a text

formality language which observes agreed conventions, which would be used in business or professional contexts, particularly in less personal contexts

informality language best suited to close or personal contexts, in which accepted rules or conventions can be adapted, abbreviated or otherwise altered, for example, in writing that sounds more like speaking

symbol a word or phrase that can represent an idea; for example, in paragraph A above the condor represents freedom

imagery language that draws on visual depictions to suggest ideas, for example, *The road through the mountains was a necklace of lights that shimmered and twinkled*

ACTIVITY 1.3

1   With a partner, talk about each text in turn. Consider:
   - the **voice** of the writer (Who is speaking? Do we know? What form of address do they use? What tense? Is the **tone** humorous, reflective, angry?)
   - the **formality** or **informality** (How 'close' to the reader is the tone? Is it chatty? Does it use speech-like language or punctuation?)
   - other language choices (e.g. use of particular vocabulary)
   - the **types or variety of sentence** used (Short? Long? Simple? Complex?)
   - **symbols** or **imagery**
   - the **order or structure** of the text (Does it matter? What can we learn from it?).

2   Share your ideas with another pair and then feed back responses to the rest of the class or group.
   - Did you find a way of describing the style and language for each of these texts?
   - Did any of the texts share similar elements of style and language? Which? How?

Summary

Remember these key points from this section:

- Questions can be general and focus broadly on style and language, or can be more specific and direct you towards key aspects.
- Understanding what style and language consist of will help you focus on the key elements you need to comment on.

Key reading skills for responding to passages

In this section you will:

- understand key success criteria for commenting on passages
- explore how to interpret selected words and phrases from texts
- evaluate commentary skills.

How to approach passage-based questions

Having a system for approaching passage-based questions is key to a successful commentary on them. But what kind of things should you do in the reading and writing stages?

Here are some key success criteria:

Do:

- read the text at least twice
- list or highlight key words and phrases from the text before you begin to write
- start your commentary with a clear, brief introduction in which you offer an overview or framework for your interpretation of, or commentary on, the set passage
- focus on what the writer **does** (the techniques he or she uses) and the **features** presented
- describe the **effects** of those techniques and features on the reader
- support what you say with well-chosen, **selective evidence** and **apt quotation**
- write in a **coherent**, **fluent** way which **links** rather than lists ideas
- keep your focus on style and language
- check your work as you write and tweak or adapt carefully to make sure your expression is succinct, yet sufficiently detailed.

Don't:

- start writing before you have read the text properly
- simply list or highlight everything in the text (!) – be selective
- **assert** an idea or opinion without supporting evidence
- simply 'feature-spot' – that is, point out a technique or a language device without explaining its effect or purpose (for example, mention that the writer has used alliteration without saying what its effect is)
- just summarise what happens or paraphrase without offering any commentary or interpretation
- list points or ideas in an unconnected way
- drift off into discussing aspects outside the question set.

KEY TERMS

assert state something as a fact with no real support or proof

Read these two short paragraphs from students' commentaries. You do not need to have read the original passage but they are based on the extract from *Shooting an Elephant* by George Orwell on page 9 of this unit.

A On the whole, this is an easy-to-read passage in which the writer uses short and long sentences to good effect. It is a direct and descriptive account of how an animal was shot. The writer lets the readers get acquainted with the scene and the atmosphere. The writer uses *if* clauses which add variety.

B Orwell gives a direct, straightforward account in broadly chronological order, establishing the setting and then the events that ensue. He demonstrates the thought-processes he went through at the time, using *if* clauses to consider the consequences of what he might do, for example, saying *If he charged, I could shoot* ... to explain how the situation would be taken out of his hands.

ACTIVITY 1.4

1 On your own, based on the relevant success criteria on page 6:
   - note down which of the success criteria are evident
   - decide which of the responses is more effective
   - decide what is wrong with, or could be improved in, the other response.
2 Once you have done this, compare your ideas with a partner.
   - Did you agree on which extract was better and why?
   - What two important things, in particular, should have been done?

Highlighting or listing key words or phrases

Passages of writing contain an enormous variety of possibilities which you can choose to comment on. In fact, you could probably comment on every single word or phrase! However, this is not practical, nor desirable. By highlighting or listing key words and phrases you will be able to interact with the text, however dense and complex it might first appear, and focus on key patterns or features that create the tone or mood.

You will be looking at how to plan and structure responses to texts later in this unit but first, read the extract below. The annotations in the first four paragraphs provide an idea of the sorts of aspects you might draw from a text.

| Short, simple sentence introduces the focus for the piece. |
| Metaphor captures the sense of mental imprisonment. |
| The writer's appetite to find out as much as he can. |

I never met my grandfather. He died nine years to the day before I was born. What I knew of him was pieced together from conversations with my grandmother...

We gathered in her garden on the day of her funeral, steeling ourselves against the encroaching sadness of final farewell. I left the stilted conversation that caged in our grief and walked through her house, drinking in every detail of a place I would never see again. I paused in front of an old cedar-wood bookcase where my grandmother had arranged her most prized photos. Amid all the weddings, Christmas dinners, birthdays, graduations, grandchildren

Withholds the name of the grandfather till the end of the sentence; he comes alive at this point, following the list of items viewed.

The repeating structure mimics the sense of the writer's eyes moving from one image to the next, as if we are seeing them too.

Long, extended noun phrase captures Bryan's charisma and achievements.

Return to the first person, *I*, relocates the text as being as much about the writer as the subject.

Final clause creates a sense of drama; suggests something mysterious or interesting is to be revealed.

8

and great-grandchildren <u>were pictures of Bryan</u>. They were sundry keepsakes of a life of staggering high achievement.

<u>Here was Bryan</u> at the foot of a satellite whose construction he oversaw, moments before a rocket launched it into outer space; <u>here he was</u> in a park in Leningrad at the height of the Cold War, the delegate representing Australia at an international space conference; here he was in Maralinga, the distinguished scientist observing the atomic-bomb tests; here he posed for his official photograph as director of Australia's Antarctic Division; and here he was looking like **Errol Flynn**[1], <u>the decorated squadron leader with moustache neatly clipped and hat rakishly angled</u>.

<u>I had never felt as remote from my grandfather as I did at that moment.</u> There were no photos of him holding a baby or laughing with his children or smiling with his bride on his wedding day. He was on his own in all of them, <u>but for one exception</u>.

The photo was smaller than the others, discreetly placed at the edge of the bookcase. It captured my grandfather later in his life standing shoulder-to-shoulder with a man of similar age and proportions, both of them dressed in dark suits and ties. A wintry background of leafless trees and cloudy sky scarcely dimmed the quiet enthusiasm each man exuded in the other's company. I picked it up in the hope that closer inspection might put a name to the man whose life was sufficiently exalted to share space with my grandfather. I took it out of the frame and flipped it around. On the back, my grandmother had scrawled a name in pencil: Hiram Cassedy.

Cassedy. The very sight of the name called forth images formed in my youth. In my mind's eye, I could see a party of emaciated castaways covered in tropical ulcers gathered on a beach, a full moon lighting up the crashing surf. A bare-chested Timorese man moves among the group clutching a fistful of Dutch guilders. A radioman, malaria-ravaged and undernourished, crouches alongside an enormous transceiver, frantically scribbling an encoded message on the back of a corn leaf. Nearby, a crucifix fashioned from palm branches tilts at an angle above a freshly dug grave. And, standing slightly apart – his face bearded and gaunt, his clothes torn and filthy – is my grandfather. In one hand, he clasps a letter sent from the Japanese Army demanding surrender; in the other, he holds a torch. Later that night, my grandfather would meet Hiram Cassedy, the lynchpin in an event that most believed defined my grandfather's life and some thought ended it prematurely.

The photo I held was taken years later, on the occasion of his second encounter with Cassedy. It was a rare souvenir honouring a rescue mission of such implausibility that the Allies covered it up in the hope of using it again. When the press eventually reported the event, the story was lost in a war filled with like tales of bravery, heroism and despair.

I placed the photo back in its frame and drew it close. The key to understanding my grandfather lay at the heart of this photo and in understanding the event it commemorated. I placed it back on the bookcase and returned to my grieving family. That was when I decided to go to Timor.

From *Rescue at 21.00 Hours* by Tom Trumble.

[1] **Errol Flynn** swashbuckling actor from the 1930s to 1950s

TIP
It is vital that you refer to the **effect** of particular language features, devices or patterns when you comment on a text otherwise your comments will reveal little of the mood or tone.

ACTIVITY 1.5

1 Basing your answer solely on the annotations to the text, what do you feel you have learned about the writer and his style and language?

With a partner, discuss how useful the annotations were.

juxtapose to place ideas or words/phrases in close proximity to each other to convey an idea, or to balance contrasting points

figurative language language such as imagery, in which the literal meaning is less relevant than what the word/phrase suggests or symbolises. For example, *My heart was stone* does not mean that the writer's heart was literally made of stone, but perhaps that it was unfeeling

TIP

Being aware of things to avoid can be as useful as remembering what you should do when answering passage-based questions.

2 Now have a go yourself. Read the extract again including the second, unannotated part. Using the **first four paragraphs as a model**, list key words or phrases that stand out to you.

These might include any of the following:

- particularly vivid descriptions (perhaps adjectives and nouns)
- repetitions of words/phrases or patterns of language
- groups of similar or related words
- contrasting or juxtaposed ideas or phrases
- imagery, symbols or other forms of figurative language
- changes in tone or focus.

3 Once you have done this, choose one or two of these aspects and make your own notes about what they reveal about the writer and his tone. Make sure you are able to:

- relate what you say to the words or phrases you have listed
- refer to the **effect** of these words or phrases on the reader and the mood conveyed.

Evaluating commentary skills

What makes a good commentary? While no two commentaries on a text should be the same and while each should reflect the student's own interpretation and 'take' on the text, there are key skills that everyone should apply, as indicated by the success criteria on page 6.

Now read this task and the passage that follows it:

1 *The passage below describes the writer's experience in Burma when he was serving as a police officer at a time when the British ruled the country. He has been ordered to deal with a possible threat posed by an elephant.*
(a) Comment on the style and language of the passage.

Cambridge International AS and A Level English Language 8693 Paper 1 (May/June 2009), Q1a.

But I did not want to shoot the elephant. I watched him beating his bunch of grass against his knees, with that preoccupied grandmotherly air that elephants have. It seemed to me that it would be murder to shoot him. At that age I was not squeamish about killing animals, but I had never shot an elephant and never wanted to. (Somehow it always seems worse to kill a large animal). Besides, there was the beast's owner to be considered. Alive, the elephant was worth at least a hundred pounds; dead, he would only be worth the value of his tusks, five pounds, possibly. But I had got to act quickly. I turned to some experienced-looking Burmans who had been there when we arrived, and asked them how the elephant had been behaving. They all said the same thing: he took no notice of you if you left him alone, but he might charge if you went too close to him.

It was perfectly clear to me what I ought to do. I ought to walk up to within, say, twenty-five yards of the elephant and test his behaviour. If he charged, I could shoot; if he took no notice of me, it would be safe to leave him until the **mahout**[1] came back. But also I knew that I was going to do no such thing. I was a poor shot with a rifle and the ground was soft mud into which one would sink at every step. If the elephant charged and I missed him, I should have about as much chance as a toad under a steam-roller.

There was only one alternative. I shoved the cartridges into the magazine and lay down on the road to get a better aim. The crowd grew very still, and a deep, low, happy sigh, as of people who see the theatre curtain go up at last, breathed from innumerable throats. They were going to have their bit of fun after all. The rifle was a beautiful German thing with cross-hair sights. I did not then know that in shooting an elephant one would shoot to cut an imaginary bar running from ear-hole to ear-hole. I ought, therefore, as the elephant was sideways on, to have aimed straight at his ear-hole; actually I aimed several inches in front of this, thinking the brain would be further forward.

When I pulled the trigger I did not hear the bang or feel the kick – one never does when a shot goes home – but I heard the devilish roar of glee that went up from the crowd. In that instant, in too short a time, one would have thought, even for the bullet to get there, a mysterious, terrible change had come over the elephant. He neither stirred nor fell, but every line of his body had altered. He looked suddenly stricken, shrunken, immensely old, as though the frightful impact of the bullet had paralysed him without knocking him down. At last, after what seemed a long time – it might have been five seconds, I dare say – he sagged flabbily to his knees. His mouth slobbered. An enormous senility seemed to have settled upon him. One could have imagined him thousands of years old. I fired again into the same spot. At the second shot he did not collapse but climbed with desperate slowness to his feet and stood weakly upright, with legs sagging and head drooping. I fired a third time. That was the shot that did for him. You could see the agony of it jolt his whole body and knock the last remnant of strength from his legs. But in falling he seemed for a moment to rise, for as his hind legs collapsed beneath him he seemed to tower upward like a huge rock toppling, his trunk reaching skyward like a tree. He trumpeted, for the first and only time. And then down he came, his belly towards me, with a crash that seemed to shake the ground even where I lay.

I got up. The Burmans were already racing past me across the mud. It was obvious that the elephant would never rise again, but he was not dead. He was breathing very rhythmically with long rattling gasps, his great mound of a side painfully rising and falling. His mouth was wide open – I could see far down into caverns of pale pink throat. I waited a long time for him to die, but his breathing did not weaken. Finally I fired my two remaining shots into the spot where I thought his heart must be. The thick blood welled out of him like red velvet, but still he did not die. His body did not even jerk when the shots hit him, the tortured breathing continued without a pause. He was dying, very slowly and in great agony, but in some world remote from me where not even a bullet could damage him further. I felt that I had got to put an end to that dreadful noise. It seemed dreadful to see the great beast lying there, powerless to move and yet powerless to die, and not even to be able to finish him. I sent back for my small rifle and poured shot after shot into his heart and down his throat. They seemed to make no impression. The tortured gasps continued as steadily as the ticking of a clock.

In the end I could not stand it any longer and went away.

From *Shooting an Elephant* by George Orwell.

¹ **mahout** an elephant owner or keeper

ACTIVITY 1.6

1 Discuss with a partner:
- What happens in the passage?
- What do you find particularly effective or striking about the account?
- What kinds of things might you write about if commenting on the style and language?

2 Now read this sample response to the task. As you read it, consider to what extent it meets the success criteria for such a response.

This doesn't really tell us anything other than what the passage is about.

There is no comment on how this is done, and whilst true, does not really offer any overall comment on style or language.

This is an assertion – where is the evidence? A quotation?

SAMPLE RESPONSE

This is an easy-to-read passage in which the writer describes how an animal was shot. The writer lets the readers get acquainted with the scene and the atmosphere. Shooting the elephant was like something he was forced to do. He thought it would be like doing murder to kill the elephant itself. As the passage goes on he begins to care less. His first feelings go away and his worry about killing the animal goes away. He was now obsessed with getting the animal to die. He is confused about what he should do and the elephant could be a possible threat. The police officer was still not that old and unsure what kind of things he should do at this point. He is over-reacting and behaving in a not very good way for a police officer.

The writer uses **stream of consciousness** to describe a memory as seen through a first person view. This can be seen in the way in which the word *I* is used several times in the opening sentences. The writer uses various literary devices and metaphorical tools. For example, in the first paragraph, the author uses a **metaphor** in comparing the elephant to someone with a *grandmotherly air*. The **alliteration** of *beating his bunch* creates the harsh mood at the start and there is a sense of the same idea in the way that the author uses the repetition of *never* and *never* in order to show his state of mind.

The almost **anaphoric** contrast between *alive* and *dead* stands out to also show the way the officer was thinking. He is unsure about killing the animal and uses parenthesis around a sentence to show his inner thought. There are also simple sentences which show his inner thoughts and these are placed alongside longer complex sentences which show the action going on outside his stream of consciousness. The punctuation also adds to the dramatic effect. Commas come after certain words to create tension and suspense: *killing animals, but … Besides, there … Alive, dead, …*

The point of view of the passage is **first person** and we see things through the eyes of the writer. The diary dictated style gives an insight into the police officer's thoughts. Yet there are also outside sources, which give another perspective to the first-person point of view. There were *experienced-looking Burmans* and also there was *the beast's owner to be considered*. Besides that there was the excited crowd. While the police officer's thoughts come first, an atmosphere is created by inserting other people's actions and position.

Throughout the passage the author uses many metaphors and **similes** to good effect. The figurative language gives a more entertaining feel to the passage and helps the reader participate as if one is actually witnessing the events as they happen. The reader is fascinated as they hear the *happy sigh* and witness the blood that flowed in the simile *like red velvet*. The passage contains many such descriptive details, which help bring the story to life. The reader can visualise the agony the elephant went through and the excitement of the rather bored and aggressive crowd. With the use of many similes, it implies that the officer feels guilt.

🔑 KEY TERMS

stream of consciousness how words reflect the way in which a narrator's or speaker's mind is actually working at a given point

metaphor a direct comparison between two things which is not literally true

alliteration the repetition of the same sounds or of the same kinds of sounds at the beginning of words

anaphoric a reference which depends on, or connects back to, a previous, related word or phrase

first person the mode of narration in which the writer uses the *I* form.

simile a comparison between two things which uses *like* or *as*

ACTIVITY 1.7

Discuss with a partner:

- What works well and what doesn't work in this response?
- Which success criteria have *not* been met?
- What single thing do you feel would most have improved the response?

LINK

See page 17 of this unit for more about how to use the **point/quotation/comment** technique.

TIP

Get into the habit of regularly selecting articles or reports from reputable publications and reading them with an 'exam head' on – in other words, analysing them for style and language as much as for what they have to say.

It is important to support your points with evidence and then provide some sort of comment or further explanation of the point you have made. You will learn more about how to use this technique in a later section of this unit. As a first practice of this skill, write one or two sentences about the passage with one aspect of the style mentioned here – the use of **metaphor** to describe the elephant.

Try to:

- say something about what the use of *grandmotherly* conveys about the writer's feelings towards the elephant
- link this with any other way in which the elephant is described later in the passage.

The writer's use of a metaphor to describe the way the elephant behaves with a 'grandmotherly air' suggests that …

Summary

Remember these key points from this section:

- Non-fiction writing shares many similarities with fiction writing.
- The reading and analysis skills you develop for commentary will help your own writing.
- Highlighting, listing or annotating key words and phrases in a text is an essential part of commentary.
- The best responses to texts always support the points made with apt, direct quotations.
- These should always be explained in terms of their effect on tone, mood or the perspective of the writer.

Planning and structuring a commentary

In this section, you will:

- learn how to read and plan your response
- select key words to help shape your introduction and response
- learn how different introductions can focus on different elements in the text.

It is important to have a mental or actual plan of how your commentary will be organised. Without it, you may spend too long on one aspect and not enough on another.

A process for response

In order to respond to a passage effectively, you should follow this guidance.

1 Read the passage closely **at least twice**.
  Why? The first reading should be to get the overall sense of the passage, what happens and how it all fits together. The second will allow you to focus on the way the passage works, the specific language style and the mood created.

2 **Divide the passage into equal sections**. This can be done quite easily if the paragraphs are of regular and fairly equal length. If they are not of equal length, then divide the passage into roughly equal sections based on dividing the number of lines into, say, four parts.
  Why? In this way, you will give equal attention to the different sections.

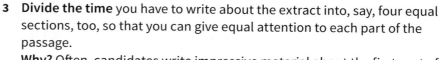

3   **Divide the time** you have to write about the extract into, say, four equal sections, too, so that you can give equal attention to each part of the passage.
     Why? Often, candidates write impressive material about the first part of an extract but you need to ensure that you deal with **all** the passage – especially the conclusion – in the same depth.

4   **Make a list of key words and phrases** (no longer than six or seven words).
     Why? You cannot write about everything, but you do need some particularly powerful, vivid or meaningful words or phrases to hang your key ideas around. You may wish to colour-code words and phrases which seem to be related to each other.

5   **Plan your response**.
     Why? Even if you do not have time to write out a plan, mentally you need to consider the structure of your response. You have a list of key words/phrases and you have divided up the passage, but you also need to consider your own writing. You can, of course, write one paragraph on point of view, one on the use of imagery to convey the setting, etc. However it is probably better to plan to show the **progression of the passage**. This is the way it **develops** and **unfolds** and this approach allows you to:

     ■ comment on similarities and contrasts within the passage
     ■ show how attitudes develop or change
     ■ explain how focuses shift from one thing, person or place to another.

13

TIP
Remember that you are not expected to comment on everything!

KEY TERMS

mood atmosphere, feeling

perspective the viewpoint or 'angle' the writer has on a situation, person or experience

voice the individual or specific tone or perspective of a writer

What kind of words or phrases should you list?

You should make a list of words or phrases that:

■ suggest a particular **mood** or attitude of the writer at that point in the passage
■ seem to suggest certain qualities or ideas
■ seem to echo others in the extract
■ seem to contrast with others in the extract
■ you can use for your introduction.

How should you use the words and phrases you have listed?

Focus on the following four ideas:

■ what **voice** or **perspective** is exemplified through these selected words?
■ what is the passage or writer implying or what kind of message is being given?
■ what relationships and/or social positions in the passage are presented and how do they change or develop, if at all?
■ what **contexts** are shown? Are they, for example, cultural, social, economic, geographical or historical?

Sometimes all four of these ideas might apply, sometimes two or just one. You should prioritise them according to the passage. These ideas will form the basis for your introduction/overview and the framework for your analysis as a whole.

Imagine you have been given the following task and need to plan your response. For the purposes of this practice, you have 45 minutes for the plan and the writing. You are **not** going to write the commentary, this is about how you would approach it.

Comment on the ways in which language and style are used in the following extract to persuade readers to visit Kenya.

Remember, you will need to follow this process:

- Read the extract twice.
- Divide the passage into equal sections – perhaps three or four.
- Divide the time you have equally (so, perhaps 12–15 minutes on each part).
- List your key words or phrases.
- Colour-code or link any of these according to contrast/similarity/use, etc.
- Decide how you will approach your response. (Will you write one paragraph on your first section?)

ACTIVITY 1.8

This is the first part of the process. Read the following text twice. It is an extract from a website advertising a destination in Africa. Then complete the rest of the planning process – the other stages in the list.

When you have finished reading and planning, evaluate how well you dealt with the task.

- Did you do all the parts of the process that were recommended?
- Were you able to select enough key words and phrases?
- Would your planning make you feel confident enough to answer the set task? If not, what do you need to do better?

The coastline south of Mombassa is a tropical paradise of palm fringed white sand beaches, where the turquoise waters of the Indian Ocean meet beautiful coral reefs. The protective reefs have created ideal beaches with calm, inviting waters.

Days are filled with sunshine and nights are balmy and warm with gentle sea breezes. The offshore reefs are alive with coral, myriad fish, sea turtles and dolphins. Both outer and inner reef walls offer world class diving with spectacular coral gardens and drop offs. At Kisite-Mpunguti, a Marine Reserve has been established around beautiful Wasini Island, an ideal day trip for divers and snorkellers.

The beaches are bordered by lush green coastal rainforests with prolific birdlife and variety of wildlife including baboons, rare colobus monkeys and even leopard. A wide range of World Class resorts, centred around Diani Beach, allow visitors to relax and enjoy this natural paradise with the best standards of accommodation, service and cuisine.

The south coast also has many smaller quiet getaways such as Tiwi Beach, ideal for travellers looking for a low key break. Inland, the fertile hinterland of Kwale District consists of small villages inhabited by the Wakamba, Digo and Duruma tribes.

Further south, the small fishing village of Shimoni is home to a series of deep, mysterious coastal caves that stretch from the sea to deep into the jungles. Historically, these caves were long used as a refuge for Dhow Sailors and explorers. Shimoni is also an excellent base for big game fishing in the waters of the Pemba Channel.

Whether you are looking for a base to actively explore this fascinating region, or just somewhere to unwind and find peace, Kenya's south coast has everything you could wish for.

Kenya Tourist Board

Further practice

If you wish to, write the commentary based on the process you completed. Alternatively, come back to the passage after you have worked on the skills in the rest of this section.

Introductions to commentaries

Now that you have considered how to plan for your commentary, it is time to deal with a commentary itself.

Your response should begin with a **brief introduction** to the passage so that an overview or framework is established. It is the framework outlined in this introduction which shapes the analysis of the piece. The words and phrases you select when planning will help shape your overall interpretation of the passage and can help shape your introduction.

Read this new introduction to the commentary based on the Orwell passage on page 9.

COMMENTARY

The writer gives a direct, straightforward account in broadly chronological order, establishing the setting and then trying to make sense of the events that ensue. However, he seems to be out of place in the world he finds himself in. His feelings for the elephant appear not only to be fighting against his own conscience but also against the contrasting and alien emotions of the crowd. As a result, he struggles to come to terms with his situation on both a practical and mental level.

This works well because:

- it is **brief** – four to five lines long
- where it talks about **purpose** it does so in a general way which does not close down other possibilities
- it does **not** use any quotations or unnecessary linguistic terminology
- it tries to offer an overview/interpretation of the **entire** extract
- it looks for some sort of **contrast** or **development**
- it does not fall into the trap of offering one final and fixed interpretation – words such as *seems* and *appears* are carefully used. As you begin your answer, you may not be aware of things that become clearer to you the more you study and write about the extract. Such words allow for some flexibility as your answer unfolds.

> 🔑 **KEY TERMS**
>
> **contrast** opposites or differences between things, such as contrasts in characters or places (either within a character – here the writer himself; or between different characters – here the writer and the crowd)

LINK

You may wish to refer to this example as you write introductions in response to other extracts in the book.

ACTIVITY 1.9

Write your own introduction to the commentary on the Kenya tourism passage on page 14. You can keep it and then have another go once you have completed more work on writing introductions.

TIP

You can use conjunctions or adverbials such as *However, as … develops*, etc. to signal your use of contrasting or additional ideas. They can also guide **how** you divide your commentary. For example, in Introduction A, *however* could signal the second part of the commentary.

- it does not focus on audience – as this is not something referred to in the original task.

The introduction works particularly well because the introduction 'sets up' what the commentary might focus on:

- the sense of cultural contexts meeting (being out of place in the world the writer finds himself in)
- his relationships in the extract (with the elephant and with the crowd).

Different types of introduction

The focus you choose for your introduction can reflect the focus of your commentary.

Read two more introductions to commentaries on the Orwell passage:

COMMENTARIES

A The writer seems to explore the contrasting attitudes of the police officer. Initially, the officer seems aware that he has a job to do, although there is some reluctance on his part to do so. However, as the extract develops, this underlying reluctance seems to grow in strength and undermine his professional approach to the situation and eat away at his very conscience.

B In the extract the writer seems to begin with a negative and almost hostile attitude towards the task he has been given. He appears to be at war with himself mentally, his instincts battling his conscientious sense of duty as a police officer. As the passage develops this struggle becomes even more intense and the officer views the experience with increasing horror and revulsion, with a sense of disbelief at what he has seen and done.

ACTIVITY 1.10

Which of these two introductions:

- suggests the *Shooting an Elephant* passage develops and becomes more and more powerful in terms of the feelings experienced by the writer?
- suggests there is a marked contrast between the writer/officer's feelings at the start and at the end?

Summary

Remember these key points from this section:

- Plan your response to the passage in the methodical way you have learned.
- Select words and phrases from the passage which will help to shape your response.
- Write an introduction which uses its focus to help set the framework for the commentary.

Using evidence and quotations

In this section you will:

- learn how to analyse specific language features and explain their effects
- quote effectively and selectively.

Being able to select specific language features or devices, quote directly from the text and explain or analyse their effect in a fluent way, is fundamental to successful commentary.

Point/quotation/comment

In the previous section, you looked at how selecting specific words and phrases could guide your interpretation of a passage and help to structure your response. However, you also need an approach to these words and phrases that allows you to comment on them *and* explain their effects.

One simple way of doing this is to follow this sequence:

- Make a POINT.
- Support it with a QUOTATION.
- Explain or develop it with a COMMENT, usually on the effect created or the meaning suggested.
- **Connect** or link your point with other points or observations you make.

When writing your commentary, you should ensure that you **avoid**:

- **using quotations as a substitute for your own words.** For example: 'We see in this extract that the officer is going to shoot *an elephant* but he does not *want to*. He feels that it *would be murder to shoot him* and he realises he *had never shot an elephant*. He also realises that *there was the beast's owner to be considered* and this creates a problem for him'. This kind of material is really just another form of paraphrase or narrative summary of the content of the extract.
- **relying on phrases such as** *this means, the writer explains* **or** *this tells us*. You will end up offering a kind of translation of the quoted word or phrase rather than commenting upon it. You may also suggest there is only one 'right' meaning to a selected phrase; it is better to suggest your ideas.
- **comments which rely on vague generalisation.** Try not to use phrases like *this draws the reader in, this makes the reader want to read on,* or *this engages the reader*. These phrases tend to lead nowhere and could be applied to almost any word or phrase used in the extract!

In order to avoid these pitfalls, you may find it helpful to use the following phrases to introduce ideas:

- *This suggests …*
- *This evokes a sense of …*
- *This conveys …*
- *This implies …*
- *This conjures up …*
- *This establishes a sense of …*

TIP

The way you express your ideas must not become a list of unconnected PQCs (point, quotation, comment) followed by more PQCs.

Do not allow your use of the PQC structure to become robotic and list-like. Use connectives and other **cohesive devices** such as pronouns (they/it etc) or demonstratives (that, those, this etc) to make your writing fluent and to link your points together.

TIP

Use modal verbs such as *could, should, might, would* to help you suggest ideas in a non-definitive way. For example, consider the difference between, *This means …* and *This* **might** *mean…*

Applying the skills

Here is another example of a response to the Orwell passage on page 9.
Examples of point/quotation/comment are highlighted in the first paragraph.

The first paragraph seems to introduce a sense of indecision and a conflict between private and public responsibilities at once. The writer is directly honest about the problems he is facing [point], accepting that he has a negative attitude towards the issue placed before him – *But I did not want to shoot the elephant* [quotation] – which immediately appears to establish a dilemma for him. He is torn between his natural empathy for the creature and the public role he is expected to follow. The strong attachment, moreover [linking word], which he has for the animal [point] is shown by the use of *the* instead of *that elephant* or *an* [quotation]; this conveys how he considers it an individual, a separate being, instead of just one of a kind [comment].

This apparently subconscious sense of human attachment is exemplified further by the *grandmotherly air*, a rather unusual phrase, evoking a sense of extreme gentleness and slowness. His internal dilemma is hinted at by the choice of the harsh and stark word *murder* which seems to highlight his awareness from the beginning that to commit such a deed would be a kind of sin. Furthermore, this dilemma is reinforced by the addition of the single word *Besides* which suggests that he is still hesitating, trying to persuade himself against his will.

He is aware of his own ineptitude, the reference to *at that age* suggests he is still relatively young for the position he is in. He recognises that he *has to act quickly*, suggesting he is aware he might be wasting time. Indeed, his almost thankful reference to *experienced-looking Burmans* could indicate further delaying tactics, as well as implying his own youthful innocence compared to the knowledge and awareness they seem to possess.

ACTIVITY 1.11

1 With a partner, read the unannotated remainder of the response and identify:
   - all the other examples of the point/quotation/comment approach
   - any examples where the writer (of the commentary) has used linking or contrasting words or phrases to emphasise or develop points.

2 Now look at these notes made by the same student about Orwell's attitude to what he has to do.
   - Copy and complete the table opposite, adding a comment or effect to the last two points.
   - Then, take any of the last three points and turn them into a longer sentence, like this (the sections from the table are highlighted):

*The second paragraph introduces **a more definite tone** in the use of the phrase **'perfectly clear'**, implying he has moved on from a sense of doubt.*

Here are three possible sentence starters to help you:
   - *The apparent certainty in the repeated phrase, 'I ought' …*
   - *Yet, immediately a sudden change of tack and the writer's mood is indicated by …*
   - *The vivid simile to explain his dilemma in which he compares his chances to those of a '…'*

Point	Quote	Comment/effect
More definite tone (2nd paragraph).	*perfectly clear*	Implies a change from earlier sense of doubt.
Apparent certainty in repeated phrase.	*I ought ...*	Suggests initial confusion between private feelings and public responsibility has passed.
Sudden change of tack indicated.	*But I also knew I was going to do no such thing.*	Implies he is feeling ...
Uses a vivid simile to explain his dilemma.	*I should have about as much chance as a toad under a steam-roller.*	Conveys a sense of his ...

Further practice

For further practice of the selection of key words and phrases and the use of the point/quotation/comment approach, read the final text in this section. The extract describes some of the writer's feelings when she visited Bolivia in South America.

But the area is also a spectacular place for hiking. We roamed higher, over plains of green moss and quinoa fields, among herds of llama and alpaca. The world's highest forest grows here and there were bubbling multi-coloured geysers and hot springs where we swam down peaty channels. And then, one late afternoon, as the sky turned purple behind the snow-capped volcanos, the village suddenly came out. The boys mounted wild-looking ponies, women in frilly shiny skirts began to dance, and the men got out their flutes. They all formed a small but beautiful procession on the cold muddy streets and we followed them as they blessed each corner of their shabby little village for what had passed that year, and what might lie ahead.

Gemma Bowes, *The Guardian.*

ACTIVITY 1.12

1 Highlight four or five key words and phrases which you think are central to the perspective of the writer and her experiences.

2 Write a paragraph in which you explain what feelings are evoked by the description and the effects created. You could begin:

There is a sense of movement, energy and freedom that emerges from this passage. At the start, for example, the travellers …

Summary

Remember these key points from this section:

- Highlight or list key words or phrases with a view to the mood, perspective, tone and changing effects across the text.
- Use the point/quotation/comment approach but in a way that allows for fluent expression.
- Always comment on the effect of particular words or phrases.
- Use a range of expressions (such as *suggest*, *appears to*) or modal forms (*might*, *could*, etc.) to make what you say suggestive rather than definitive.

TYPES OF NON-FICTION TEXT

Reading or encountering a wide variety of different forms and types of text is vital. Only by familiarising yourself with the individual styles of different writers will you be able to deal with an unfamiliar text you are encountering for the first time.

As you have already seen, you will come across a range of non-fiction texts, some of which will share features with aspects of fiction writing.

Descriptive writing

In this section, you will:

- consider what descriptive writing is
- read a range of passages which contain descriptive writing
- explore a range of features which are typical of much descriptive writing.

Descriptive writing is a 'catch-all' term that seems to encompass many forms and types of text. You may see descriptive writing in newspaper reports and in imaginative narratives, but what are the shared conventions and features you should look out for? Here are some possibilities:

Descriptive writing often:

- tries to create a very particular or vivid mood or atmosphere
- conveys a strong sense of individual settings, people, events or experiences
- focuses in on detail but can also 'zoom out' to over-views or panoramas
- draws on a range of sensory experiences, such as taste, sight, sound, touch and smell.

Examples of descriptive writing might include:

- an account of an incident from an expedition across the Antarctic
- an advert for a city and its key attractions on a tourist website
- a diary entry describing attendance at a World Cup match
- a biographical account of a historical event such as the eruptions at Pompeii
- a newspaper report of a natural disaster such as a tsunami
- a fictional description of a memorable character.

Introducing key aspects of descriptive writing

The following passage exemplifies many of the language techniques and elements we might expect to see in descriptive writing.

Vivid visual detail immediately locates reader in tent.

Snoring – the sense of sound adds to the overall picture.

Close detail of individual items and events draws all the senses together.

Filmic sense of 'cutting' from an interior to exterior shot.

Writer's own imaginative sense – he cannot actually see the condor at this point.

Geographical, factual detail adds to the whole picture being built up.

Long noun phrase uses several adjectives to convey the scene's majesty.

Camp 6 near Pacchanta in the Andes Mountains, Peru.

I was lying in my sleeping bag, <u>staring at the light filtering through the red and green fabric</u> of the dome tent. <u>Simon was snoring loudly</u>, occasionally twitching in his dream world. We could have been anywhere. There is a peculiar anonymity about being in tents. Once the zip is closed and the outside world barred from sight, all sense of location disappears. Scotland, the French Alps, the Karakoram, it was always the same. <u>The sounds of rustling, of fabric flapping in the wind, or of rainfall, the feel of hard lumps under the ground sheet, the smell of rancid socks and sweat – these are universals</u>, as comforting as the warmth of the down sleeping bag.

<u>Outside, in a lightening sky, the peaks would be catching the first of the morning sun</u>, with <u>perhaps even a condor cresting the thermals above the tent</u>. That wasn't too fanciful either since I had seen one circling the camp the previous afternoon. We were <u>in the middle of the Cordillera Huayhuash</u>, in the Peruvian Andes, separated from the nearest village by twenty-eight miles of rough walking, and surrounded by the <u>most spectacular ring of ice mountains</u> I had ever seen, and the only indication of this from within our tent was the regular roaring of avalanches falling off Cerro Sarapo.

I felt a homely affection for the warm security of the tent, and reluctantly wormed out of my bag to face the prospect of lighting the stove. It had snowed a little during the night, and the grass crunched frostily under my feet as I padded over to the cooking rock. There was no sign of Richard stirring as I passed his tiny one-man tent, half collapsed and whitened with hoar frost.

Squatting under the lee of the huge overhanging boulder that had become our kitchen, I relished this moment when I could be entirely alone. I fiddled with the petrol stove which was mulishly objecting to both the temperature and the rusty petrol with which I had filled it. I resorted to brutal coercion when coaxing failed and sat it atop a propane gas stove going full blast. It burst into vigorous life, spluttering out two-foot-high flames in petulant revolt against the dirty petrol.

As the pan of water slowly heated, I looked around at the wide, dry and rock-strewn river bed, the erratic boulder under which I crouched marking the site at a distance in all but the very worst weather. A huge, almost vertical wall of ice and snow soared upwards to the summit of Cerro Sarapo directly in front of the camp, no more than a mile and a half away. Rising from the sea of moraine to my left, two spectacular and extravagant castles of sugar icing, Yerupaja and Rasac, dominated the camp site. The majestic 21,000-foot Siula Grande lay behind Sarapo and was not visible. It had been climbed for the first time in 1936 by two bold Germans via the North Ridge. There had been few ascents since then, and the true prize, the daunting 4,500-foot West Face had so far defeated all attempts.

I turned off the stove and gingerly slopped the water into three large mugs. The sun hadn't cleared the ridge of mountains opposite and it was still chilly in the shadows.

From *Touching the Void* by Joe Simpson.

The writer builds this detailed and evocative picture of the environment by focusing on **three** particular things: the world inside the tent; the world outside the tent; his actions as he wakes and prepares tea. How does he do this?

ACTIVITY 1.13

1   Re-read the un-annotated section of the passage. Note down:
    - any further examples of actions or observations which involve the senses
    - references to specific objects/items rather than general reflections
    - use of imagery or figurative language to describe the writer's actions or the world around him
    - places where, as a writer, he **positions** the reader to look at or turn their attention to certain objects, natural places, etc., rather like a camera.

2   Now think about the style of the piece in terms of the tone or mood that it creates. What impressions do you get of how the writer **feels** about his experiences? Do these change at all as he wakes, moves around the tent and goes outside?

3   Write two or three paragraphs in which you consider the language of description *and* the style and mood created.

22

TIP

When you come to write your own descriptive pieces (for example for the Unit 3 task on page 114 when a character is confined within one place), consider how you could use the technique of moving from describing an internal to external setting.

KEY TERMS

external or **exterior location** a place or setting outside

Describing an external location

Descriptive passages, such as the one above, can mix internal and **external location** descriptions. This can be literal – for example, inside a building and outside in the street, or more emotional – a writer's private thoughts versus his or her public expressions or behaviour. However, similar skills apply when it comes to commenting on the effect of language.

It can be especially important to look for how groups of similar words or usages (for examples **adjectives**, or **noun phrases**) convey a particular mood or atmosphere. This mood or atmosphere can be broadly positive or negative, but you will need to go beyond generality and try to be more specific. For example, for the text above, you might write that:

The writer creates a <u>very positive impression</u> of the landscape with his reference to the mountains which are 'spectacular and magnificent castles,' <u>showing how much he likes the scenery</u>.

None of this is 'wrong' but it does not really capture the style of the language. It would be more effective to write:

> *The writer focuses the reader's attention on the mountain peaks which he describes as 'spectacular and magnificent castles.' This metaphor, containing these two powerful adjectives, suggests there is something glorious, almost mythic, about the landscape.*

This second version is more effective because it is able to refer to the specific words/phrases used and their linguistic function, but more importantly it comments in a more specific way on the particular effect of the chosen words.

Adjectives or adjectival / noun phrases	Effect or mood the writer wishes to create
protective, ideal, calm, inviting, balmy, gentle	
filled with sunshine alive with coral myriad fish lush green coastal rainforests	

Key technique: lists of three

Lists or patterns **of three** ideas or items in texts are often used for rhetorical impact, in that they help build and emphasise an idea. For example, in the Kenya text, the idea of a complete variety of wildlife is conveyed in the three references to *baboons, rare Colobus monkeys and even leopard*, suggesting a sense of diversity and an area teeming with life.

23

ACTIVITY 1.14

Look at these words and phrases taken from the extract describing Kenya on page 14.

Discuss with a partner what overall effect or mood you think is created by each set of words and phrases. Then copy and complete the table.

KEY TERMS

list of three a sequence of three items, one after the other, often used to create a particular effect

ACTIVITY 1.15

Read this sentence from the extract about Kenya on page 14.

> *A wide range of World Class resorts, centred around Diani Beach, allow visitors to relax and enjoy this natural paradise with the best standards of accommodation, service and cuisine.*

Discuss with a partner:
- What list or pattern of three is referred to here?
- What is the message the writer intends to convey about the resort?

Now, read the following text about an external landscape and location. As you do so, begin to think about the overall tone and mood that is created.

A pair of scarlet macaws breaks out of the treetops and soars over a beach where the only tracks are those of last night's nesting turtles. You ride your horse over the sands to a small stream where blue butterflies play over brilliant pink flowers. Sounds of jungle and surf are strangely intermingled. This is where rain forest and beach meet in Costa Rica's Corcovado National Park, the day-glo tropical version of "**Where the Wild Things Are.**"[1] But could any writer's imagined fantasyland be as wondrous as this?

The Pacific Coast of Costa Rica is shaped like a giant crab with two great claws. Within this wide embrace lies a natural paradise so dazzling and diverse that it defies any adequate description. With 9,000 higher plant species, 850 bird species, hundreds of frogs and reptiles and 10 percent of all mammals on earth, today it is human visitors who find welcome refuge.

From the stunning volcanic peaks of Nicaragua down to the rustic scenery of Panama, Central America's breathtaking beauty allows you to just sit, stand, lie or look in any direction and watch nature perform around you. Howler monkeys roam freely through the jungle canopy above while manta rays weightlessly glide through the waters below.

Join us in a rare adventure of nature unbounded.

A Star Clipper's voyage is everything a conventional cruise is not. Thousands of square feet of cream-coloured sails billowing above you, warm teak decks under your bare feet and with a good wind, no sound apart from the splash of the waves against the hull.

They are the stars of the sea, as fleet as the wind and as graceful as swans.

These are true clipper ships reflecting their proud heritage in every inch of their polished brass and gleaming brightwork. Step aboard these unique vessels and discover a new age of sail, where the traditions of the past are happily married to the comforts and amenities of the present day. They are modern cruise ships in every way, created for luxury-loving passengers who also love the traditions and romance of the legendary era of sailing ships.

Life aboard is blissfully relaxed, much like traveling on a private yacht. You'll never feel confined. Each ship offers spacious accommodations and expansive teak decks with ample space and not one, but two swimming pools. In fact, you'll find that these ships offer more outdoor space per passenger than most conventional cruise ships.

When you rise, help yourself to a continental breakfast with croissants, toasted English muffins or sweet Danish pastries. Or savor a full breakfast with fresh tropical fruits and crisp bacon, grilled sausage, smoked salmon and omelettes cooked to order in the dining room. At lunch, a marvellous buffet of seafood, salads and grilled favourites awaits your pleasure. If the day includes a stop at one of the paradisiacal islands we frequent, you might also be treated to a festive outdoor barbecue on shore.

When evening comes, our elegantly appointed dining room featuring a splendid collection of paintings of sailing ships becomes the setting for the chef's finest culinary presentations, designed to please the eye and the palate. All complemented by equally fine wines. You'll find our service to be friendly and gracious, befitting a sophisticated restaurant. Of course, we would not presume to dictate your seating preferences. On all three ships, you are free to dine when and with whomever you wish – including officers, who join our guests in the dining room most nights. The dress code? No need for formal gowns and black tie, casual elegance is the order of the day and each night.

Friends gather round the Piano Bar and join in singing a few favourites. And in the Tropical Bar, the bartender shakes a pitcher full of some delicious cooling concoction. Now, is there anything more relaxing than this? Up on deck, a couple watch the sun drop slowly into the sea as gulls circle one last time in the sky.

Like a fine resort, all the amenities are here: double bed or twin beds that can be converted to queen, marble bathroom, private safe, television with in-cabin video, DVD player, direct-dial telephone, hairdryer and comfortable furnishings. The décor is tastefully traditional. You'll find the accoutrements of a luxurious classic yacht, where everything is ingeniously designed for comfort, ease and efficiency. Burnished brass fittings and mahogany brightwork recall our nautical heritage. Soft natural fabrics reflect the colors of the sun, sea and sky. Prints of famous clipper ships and sailing yachts grace the walls. Everything is immaculately maintained and your steward knows exactly when to appear or disappear.

There's nothing so easy and pleasurable as falling asleep to the gentle rhythms of the ship and sea – unless it's awakening refreshed the next morning to a newborn day.

Star Clippers, www.starclippers.com.

[1] *Where the Wild Things Are* is a 1963 children's picture book by Maurice Sendak

ACTIVITY 1.16

1 Working on your own, look at the first half of the passage up to *Join us in a rare adventure of nature unbounded*. List the key words or phrases that stand out in this part of the text. For the purposes of this task you could focus on:

- the **positive** adjectives used to describe landscape and nature (e.g. *dazzling*)

- particular **nouns** or **noun phrases** related to the natural world (*scarlet macaws*)
- **verbs** suggesting what can be done, or the behaviour of people and natural elements (*ride your horse*).

2 Then, compare your list with a partner.

- Can you see any connections or groups of words/phrases that seem to go together?
- Are there any key patterns of language such as lists of three?
- Does the writer use descriptions to create contrasts of any sort?

3 Once you have discussed and made notes on these issues, agree with your partner two or three key observations about the style and language based on the words, phrases and patterns you have highlighted.

Key technique: simile and metaphor

In the text, the writer does not just use specific nouns, verbs, etc. to convey the experience of a holiday with Star Clippers; he or she also uses some evocative imagery. For example:

Simile compares the shape of the coast to a huge crab.

Metaphor suggests the crab's clutches are more like a kiss or hug.

The Pacific Coast of Costa Rica <u>is shaped like a giant crab with two great claws</u>. Within this <u>wide embrace</u> lies a natural paradise so dazzling and diverse that it defies any adequate description.

This might be expressed in a commentary as follows:

COMMENTARY

The two ideas of the traveller being in the heart of the natural world, and yet being welcomed by it are expressed in the two phrases which describe the coast. In being *shaped like a giant crab with two great claws* the writer conflates the landscape with the wildlife that inhabits it; yet, by referring to the crab's *wide embrace* it is suggested that the landscape, and by association the people and wildlife, welcome the visitor, thus making the description doubly attractive.

ACTIVITY 1.17

1 Identify in the commentary:

- the point/s, quotations and comments
- the effect of the selected words.

2 Now, look at this sentence from the text:

From the stunning volcanic peaks of Nicaragua down to the rustic scenery of Panama, Central America's breathtaking beauty allows you to just sit, stand, lie or look in any direction <u>and watch nature perform around you</u>.

25

KEY TERMS

personification giving human characteristics to animals, objects and so on

TIP
Remember not to use excessive linguistic terminology or try to spot techniques and features of language (for example, alliteration) just for their own sake.

- On your own, look at the underlined section.
- Decide how the writer has used **personification** here.
- When you have done so, write a sentence or two making a point, quoting words or phrases and then commenting on the effect. Remember, you need to go beyond saying whether it is a positive mood or message.

Further practice

Now work through the remainder of the Star Clippers extract on page 24 and follow the plan you learned about in Section 1:

- Divide what remains into sections.
- Highlight key words and phrases and identify groups or patterns of words.
- Practise writing two paragraphs based on this section of the text, commenting on: the style and language; how this links to the purpose or perspective.

Remember to use phrases such as *this suggests/seems/appears…*

Key technique: understanding voice

You can use the same techniques of analysis and commentary regardless of the mood, tone or voice of the text.

Read the passage below which describes the author's feelings when he visits a particular place in India, looking for a particular drink called a *toddy*. As you read, consider the mood or tone created by the voice of the writer.

Kariumpumkala today is a slightly ghastly brick-and-mortar structure, painted in shades of green and pink. Its top two storeys are air-conditioned, every floor is tiled, and the tabletops are made of granite. Over the billing counter is a shelf full of trophies that Kariumpumkala has won in something called the Philips Food Fest. But most heartbreaking of all is a perverse remembrance of times past—a sign that says 'Smoking, alcohols strictly prohibited.'

Kariumpumkala's present owner would talk of none of this. He was obsessed, instead, with his legal battle with Karimpinkala, the upstart establishment down the road that, he claimed, had stolen and only slightly modified his restaurant's name. 'That isn't the real one,' he said repeatedly. But Karimpinkala still serves toddy, and Kariumpumkala does not. That little edge makes all the difference in the sweeps to win Kerala's hearts and minds.

In the leafy parking lot of Karimpinkala, a 'Toddy Shop And A/c Family Restaurant,' we found Maruti Swift cars and gleaming SUVs, and cabanas that were closer in size to a middling dorm room. We sat under fans, on plastic chairs that skidded on the tiled floors, and drummed our fingers on a glass-topped table. We were handed a menu, laminated in clear plastic. Apart from the 'Sweet and cold coconut toddy,' we could have ordered Diet Coke, Fanta, the enigmatic 'Soda B & S,' or ice cream. We could even have asked for that most pan-Indian of dishes, *Gobi Manchurian*. As we sat staring a little disbelievingly at that menu, another SUV pulled up outside. A family dismounted—parents, little children, and even a grandmother—and stormed into one of the other cabanas.

From 'Shaaaping in God's Own Land'
by Samanth Subramanian.

Now read this initial response to the first part of the passage.

SAMPLE RESPONSE

The initial feeling which comes through the voice of the writer is one of dislike and appalled horror. This disdain is apparent when the writer describes the location as *a slightly ghastly brick-and-mortar structure*, words which suggest not only his detachment and repulsion (*ghastly*) but his inability to see the building in any particular shape or form – it is simply a *structure*. The **adjectives** in *shades of green and pink* add to this sense of a rather unattractive combination of features.

ACTIVITY 1.18

1 Discuss with a partner:
   - What 'voice' does this commentary suggests emerges from the text?
   - What evidence does the student provide to support this view?
   - Do you agree with the commentary?

2 Now, look at the rest of the text. Can you find evidence to support the points made in the table?

Point	Evidence/quotation	Comment
There are some **unexpected** compliments in the way the building is described.		However, it is implied that …
The writer, however, qualifies what he says, and this undermines the compliments.		

27

KEY TERMS

unexpected something which surprises the reader or comes as a shock

qualification casting some uncertainty on an initial statement or a way of undermining what is apparently being said

ambivalent being undecided or having contrasting feelings about something

TIP

In texts, look out for the use of **qualification** – a way of undermining what is apparently being said. This can point to the writer's **ambivalent** or less positive perspective or viewpoint.

Key technique: connotations

You have already been using your knowledge of word/phrase connotations, even if you were not aware of it! But what are connotations?

Many words, phrases or sentences do not simply describe literal or surface meanings. They can also suggest, or bring to mind, other words, phrases, ideas, feelings and so on.

For example, on a simple level, *green* denotes a colour we can all recognise. However, it also **suggests** all sorts of other ideas: some of these might be concrete images such as lawns, grass, trees and so on; others might be abstract notions such as freshness, innocence (and possibly naivety), organic concerns, or 'Nature' more generally. It may also bring to mind idioms, such as *green with envy*. All of these ideas might be said to be 'carried' by the word *green* without being stated directly.

Connotations are often linked to positive or negative views. For example, imagine these choices when writing a letter to an employer:

TIP

Making a list of key individual words, groups of words, phrases and ideas which contrast or oppose each other, can help you, as the reader, to pull out opposing strands of style and language.

ACTIVITY 1.19

Discuss with a partner:

- what each of the underlined adjectives suggests/connotes
- how each one is subtly (or perhaps completely) different from the alternatives (e.g. what is the difference between someone who is *cunning* and someone who is *clever*?)
- which are broadly positive and which are negative. (Take care: this may depend on the context – what may not be suitable or relevant to a job application might be entirely suitable in a less formal context.)

I believe I am ideal for this challenging post as I am very <u>assertive/confident/pushy/ dominant/self-possessed</u>. My academic record also shows that I am <u>brainy/geeky/ intelligent/clever/cunning</u>, so will be able to deal with the complex demands of the role.

In longer descriptions, we can see the greater range of language choices available and also the wider connotations these imply. For example, read these two descriptions:

- *the thin urchin fading without trace behind twisted posts in the suffocating traffic*
- *the lithe youth moving effortlessly from lamp to lamp in the busy avenue.*

Both describe a broadly similar event, but the first has connotations of hunger, poverty and invisibility in a choked-up town; the second suggests health, athleticism and an energetic environment.

Positive and negative aspects of a place can occur within the same text of course. For example, read this extract which is taken from an autobiography and explores the writer's memories of living in a certain part of Australia.

Above the plants that creep across the ground are the bushes, which grow wherever an indentation in the earth, scarcely visible to the eye, allows for the concentration of more moisture from the dew and the reluctant rain. There is the ever-present round mound of prickly weed, which begins its life a strong acid green with hints of yellow, and then is burnt by the sun or the frost to a pale whitish yellow. As it ages, its root system weakens so that on windy days the wind will pick it out of the earth and roll it slowly and majestically about like whirling suns in a Van Gogh painting. Where the soil contains limestone, stronger bushes grow, sometimes two to three feet high, with the delicate narrow-leaved foliage of arid climates, bluish green and dusty grey in color, perfectly adapted to resist the drying sun. Where the soil is less porous and water will lie for a while after rain, comes the annual saltbush, a miraculous silvery-grey plant which stores its own water in small balloonlike round leaves and thrives long after the rains have vanished. Its sterner perennial cousin, which resembles sagebrush, rises on woody branches and rides out the strongest wind.

From *The Road from Coorain* by Jill Kerr Conway.

ACTIVITY 1.20

1 Read through the text again and pick out any words or phrases that suggest contrasting moods, such as a weakness/strength in nature.
2 Can you identify what sorts or words you have selected? (e.g are some verbs? Nouns? If so, which?)
3 What part, if any, does imagery play in the world described? (Think about similes or metaphors.) What connotations are suggested by these images?

Now read this short commentary on the text:

KEY TERMS

verb a word that conveys an action, a state of being or a happening

COMMENTARY

A sense of contrast but also of ideas which echo each other come together to create two opposing moods in the landscape. There are negative connotations in the sense of the struggle for life (*plants that creep … scarcely visible … reluctant rain … burnt by the sun … root systems weakens … wintry days*). The **verbs** here such as *creep* and *weakens* suggest a sense of tentative, fragile life.

The whole scene seems to be a world of elements where the struggle for life is marked out by the colours themselves. The deathly lifelessness of this world is suggested by the *acid green*, the *pale whitish yellow* and the *dusty grey*.

Yet, there are also groups of words which convey life and energy emerging (*delicate narrowed leaved foliage … a miraculous silvery-grey plant … thrives long after … sterner perennial cousin … rises and rides*).

The writer even uses a simile (where two things are compared using *like* or *as*) which gives an unexpected quality to the passage – it conveys how what should be a potential source of life (the sun) seems to be a mixture of beautiful energy and destruction (*the wind will pick it out of the earth and roll it slowly and majestically about like whirling suns*) so that both opposing moods are joined in the image.

ACTIVITY 1.21

1 Which contrasts has the writer of the commentary picked out?
2 How has the writer of the commentary used connotation to explore particular words or phrases? (Look for words such as *suggest, seems, convey, implications*.)

KEY TERMS

internal inside a particular location

Describing an internal location

As can be seen in the commentaries on the two texts above, descriptions of people and places are not always as straightforward as they seem. The view of the writer may both admire *and* condemn, be shocked and yet spellbound.

Read this extract in which George Orwell describes a visit to an underground mine.

The time to go there is when the machines are roaring and the air is black with coal dust, and when you can actually see what the miners have to do. At those times the place is like hell, or at any rate like my own mental picture of hell. Most of the things one imagines in hell are if there — heat, noise, confusion, darkness, foul air, and, above all, unbearably cramped space. Everything except the fire, for there is no fire down there except the feeble beams of Davy lamps and electric torches which scarcely penetrate the clouds of coal dust.

When you have finally got there... you crawl through the last line of pit props and see opposite you a shiny black wall three or four feet high. This is the coal face. Overhead is the smooth ceiling made by the rock from which the coal has been cut; underneath is the rock again, so that the gallery you are in is only as high as the ledge of coal itself, probably not much more than a yard. The first impression of all, overmastering everything else for a while, is the frightful, deafening din from the conveyor belt which carries the coal away. You cannot see very far, because the fog of coal dust throws back the beam of your lamp, but you can see on either side of you the line of half-naked kneeling men, one to every four or five yards, driving their shovels under the fallen coal and flinging it swiftly over their left shoulders. They are feeding it on to the conveyor belt, a moving rubber belt a couple of feet wide which runs a yard or two behind them. Down this belt a glittering river of coal races constantly. In a

big mine it is carrying away several tons of coal every minute. It bears it off to some place in the main roads where it is shot into tubs holding half a tun, and thence dragged to the cages and hoisted to the outer air...

It is impossible to watch the 'fillers' at work without feeling a pang of envy for their toughness. It is a dreadful job that they do, an almost superhuman job by the standard of an ordinary person. For they are not only shifting monstrous quantities of coal, they are also doing, it in a position that doubles or trebles the work. They have got to remain kneeling all the while — they could hardly rise from their knees without hitting the ceiling — and you can easily see by trying it what a tremendous effort this means. Shovelling is comparatively easy when you are standing up, because you can use your knee and thigh to drive the shovel along; kneeling down, the whole of the strain is thrown upon your arm and belly muscles. And the other conditions do not exactly make things easier. There is the heat — it varies, but in some mines it is suffocating — and the coal dust that stuffs up your throat and nostrils and collects along your eyelids, and the unending rattle of the conveyor belt, which in that confined space is rather like the rattle of a machine gun. But the fillers look and work as though they were made of iron. They really do look like iron hammered iron statues — under the smooth coat of coal dust which clings to them from head to foot.

From *Down the Mine* by George Orwell.

ACTIVITY 1.22

Discuss with a partner what evidence you can find that the writer is both appalled *and* impressed by what he encounters?

Key technique: using the senses

We have already seen how writers, particularly of highly descriptive passages, use the senses to convey ideas and feelings. This is especially true in the text you have just read. For example, the very opening sentence:

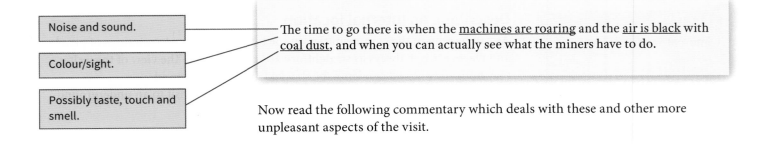

Noise and sound.

Colour/sight.

Possibly taste, touch and smell.

The time to go there is when the <u>machines are roaring</u> and the <u>air is black</u> with <u>coal dust</u>, and when you can actually see what the miners have to do.

Now read the following commentary which deals with these and other more unpleasant aspects of the visit.

TIP

Look for references to the senses in descriptive passages to find clues about the positive or negative impressions of a place.

LINK

Using the senses can be particularly effective when one specific experience or detail is explored. For example, look at the different ways snow is described in Chenjerai Hove's, *A Letter To My Mother* on page 34.

COMMENTARY

The writer conveys a feeling of oppression through selection of words such as *roaring* and *noise*, for example, and evokes a world where the senses – physical aspects such as sight, smell, taste, touch, hearing of the visitor – seem to be physically attacked. In addition, the sense of an alien landscape is conveyed by the simile *the place is like hell*, suggesting an almost demonic and corrupting location. The sense of complete oppression is also clarified by the writer's selection of a detailed list (*heat, noise, confusion, darkness, foul air*), as if one thing after another hits the visitor to the mine, as if there is no escape.

ACTIVITY 1.23

1 Read the text again and note down any *positive* impressions Orwell gets. You should already have some ideas from the discussion activity opposite.
2 Note down whether these are contrasted with other, unpleasant aspects, for example, the strange sense of beauty in the mine.

Key technique: verbs, adjectives and similes

When commenting on a passage, you should look for content ideas such as 'reference to the senses' but also for particular words or linguistic functions, such as action verbs; adjectives related to shape or size; and imagery such as the use of simile.

ACTIVITY 1.24

Read the first four paragraphs of this long extract, listing key words and phrases. Identify examples of **similes**, **adjectives** and **verbs**, and what their effects might be.

31

A quite different world opens before me when I only just push at the heavy door that separates the shop from our apartment.

It is a door entirely covered with tin. Instead of a latch it has a big key that is always in the lock. In the dark rear shop, into which I tumble first, I grope along the walls as though I were blind. Thick yellow sheets of paper rustle underfoot.

Wrapped-up wall clocks rest on the floor here. Until they are hung on walls, they do not move; they lie quiet and soundless, as if buried alive. But the stuffy air of the dark chamber seems swollen with the voices that seep in from the shop. The voices crowd against the high wooden wall and recoil from it again. I stand behind it as in a prison, and listen to what is being said. I want to make out whose voice is talking. And if I catch mother's voice, I am content.

But wait! Is her voice quiet, calm, or, God forbid, angry? Mother's voice will give me warning, tell me whether to go into the shop or not.

Her high tones encourage me. I touch the curtain of the last door, which leads to the shop. I become dizzy at once because of the mirrors and glass. All the clocks are being wound in my ears. The shop is full of glitter on every side. The flashing of silver and gold blinds me like fire; it is reflected in the mirrors, roams over the glass drawers. It dazzles my eyes.

Two large gas chandeliers burn high up under the ceiling, humming loudly; the sound becomes a moan of pain. Fire spatters from the close-netted caps on the burners that barely hold back the sparks.

There are two high walls entirely lined from top to bottom with glass cupboards. The cupboards reach up to the ceiling and are so solidly built that they seem to have grown into it. Their glass doors slide easily back and forth. Through the glass one can clearly see all the objects on display, almost touch them with one's hand. On the shelves are goblets, wineglasses, sugar bowls, saucers, braided baskets, milk and water pitchers, fruit bowls. Everything shines and glitters with a newly polished look. Whenever I move, all the objects run after me in reflection. The fire of the lamps and the light of the silver cross each other. Now the silver drowns in a flash of the lamplight, now it re-emerges with an even sharper glitter.

On the opposite wall there is another glass cupboard. Behind its panes are objects not of silver but of white metal, and their gleam is much more modest, and quieter.

In the center of the shop, on three sides, there rise, as if from the floor itself, three inner walls – long counters with drawers. They divide the shop into two sections. All laid out with glass, full of gold objects, they glitter like magical arks. Little stones of all colors, framed in gold rings, earrings, brooches, bracelets, flicker there like lighted matches.

In this air full of fire it is quite impossible to see that the floor is dark. At the front, at the very feet of the customers, entire silver services shine through the glass. And so even the customers' black shoes glitter and catch reflections along with the silver.

The third wall is dim even by day. Overgrown with long hanging clocks, it looks like a forest of dark trees. There are wall clocks of various sizes. Some have big, squat cases with thick hanging chains supporting heavy copper weights. Other wall clocks have narrower, slimmer bodies. Their chains are lighter, more movable, with smaller weights attached. In the bellies of all of them pointed pendulums dangle like swords, swinging restlessly back and forth.

Among the large wall clocks smaller ones are hiding, and even tiny ones; one can see only the white dials, their round moon faces. They have no wooden bellies, and their chain legs move in the open, before everyone's eyes, up and down. The whole wall of clocks sighs and breathes heavily. From each box come smothered groans, as though at every moment someone were being killed on the dark wall.

From *Burning Lights* by Bella Chagall.

Now read the following commentary on the first four paragraphs of the passage.

COMMENTARY

The writer creates a sense of the oppressive nature of the interior (a similar quality to that we saw in the passage about the mine) in the way that the narrator seems to be in a location where there is a sense of slow progress.

The use of adjectives in *heavy door*, *dark rear shop* and *Thick yellow sheets of paper* create a feeling of weight and difficulty. Similar phrases, especially in the use of verbs, add to this sense of limited progress: *just push at*, *tumble* and *grope* convey a mood of stumbling progress.

The atmosphere seems deathly and lifeless; the simile describing how the clocks *lie quiet and soundless, as if buried alive* develops this atmosphere and the mood of limited opportunities for escape. Further similes – such as *as though I were blind* and *I stand behind it as in a prison* – highlight the narrator's suspicion that there is no certainty in or escape from this world.

References to noise add to this sense of a sinister and threatening atmosphere. We are told of *voices that seep in*, implying a gradual and persistent challenge but that gradually they start to *crowd* the shop, as if approaching closer and closer.

- Which of these elements were ones you selected or identified?
- How well does the student link his or her ideas in this commentary? (Look at the connective words or phrases used.)

- Now read the rest of the extract on pages 31 and 32 and list further key words and phrases. You may wish to move beyond looking at verbs, adjectives and similes and draw upon other skills or features you have learned about.

ACTIVITY 1.25

Write a commentary on the style and language of the second part of the text, from *Her high tones encourage me …* In addition to references to similes, metaphors and verb usages, comment on the impact of the **present tense**.

Summary

Remember these key points from this section:

- Whilst descriptive writing can be found in both fiction and non-fiction writing there are specific features and elements which are often common to both.
- Look for specific, rather than general vocabulary; powerful and vivid detail; reference to the senses; patterns and groups of words which build a whole picture.
- Comment on the effect of language use and in particular on imagery.
- The voice of the writer can encompass both positive and negative perspectives; it may be ambivalent or qualify what is said.

Personal writing

In this section you will:

- read a range of personal texts, including diaries, letters, memoirs and autobiographies
- explore the impact of first person accounts
- develop your understanding of 'voice' in texts
- explore a number of key techniques, such as how writers use dialogue.

What is personal writing?

We could say that all writing is to some extent 'personal' in that someone had to author it, but clearly some texts are explicitly personal in that we know who the writer is, what their situation is and, often, why they are writing.

Personal writing can allow the reader to:

- witness characters and events from the point of view of the narrator, especially when written in the first person (that is, using *I*)
- provide a glimpse of the writer's more private thoughts and attitudes
- explore reasons and motives for behaving in particular ways or feeling particular emotions.

Letters

Whilst written and posted letters have been superseded in many places by email or the ease of making a phone call, letters still offer the writer a chance to be reflective and thoughtful.

Read this text which is taken from a letter written by a son, now living in Norway, to his mother back home in Zimbabwe.

Remember the day I arrived in my new town, one of my many stops on this journey that is life. The rains at the airport in Stavanger brought me memories of you working in the fields, not shielding yourself from the warm raindrops. I remembered you then, way back. For, I knew you would have composed an instant poem to celebrate first raindrops, those songs about the fish eagle up in the sky, the harbinger of rain, giving life to people, animals and plants.

Here they still have not stopped cursing the rain. I always remind them that one who curses the rain is a witch who wishes that life should not be brought to this earth. But no, they still curse at their gentle, thunderless rain. They prefer the sun instead. Or the white snow which paints the street white as if cotton wool has embraced the whole earth. My fear of snow still persists, especially when it hardens and becomes slippery ice.

For me, a step on ice is a potential disaster. Ice is more slippery than the muddy clay soils of your maize fields. Norwegians hardly fall on ice. They float on it like Arabs walking on sand, never sinking, never falling. They even run races on the ice and win competitions! Can you imagine?

...By the way, I forget that you have never seen the sea. I remember you telling me stories about the place where all rivers poured their waters, in our language, gungwa (the water to quench all thirsts). It is just that,

and Norwegians are people of the sea. They play in it, swim in it, dive in it, ride fast boats in it and fish there. They travel over the sea to many places. All their towns and villages are by the sea: it brings them everything they want, friends and enemies, food from far away places, and petrol which they discovered under the depths of the sea. The sea is full of so many creatures which you find on their plate for almost every meal. According to Norwegians, if you don't eat fish, like me, you are supposed to be miserable...

I hope the thunderous rains have come by now. Maybe the maize you planted is already the height of a small child. Every sun which rises gives me fresh memories of you, and every early sunset reminds me that I am in other lands. Maybe one day we will sit together, switch off the street lights and gaze at the beauty of that lovely African moon which displays the image of a rabbit with large ears. Maybe I will be older, but I will not have given up the idea of being young.

Now I know that there are so many streams to the river of knowledge, and one of them is to live in other lands.

Your Son,
Chenjerai

From *A Letter To My Mother* by Chenjerai Hove.

Key technique: improving your expression

So far, in this book, most of the attention has been on the features you should look for and comment on in a text, but none of this information is of any value to you unless you are able to express yourself fluently and clearly.

ACTIVITY 1.26

1   As for previous passages, begin by listing key words and phrases in this extract which might tell us something about the mood and feelings of the writer.

2   Now look at this word bank describing tone and mood. Select the words that you think *best describe the writer's mood* (or moods) in the text.

intimate	personal	reflective	observational	gently comic	nostalgic	angry
anxious	determined	disbelieving	elegiac	ironic	loving	tender
direct	conversational	poetic	sharp	playful	impatient	thoughtful

3 If you think the moods change or develop, write the appropriate word (e.g. *gently comic*) on a copy of the extract alongside the relevant paragraph. Alternatively, write the term down with the number of the paragraph next to it (e.g. *thoughtful*, paragraph 1).

4 Discuss your findings with a partner and then share with another pair. Try to build a clear picture of how the text works and reference your ideas to specific words or phrases in the text.

Now read this extract from a commentary on the text and look at the annotations around it.

Key point about tone with these two adjectives.

Supporting quotation but needs reference to imperative verb which speaks directly, as if in conversation.

Language device.

Good expression suggesting an interpretation.

Effect clearly stated.

COMMENTARY

The tone is personal and intimate, with the writer inviting his mother to participate in shared knowledge (*Remember*). From the beginning he creates a philosophical mood with his reference to the *journey that is life*. The use of the metaphor seems to imply that this is a moment of pause, a stop, for reflection on his constant travels. His words are nostalgic and gentle as he reminisces about the past. The references to the *rain* and the *warm raindrops* suggest a mood of refreshing memories, echoed in the way he describes such weather as *giving life*, associating water with vitality and creation.

The writer contrasts his own fond and positive memories of the African landscape and weather with the ways in which the rain is viewed in his current homeland. There is a contrast in the way the harsh sounding *cursing … curses … curse* is repeated to convey this sense of negativity on the part of his fellow residents. There is almost a sense of disbelief in his use of the phrase *But no*, as if the writer cannot come to terms with their exasperating attitude.

Working on your own, find other words in the second part of the commentary which have been used to explain the mood of the writer. These are likely to be, but are not exclusively, adjectives such as the ones in the word bank opposite.

Further practice

Look at the rest of the extract and write two further paragraphs.

■ In the first, comment on what the writer has to say about the Norwegians' love of the sea and what mood this creates.

■ In the second, comment on his thoughts about his homeland and his thoughts for the future.

Diaries

Diaries can provide windows into people's thoughts whilst at the same time conveying narrative accounts of events and people encountered. As one might expect, a strong sense of voice is often present.

Here are the most common key conventions found in diaries:

■ Like personal letters, we expect diaries to have an element of reflection and thought.

■ They also share elements of narrative texts in that they recount events.

TIP

When writing about a passage, try to use 'mood/tone' words such as the ones from the word bank opposite, or any others you feel are appropriate to describe the style of the text.

35

- They are usually organised into chronological 'chunks' so that entries follow consecutively.
- They mix factual detail with personal observation.
- They often mix tenses, so that we are taken 'into the moment' with present tense: glimpse events that have just happened (past) or are in the process of happening (present continuous). We also get the sense of what *might* happen or is about to occur (future tenses).

Key technique: understanding tenses

It is important to understand how a writer positions the reader through the use of tenses. Whilst you do not need to show detailed knowledge of the names of specific tenses, understanding how tenses differ can help you interpret voice and perspective.

ACTIVITY 1.27

Look at this entry by a student in his/her diary. It displays several tenses.

1 Can you identify what they are? The first two have been highlighted for you.
2 What do these tenses and what they describe tell us about the situation and the events?

ACTIVITY 1.28

Write the next diary entry from the student's point of view. In it he/she reveals more information about Miss Cheung's disappearance. Use the past, present and future tenses.

<u>Today the most terrible thing happened</u>.[1] Our beloved teacher, Miss Li, has disappeared, and so, apparently, has the school money! <u>We had been waiting</u>[2] in the classroom for her when the Principal rushed in. His face was ashen. He asked us if we had seen Miss Li.

I am so upset! I cannot believe she has done this. She must have a very important reason. I am going to see what I can find out tonight when I go for piano lessons with Miss Cheung. She is a friend of Miss Li's and will tell me what she knows. Outside, the little flame-coloured bird that sits on our white fence and sings is silent. He knows how I feel!

[1] past simple
[2] past perfect continuous

•••• FURTHER READING

Search in a library and online to find extracts from a range of different personal diaries. Read these extracts to gain an appreciation of how writers respond to different conditions and situations.

Knowledge of the tenses used (or at least of the past, present and future situations) can help you make sense of the text. For example, the writer is able to inform the reader:

- what definitely **happened**
- what is **yet to happen** (which creates a sense of uncertainty)
- what is **happening now**. (The final reference to the bird who is *silent* now, in the present, creates an ongoing, feeling of unhappiness.)

Now read the extracts below which are taken from the diary of Captain Scott, a British explorer whose expedition to the South Pole in the early 20th century ended in tragedy and loss.

March 17th, 1912

...I can only write at lunch and then only occasionally. The cold is intense, −40° at midday. My companions are unendingly cheerful, but we are all on the verge of serious frostbites, and though we constantly talk of fetching through I don't think anyone of us believes it in his heart.

We are cold on the march now, and at all times except meals. Yesterday we had to lay up for a blizzard and to-day we move dreadfully slowly. We are at No. 14 pony camp, only two pony marches from One Ton Depot. We leave here our theodolite, a camera, and Oates' sleeping-bags. Diaries, &c., and geological specimens carried at Wilson's special request, will be found with us or on our sledge.

March 18th, 1912

To-day, lunch, we are 21 miles from the depot. Ill fortune presses, but better may come. We have had more wind and drift from ahead yesterday; had to stop marching; wind N.W., force 4, temp. −35°. No human being could face it, and we are worn out *nearly*.

LINK

Look back to page 27 for more about connotations

TIP

'Reading between the lines' is a useful way of describing the act of looking for what is suggested rather than stated directly.

ACTIVITY 1.29

1. Make a list of key words and phrases in the first two of Captain Scott's diary extracts. Also note down the tenses that are used.

2. Now answer these questions independently:
   - What do these words, phrases and tenses tell us about Scott's past, current and future situation?
   - How do they help us to understand Scott's mood and state of mind?

Key technique: inference and deduction

One of the key reading skills that you have already begun to develop is that of being able to **infer** meaning from what is said, especially when information or feelings are implied rather than stated directly.

Read these further extracts from Scott's diaries.

March 18th, 1912

My right foot has gone, nearly all the toes – two days ago I was proud possessor of best feet. These are the steps of my downfall. Like an ass I mixed a small spoonful of curry powder with my melted pemmican – it gave me violent indigestion. I lay awake and in pain all night; woke and felt done on the march; foot went and I didn't know it. A very small measure of neglect and have a foot which is not pleasant to contemplate. Bowers takes first place in condition, but there is not much to choose after all. The others are still confident of getting through – or pretend to be – I don't know! We have the last *half* fill of oil in our primus and a very small quantity of spirit – this alone between us and thirst. The wind is fair for the moment, and that is perhaps a fact to help. The mileage would have seemed ridiculously small on our outward journey.

March 19th, 1912

Lunch. We camped with difficulty last night, and were dreadfully cold till after our supper of cold pemmican and biscuit and a half a pannikin of cocoa cooked over the spirit. Then, contrary to expectation, we got warm and all slept well. To-day we started in the usual dragging manner. Sledge dreadfully heavy. We are 15½ miles from the depot and ought to get there in three days. What progress! We have two days' food but barely a day's fuel. All our feet are getting bad – Wilson's best, my right foot worst, left all right. There is no chance to nurse one's feet till we can get hot food into us. Amputation is the least I can hope for now, but will the trouble spread? That is the serious question. The weather doesn't give us a chance – the wind from N. to N.W. and –40° temp, to-day.

March 23rd, 1912

Blizzard bad as ever – Wilson and Bowers unable to start – to-morrow last chance – no fuel and only one or two of food left – must be near the end. Have decided it shall be natural – we shall march for the depot with or without our effects and die in our tracks...

R. Scott.

Work through Activity 1.30 then read this commentary about Scott's diaries.

ACTIVITY 1.30

Discuss with a partner:

- What does Scott tell us directly (i.e what he tells us as plain fact or **direct statement**)?
- What can we *infer* from what he says, by understanding the clues or hints in what he writes?

KEY TERMS

direct statement something stated as a definite fact, opinion or truth, with no sense of doubt

syntax the order of words and phrases in a sentence

COMMENTARY

There seems to be a sense of conflict in the moods right from the start. Scott himself seems negative and pessimistic from the opening without any doubt or qualification: *The cold is intense* is a direct statement allowing no doubt at all to his thoughts and feelings and his reference to how *I don't think anyone of us believes it in his heart* reveals his very private thoughts and beliefs expressed to himself but not his colleagues.

Yet those around him are more positive, trying to be *unendingly cheerful*, the first word a contrast to Scott's own sense of certainty and finality. His sense of foreboding is illuminated by his use of words like *dreadfully* (repeated later on) but at times he tries to see the more optimistic frame of mind conveyed by his colleagues: *Ill fortune presses, but better may come*, perhaps the syntax suggesting that his first view is the one that dominates his mind. Indeed, his negativity seems to take over again as he resorts to direct statement without qualification once more: *No human being could face it*, words implying the dark state of his mind and a sense that little hope remains and that the shadow of death hovers over everything they do.

LINK

Inference and deduction are skills you can apply to almost any text: in R. H. Tawney's *The Attack* on page 41, we are not told what happens to the officer but consider how inference might help you draw your own conclusions.

ACTIVITY 1.31

Working with the same partner, discuss:

- how effectively the commentary picks up on what is directly stated and what is implied
- whether the commentary captures Scott's mood and how it changes.

Other diary writers, especially in times of crisis like wartime, may respond to a particular experience using opposing moods as in Scott's diary entries, yet with a more psychological and reflective outlook.

The following diary extracts were written at the time of the outbreak of the Second World War.

ACTIVITY 1.32

1 Read the diary extracts. As you do so, consider how they link back to some of the descriptive passages you have already encountered, in particular the extract from *Touching the Void* on page 21.
2 List key words and phrases and identify the ways in which the writer creates opposing moods in his writing.
3 Find examples of lists of three or any other techniques or features you have encountered in the book so far (e.g. imagery, moving from an internal to an external location).

20 April
Yesterday, up early in the morning – the washing, the dressing, the brushing, then to the station on my bicycle. Everything planned, everything done, the ticket bought, the clean gloves in the pocket.

How late the train was – waiting, waiting there. Then the bursting carriages and all the passage filled with soldiers – their tin hats, bottles, knapsacks hitting on the walls when they turned. I wondered how I could stand ... I tried to sit down in the loop of a strap, then on a fire extinguisher. Sore, painful, I felt desperate. How ill and tired I would be if I could not sit down. I gazed at the fat suitcase for some time, then at last I dared to sit down on it. Pleasure, bliss, gazing out of the window, sitting down at last.

The fields, the feathery trees, wonderful poison green, fresh as new lettuce. The large lonely young man carrying a huge implement across unending fields. Then the long, long tunnel with its whistle and the belching white smoke, not escaping, flowing over the train in a thick cape. Sparks flew and faded. The red demon glow on the white smoke belchings and the growing of it till I was really ready for some catastrophe. Can something be on fire? Will the engine burst and the driver be burnt to death in the steam, as I have read? Will I be groping in wreckage in the dark tunnel? All this through my mind and more. No change from early childhood.

Then the sooted wall seen faintly, the lamps of some workers, like miners' lamps or the lamps of gaolers in a dungeon. It is like a haunted house ...The green, luminous skeleton should descend, champing its terrible jaws, grinning. The concrete grime, then at last the air, on, on. Quite happy now, almost peaceful.

From *The Journals of Denton Welch*.

39

ACTIVITY 1.33

Now write a short commentary on the passage. You could use the following prompts to help you structure what you have to say:

The account begins briskly, almost matter-of-factly with routines such as ...

Then, there is a change of mood as the writer recounts the physical aspects of the journey ...

After that, the description is laced with striking, often nightmarish images and visions, as shown by ...

••• **FURTHER READING**

For more examples of war diaries visit http://www.firstworldwar.com/diaries/index.htm

Now read this somewhat different diary entry.

I look back and see visions of my country as for twenty-three years I have known it, peaceful, blooming, full of abundance, its vast plain an ocean of waving corn amongst which diligent peasants move to and fro gathering in the harvest, the land's dearest pride.

I see its humble villages hidden amongst fruit trees, I see the autumn splendour of its forests, I see the grand solitude of its mountain summits, I see its noble convents, corners of hidden beauty, treasures of ancient art, I hear the sound of the shepherd's horn, the sweet complaint of his ditties.

I see long roads with clouds of dust rising from them, many carts in a file, I see gaily clad peasants flocking to market. I see naked plains and long stretches of sand by the sea.

I also see our broad, proud Danube rolling its many waters past quaint little villages and boroughs inhabited by motley crowds of different nationalities, past towns of which the rising industries are a promise of future wealth. I see our port of Constanza with its bustle, its noise and its hopes.

From the diaries of Queen Marie of Romania.

TIP

Remember not to organise your answer around each technique (e.g. a paragraph on first person and then a paragraph on the use of lists), but work through the extract in sections.

FURTHER READING

For more examples of different types of diaries look at *The Penguin Book of Diaries* selected by Ronald Blythe (Penguin, 1991).

ACTIVITY 1.34

1   Identify where and how the following techniques are used in this diary extract:
  ■ the use of the **first person**, repeated in the same form of **syntax** and sentence
  ■ the sense of the writer's **voice**
  ■ how the writer also uses the **present tense** and what it tells us about the past
  ■ the use of **lists of three**
  ■ the use of **adjectives** and **verbs** to create a certain kind of mood.

2   Now, referring to the techniques you have identified, write a short commentary on this diary extract, ensuring that you use point/quotation/comment and words and phrases like *seems*, *appears*, *this suggests*, *this implies*.

Memoirs and autobiographies

Memoirs and autobiographies are generally first-person accounts of a real person's life or of a specific time or event from their life.

All memoirs differ but most share common conventions such as:

■ reference to particularly memorable or vivid events or experiences that had an impact on the life of the narrator
■ the evocation of past times or places, sometimes seen nostalgically, but also with regret, gratitude, anger, etc.
■ the 'bringing back to life' of people or interesting characters from the past
■ reflection on one's earlier life through adult eyes.

40

ACTIVITY 1.35

Write a short passage about your own life recalling an experience or event from when you were very young. Try to evoke what you felt then, as a child, and how you look at the same event now as an older person.

You need not share this work with anyone, as it may be something you would prefer to keep private. However, keep in mind the skills you had to deploy in writing it as you read the accounts that follow.

Writers may express their thoughts and feelings in memoirs and autobiographies, often relying on descriptive language to convey the sense of a particular location in which their experience occurred.

Memoirs tend to focus on a particular memory or heightened experience in the author's life. For example, the text below the photo is not a diary entry about war, but a memoir recalling a very dramatic experience in the writer's time as a soldier. The external world he found himself in seemed to encapsulate his intense feelings at the time.

A British trench during the Battle of the Somme.

ACTIVITY 1.36

Look at the extract below. List key words and phrases from the passage. Are there any you could group together or link by a particular mood? For example, *wonderful* and *peaceful* would be in a different mood category from *agonised*.

Beside, something wonderful was happening outside. Some evenings before, I had watched with some friends from a peaceful little **butte**[1] some miles behind our front the opening hours of the great bombardment. We had seen it from above, beneath a slowly sinking sun, as a long white line of surf breaking without pause on a shore that faded at its extremities into horizons beyond our sight, and had marveled that, by some trick of the ground, not a whisper from that awe-inspiring racket reached us. Now, at the tremendous climax of the last hour of the inferno – the last, I mean, before we went over the top – another miracle was being worked.

It was a glorious morning, and, as though there were some mysterious sympathy between the wonders of the ear and of the eye, the bewildering tumult seemed to grow more insistent with the growing brilliance of the atmosphere and the intenser blue of the July sky. The sound was different, not only in magnitude, but in quality, from anything known to me. It was not a succession of explosions or a continuous roar; I, at least, never heard either a gun or a bursting shell. It was not a noise; it was a symphony. It did not move; it hung over us. It was as though the air were full of a vast and agonized passion, bursting now into groans and sighs, now into shrill screams and pitiful whimpers, shuddering beneath terrible blows, torn by unearthly whips, vibrating with the solemn pulse of enormous wings. And the supernatural tumult did not pass in this direction or that. It did not begin, intensify, decline, and end. It was poised in the air, a stationary panorama of sound, a condition of the atmosphere, not the creation of man. It seemed that one had only to lift one's eyes to be appalled by the writhing of the tormented element above one, that a hand raised ever so little above the level of the trench would be sucked away into a whirlpool revolving with cruel and incredible velocity over infinite depths. And this feeling, while it filled one with awe, filled one also with triumphant exultation, the exultation of struggling against a storm in mountains, or watching the irresistible course of a swift and destructive river.

Yet at the same time one was intent on practical details, wiping the trench dirt off the bolt of one's rifle, reminding the men of what each was to do, and when the message went round, "five minutes to go," seeing that all bayonets were fixed. My captain, a brave man and a good officer, came along and borrowed a spare watch off me. It was the last time I saw him. At 7:30 we went up the ladders, doubled through the gaps in the wire, and lay down, waiting for the line to form up on each side of us. When it was ready we went forward, not doubling, but at a walk. For we had nine hundred yards of rough ground to the trench which was our first objective, and about fifteen hundred to a further trench where we were to wait for orders. There was a bright light in the air, and the tufts of coarse grass were gray with dew.

I hadn't gone ten yards before I felt a load fall from me.

From *The Attack* by R. H. Tawney.

¹ **butte** a small hill

Key technique: grouping words and phrases

Look at how grouping words and phrases together by mood can help make sense of the passage. The following diagram shows how one set of words and phrases has been linked.

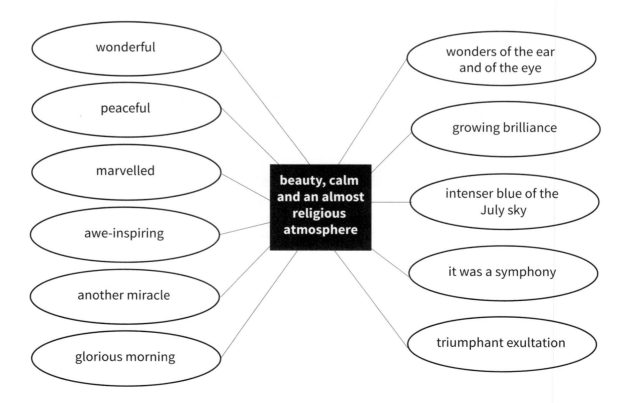

1 Now do the same for the aspect shown below. Copy and complete the diagram, finding as many words or phrases as you can.

2 Once you have completed the diagram, write a paragraph on that particular aspect. Select three or four words from the diagram and, in your paragraph, comment on them and the effects created.

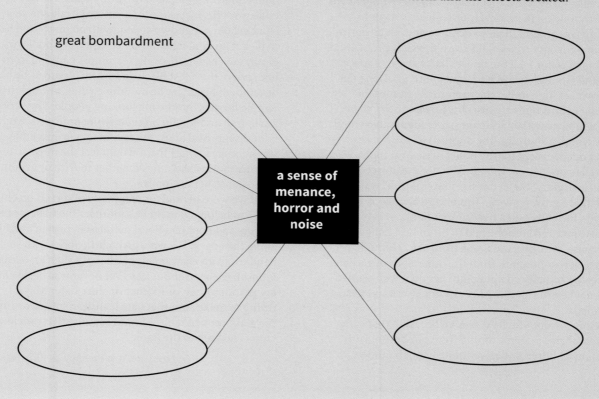

Further practice

Notice how towards the end of the extract, where the writer refers to how *one was intent on practical detail*, the rest of the passage seems to change in style and mood. Write a sentence explaining how and why this happens.

Characters in memoirs

Writers of memoirs and autobiographies sometimes use descriptive language to portray a certain location as a way of telling us about a particular character who lives there and their own reactions to the world in which they find themselves.

When we speak about 'character' what we are really talking about are the various elements that contribute to the 'picture' of someone. These might include:

- their appearance
- what they say and do
- what others say to them, about them, etc.
- how others respond to them
- the circumstances or locations they are found in.

Places as reflections of character are very common in both fiction and non-fiction. This is most obviously the case when the place is the home of the person described.

Make a list of key words and phrases in the extract on page 44 to explore what the language and style imply about the character of the writer's godmother.

For example, the following extract describes the place where the writer's godmother (Stella) lives in India.

The houses all had high ceilings and sloping roofs made of corrugated asbestos that monsoon rains would drum on, then slide off in vertical lines. (Once in a while, during a storm, milk-heavy coconuts or even an entire head of a coconut tree would crash through a roof amid torrents of water.) All the houses had a sense of space, light and circulating air, with open porches. Long flat windows set high under the roofs made frames for swirling palm fronds against sky. Lower down, there were windows with black panes, rectangular bars, and white wooden shutters. The doors to all the houses were always open, except for the hours of sleep at night.

Stella's open door, though, did not mean free visitation rights. "Stella doesn't like children" was an adage that I grew up with. There were occasions when we were formally taken over to visit Stella, scrubbed and brushed and admonished to be on best behavior. Otherwise, we observed Stella from afar: through hedges, across porches, from the other ends of gardens, or even by actually creeping into her own well-tended garden when the air hung heavy with afternoon siestas of adults...

"Going over to Stella's" was an occasion that came twice or thrice a year. Coming from our house, with too many children and never quite enough money,

Stella's house — so similar with its white walls and high windows — seemed dreamily opulent. An entire table was often set aside for a jigsaw puzzle she was working on, at her own speed, with no one to tell her to pick it up. She read the latest expensive books with glossy covers. On the walls, or simply hanging from lines, were the latest black and white pictures she had developed: beach patterns, jungle ruins, animals from temple friezes, interesting looking people. The servants, Zachariah and Raghu, in their white uniforms, exuded faint disapproval at us, the raggle-taggle ensemble. It was at Stella's house that I would feel the most acutely that my mother did not remember to trim or groom, let alone paint, her toe-nails.

If we were invited for tea, we were served on china that had belonged to Stella's mother. The delicate plates, saucers and cups had floral patterns in brown and black along the edges. We were given little forks with shell handles. In an early memory I have of such an occasion, I must have been about four. Whoever was beside me — my grandmother, or mother or elder sister Maya — was trying to make sure that I ate leaning forward towards the glass-topped table without sending that precious china crashing to the floor.

From *Stella in Bombay* by Kirin Naravan.

Key technique: characterisation through setting

You may have noticed how the writer creates a sense of freedom (*had a sense of space, light and circulating air, with open porches*) and the way in which a sense of order is suggested (*flat windows set high under the roofs made frames for swirling palm fronds against sky*).

The interior world seems to offer a sense of regularity and protection from the intrusion of the wilder elements of the outside world, an idea echoed in the way that the roofs would make the threatening rain *then slide off in vertical lines*. Such a sense of an ordered and safe world is echoed by the description of how *there were windows with black panes, rectangular bars, and white wooden shutters*.

TIP

An unusual or older character – often a relative – can be represented in memoirs or autobiographies by the writer creating a sense of mystery and offering no real **narrative**.

KEY TERMS

narrative the development or unfolding of a plot, account or story

ACTIVITY 1.39

Having read the explanation about characterisation above, and the extract as a whole, discuss with a partner:

- What might the description of the location suggest about its occupant?
- What do we learn about the children's thoughts about their grandmother from the descriptions of the location? (For example, why the words *black* and *white* are repeated and what this suggests.)

The next extract describes another writer's attempts to work out her identity and origins.

My grandfather said he knew what people we came from. I reeled off all the names I knew. Yoruba? Ibo? Ashanti? Mandingo? He said no to all of them, saying that he would know it if he heard it. I was thirteen. I was anxious for him to remember.

I pestered him for days. He told me to stop bothering him and that he would remember. Or stop bothering or else he would not remember. I hovered about him in any room in which he rested. I followed him around asking him if he wanted me to do this or that for him, clean his glasses, polish his shoes, bring his tea. I studied him intently when he came home. I searched the grey bristles of his moustache for any flicker which might suggest he was about to speak. He raised his *Sunday Guardian* newspaper to block my view. He shooed me away, telling me to find some book to read or work to do. At times it seemed as if Papa was on the brink of remembering. I imagined pulling the word off his tongue if only I knew the first syllable.

I scoured the San Fernando library and found no other lists of names at the time. Having no way of finding other names, I could only repeat the ones I knew, asking him if he was sure it wasn't Yoruba, how about Ashanti? I couldn't help myself. I wanted to be either one. I had heard that they were noble people. But I could also be Ibo; I had heard that they were gentle. And I had followed the war in Biafra. I was on their side.

Papa never remembered. Each week he came I asked him had he remembered. Each week he told me no. Then I stopped asking. He was disappointed. I was disappointed. We lived after that in this mutual disappointment. It was a rift between us. It gathered into a kind of estrangement. After that he grew old. I grew young. A small space opened in me.

From *A Map to the Door of No Return* by Dionne Brand.

45

ACTIVITY 1.40

Highlight key words and phrases in this extract. Then discuss with a partner what we learn about the grandfather and the narrator's perspective towards him.

KEY TERMS

repeated syntactical structures or **patterning** the use of the same types of word or phrase order

inner thoughts ideas in the mind of a character or narrator

ACTIVITY 1.41

Can you find further examples of the techniques of short sentences, syntactical patterns and repetitions in the text by Dionne Brand?

The first person usage (*I*) keeps the focus on the narrator throughout, but there are other aspects and techniques you might have identified:

- **lists of three** (*clean his glasses*, *polish his shoes*, *bring his tea*) to create a sense of everything the writer does in a frustrated attempt to please her grandfather
- **repeated syntactical structures** such as *I hovered about him… I followed him…* in order to create the sense of perseverance and repetitive obsession of the author's search
- **short sentences and repeated vocabulary** as a way of expressing the limited amount of progress she made and the sense of an ongoing routine that prevents any possible progress being made (*Papa never remembered. Each week he came I asked him had he remembered. Each week he told me no.*)
- a sense of **voice** expressed by conveying her **inner thoughts**.

 LINK

Drawing conclusions about people from the settings or locations is something you can apply to a range of texts. Look back at the extract from *Touching the Void* on page 21. What does the environment, and the narrator's response to it, tell us about him?

Third person memoirs

The memoirs and autobiographies you have analysed so far in this section have been written in first person. Writers of these types of texts may also choose to write in **third person singular** in order to distance themselves from their subject.

For example, the writer may adopt the voice of a child to convey how she or he was feeling (rather than the events which were happening around them) at certain points of their upbringing.

Read this autobiographical account in which a South African writer looks back to a time earlier in his career when he visited London, aspiring to become a poet.

The British Museum Library Reading Room.

ACTIVITY 1.42

By listing key words and phrases in this extract, explore the use of present tense, voice and expression of inner thoughts in the first two paragraphs.

46

It is three o'clock on a Saturday afternoon. He has been in the Reading Room since opening time, reading Ford's *Mr Humpty Dumpty*, a novel so tedious that he has to fight to stay awake. In a short while the Reading Room will close for the day, the whole great Museum will close. On Sundays the Reading Room does not open; between now and next Saturday, reading will be a matter of an hour snatched here and there of an evening. Should he soldier on until closing time, though he is racked with yawns? What is the point of this enterprise anyway?

What is the good to a computer programmer, if computer programming is to be his life, to have an MA in English literature? And where are the unrecognised masterpieces that he was going to uncover? *Mr Humpty Dumpty* is certainly not one of them. He shuts the book, packs up.

Outside the daylight is already waning. Along Great Russell Street he trudges to Tottenham Court Road, then south toward Charing Cross. Of the throng on the sidewalks, most are young people. Strictly speaking he is their contemporary, but he does not feel like that. He feels middle-aged, prematurely middle-aged: one of those bloodless, high-domed, exhausted scholars whose skin flakes at the merest touch. Deeper than that he is still a child ignorant of his place in the world, frightened, indecisive. What is he doing in this huge, cold city where merely to stay alive means holding tight all the time, trying not to fall?

The bookshops on Charing Cross Road stay open until six. Until six he has somewhere to go. After that he will be adrift amid the Saturday-night fun-seekers. For a while he can follow the flow, pretending he too is seeking fun, pretending he has somewhere to go, someone to meet; but in the end he will have to give up and catch the train back to Archway station and the solitude of his room.

From *Lost in London* by J.M.Coetzee.

ACTIVITY 1.43

1   Find examples of the following techniques in the extract:
   - the sense of endless boredom conveyed by the present tense
   - how the writer uses certain phrases and adjectives (like *tedious*) and verbs (such as *soldier on*) and what this expresses
   - how he vocalises his inner thoughts through a series of questions.

2   Now write a paragraph explaining what you think the effect of the writer using the third person is. What does Coetzee achieve through this? (Think about when in his life he might have actually written this account and also about the dual perspective of narrator and 'character'.)

Further practice

Look at the final two paragraphs of the extract and the ways in which it starts to draw on more descriptive language.

Dialogue and action

When writers focus descriptions on other people, they can reveal as much about themselves as the people they present. **Dialogue**, is of course, a key signal of character and behaviour. Writers do not use dialogue as 'filler' but to convey important ideas about people or, in narratives, to forward the plot/**action**.

For example, in the following extract the writer visits her apparently high-achieving sister and her family. Through the dialogue, and what happens around it, a number of things emerge about the narrator.

KEY TERMS

dialogue speech or conversation of, or between, characters

actions things done or decisions taken

47

When I arrived at my sister's new home, she was still at work. I was greeted at the door by my 7-year-old niece, Sophie, still recovering from a cold, and the nanny who, I later found out, makes more money than I do.

"Aunt Tobin, come see my room!" said Sophie, grabbing my hand and pulling me up the stairs to her room, which was bright, clean, organized.

"It's amazing," I said with a tinge of sadness she's too young to have noticed.

Sophie continued the tour around the home – not ostentatious or a mansion, by any stretch, but big and two stories and beautiful. She took me into my sister's room, a gigantic spread with a king-size bed and large flat-screen TV hanging above a fireplace. Her bathroom has two sinks, the biggest bathtub I've ever seen, marble counter tops, and makeup drawers that stop short of the cabinet then slowly, quietly close on their own, like the trunk lids on fancy cars...

The morning after I arrived in Los Angeles was frenetic. The rustling began at 6 a.m., when my brother-in-law got up to make the kids' lunch.

"Can you wake up Sophie and make sure she gets dressed?" my sister asked.

"Sure, no problem," I said, needing to be useful in some way, wanting to feel like a part of the family, and hoping to disprove my sister's conviction that I'm wholly incapable of being functional before 10 a.m.

But my niece didn't want to get out of bed. Apparently, acquiescence costs $2.

On the drive to school, Sophie sat behind me, elevated by a kid seat that I needed her help to install in my manual-windows-only Kia rental. I was wearing old jeans and the sweat shirt I'd slept in, trying and failing to engage in a conversation through the rear-view mirror. Then the Violent Femmes came on the radio. "Kiss off," I love that song, so I started singing, hoping she'd appreciate the entertainment. *I said one one one cause you left me / And two two two for my sorrow / And three three three for my heartache ...*

"Stop!" said my niece. "You're weird, Aunt Tobin."

From *My Sister's Perfect Life* by Tobin Levy.

Read this commentary which focuses largely on the dialogue.

KEY TERMS

imperative order or command

understatement phrasing ideas so that they do not sound as impressive as they might appear; offering faint praise or a sense of disapproval

COMMENTARY

At first the niece uses positive, inviting language which is in fact an **imperative** without any sense of formal greeting, an indication that she is at ease with her aunt. The enthusiasm and urgency of the invitation is accompanied by the child's instinctive *grabbing* and *pulling* which suggest a sense of intimacy and an equal level of familiarity. The aunt's reply (*It's amazing*) does not seem to mirror the initial enthusiasm of the niece's words; the absence of the exclamation mark in comparison to Sophie's greeting an indication of this sense of **understatement** or sense of inferiority as the writer realises the kind of environment Sophie and her family inhabit.

ACTIVITY 1.44

1 Discuss with a partner:
   - Which character does the commentary focus on?
   - What particular actions and spoken words does the commentary pick up on to explore the relationship?
   - Why does the commentary draw attention to the omission of the exclamation mark?

2 Now, working on your own, copy and complete this table which selects some other aspects of dialogue and actions from the passage:

Point	Quotation	Comment/effect on how we view narrator/Sophie
Mother's words in morning echo Sophie's opening words	"Come see my room." "Can you wake up Sophie …"	Suggests both mother and daughter are telling the compliant narrator what to do
Sophie's refusal to do what she's told at first	But my niece didn't want to get out of bed…	Suggests …
Sophie helping her aunt to fix the car seat		
Sophie telling her aunt not to sing		Implies that …

3 Look at some of the other elements of the passage and make notes on:
   - the physical descriptions of the house and the gadgets in it
   - the appearance and behaviour of the narrator herself
   - asides or apparently 'throwaway' comments which reveal something about the writer and her situation.

4 Finally, write a full commentary on the whole passage in answer to the following task:

   How does the writer present her situation and relationships in the passage through the style and language used?

   Include the notes you have made on *all* the aspects you explored, including dialogue.

Humour and hyperbole

One of the key techniques writers use is to take a situation or experience and use exaggerated language or ideas for effect. This device is often used by feature writers in magazines or newspapers who reflect with an element of amusement upon their own lives, or those of people they know well.

KEY TERMS

hyperbole exaggeration

anecdotal relating to minor personal events or moments

In the following extract, the writer uses a number of devices to paint a vivid portrait of his father. These include:

- **anecdotal** accounts – examples of things his father has said and done
- **hyperbole** – exaggerated images, descriptions or comparisons
- the use of a variety of tenses to convey past behaviour or experiences with his father, and the current situation.

There is little description, if any, of his father's physical appearance, other than his voice. It is therefore important to understand how the writer is able to convey such an effective portrait of his father.

ACTIVITY 1.45

Read the extract and make your usual list of key words and phrases, ready to write up for a commentary on the style and language.

"Try not to overdo the exercise," I tell my dad. "I'M FINE," he replies, loudly. "I'VE ALREADY BEEN FOR A SEVEN MILE RUN, SWAM FORTY LENGTHS AND CHOPPED A BIG LOAD OF WOOD THIS MORNING." I live over a hundred miles from my parents, and I haven't seen them since two months ago, when my dad first reignited his exercise regime, but I already feel tired merely from hearing about it. Could he not just do the same things in moderation? I ask him.

I know from historical evidence that this is a bit like trying to persuade a lion to ignore a gazelle carcass and eat some tapas with a fork, but it has become my job to worry.

He has been having violently energetic sporting dreams again. This is a customary byproduct of the punishing regimes of physical exercise he plunges into every couple of years or so. "LAST NIGHT'S ONE WAS ABOUT A WINNING HEADER IN A FOOTBALL MATCH," he told me. "I WOKE UP ON THE FLOOR. I HIT THE BEDSIDE TABLE ON THE WAY. I EMAILED THE BBC WEATHER TEAM TO SAY THEY'RE RUBBISH AND COULDN'T FORECAST THE DAYS OF THE WEEK. THEY HAVEN'T GOT BACK TO ME."

A few years ago, my dad successfully completed a marathon in a superhero suit, seventeen months shy of his sixtieth birthday. During his warm-up for this, his nocturnal adventures included another top flight football clash, which left him with a deep cut on his forehead (same bedside table) and a rugby match which climaxed with him drop-kicking my mum across the bed. After a slightly sedentary period, he's started exercising a lot again of late: running several miles a day and getting up at 6am to swim competitively against his friend Malcolm.

As my dad reports incidents from his recent athletic life to me, he will switch subjects mid-flow, without pausing for breath. He might come back to the original subject, but you never know for sure, or at what point. "I LET THE POSTWOMAN FEEL MY STOMACH TODAY," he told me on the phone yesterday. "SHE SAID IT WAS REALLY FLAT. I RUN AROUND THE VILLAGE CRICKET PITCH BECAUSE THEN YOUR MUM KNOWS THERE'S ROOM FOR AN AIR AMBULANCE IF I HAVE A HEART ATTACK."

He is the worst kind of wing man to have as a storyteller, constantly charging in and riding roughshod over the crescendo of my mum's gently told anecdotes. "Mick," she'll say. "Who's telling this story?" But it has little effect. We've now almost cured him of his habit of quietly picking up their second telephone and adding his bellowing input to our conversations at comically inopportune moments, but a chat with him in the flesh can leave you feeling spent and dizzy.

My parents come from families of vastly contrasting volumes: one excitable, one deferentially quiet. Whereas my late nan – my mum's mum – tended to pick up the phone in the manner of a woman who'd been hiding from an angry dragon for her entire life and was worried it might have finally tracked her down using the phonebook, my dad's parents would often bellow for several minutes into answer phones before realising they weren't speaking to a real human, so accustomed were they to their voices drowning out those of others. My grandma and granddad are gone now, and my dad doesn't have a similarly loud spouse, or siblings, so he makes up for it by adding two or three extra raucous conversations to every room he's in.

"THAT WAS THE OTHER THING ABOUT MICK GALLAGHER FROM MY GANG IN THE EARLY SIXTIES," my dad – who, though still some way from his dotage, has definitely reached his anecdotage – will explain. "HE LATER WENT OUT WITH THREE WOMEN. LOOK AT THE SIZE OF THAT BUZZARD! I DON'T LIKE THAT BLOKE OFF *GRAND DESIGNS*[1]. HE OWNS TOO MANY JACKETS."

Being at the wheel of the car will not stem the flow. "IMAGINE WHAT IT WOULD HAVE BEEN LIKE TO LIVE ON THAT FARM IN THE SEVENTEEN HUNDREDS," he'll say, slowing down his VW Golf.

[1] *Grand Designs* a UK television programme

"BRILLIANT! I USED TO MAKE GREAT DENS AS A KID. SEE THAT SPEED CAMERA? IT'S FAKE."

Of course, with all this exercising, the adrenaline is pumping all the harder, and his storytelling even more enthusiastic and freeform. My mum claims my dad "doesn't have an off switch" but I'm not sure that's strictly true. He can fall asleep instantly in pretty much any environment, on any vaguely horizontal surface. When he's off, he's completely off. It's just that when he's on, he's also completely on. He's like a TV in that sense: an old one, without the standby function.

From *Loud Dad* by Tom Cox.

ACTIVITY 1.46

Write a commentary on the style and language of the extract:

- Write a brief, focused introduction for the extract.
- Work through the extract in sections, looking for contrasts, differences and similarities between them.
- Use the words and phrases that have been highlighted as the basis for the quotations commented on.
- Try not to assert ideas but use words like *seems*, *appears* and *apparent*.
- Don't use excessive linguistic terminology or try to spot techniques and language features for their own sake.

Summary

Remember these key points from this section:

- Personal writing can take many forms and will contain elements of other types of text.
- A sense of 'voice' is central to personal writing.
- Characterisation, whether of the writer or of the people they are describing, is an important component of much personal writing.
- Exploring the use of a variety of tenses can provide insights into the writer's perspective.

Persuasive writing

In this section you will:

- read a range of **persuasive** texts
- explore some of their key features.

What is persuasive writing?

Persuasive writing can take many forms:

- **reviews** of cultural events or experiences such as plays or films
- reviews of texts such as novels, poetry or non-fiction

KEY TERMS

persuasive trying to convince others about a particular idea, viewpoint or product

review a critical assessment of something – such as a film, book, television or radio programme

- feature articles in magazine or newspapers which tackle a particular issue or topic
- opinion pieces with a more direct and straightforward angle on a subject of debate
- letters in newspapers or other media.

The style and language of persuasive writing is driven by the form, the audience and the stance of the writer. Some use highly emotive, charged language to create maximum impact; others employ a more balanced tone, using measured argument to make their point. Other writers might take an amused or slightly ironic approach.

The conventions writers use in persuasive writing will therefore change according to the tone they wish to strike. These might include:

- loaded, emotive language (e.g. *he gives an <u>appallingly dull, wooden performance</u>*)
- rhetorical effects and devices, for example, rhetorical questions (e.g. <u>*Are we really meant to believe so many men would fall for her?*</u>)
- humour or **ironic** comment (e.g. *The only chemistry between them was <u>the hot air they kept on speaking</u>*)
- expanded noun phrases, especially in reviews (e.g. *'He is the <u>usual all-American downtrodden fall-guy we all root for</u>*)
- hyperbole, or exaggeration for comic, **sarcastic** or dramatic impact (e.g. *The music continues <u>to rattle the lonely glassware</u>. This is a very quiet restaurant.*)
- direct appeal to the reader through a conversational tone, for example using **question tags** or other informal forms (e.g. <u>*You'll*</u> *come out of the cinema smiling, <u>which can't be a bad thing, can it?</u>*)
- technical or specialist/subject-specific vocabulary that casts the writer as an expert (e.g. *The opening <u>montage</u> clearly shot <u>on location</u> in Turkey features a roof-top chase which introduces our charismatic <u>protagonist</u>*)
- often, but not exclusively, expressed mainly in the present tense to describe the immediate experience.

51

> 🔑 **KEY TERMS**
>
> **ironic** suggesting the opposite to what is expected
>
> **sarcastic** sharp and mocking
>
> **question tag** a verbal addition to statements to add rhetorical emphasis or to elicit a reaction (e.g. *We'll be home by tea, **won't we**, Mum? It's a terrible indictment of our government, **isn't it?**)

●●● FURTHER RESEARCH

In some cases a writer may try to persuade in a balanced piece of writing such as a newspaper article, but sometimes editorial opinion can be much more biased. Try to find examples of:

- a balanced news article
- a biased editorial or opinion piece
- a blog in which the writer expresses his or her opinion.

In each case, try to identify the techniques and language the writer uses in order to persuade their readers towards their point of view.

A theatre review

Read the following text which describes the writer's experience of watching a particular show in a theatre.

Taken on its own terms, however, my first brush with the show on stage (I saw the film version with Madonna) leaves little impression. Most of the numbers blend together and the strongest melody is reprised throughout beginning with "What A Circus," the famed peak "Don't Cry For Me, Argentina" and the finale. This unfolding of a melody throughout a show can climax with a powerful "reveal" of the number. Here it simply feels like leaning on a good tune too often.

Still, this is a handsome production with a full orchestra sounding marvelous. One can imagine a hungry, attention-grabbing actress like Patti Lupone making the most of the spotlight. Unfortunately, the acclaimed actress Elena Roger can barely hold the stage. Her voice is not remotely equipped for the part and her stage presence is minimal. You look at the spectacle of this *Evita* when you should be riveted on Eva Peron herself. An entire nation prostrates itself at her feet? You doubt they'd even notice her...

Evita should be a fiercely ambitious character as embodied in her singing. But Roger's voice is so thin and small (she played Edith Piaf in another hit show in London) that it simply disappears in the higher register. You're more worried for her than intimidated or magnetized. Her best moments occur when she can stay in that lower register and speak-sing a song, such as the duet "I'd Be Surprisingly Good For You," with Cerveris. He, by the way, is a marvelous performer, but paired with Roger and singing what is essentially a dull and uninteresting role, even Cerveris can't do much. Also less demanding vocally (though during this song she's dancing quite a bit) is "Buenos Aires" with Martin. He's an amiable presence on stage albeit with little of the ability to give Che the edginess and cynicism the role desperately needs.

When it comes to that iconic number "Don't Cry For Me Argentina," Roger simply makes you feel nervous. It works better at the end when her frail voice can be seen as in character, since Evita is dying when she reprises the tune from her deathbed (where, frankly, it makes more emotional sense than it does on the balcony anyway). She's especially exposed on "You Must Love Me," the ballad written for the film which she sings alone on a stage with Cerveris. Without sets and dancing and other cast members to distract, you have nothing to focus on but her unconvincing vocals.

Frankly, it's difficult to understand why she was cast in London, much less here, where the standards for musicals are and should be the highest in the world. Roger unquestionably does not possess the pipes to sing this part. Since this isn't a dance show where dancing might be the most important talent and she certainly doesn't act anyone off the stage, why would her ability to—at best—get through the big numbers rather than nail them be acceptable? The entire show is built around what should be the fiery performance at its heart, making this *Evita* very cool indeed...

'Do Cry for Argentina' by Michael Giltz, from *The Huffington Post*.

ACTIVITY 1.47

Make brief notes on the following questions:

■ What is the writer's viewpoint on the show?
■ Which of the techniques or language features mentioned on page 51 can be seen here? (Look particularly for examples of loaded language – either positive or negative.)

Key technique: the expert view

One key feature of many reviews is the **expert** view. This can be seen in:

■ specialist or technical terms which the writer is competent in using
■ the perspective or viewpoint expressed (a confidence that they know what they're talking about)
■ references to other, similar texts, plays, etc.

Read the extended commentary opposite, which begins by commenting on this aspect in particular.

KEY TERMS

expert a person who is a great authority on a subject

Reference to the expert tone of the piece.

Evidence in the **modal form** *should be* – what the production ought to have and in the specialist terms, *melody* and *reprised*.

Additional noun phrases emphasise the writer's knowledge.

COMMENTARY

In the passage, the writer expresses his views by seeming to develop a clear sense of voice, that <u>of someone who is an expert</u>, someone who knows what should be expected as evidenced in the **modal** form ('<u>Evita should be… the strongest melody is reprised throughout</u>') and appears to further demonstrate that knowledge by offering some apparent compliments(*this is <u>a handsome production</u> with a <u>full orchestra sounding marvellous</u> … is a marvellous performer … <u>the acclaimed actress</u> … an amiable presence on stage*).

Yet, a number of direct statements (*leaves little impression … it's difficult to understand why she was cast*) leave no doubt about his real opinion. Indeed, an apparent compliment (*This unfolding of a melody throughout a show can climax …*) is sometimes undermined straight away by such a direct statement – *Here it simply feels like leaning on a good tune too often* – so that the syntax creates a rather downbeat tone with the final words here suggesting a lack of effort on the production's part.

The more forthright comments leave little doubt about the writer's true sentiments as he highlights the central performer, in particular, as his target. She is described in negative terms and there is little attempt to offer any apparent compliments as the reviewer draws on contrasts between the expectations of the audience and the unexpected experience they come across: where the lead character should be *fiercely ambitious* the performer's voice *is so thin and small*, suggesting a sense of frailty and inadequacy symbolic of her entire performance and not just her voice. A further contrast is used to suggest how low the reviewer estimates her. He employs strong adjectives to describe one of her rivals – a *hungry, attention-grabbing … Patti Lupone* – conveying her sense of passion and self-centred demands in comparison to the current star who *can barely hold the stage*, the **adverb** implying her limitations and frailty once more.

Other adverbs are also used by the writer, as if he is taking us into his own private thoughts and opening up to us – he repeats the word *frankly* as if reaching a decisive and revealing moment of recognition and understanding about his feelings for the show. Yet, there are some occasions where he cannot hide his sense of voice, his rather sarcastic tone, expressing his inner thoughts. He follows the rhetorical question *An entire nation prostrates itself at her feet?* – where he blurs the line between the real Eva Peron who was adored by some of her followers in her lifetime – with the actual actor playing her so that there is again an answer which adds to the other aspects of the downbeat tone in the article: *You doubt they'd even notice her…*

53

KEY TERMS

modal a form or type of verb that modifies the meaning of another one (e.g. *I **might** go* alters or modifies the meaning of the verb *to go* so that it suggests possibility; another modal, *will*, when added to *go* modifies the meaning again, so that it expresses certainty)

adverb a word which tells us more about a verb

ACTIVITY 1.48

1 Which of the *other* features or techniques you picked up in the activity opposite have been identified in the commentary?
2 Which have been missed, if any?
3 What comments are made in the commentary about the mood and perspective of the reviewer?

A film review

By reading other reviews for different art forms, you can begin to pick up on common conventions that they share, whilst at the same time beginning to appreciate the distinctive voice of individual critics.

Read this extract from a review of a different art form – a film about Princess Diana. Begin by listing key words and phrases, preparing to comment on the kinds of techniques and effects the writer employs to express her opinions about the film.

What was Naomi Watts thinking? No sooner has she landed her second Oscar nod for tsunami drama *The Impossible* than she's in over her head trying to pass herself off as **Princess Diana**[1]. She must have some nerve, too, tackling the last days of "the most famous woman in the world" when no film-maker in this country would dare touch the story.

As it turns out, Watts and Hirschbiegel aren't that plucky at all. Their approach to Diana is tentative, like a couple of tourists on a British beach, dipping their toes in shallow water and running out again at the first nip of cold. For Hirschbiegel there is a more bitter irony in that almost a decade after making Hitler look human in *Downfall* (and earning an Oscar nomination), he has failed to do for Diana what he did for the most evil man who ever lived.

The cocked head, the tilted chin, the searching gaze beneath fluttering eyelashes; it's as if Naomi Watts is being mildly electrocuted to reproduce all the ticks and quirks that Diana exhibited in her **1995 interview with Martin Bashir**[2]. It's easy to imagine Hirschbiegel behind the camera with his finger on the buzzer, pressing every time he wants an emotional reaction. Unfortunately, it does not have the desired effect.

What was Diana thinking? It's difficult to tell behind the mascara and the nervous mannerisms. This rendering is very blonde and very bland.

That interview with Bashir is a flashpoint for the film, but it's Diana's romance with Pakistani heart surgeon Hasnat Khan (much too earnestly played by *Lost* star Naveen Andrews) that provides its framework. He falls hook, line and sinker for that eyelash thing, but if this is a love story between sinner and saint, he's the one wearing the halo. "I save lives," he says (more than once) and Diana is suitably impressed.

Not to be outdone, though, she wanders through minefields, kisses sick children and invites an old blind man in a crowd to touch her face. Her humanitarian work is reductively portrayed – just another way to elicit sympathy for her troubles, because long eyelashes will only get you so far.

It's tempting to think that Diana's charitable efforts were, in some way, an attempt to redeem her less attractive features, but Hirschbiegel doesn't bridge the gap between the conflicting sides of her character. He doesn't even try. He only hints at her manipulative tendencies. Diana makes light of being "a mad bitch stalker" after breaking into Khan's flat, donning rubber gloves and proceeding to (shock, horror) clean the kitchen.

She's also seen playing cat-and-mouse games with the press when **Dodi Fayed**[3] enters the picture. Of course no one could sympathise with a bunch of slobbering press hounds, but what of the man who was killed alongside her? He only gets two lines in the script (bad news for jobbing actor Cas Anvar), but according to this film, he was only bait to make Khan jealous. Best to keep him in the background then, in case he starts looking like the forgotten victim in all this.

The thing is, Diana was lonely. Oh so lonely ... That's how Geraldine James explains away her questionable behaviour as acupuncturist and friend Oonagh Toffolo. Diana's relationship with Khan is marked by separation because he firmly insists that he is "a private man", unable to see how he can operate on people's hearts ("saving people's lives!") with paps shoving cameras in his face.

On the other hand, he can't live without Diana and the montage-friendly fun they had: watching telly on the sofa, frolicking on the beach and in the bedroom, her head thrown back in rapturous laughter – often at serious risk of tipping the wig she wore to disguise herself. Then there were the late-night dinners at Chicken Cottage, presumably because that's the only place open after midnight.

The dialogue is as stodgy as the contents of a bargain bucket. Khan occasionally throws a little poetry into the mix, but very often they're just attacking each other with the blunt realities of the situation, i.e. that she is the most famous woman in the world and he's busy (saving lives!).

When Hasnat calls Diana to the middle of Hyde Park in the dead of the night for yet another round of stating the blindingly obvious, the only burning question that springs to mind is, 'Was the Chicken Cottage not open?' The park is a strange place to meet except that it offers Watts the chance to do a Tom Cruise and run off at speed through the dark empty streets, with strained expression, cursing a world that seems to be against her. And Hirschbiegel gets to tick off yet another cliché.

Truth? Maybe you can't handle the truth.

From a review by Stella Papamichael, *Radio Times*.

[1] **Princess Diana** formerly married to Prince Charles, heir to the British throne

[2] **1995 interview with Martin Bashir** a famous TV interview after her divorce

[3] **Dodi Fayed** Diana's partner at the time of her death

ACTIVITY 1.50

1 Working in small groups, divide up the following features and look for them in this extract:
   - the use of apparent compliments which are then undercut
   - the use of direct statements to state a viewpoint clearly
   - words and phrases that create a downbeat tone
   - the use of contrasts
   - the use of adjectives and adverbs which reveal tone or perspective
   - the use of internal thoughts as if the reviewer is thinking out loud
   - points where the reviewer's voice emerges openly.

2 When you have finished, discuss:
   - what you think the reviewer's opinion is,
   - how you would describe it.

   You will need to go beyond saying that she likes/dislikes the film and find a way of expressing the tone of the critic.

FURTHER RESEARCH

Look for other reviews of plays, film, books, concerts or television programmes in newspapers, magazines and online. Choose two or three and use them to practise writing further analyses, adopting the techniques suggested above.

Further practice

Now, take at least two or three of the aspects from the bulleted list above and write a partial analysis of the language and style of this film review. Explore how the writer's response to the film is presented.

A restaurant review

Read this review. It is a food critic's opinion about his experience of eating in a particular restaurant. As you read, pick out words and phrases that indicate:

- the writer's state of mind, and how thoughts 'pop' up in the review
- his observations about the place and the food, and how that changes or develops
- specific details that indicate his own knowledge, or lack of it (how much is he pretending not to know a lot?)

This week's restaurant is housed in what, from the outside, is a lovely hunk of oldness. I want to say Victorian, but perhaps it's Georgian. Or older. Or younger. I don't know. It's pretty. What do I know about architecture? And the mere fact that I am banging on about the outside of the restaurant, as if standing with my toe on the threshold, hesitating before taking you inside, speaks volumes. Can I also say that the people inside seem nice? Smiley. Rather sweet. Welcoming. Oh God.

This is tough. Not as tough as it's going to be for them to read, but less than easy all the same. I considered reviewing without naming them; holding up the faults as ones from which others could learn. But that, I realised, was a stupid idea. They may be nice people. They may have their hearts in the right place. But they are still charging money – £90 for two is not peanuts – and, after all, who am I writing for?

So come with me then, into the flag-stoned hallway, which is brightly lit. Not just "Oh, I can see my way" brightly lit but "Blimey, that's a bit sharp" brightly lit. And from there into the "lounge", which is the last place you'd want to do such a thing. The lights are up so high you can see every scuff mark on the walls, every tatty seam on the oddly positioned dun-coloured sofas. Young people's music clatters and bangs off every hard surface.

We order a couple of "Kia Royals". It's viciously sweet. Then I think: maybe it's my fault. When what should be a mix of champagne and a blush of cassis costs £4 the clue is in the price. One of the staff gets out a mop and starts slopping down the floor in the doorway. Through to the completely empty dining room, which is equally brightly lit. The music continues to rattle the lonely glassware. This is a very quiet restaurant. It is trying. To which I immediately want to add "very". It

feels like a place that hasn't worked out how to do the thing it wants to do.

The food is a mix of odd and uncertain and not quite. Sautéed field mushrooms come on what feel like toasted pieces of pre-sliced brown bread. The advertised smoked stilton – why would you smoke stilton? – makes no impact. It's a pile of things, as though cobbled together from ingredients at the back of the fridge. Dense cod fritters come on a big, dry pile of garden peas with hunks of chorizo. There is meant to be a butter and sage sauce, but there is no sign of it. A main-course duck dish is brown. Very, very brown: a few squares of roasted brown root vegetables, a huge brown breaded mashed potato croquette like a draught excluder, some slices of overdone brown duck. A brown sauce. It's a strange plateful for £17.50. Better are some plaice fillets with planks of crisp bacon and vast amounts of mash. We console ourselves with a well-priced bottle of wine.

Desserts are the one clear success. A crème brûlée with Kahlua is a bit solid, but at least you can't taste the Kahlua. A pear and almond tart is an expert piece of tart making. Pastry seems to be something the kitchen is good at. From time to time someone wanders into the dining room to ask if everything is all right, but we don't want to intrude on private grief by being honest so we say fine.

This restaurant was chosen for review after much research. Views were sourced, temperatures taken. The website looked convincing. I did not want to go to the obvious places. It was with the best of intentions. The team here have a lovely site, they really do. But if they want it to work, they have to change. And they could start by turning down the lights, before somebody else comes along and switches them off altogether.

From a review by Jay Rayner, *The Observer*.

Key technique: evoking thought processes

Writers often use sentence structure and types of sentence (long, short, simple, complex, etc.) to convey their state of mind. For example, an account of a match might read:

> *I wondered if I was watching the same team I'd seen last year. It was bizarre. United players kept falling over or passing to the other team. What was going on? I found my mind drifting. When was half-time? Oh… they'd scored. The other team, that is. No surprise there. Time for my half-time pie and cup of tea.*

From this we get a sense of the way the writer's mind is drifting, uninvolved with the game. The short questions are unanswered, and when something does happen, the writer expresses his weary acceptance in a short minor sentence with no verb – *No surprise there* – a throwaway line soon replaced by another minor sentence as a more important thought pops into his mind – *pie and cup of tea*.

ACTIVITY 1.51

Now read this commentary below on the restaurant review. As you read, ask yourself:

- Do you agree with the comments made? (e.g. that the writer *does not set himself up as an expert*)
- What new or different techniques that you haven't come across before does the writer of the commentary draw our attention to?

COMMENTARY

The review begins with a direct statement suggesting a positive frame of mind – *This week's restaurant is housed in what, from the outside, is a lovely hunk of oldness* – conveying a sense of the restaurant's tradition and solidity in the final words; and yet on closer reading there is a degree of qualification in the words *from the outside*, implying that inside may not sustain this initial impression.

Unlike the other reviews so far, the writer does not set himself up as an expert. A form of stream of conscious uncertainty begins to take over and we see the use of short sentences to create an impression of rapid, alternating thoughts (*Or older. Or younger.*), accompanied by further qualification (*perhaps*), culminating in doubt (*I don't know.*) and the expression of inner thoughts which seem to move from a degree of certainty (*It's pretty*) to issues of further uncertainty and confusion (*I don't know. It's pretty. What do I know about architecture? … Can I also say that the people inside seem nice?*)

We see the writer's thoughts progress in terms of syntactical patterning (*This is tough. Not as tough as it's going to be for them to read*) as word associations and repetitive vocabulary show him making tentative progress in coming to a decision. Further use of repetitive syntax seems to confirm the decision he has taken – and the reason for it; the use of *They may … They may … they are* shows an increasing degree of certainty and confirmation on his part.

The third paragraph seems to switch to a more inviting and personal tone as the writer, far from being an expert, assumes we are on the same

---

KEY TERMS

word associations ideas suggested by particular words or phrases

syntactical patterning the use and order of similar words and structures

KEY TERMS

register language associated with a particular subject or situation

level as him (*So come with me then*) now that he has made his decision and got beyond his doubts. The adjectives in the phrases *flag-stoned* and *brightly lit* suggest an air of solid tradition and a positive atmosphere once more. However, the **register** seems to become more colloquial and critical (*Not just "Oh, I can see my way" brightly lit but "Blimey, that's a bit sharp" brightly lit*) and the balanced and repetitive syntactical phrasing of *Not just … brightly lit … but brightly lit* creates a sense of one view outweighing another.

Furthermore, the way in which the writer seems to quote the words of contrast from an actual customer (*"Oh, I can see my way" … "Blimey, that's a bit sharp"*) again suggest that he is on our level and using the down-to-earth vocabulary of the average customer.

The negative atmosphere of the interior world or setting, in contrast to the sense of solid tradition conveyed in the opening sentence of the review, is expressed by the groups of words (*scuff … tatty … oddly positioned*) associated with an untidy and disorganised presentation. The initial impression of the rather harsh lighting is echoed by the way in which the writer feels *music clatters and bangs off every hard surface*, words inferring how he feels oppressed by harsh and aggressive elements.

Further practice

Re-read the last three paragraphs of the review. Comment on the kinds of techniques and effects the writer employs to express his views.

Look particularly for examples of the following:

- a mixture of direct statement and doubt
- the use of adjectives
- further negative and harsh vocabulary
- further use of word associations
- the use of internal thoughts.

Scripted speeches

Scripted speeches are those that are prepared and written down in advance in contrast to the kind of spontaneous conversation and dialogue we use in everyday situations. Scripted speeches may be political speeches or speeches addressed to particular organisations or gatherings. They may be intended for public mass audiences or for more local and private meetings. Such speeches:

- seek to engage their audience in a range of ways, often with rhetorical techniques similar to those used in persuasive writing; they may or may not offer counter-arguments
- tend to offer a particular line or point of view and attempt to persuade listeners to share their vision
- may try to establish a particular mood, a particular attempt to come to terms with issues or events or a vision of the future; they may draw on a range of techniques to achieve these ends.

KEY TERMS

ideal a vision of something perfect, a desire to aim for

Key technique: the direct approach

Some scripted speeches may adopt a plain and direct style, whilst encouraging some future **ideal**. Read the following text, which is an extract from a speech given by Aung San Suu Kyi of Burma.

I believe that all the people who have assembled here have without exception come with the unshakeable desire to strive for and win a multi-party democratic system. In order to arrive at this objective, all the people should march unitedly in a disciplined manner towards the goal of democracy...

A number of people are saying that since I have spent most of my time abroad and am married to a foreigner I could not be familiar with the ramifications of this country's politics. I wish to speak from this platform very frankly and openly to the people. It is true that I have lived abroad. It is also true that I am married to a foreigner. These facts have never interfered and will never interfere with or lessen my love and devotion for my country by any measure or degree.

We must make democracy the popular creed. We must try to build up a free Burma in accordance with such a creed. If we should fail to do this, our people are bound to suffer. If democracy should fail the world cannot stand back and just look on, and therefore Burma would one day, like Japan and Germany, be despised. Democracy is the only ideology which is consistent with freedom. It is also an ideology that promotes and strengthens peace. It is therefore the only ideology we should aim for.

That is what my father said. It is the reason why I am participating in this struggle for freedom and democracy in the footsteps and traditions of my father. To achieve democracy the people should be united. That is very clear. It is a very plain fact. If there is no unity of purpose we shall be unable to achieve anything at all. If the people are disunited, no ideology or form of government can bring much benefit to the country. This must be firmly fixed in the minds of the people. If there is no discipline, no system can succeed. Therefore one people should always be united and disciplined.

From a speech by Aung San Suu Kyi.

59

ACTIVITY 1.52

Discuss with a partner:

- What is the main point that Aung San Suu Kyi makes in this speech?
- How would you describe the mode of address? Is it direct and straightforward? Or more subtle and complex?
- How can you tell?

 KEY TERMS

future tense as if happening later in time

Work through Activity 1.52 then read this extract from a commentary on the speech. It deals in particular with the first three paragraphs.

COMMENTARY

The speaker adopts a personal and open tone, attitude or mood in her use of direct statements (*I believe that all the people*), drawing on the literal and metaphoric idea that the group is on some kind of journey towards an ideal (*march … towards the goal of democracy*). At the same time, the speaker tries to establish a personal connection with the audience by referring to her own situation and circumstances in order to alleviate any negative impression listeners might have about her (*people are saying that since I have spent most of my time abroad and am married to a foreigner*). She uses adverbs (*frankly and openly*) to express her efforts to be honest with them. The use of repeated structures and their syntactical positioning at the beginning of her sentences attempts to reinforce this impression (*It is true … It is also true*), as does the choice of repeated key words (*have never interfered and will never interfere*), the switch from past to **future tense** – an indication of her conviction then and now.

Indeed, this sense of personal conviction is then directed towards certainty about future actions. The use of repeated key phrases and structures create a sense of purpose and intention (*We must … We must*), drawing on the sense of unity in the use of the first person plural (*We*). The repeated phrases create a feeling of logical, step by step building blocks which make the arguments seem clear and sound (*If democracy … Democracy is*), the syntactical positioning of the key word again drawing emphasis to its centrality. This logical sequencing of arguments leads on to a seemingly natural conclusion, conveyed by the use of *Therefore*.

ACTIVITY 1.53

How does the final paragraph:

- use references to Aung San Suu Kyi's personal background to endorse her ideas?
- use clear and authoritative language to suggest clarity of thought and belief?
- use *if* clauses to foreground the dangers of *not* listening to what she says?

Some types of speech may need to adopt a different style in order to create a special sense of mood and occasion. Read the text below, which is an extract from a speech given by the Prime Minister of India, Jawaharlal Nehru, after the assassination of Mahatma Gandhi, leader of Indian independence.

As you read, list any words or phrases that convey the tone or mood of the speech.

Friends and comrades, the light has gone out of our lives and there is darkness everywhere. I do not know what to tell you and how to say it. Our beloved leader, Bapu as we called him, the father of the nation, is no more. Perhaps I am wrong to say that. Nevertheless, we will not see him again as we have seen him for these many years. We will not run to him for advise and seek solace from him, and that is a terrible blow, not to me only, but to millions and millions in this country, and it is a little difficult to soften the blow by any other advice that I or anyone else can give you.

The light has gone out, I said, and yet I was wrong. For the light that shone in this country was no ordinary light. The light that has illumined this country for these many years will illumine this country for many more years, and a thousand years later that light will still be seen in this country, and the world will see it and it will give solace to innumerable hearts. For that light represented the living truth … the eternal truths, reminding us of the right path, drawing us from error, taking this ancient country to freedom.

From a speech by Jawaharlal Nehru.

●●● FURTHER RESEARCH

For more examples of formal scripted speeches visit the following websites:
www.historyplace.com/speeches
http://www.nobelprize.org/index.html
or look at a copy of *The Penguin Book of Twentieth Century Speeches*.

More examples of informal speeches can be found at:
www.cnn.com/TRANSCRIPTS/index.html

Key technique: imagery

> ### ACTIVITY 1.54
>
> Read the following commentary on the Indian Prime Minister's speech which explores the tone and mood.
>
> - How well has the writer of the commentary explored the mood of the speech?
> - Do you agree with his or her comments?
> - What role does the writer say imagery plays in creating the tone and mood?

KEY TERMS

imagery descriptive language, referring to adjectives, similes and metaphors

extended image a comparison of two things which is returned to throughout the text

parallel structures words and phrases that are similar in length and order

COMMENTARY

The speaker adopts a solemn voice, using **imagery** based on contrasts to suggest the change from a mood of hope (*light*) to a present and future empty and forlorn world (*darkness everywhere*). Syntactically, the speaker appears uncertain initially (*I do not know what to tell you*) but confirms the one truth he does now know (*we will not see him again … that is a terrible blow*) and confirms that truth by the use of direct statements (*We will not run to him*), the use of the future tense underlining the idea of a bleak outlook. There is a sense of unity in the way that the speaker places himself on the same level as those he governs (*I do not know what to tell you … Our … we called him*), conveying the idea that they are part of the same family which has lost its role model and figurehead, its 'father'.

The speaker proves his fallibility again by admitting he *was wrong*, doubling back to develop and sustain his **extended image** of light and dark: the future is not bleak. The repeated reference to the *light*, the progressive change in **tenses** (*was no ordinary light … illumined … will illumine*) and the **parallel structures** (*for these many years … for many more years … and a thousand years later*) create a sense of a progressively uplifting note of hope and vision. The words move from one particular place (*this country*) to a reference to *the world*, offering an impression that the hope symbolized by the lost leader is an inspiration far beyond the reaches of this time and place. The phrases draw on ideas of expansion and immortality, a sense that though the physical being of their leader may be gone, his spirit will live forever (*innumerable … eternal*), infusing the rest of humanity in their *hearts*.

There is a structural contrast in evidence: although the speaker may have shown that he himself is human in the way he has been uncertain and changed his initial observation, Gandhi has moved beyond that mortal level.

61

⊙⊙⊙ FURTHER RESEARCH

For further information about the use of specific devices used in speeches go to:
http://www.virtualsalt.com/rhetoric.htm

Persuasive articles

Other forms of individual opinions about particular issues can be found in the writing of newspaper and magazine columnists. Persuasive articles use many of the same techniques as scripted speeches. Indeed, we might even see some persuasive articles as a form of monologue by a writer hoping to reach an (unseen) audience. Framed in the guise of personal writing, such columnists often give vent to their views about a particular matter which affects them in some way and turn this into a topic that has wider concerns.

Key technique: the mode of address

One key technique used in persuasive articles is adapting the **mode of address**. This is often tied up with formality and informality, but it can go beyond this. For example, we might notice very direct language which speaks to the reader/audience as if they are the only person listening or reading. This can be a feature of other types of article, too.

Read these two travel accounts:

A   *I know what you're thinking. What was I doing in a bar in the depths of Eastern Europe at midnight, playing cards with a bunch of shady characters in motorcycle jackets? Me, a naïve, young woman who had only ever been abroad once … on a day trip with my mum and dad. Well, don't worry. I was asking myself the very same question.*

B   *Everything about the bar was of concern. There were a number of men, of a certain age, gathered round a beer-soaked table, playing a card-game. The lights above were fizzing, and cigarette smoke wafted about, hiding their shadowy faces from time to time.*

Now read the text below taken from an article by a newspaper columnist. In it, she addresses the issue of parenthood.

KEY TERMS

mode of address the way in which the reader is 'spoken to' by the writer

ACTIVITY 1.55

Make notes on these questions:

- How do the modes of address differ in these two accounts?
- What effect does this have on the mood of each piece? (Which one seems more humorous, for example?)

Enough. Enough already. I don't want to hear any more. I am sick of reading about mums feeling desolate, how hard motherhood is … The joy around Victoria Beckham having a girl after three boys was as ridiculous as her heels. Thank God! Yes, her life making frocks in LA with David and three gorgeous boys must have been torture before.

I don't want to mum-bash, but I do want mums to open their eyes and see what they have. At the risk of being lynched – give it a break. Give *me* a break. Give women like me, who wanted children but don't have them, a break. You mums do not know how blessed you are – so please just be happy and quit complaining. You got the prize. You have the child. Rejoice.

Of course being a mum has its difficulties – but they are finite and surmountable. If you haven't had a child, that devastating problem can never be solved. So raising a child is expensive? So is being single and living alone. You are tired and shattered? That must be horrible – but that feeling can be short-term and the pros (snuggling up to your warm, chubby baby) surely outweigh that particular con? (And let me tell you, the emotional upset of crying congratulations down the phone when your sister nervously tells you she is pregnant, just days after you've been told you most probably never will be, can be exhausting too.)

You feel you have lost your identity? Well, I'd say you've gained a better one. And the women who write "mum" on their Twitter and Facebook bios know that too. Mothers are treated as superior citizens. Pavements and public transport become yours (I was once asked to get off a bus so a woman with a pram could get on, but let's not re-enact that ugly scene here) and the world can't get enough of you.

From an article by Bibi Lynch, *The Guardian*

TIP

Terms such as *voice* and *mode of address* refer to similar aspects of texts so don't get too concerned about which one you use. The key thing is that, whatever the term, you consider the *manner* and *language* in which a writer expresses his or her thoughts.

●●● **FURTHER READING**

For other examples of columnists with strong opinions look at newspapers and magazines on a regular basis.

ACTIVITY 1.56

1 Read the passage again and identify examples of any of the techniques and effects you have learned about in this section on persuasive writing. You might look in particular at:

- the mode of address (e.g. does the writer address the reader directly or indirectly?)
- repetitions and patterns, repeated words and phrases
- emotive language and rhetorical questions
- use of personal anecdotes, references to the writer's own life
- vivid images or use of imagery.

2 Write your own commentary on the style and language of the extract.

Read the following comments on the longer article about motherhood. You may have noticed:

- the use of short dramatic sentences offering a strong opinion [*Enough. Enough already … Thank God! … Rejoice.*]
- the use of lists of three [*I am sick of reading about mums feeling desolate, how hard motherhood is, and how some women can't quite cope*] and repetitive syntactical structures [*give it a break. Give me a break. Give women like me, who wanted children but don't have them, a break.*] to convey the writer's sense of being overwhelmed and exhausted
- how the mode of address appears to be informal in terms of sharing the same gender but also appears quite aggressive as the writer feels her difference to those who can have children [*You mums do not know how blessed you are – so please just be happy and quit complaining. You got the prize. You have the child*], with the use of imperatives and further syntactical patterning
- the use of questions, as if the writer is addressing counter-arguments in order to dismiss them [*So raising a child is expensive? So is being single and living alone. You are tired and shattered? That must be horrible.*] with abrupt and dismissive direct statements which contain her certainty.

Summary

Remember these key points from this section:

- Persuasive writing texts share many similar conventions.
- Pay attention to the mode of address, which can affect mood and tone.
- Consider how syntactical patterning and use of sentence variety can convey thoughts and reflections.

Practice and self-evaluation

In this section you will:

- have the opportunity to apply and practise independently the techniques and effects you have learned about
- evaluate what you have learned and what you need to improve.

Applying what you have learned

You have learned about a wide range of techniques and devices used by writers in non-fiction texts. You have also learned about a useful process to follow when doing your own commentary. Now you have the chance, without additional guidance, to put what you have learned into practice.

The task is as follows:

Comment on the language and style used by the writer to convey his experience of a visit to the salt flats of Bolivia.

(Ask your teacher to set you an appropriate time limit to complete the reading and the task.)

Solitude, serenity and salt

As I stepped out of the Toyota Land Cruiser, it felt like walking on shattered glass. Spinning around, all I could see was a white void stretching to the horizon, a surreal, almost lunar landscape. It struck me that this might be the closest the planet has to complete, timeless nothingness; from pre-Incan peoples to the present day, humanity has made almost no impression on this endless expanse of white.

Covering some 4,000 square miles at an altitude of 3,650m, the Salar de Uyuni in Bolivia is the world's largest salt flat. It has long been a popular destination for backpackers, who come and stay in the handful of basic hotels around its perimeter and make day-trip excursions out into the salty desert. Now, though, travellers can stay right in the middle of the mesmerising emptiness, camping out in a shiny Airstream caravan.

The trips have been created by Darius Morgan, a local tour operator and hotelier who has imported three 25ft-long Airstream Safari caravans from the US so that guests can view the bizarre landscape in glorious solitude. "Now you can pay for the indulgence of being completely alone – you feel as if you actually own time and space," he told me when I flew down from La Paz earlier this month to be his first guest.

The hour-long flight landed at the recently opened airstrip outside the unattractive mining town of Uyuni. A driver and guide were waiting and we set off in the Land Cruiser, quickly passing through the town of Colchani, a cluster of adobe houses where most of the salt gatherers who work in the desert live. Geological studies have found the salt is up to 120m deep in places; in total the Salar contains an estimated 10bn tonnes, of which 25,000 tonnes are extracted annually.

We drove out on to the surface of the salt pan – flat but cracked into a billion naturally occurring hexagon shapes. Its appearance can change dramatically: in dry conditions the surface can look like snow or ice while at night it glows with reflected moonlight; when wet it takes on the appearance of a colossal mirror fringed by distant, snow-capped peaks.

After two hours' driving, we made our first stop at Incahuasi, the remains of a volcanic cone that now looks like a small rocky island rising out from the salt, about 45 miles west of Colchani. The Salar was formed some 30,000 years ago by the drying up of a vast prehistoric lake, Lago Minchin, and Incahuasi's rocks show traces of seashells and coral. Its slopes are dotted with thousand-year-old cacti, and as I climbed up among them with my guide Iván Blanco we began to pant in the thinning air. The view from the summit, 100 or so metres above the surface of the salt sea, is astounding. "Look around," said Blanco. "I'd venture to say that this is the last truly virgin spot on Earth."

It's easy to see his point but, nevertheless, the island is a stopping point for most tours of the Salar and can get busy with day-trippers, so we pressed on farther into the wilderness. We drove north for another hour, to the camp where Morgan and his Airstream were waiting for us.

"This is the loneliest spot of the salty desert – and it is all here just for you," said Morgan, as we prepared to eat a dinner of juicy roast llama steak, served with some decent Bolivian red wine from the southern region of Tarija, under an umbrella in the middle of the desert.

The next morning, from the comfort of my warm bed, I witnessed an orange dawn lighting up one of the most extraordinary landscapes I have ever seen. Soon after, the ever-courteous chef, Isaac Quispe, knocked on the door, bringing freshly squeezed orange and pineapple juices and sweet papayas served alongside fresh coffee, all produce coming from Bolivia's western Amazon basin. He left quickly, telling me: "The idea is to leave the traveller completely alone, so you can enjoy the experience the way you want. So, please, excuse me."

But there are benefits beyond solitude. Having a mobile base makes it easier to explore the area –

cycling or trekking across remote parts of the salt flats, visiting local communities or climbing the volcanoes at its edges.

Later, we drove north to the tiny villages of Jirira and Coqueza in the shadow of Thunupa, the extinct volcano that looms over the salt pan.

"For us, the salt flats are almost sacred," said Doña Lupe, an Aymaran elder wearing a bowler hat and pleated skirt, who owns a humble but comfortable eight-room hotel made of salt bricks in Jirira. "We would like more people to be able to feel that."

Andres Schipani, www.ft.com

Evaluation

Once you have completed your commentary, it is important that you consider what you have done effectively and what you need to do to improve your weaker points.

In order to do this, look at the table. Read each skill carefully and then make a judgement about whether you have mastered it, or if it needs more work.

If you need to revisit key skills or areas of knowledge, use the final column to find the relevant section of the book. Go to that section, and reread it, or try out the activities a second time.

Skill	Yes	No	Go to
I was able to follow a clear process and complete the task in the time set.			pages 12–13
I was able to group words and see patterns.			pages 13–14, 42
I had an introduction which had a focus that guided my commentary as a whole.			page 15
I used the point/quotation/comment process effectively.			page 17
I expressed my ideas fluently and coherently rather than as a list of disconnected items.			page 18
I was able to comment on the connotations of particular words and phrases.			page 27

Unit 2: Writing non-fiction

In this unit, you will explore the types of writing, purposes and forms which you might meet in an exam situation: in directed writing tasks and when writing for a specified audience.

However, whatever the task, much of your writing of non-fiction will benefit from the skills you developed in *reading* non-fiction. This is true both of exam responses which expect you to build on passages you have read, as well as those you have to write without a stimulus text. By reading and exploring a wide range of non-fiction texts, from modern newspaper articles to personal travel accounts or promotional brochures, you will encounter a variety of skills and techniques which you can apply to your own writing.

Approaching 'directed writing' questions

In this section you will learn:

- what the different sorts of non-fiction tasks are
- how to identify and extract the key information from them.

What is a 'directed writing' task?

A **directed writing task** is a piece of writing based on **either**:

- the **style and language** of the original passage

or

- the **material** of the original passage.

'Directed writing' may involve:

- adapting a piece of writing for a similar task, but maybe with a different context, using the same language and style
- rewriting a passage with a different purpose and/or viewpoint (for example, from the perspective of a different character mentioned in the passage) using the same material.

In an exam situation you will be asked to write between 120 and 150 words for a directed writing task.

Same style, different context

Tasks might ask you to remain 'in role' as the same speaker or writer of the original passage, keeping a similar style and language, but changing the **topic**, **focus** or **content** of the writing. Here is a typical task:

> *The following text is from an online promotion for an adventure trek by pony in South America. The same company decides to organise a trek, using a different means of transport, in your own country.*
>
> *Write the opening (120–150 words) for this promotion. Base your answer closely on the style and language of the original text.*

From this, (even though we cannot see the original text) you can see that the task tells you:

- the **writer/role**: someone from the travel company (the same writer as the original)
- the **purpose/type of text**: to promote the trek, still an online promotion
- the **style** of the text: to be based *closely* on the original
- the **length**: 120–150 words
- the **content/context**: the different elements you must include – just the *opening*; different *means of transport* and *own country*.

ACTIVITY 2.1

Read this similar task.

1 *The following passage is part of a speech delivered by Hilary Clinton, wife of the American president at the time. In it she considers the issue of women's rights.*

   (a) *Comment on the style and language of the passage.*
   (b) *The same speaker delivers another speech to an international audience. In it she considers the rights of children. Write the opening of her speech (between 120–150 words). Base your answer closely on the style and language of the original extract.*

Cambridge International AS and A Level English Language 8693
Paper 1 (May/June 2011), Q1. a, b.

On your own, note down:

- the **writer/role** (whose perspective you will be writing from)
- the **purpose/type of text**
- the **style** (if stated)
- the **length**
- the **content/context** (different elements, if any, you must include or change).

Further practice

Write a response to the task given in Activity 2.1.

Same material, different perspective

In directed writing tasks you may also have to use the material in a different way, or write from a new person's perspective.

Look again at the restaurant review on page 56 in **Unit 1: Reading non-fiction** and this directed writing task:

Another reviewer visits the same restaurant at the same time, but has a different viewpoint on his/her dining experience. Basing your answer closely on the material of the original extract, write the opening section (120–150 words) of the review.

Remember that you would need to bear in mind the following points:

- the **writer/role**: this will be a different reviewer (not the original one)
- the **purpose/type of text**: this is the same – to review the meal/visit
- the **style**: this is not mentioned, but as it is a review you should use similar language features and conventions as those in the original passage

ACTIVITY 2.2

Now read this similar task based on the same passage:

The manager of the restaurant writes a letter to the reviewer complaining about his review. Basing your answer closely on the material of the original extract, write the opening section (120–150 words) of the letter.

Note down:

- the **writer/role** (whose perspective you will be writing from)
- the likely **purpose/type of text**
- the **style**
- the **content/context** (what elements to include, what viewpoint, etc.)

Discuss with a partner:

- What are the main differences from the original text?
- What do you think the main challenges will be?

LINK

There is a follow-up task in the section on **Planning directed writing responses** on page 71.

- the **content/context** (what elements to include, what viewpoint, etc.): the viewpoint is to be *different*; the original was very negative, so it is implied that your response should be a positive one. You only have to write the opening section of the review, so this might deal with the arrival and first course, for example.

Whether the tasks require you to maintain a similar voice and style, or to take on a new role or perspective, the important thing is to take what you can from the original passage and shape it carefully to your needs.

Remember:

- directed writing tasks will be short texts of 125–150 words based on a passage you have already commented on
- read the questions carefully to identify whether it is a 'style' or 'material' type of question, and perhaps, even a combination of the two (e.g. as shown in the restaurant review task above).

Approaching 'writing for a specified audience' questions

In this section, you will:

- read a range of typical tasks with this focus
- learn how to identify the key aspects to base your response on.

What is 'writing for a specified audience'?

When you write for a specified audience the task is likely to:

- tell you what **voice or perspective** you need to write from
- set out the **type and purpose** of text you will be expected to write, as it will not be based on a passage you have already read. In some cases, the **audience or likely reader** will be mentioned, or implied by the type of text mentioned.
- give guidance on the **mood or tone** you are required to create though those words may not be mentioned (the word **sense** may replace them).

FURTHER RESEARCH

You can usefully practise your understanding of *audience* by looking at four or five types of magazine (either online or in a shop) and trying to work out what their target readership is.

TIP

In exam situations, specified *audiences* can be defined quite broadly by age, gender, shared interests, family/social roles, hobbies or other aspects of lifestyle.

Typical tasks and questions

Read this typical task:

The owner of a shop writes an article called Small change. *The article discusses the challenges and rewards of starting a small business. Write the text for the article. In your writing, create a sense of excitement but also the worries that such a path can bring. You should write 600–900 words.*

From this, you can see that:

- the **text type** is an article (magazine or newspaper)
- the **purpose** is to *discuss*
- the **writer/role** (the person you have to 'pretend' to be) is a small business owner/shop keeper
- the **content** is the *challenges and rewards of starting a small business*
- the **tone** (referred to as *sense* here) is one of *excitement* but also *worries*
- the **length** is 600–900 words (just one article).

What do you need to do next?

To write a successful response to the task, you will need to:

- Draw on what you know about the **conventions** of a **magazine or newspaper article**: this might be related to form/layout/structure, typical modes of address to readers, likely vocabulary, turns of phrase, and so on.
- **Imagine yourself** in the shoes of the writer: what kind of things might he/she choose to write about? What **'voice'** will he/she have? Level of **formality** or **informality**?

- Draw on what you know about **how to create a 'sense'/mood/tone**: for example, particular vocabulary, figures of speech, types of sentences, etc.
- Think about the **purpose of the text** and what **writing techniques** that suggests. In this case, there is *discussion*; what devices and ways of writing fit this purpose?
- Plan the **content/structure**: what *challenges and rewards* will you mention? How will you start, develop and end your piece?

Here are some brief notes written by one student after considering the task:

ACTIVITY 2.3

Consider these questions:

- How well do you think the student considered what he or she has to do?
- Are there any elements he or she has left out of their thinking?
- This is the 'thinking' part – the reading of the task carefully. What should the student do next?

SAMPLE RESPONSE

I think that as it is an article about a small business then it shouldn't read like a story, as such, more like an exploration of the main issues. Of course, it is written for an audience … the newspaper or magazine readership … so it must interest and engage them, not lecture them. I know that newspaper articles usually begin with key information in the first paragraph or so, but this is not a news report as such, so that might not work. I need to sound well-informed and also give a balanced view (*challenges and rewards*) … this isn't all about the difficulties! To keep readers interested, I might need to include some sort of personal anecdotes and information about myself. Hmm. I could start with that perhaps … an anecdote.

TIP

Make sure you select the kind of language appropriate to the specified form, purpose and intended audience. A magazine feature aimed at an older reader (if specified) may not make use of the same words and phrases as one intended for teenage readers.

ACTIVITY 2.4

Here is a similar task.

A newspaper invites its readers to enter a competition called What This Country Needs *by sending in articles exploring contemporary issues. Write one such article. In your writing, create a sense of what you think are essential priorities and the reasons for them.*

1 Note down:
- the **text type**
- the **purpose**
- the **writer/role** (the person you have to 'pretend' to be, if anyone)
- the **content**
- the **tone** (referred to sense here)
- the **length** (600–900 words; one text or more?)

2 Now write some brief notes for yourself about the task and the required style, etc. Use the example on the previous page to help you. You could start: *As this is for a competition, and is about 'priorities', I will need to write in a …*

3 In pairs, read these three extracts from students' responses to the task. Judging from what you have discovered by analysing the task, decide which is closest to the style required.

A   *Who really cares what our country needs? I'm a happy-go-lucky kinda guy and I'm not really too fussed about this sort of thing. 'Cos I'd really prefer to hang out with my mates and talk 'bout music, baseball … the usual, y'know …*

B *The president looked through the shaded windscreen. 'Who do these people think they are?' he thought, as the chauffeur prepared to drive on to his private residence. Outside, protesters were waving placards and shouting, their faces sweating in the heat of the midday sun. 'Turn on the air-con,' he told the driver.*

C *Trying to decide what the priorities for our country are is like selecting a perfect present for a relative; you need to know all about them before you choose. Get it wrong, and you waste huge amounts of money; get it right, and you make someone very, very happy. So, let us begin by briefly looking at what needs putting right. In other words, let us get to know that relative as best we can …*

Of course, this is just the start of the process. However, identifying the sorts of elements and the kind of tone and style you will need for your own text is very important. The next thing to consider is planning the structure of your response.

Summary

Remember these key points from this section:

- Read the task carefully, identifying the key words or phrases.
- Use the clues in the task to help you gauge what is needed in your response.
- Make sure you are able to identify as much as you can about the type of text; the writer/role (if there is one); the form; the audience and purpose; the content and tone.

Planning written responses

In this section, you will learn how to:

- plan and structure written responses.

Planning directed writing responses

As directed writing responses are so short, a detailed plan or structure is generally unnecessary and is not a good use of your time. However, spending two or three minutes quickly listing key words or phrases from the wording of the task will be useful.

It is also very important to think about – and perhaps plan – your very first sentence or line. This will set the tone for the rest of your response. For example, let's look again at this task:

> *Another reviewer visits the same restaurant at the same time, but has a different viewpoint on his/her dining experience. Basing your answer closely on the material of the original extract, write the opening section (120–150 words) of the review.*

The original review:

- begins with a description of the building
- mentions the price of the meal
- moves on to the lighting
- they have a pre-meal drink ('Kia' Royal).

Based on this, you could structure your alternative review around what you thought about the building, the cost, the lighting and a pre-meal drink (probably a different one).

However, you could also begin with sitting down for the meal (the starter) and then mention some of the other things in flashback, or in a different order.

LINK

It is very important that you apply what you have learned here to the practice tasks you will complete at the end of this unit on pages 108–109.

The main thing is to remember that as this is a restaurant review, you must **stick to** commenting on **décor**, **drinks**, **atmosphere** and **food**. So, a quick plan, whether written or mental, might be:

- arrival – very welcoming staff
- drink – say what it is, describe delicious taste
- décor – the brightness, how you liked it compared with dingy places you've eaten in before …
- starter – the mushrooms and stilton, describe positively …

Further practice

If you like, have a go at writing the review. You could begin: *The friendly staff standing at the door to take our coats was a welcome surprise, and complemented the attractive building with its…*

ACTIVITY 2.5

Write a four or five point list setting out your plan/what you would cover for the following task, which you were introduced to in the previous section:

The manager of the restaurant writes a letter to the reviewer complaining about his review. Basing your answer closely on the material of the original extract, write the opening section (120–150 words) of the letter.

Be careful: would this letter cover exactly the same things as the reviewer? Would a letter, for example, start in a different way?

Further practice

Once you have jotted down your plan, write the letter.

Planning longer written responses

The challenge when writing longer responses in an exam situation is that you have between 600 and 900 words to write. Even if the task requires *two* written responses (for example, two letters or scripted speeches), this is still a minimum of 300 words each. So for these longer responses it is important to create a plan before you start writing.

The precise content of your plan will reflect the task, the text type and the purpose (where known). For example:

- **issue-based texts** (i.e. to argue or discuss a topic) are likely to be organised by **ideas** or **viewpoints**
- **descriptive** or **personal texts** (e.g. travel accounts, memoirs) are more likely to be organised by **time** (specific moments or experiences), **features** (e.g. change of place, location), **people** (e.g. new characters) or by changing, or developing, **emotions**
- **persuasive texts** are likely to be organised by **reasons**, **promotional features**, etc.

In some cases, these aspects will intersect and work as hybrid forms, so this is only a guide.

However, there are some useful success criteria for planning written responses:

- begin by **identifying the key words/phrases** in the task as you have learned from the previous section (the text type, audience, purpose, etc.)

■ **generate key ideas, features, events**, etc. by using spider-diagrams or other 'idea shower'. This might be one, or perhaps two, diagrams. For example, look again at the following task:

The owner of a shop writes an article called Small change. *The article discusses the challenges and rewards of starting a small business. Write the text for the article. In your writing, create a sense of excitement but also the worries that such a path can bring.*

For this, you could create three very quick 'idea showers'. For example, the first could deal with the imaginative content you have to invent; the second with the challenges to be discussed; and the third with the rewards.

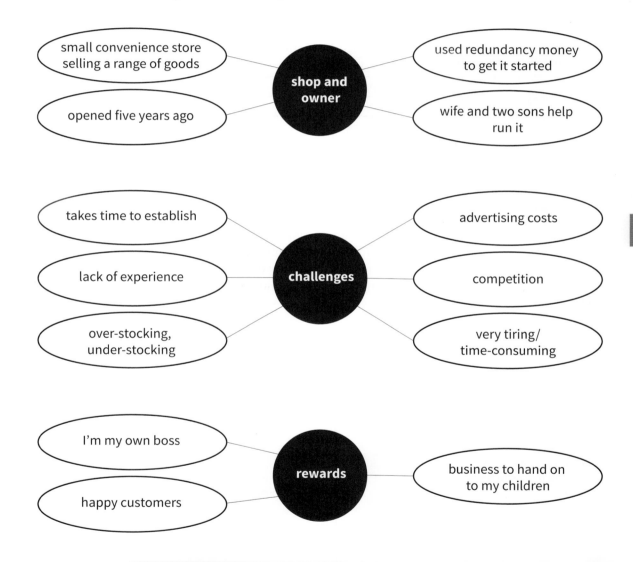

ACTIVITY 2.6

Look at the third diagram: can you add at least three more *rewards* to the diagram?

Organising the ideas

Once you have your basic ideas, you can begin to fit them into an article format.

One simple way to do this is to allocate paragraphs to the ideas you have generated. So, for the task above, spider-diagram 1 = paragraphs 1–2; diagram 2 = paragraphs 3–5; diagram 3 = paragraphs 6–8 plus concluding paragraph.

Typically, magazine or newspaper articles begin with the main facts in the early paragraphs. This isn't a news story, but it would still make sense to mention the key facts or issues in the first paragraph.

Decide whether the text type (if mentioned – e.g. letter, report, article) has a 'typical' structure to follow. If so, consider how your ideas might fit into this. For example:

Order	Focus/content
Paragraph 1 (introduction)	Introduce topic/issue: mention the shop I run
Paragraph 2	More details: why I ended up with my own shop
Paragraph 3	Challenges 1–2: lack of experience, time to set up
Paragraph 4	Challenges 3–4: costs, advertising, problems with stock, etc.
Paragraph 5	Challenges 5–6: competition, very tiring
Paragragh 6	Rewards 1–2: being my own boss, happy customers
Paragraph 7	Rewards 3–4: business to hand over, etc.
Paragraph 8	Rewards 5–6 …
Concluding paragraph	Overview: has it been worth it?

The plan, of course, does not tell you *how* to write or the language to use, but it is implied by it. For example, the plan suggests *introducing the topic*, something you would naturally do in a **discursive** article. This in turn implies what tense you might use. For example:

People <u>are opening</u> small businesses in their thousands <u>as I write</u>. <u>What is it</u> that drives people to start working for themselves? After all, there are <u>many risks and the benefits</u> aren't always obvious. This is something I know only too well, <u>as the owner of small convenience store</u> on the edge of a large city.

ACTIVITY 2.7

Discuss with a partner:

- What other ways are there of organising this content/information? (e.g. Do you have to deal with all the negatives in the first half and then the positives in the second?)

KEY TERMS

discursive a discursive text is one that explores a subject or reflects thoughtfully on it

Present tense, first person.

Present tense used to express the key question.

Words reflect the task title (*challenges and rewards*).

Informative, personal detail suggests this is the right person to be writing.

ACTIVITY 2.8

1 Choose any paragraph from the plan (except for the final one) and draft what you would write.

   When you have finished, evaluate how easy it was to write with the plan to refer to.

2 Now try planning and generating ideas for this new task:

   A magazine aimed at the over 50s publishes an article called Nothing to Fear. *The article tries to persuade readers that technology (such as computers, tablets and smart phones) and the internet can bring benefits to their lives. Write the article (600–900 words). In your writing, create a sense of enthusiasm and practical advice.*

TIP

There are lots of ways to structure and organise articles and reports – think about how the order can help you achieve your purpose.

Spend ten minutes planning your response.

- Stage 1: list the **key words or phrases** in the task that tell you text type, purpose, mood/tone, etc.
- Stage 2: use a **diagram or other 'idea shower'** (e.g. a list) to **get ideas** for the **main content** (e.g. benefits of technology)
- Stage 3: briefly, **organise your ideas/points** into a **set of eight to ten paragraphs** (or more, if you wish).

Once you have done this, compare your 'Stage 3' plan with a partner's.

Is there anything you could have improved? If so, what?

••• FURTHER RESEARCH

If you search online for 'essay planners' you will see a range of different templates and diagrams. Not all of them will be suitable for this work, but you might find particular planners that suit your own way of working and organising material.

Further practice

As already noted, a good plan/structure will vary according to the task and the text type. Apply the same planning process to the following task.

A travel company publishes its new brochure describing in detail the locations it offers visits to. The promotion outlines the journey and the attractions and qualities of each place. Write the text for one of these locations. In your writing, create a sense of a pleasurable and once-in-a-lifetime experience.

Summary

Remember these key points from this section:

- It is important to use the title/task to generate key ideas.
- Plan your writing carefully, considering the order and sequence of information.
- Different text types will imply different focuses for each paragraph or section of text.

Text types and purposes

In this section, you will:

- review the main writing types and purposes
- consider their conventions and key features
- apply them appropriately to set tasks.

For both directed writing tasks and audience-specific writing it is important that you are familiar with the different types and purposes of writing that you may be required to use. These types and purposes imply particular conventions and language features, but they will also sometimes combine styles, literary devices and structures.

What are the key text types and purposes?

From your work on **Unit 1** you have already become familiar with some of the different types of writing and purposes you may meet in an examination situation:

- descriptive writing (in texts such as travel articles or accounts)
- personal writing (in texts such as autobiographies, diaries and letters)
- writing about others (in texts such as biography and memoirs)
- persuasive, discursive or argumentative writing (in texts such as news or magazine features, speeches, promotional brochures or leaflets and reviews).

The purposes such texts and forms suggest are widespread, but might be to **inform**, **explain**, **describe**, **reflect** (on experiences), **discuss** or **explore**, **comment**, **review**, **persuade**, **argue a case**, or **promote an idea**.

ACTIVITY 2.9

Discuss with a partner:

- What do you think the *main* writing purposes are in the following forms of text? (There may be several, but think about the key focus each is likely to have.)
    - a campaign speech from a politician hoping to win an election
    - an account by a war reporter of conditions inside a refugee camp
    - an article about the pros and cons of providing free childcare.

 LINK

Throughout this unit, you may find it helpful to look back at **Unit 1** for examples of the different types of writing and formats you have studied.

Letters

In an examination situation you may be asked to write:

- **either** a section of a letter for a shorter directed writing task based on a passage you have read (120–150 words)
- **or** two contrasting letters (300–450 words each) when asked to write for a specified audience.

Whether your letter is formal or informal, it should look like this on the page (this is an informal example):

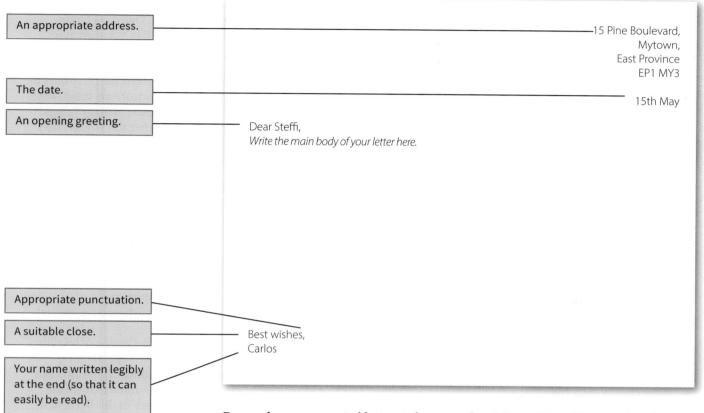

An appropriate address.

15 Pine Boulevard,
Mytown,
East Province
EP1 MY3

The date.

15th May

An opening greeting.

Dear Steffi,
Write the main body of your letter here.

Appropriate punctuation.

A suitable close.

Best wishes,
Carlos

Your name written legibly at the end (so that it can easily be read).

Remember: use a capital letter at the start of each line of the address and make sure it is written in a blocked format (aligned on a straight vertical line) or indented (sloping inwards to the right). The close of the letter can be chosen from a range of possible options such as *Best wishes*, *Yours truly*, *Regards* and so on.

If the letter is formal there are some differences:

- the address of the intended reader should be placed on the *left*-hand side of the letter below the level of the sender's address (which is on the *right*-hand side)
- if the title and surname of the intended reader is known, the letter should begin *Dear Mrs Gonzalez* or *Dear Mr Manzoor*.
- if the name of the intended reader is not known, the opening of the letter should be either *Dear Sir* or *Dear Madam* if the gender is known; if the gender is not known, *Dear Sir or Madam* is used
- the close of a letter where the name of the intended reader is known should be *Yours sincerely* (followed by a comma) followed legibly by the sender's name
- the close of a formal letter where the reader's name is not known should be *Yours faithfully* (followed by a comma) followed legibly by the sender's name
- the opening paragraph should generally state the purpose of the letter.

Read the following extract in which the writer describes her experience of visiting Antarctica and meeting her colleague, Martin, for whom she develops feelings. As you read, think about elements from the text that you might be able to re-use in a follow-up task.

We both wore seasick patches, were both vaguely dissatisfied with our jobs, wanted to write books. We would stand on deck in the early hours of the morning and watch auroras like giant scribbles of moving light in the sky, and talk endlessly of lives we didn't lead and most likely never would, of what we would do when we got back. How we'd finally have the courage to do what we really wanted to. It all seemed possible down there.

In the daytime there were icebergs that looked like pool tables or Cambodian temples or Walt Disney castles or Uluru[1], some so blue it was as if the ice had trapped a piece of the sky. We stood on the bow as the ocean changed around us from open sea to water like heaving marble with long veins of white through it.

One morning there were frozen pancakes of ice with their edges kicked up, an ocean of severed ears. Over the days the ears changed to huge waterlilies of ice, then oblong chunks 20m across, then vast sheets, ice-rink sized.

On the ice chunks were seals and their blood – it was the pupping season and there were many births. There were penguins that scurried in a panic. In the channels between floes were minke whales, their backs breaking the surface in a stately arc. And circling around the Aurora were snow petrels soaring and dipping like hundreds of angels watching over us.

Martin was contemptuous of the voyagers who spent most of their time in the video room in the bowels of the ship.

"Some of them haven't seen daylight since we left Hobart. They live in a world of virtual darkness. Maybe they're acclimatising themselves to 24-hour darkness in winter, but no one has told them that they're going down in summer."

There were 300 videos on the ship, it took five weeks to sail from Hobart to Davis, and by the end of the fourth week, the video-heads were so bored they weren't fast-forwarding through the previews any more.

"I feel so alive in this place," Martin laughed in vivid contrast, exhausting me with the ferocity of his enthusiasm. He was 37, the age of reckoning as we career into middle age, and he was gulping this world like a gleeful boy. He said that we must live differently after this trip, do all the things we really wanted to do.

He was constantly dragging me up on deck to seize the light, the sky, the ocean. One day I forgot my special-issue sunglasses, but didn't care because I wanted to see unfiltered all the different shades of white around us, but then I got snow blindness like a thick film of milk over my eyes. It took me three days to recover and from then on I always wore my sunglasses; Martin made sure of it. He made sure of many things.

That our lives would change after this voyage, they must. That they would veer from their prescribed course like an ocean liner heading off to unknown climes.

The Aurora sailed up an avenue of icebergs and cracked the sea's skin to within 3km of the coastal station, but could crack it no further. The ship parked by a line of drums on the frozen surface by a two-lane highway bulldozed freshly in the ice for the cargo operations to start. The gangplank was lowered and we walked or skied the last leg, across the surface of the Great Southern Ocean, to the continent.

Tears pricked my eyes with the sheer monumental emotion of it all.

Davis Station was a scattered collection of brightly coloured buildings that looked like large shipping containers. "Legoland", it was dubbed. The Australian mainland was "the real world". I wanted to leave the real world far behind, drown myself in this brave new existence, so vulnerable and lonely and exhilarating and replenishing, in the vastness of this unsullied continent...

I didn't want to leave this place. Didn't want to go back to my cluttered, inner-city life. Didn't want to leave Martin. He had entered my heart, was riveted to it, the relationship sanctified by the shared wonder of this land. But he was staying behind, his work wasn't finished. As we said goodbye our cheeks felt like plastic.

From *Antarctica, A Voyage into Unknown Climes*
by Nikki Gemmell.

[1] **Uluru** also known as Ayers Rock

Now read this directed writing task:

On his return to land, Martin realises he does not completely share the writer's feelings about their relationship or their possible future. He writes a brief letter to a relative to express his thoughts and feelings. Basing your answer closely on the material of the original extract, write a section of the letter (120–150 words).

A example response might be as follows:

31, Smith Square,
Hobart,
Tasmania
4GH XZ9

18th July

Dear Mother,

Both she and this journey drove me mad with boredom.

Every day I hauled her up onto the deck to try to find things to occupy the journey. Anything rather than sit watching videos like the rest of the crew. We wasted quite a lot of time till late at night pointlessly looking at the stars, conversations going back into the past trailing things up that didn't matter anymore. Most days she encouraged me do the same things in the morning, such as making me stare out into the blank white horizon where there is nothing to see, just endless water and blobs of floating ice. I suppose it's beautiful in a way, but terribly colourless. Then I had to look after her when she didn't follow my advice about wearing sunglasses. I want to be out on the ice, doing things, not watching them … which is why I'm staying on. I need this time alone now

Besides, I've still got a book to finish.

All my love,
Martin

TIP
- For the first task, base your letter on the passage.
- For the second, spend 10 to 15 minutes planning your answer using the process you learned about in the previous section of this unit.

ACTIVITY 2.10

1 In what way is this is a good answer?
   - Think about the sense of voice (has the writer captured a different perspective?)
   - Does it make use of material from the original text?
   - Is the language and layout appropriate to a letter to his mother?

2 Select one of these two tasks to complete. The first is a short task in response to the passage; the second a longer 'writing for a specified audience' task.

   A   *Imagine you are another traveller on the same trip. Write a brief letter to a friend describing your feelings as a person travelling alone without someone to share the landscape and voyage with. Base your letter closely on material from the passage.*

   B   *Write two letters to a travel company who run luxury summer cruises to islands in the Caribbean, or similar. In the first letter, you have just*

LINK

To practise your skills, take another text from this unit, for example the article about rock concerts on page 86, and write a letter from the author to a friend or relative expressing her frustration about people's behaviour. Or choose any other 'non-letter' text and invent a recipient.

✓ **TIP**

Take care over using abbreviated forms in this kind of writing: diary writers do not always use full sentences all the time and may miss out words or employ phrases as a form of diary shorthand. However, it must be clear to your reader what the intended meaning of the diary entry is.

returned from the trip and want to express how enjoyable it was and what made it so special; in the second letter, write from the point of view of another traveller who found the cruise unsatisfactory, giving his/her reasons. You should write between 300 and 400 words for each letter. (Do not base this on the passage!)

Diaries

In an exam situation you may be asked to write a single diary entry or a series of entries (120–150 words) for directed writing questions.

Diaries are often:

- written in a time of crisis or as a way of recording personal, often reflective, thoughts
- written in a confidential tone: the writer of the diary is often recording very private thoughts about herself or himself, meant for the writer's eyes alone
- written using a mix of present, future and past tense forms to express how the writer has felt about past events, is feeling at that time, and to set out what he or she might do next.

Look again at the passage by George Orwell on pages 9–10. Now read this question for a directed writing task.

One of the crowd, who has been watching events, returns home and writes an entry in her diary. In it, she describes her thoughts and feelings about what she has seen. Basing your answer closely on the material of the original extract, write a section (120–150 words) of the entry.

ACTIVITY 2.11

Write your response to this task. Make sure you have thought about the key elements of the task (e.g. whose perspective you are writing from).

Remember to:

- capture the **changing voice and mood** of the narrator as the piece progresses – you could draw on memories that come out as you watched the shooting, or that come to you later
- use 'typical' **diary language** – such as the use of incomplete sentences, or a mix of present and past tenses
- use **descriptive language** to convey the horror and pity of the situation
- use a variety of **sentence structures** to show changes in attitude, for example a sudden short sentence to switch focus from one person or memory to another.

⦿⦿⦿ FURTHER RESEARCH

Excerpts from some of the most famous diaries in history are available for reading online. For example, the Anne Frank centre in the US has a website, **www.annefrank.com** and **www.pepysdiary.com** has passages from the 17th century Englishman Samuel Pepys's famous diary.

81

ACTIVITY 2.12

Discuss with a partner which of these autobiographical memories you would find most engaging to read:

- Catching the bus to school when I was young
- Watching the battle between a mongoose and a snake in my backyard
- How I got to know my grandfather who had not spoken to me for years

Autobiography and memoirs

In an examination situation you may be asked to write:

- **either** a section (120–150 words) of an autobiography or a memoir
- **or** an extended piece (600–900 words).

Autobiographies and memoirs are ways in which people assess and recount past events that have had an impact on them, or in which particular people they have met or known have made an impression.

Generally speaking, in autobiographies or memoirs you will need to:

- write in the first person
- convey the sense of an intense experience or event, rather than a simple narrative or recording of routine everyday occurrences.

Some directed writing tasks may ask you to produce a piece of writing based either on the style and language or on the material of text extracts. The type of writing and the specific format (such as an autobiography or diary) will vary.

Read this text about the writer waiting at an airport in Japan.

I feel fragile and glassy.

Outside the rain is falling down and tattooing on the Arrivals Hall. I feel like the next person to jostle me is going to fracture me into a million serrated splinters. I feel so delicate that any moment I am going to cascade spectacularly across this Arrivals Hall at Natira Airport and leave behind a trail of detritus seventeen time zones wide. I just hope that someone will sweep up the fragments and ship them home to my son.

The queue shuffles forward a fraction.

The Arrivals Hall used to be my favourite place in Japan. Everything I love about Japan can be seen contained in this small area. There are Dowager Empresses in silky kimonos, school girls in tartan mini-skirts and big-socks, salary men leaning on No Smoking signs whilst puffing on filter-less Lark cigarettes, Buddhist monks, with shaved heads, resplendent in purple robes and worried looking mothers dabbing their brows with lacy handkerchiefs and fretting about their lives slipping by. I used to love getting off the plane and thinking: My god,

Alice is through the looking glass again. But today, after crossing the Pacific, I just feel like bits of me are rubbing against themselves trying to make some kind of unlikely connection. I need to emotionally ground myself but it seems hard to do. I am standing on the edge of a chasm of fear and longing.

I am also desperately searching for a pregnant woman.

The queue shuffles forward a fraction more. The helpful marker post tells me that I should be at the immigration desk within several hours. I wonder why no-one has hung prayer flags on the markers the way walkers pile rocks on cairns in the Highlands.

Japan emphasises my inherent loneliness. Each time I come here it affects me more profoundly and I find myself questioning, continuously, who I am. Maybe the jet-lag I suffer or the sheer, gut-wrenching level of frustration which comes from working with a Japanese company. Or perhaps after all these years, I do really want to conform and be a part of something greater than myself, which sends my head reeling. People all around me are living their lives whilst mine seems a vague world of shadows and emptiness.

We shuffle forward a few paces. I finish the first half of **War and Peace**.[1]

The young couple in front of me have just returned from their first trip to the States. To kill time, because today time is something we all have in excess, I try to draw them into conversation. Slowly, shyly, carefully they come them out of themselves and begin talking about their trip. They are beautifully shy, painfully self-conscious and wonderfully conservative. They visited something like seventy-four cities in six days. Their heads are still spinning but they are pleased to be home. After much prodding and gentle questioning they tell me that the most surprising thing for them was that you could eat McDonald's in America. I ask if they realise that McDonald's is an American company and they blush sweetly and look at their shoes. After a little more prodding they produce a mega-pixel digital camera and show me snaps of them enjoying a meal under the Golden-Arches. They typify modern Japan: charmingly naïve but with a rough techno edge.

We shuffle forward a few more paces, and I think: Even death must be more pleasurable than this. If I squint I can just make out the front of the queue. It's just beyond the curve of the earth. By the time I reach the front I will probably be a grandfather and my passport will have expired.

From *A Fragile Gaijin in Japan* by Philip Blazdell.

[1] **War and Peace** an epic novel by Leo Tolstoy

ACTIVITY 2.13

In an examination situation, you may already have written a commentary on the text, so the style/language should be fairly clear to you. However, for the purpose of this practice, discuss these questions in a small group, and then make notes about each one for yourself:

- What sense do you get of the writer's attitude to his situation? (Is it consistent? Does it change or develop in any way?)
- What particular things and people does he describe? What language techniques does he use?
- How would you describe his tone? (Mocking? Sad? Angry? Thoughtful? Hopeful? Isolated? Lonely? Or a combination of these, plus other things?)

Now read this directed writing task:

> Later, the writer publishes a further account about a different location where he also needed patience. Write a section (120–150 words) of the account. Base your answer closely on the style and language of the original extract.

Here is a possible sample response to this task.

The sun is beating down on the bus shelter and thundering on the roof, drumming into my frail and distant brain.

The crowd edges forward an inch.

The shelter in London was a cherished memory for me. All that I admired about the place is encapsulated in this microcosm. Here I can see city gents in smart black suits, bent old ladies clinging on to their faded bags, teenagers in hooded jackets with tattooed faces and large black boots, shouting loudly into microscopic mobile phones.

The crowd shambles on.

The welcoming bus stop ahead informs me that I will reach boarding point before dawn.

The crowd reinforces my sense of isolation, drawing a cloak of black gloom around me. Even a hospital must be better than this. I scan the horizon for a sign. It will be the next century before the bus arrives.

Here are some good points about this response in terms of the original extract:

- there is a sense of oppression (*beating down … thundering … black gloom*)
- there is a sense of loneliness in a crowd (*isolation*)
- there is a sense of slowness (repeated reference to crowd movement)
- there is a sense of sarcasm (*I will reach boarding point before dawn … It will be the next century before the bus arrives*)
- there is similar use of past and present tenses.

ACTIVITY 2.14

Using the same title and the original extract, write a section of another account (120–150 words) of a different location the writer might have visited, one in which patience was required.

Further practice

Extended writing: as part of descriptive or imaginative writing (see **Unit 3**) you might have to write a longer piece about arriving at a location.

Write two contrasting pieces (300–400 words each) about a memory of arrival at a place. In the first piece, write from the point of view of a younger person arriving; in the second piece, write from the point of view of the adult or older person who was waiting for them.

Here, you will have to invent your own style and language around the theme. However, you can draw on some of the skills used in the sample passage and response to give a sense of voice and perspective on emotions, surroundings, the person they are meeting/waiting for, etc.

Biography and character portraits

In an examination situation you may be asked to write:

- **either** a section (120–150 words) of a biography or a character portrait
- **or** an extended piece (600–900 words).

Biographical writing is a form of writing in which a writer focuses on the life or character of someone interesting. This might be a famous or infamous person, or someone close to them whom they believe will be of interest to the reader.

 LINK

Turn to page 125 in **Unit 3** for more on writing about **Setting and location**.

In biographical writing, you will:

- write mainly in the third person, unless the text is as much about revealing your own character or relationships
- describe an event, conversation or experience which reveals something significant about the person you are writing about
- adopt a clear position and sense of voice about the person, perhaps conveying approval or disapproval in the way material and expression are selected.

Look again at the extract about the writer's father on pages 49–50 in **Unit 1**. Now read this task:

Later, the writer publishes a further article after his father takes up another interest. Basing your answer closely on the style and language of the original extract, write a section (120–150 words) of the introduction.

Look at the sample response below and consider its effectiveness:

SAMPLE RESPONSE

Be careful with those bricks' I say to him. 'IT'S GREAT' he shouts 'I'VE ALREADY CHOPPED TWENTY TREES, MADE UP FIVE BUCKETS OF CEMENT AND POLISHED LOADS OF MY TOOLS THIS AFTERNOON.' My dad's newly kindled enthusiasm for his building scheme is already wearing me out. Why not slow down? I enquire.

Experience tells me that asking this is the same as attempting to convince a dog to ignore a cat and chase a soft toy instead.

He keeps having these powerful visions about being a master craftsman. 'YESTERDAY I BUILT A SHED. AFTER DOZING AFTER LUNCH I FOUND THIS HAMMER ON MY LAP. LOOK AT WHAT IT'S DONE TO MY HANDS. I RANG THE RADIO STATION TO TELL THEM THEIR MUSIC WAS AWFUL. NOT HAD A REPLY YET.'

TIP

When asked to write about an 'interesting character', you are really being asked to make someone you know, or have heard of, *sound* interesting – they do not have to be a celebrity or have won Olympic medals!

ACTIVITY 2.15

1 Discuss the good points about this response with a partner. Write these features on sticky notes and attach them to the response. (You may need more than one of each.)
   - characterisation of the father echoes the original
   - similar comparisons
   - what the father says
   - contrast between father and son
2 Once you have done this, make notes explaining the thinking behind where you have placed the sticky notes and what they show.

●●● FURTHER RESEARCH

For more accounts of family relationships go to **www.saga.co.uk**

84

ACTIVITY 2.16

1 Rather than complete a directed writing task on the same text, plan and write a response to extended writing task for a specific audience.

A local website wants to honour 'ordinary people', so it has asked users to send in a character portrait of someone local they know well. Send in your entry (it can be for someone imaginary) and create a sense of that person's individuality and why they are so fascinating.

If you are struggling to come up with ideas, use this ideas board – either at random (close your eyes and stick a pin in it!) or through choice.

An elderly relative who has survived hardship and trouble.	A local business-person who has made a success against the odds.	A young friend who has talents that are likely to make him/her successful in the future.
A kind person who has performed many generous acts.	A teacher who has inspired you or others.	A creative person, such as an artist or writer, who lives an unusual, somewhat mysterious life.
A homeless person who is getting their life back on track.	Someone who does an unusual job, such as an undertaker.	A member of the family who is 'larger than life' and has a very strong character!

2 Once you have decided you will need to note down:
   - a location that person may be seen/found in
   - how they might speak/what they say
   - things they do/how they behave
   - how you met them/first came across them
   - a specific example or examples of your interaction or meeting with them.

TIP

Focus on the text, *not* the layout or design. For example, you should not spend time formatting your material into columns or drawing illustrations to accompany the article.

••• FURTHER RESEARCH

How do countries and media organisations around the world promote 'ordinary people' for their achievements? Look at CNN's Heroes for 2013 page at **http://edition.cnn.com/SPECIALS/cnn.heroes/** for an example, or Sarah Ditum's article on the heroes of Fukushima in *The Guardian*, **http://www.theguardian.com/commentisfree/2011/mar/19/japan-heroic-earthquake-tsunami**

Articles and features

In an examination situation you may be asked to write:

   - **either** a section (120–150 words) of an article
   - **or** a full feature or article (600–900 words).

You may be asked to write in the format of an article for a newspaper or magazine, or perhaps for a blog. Whatever the format, you will need to have a clear structure and make use of appropriate headlines and subheadings to divide the material into sections. For example:

   - Place the most important information (who? what? why? when? where?) at the opening of the article in one or two initial paragraphs.

KEY TERMS

direct speech using speech marks to quote someone's words exactly (e.g. *Local builder, William Chung said, 'The lorries go far too quickly on this road!'*)

indirect speech a report or summary of someone else's words or account without speech marks (e.g. *Local builder William Chung **said that** the lorries went far too quickly on the road*)

- Develop with 'body' paragraphs that often record an excerpt from a witness account, or the words of an official figure (e.g. a spokesperson for the police or similar authority).
- End with a paragraph about the near future – what is about to happen (e.g. a court hearing to be held on a certain date).
- Use a mixture of **direct speech** and **indirect speech**.

Extended articles and features may come up in 'writing for a specified audience' questions. They may draw on a number of other techniques: background material about people or events, use of quotations or interviews, witness accounts, statistics and surveys, more in-depth description and analysis where the writer's own observations may come into play. They are also more likely to divert from Standard English to more informal usages, vocabulary and structures.

Read the text below, which offers advice to people attending music concerts.

Going to rock concerts has always meant dealing with a bunch of unruly people but it seems like lately things have been worse than ever. Attention spans are at an all-time low, and the ubiquity of smartphones has resulted in a huge percentage of the audience at any given show barely paying attention to the action onstage. Here are the most annoying behaviors at rock concerts.

Taking pictures the entire show
I get it. You want to show all your friends on Facebook and Twitter that you saw a cool concert. Fine. Take a photo. Take five if you want! But please, don't take 77. You always manage to hold your camera right in my line of sight. You don't even look like you're enjoying the show while you're doing this. All your attention is on the photos. You'll probably never even look at them. Also, you see those guys right in front of the stage with the giant cameras? They're taking great professional pictures. There's really no need for yours.

Checking e-mail, Facebook and Twitter every couple of minutes
Unless you're a surgeon or a firefighter, everything can wait. Live in the moment. Enjoy the show. You paid good money to be here. You can e-mail your friends when you get home. Also, that cellphone emits a very harsh and distracting glow.

Incessantly talking to your friends
You might not like whatever song is playing. You may be bored with the show in general. You may have been dragged here against your will. But you've been chattering the entire show, and I can hear every word. It's driving me crazy. Please shut up. Please. I can't tell you how many shows I attend where the two people in front of me are yelling in each other's ears the entire night. Not only is my sightline blocked when their heads come together, but I can hear them. Maybe go to a coffee shop when the show is done. Lie under an oak tree and talk until the sun comes up. I don't care. Just quiet down so I can enjoy the show.

Andy Greene, *Rolling Stone*.

ACTIVITY 2.17

Write a quick plan for an article using the structure on page 85 (opening paragraphs 1–2, main body paragraphs 3–5, conclusion paragraph 6) for a report into the sighting of an unusual or unexpected creature or animal in your neighbourhood. (You need only write notes.)

ACTIVITY 2.18

1 Spend 5–10 minutes discussing with a friend what the key features and style of this article are. You could consider:
   - informal and formal usages
   - length and type of sentences
   - use of punctuation
   - mode of address (the way of speaking to the reader).

2 Then choose one of the following headings (which come from the rest of the original article) and write one of the missing entries. They are:
   - Yelling out requests
   - Pushing your way to the front
   - Filming the entire show on your phone
   - Yelling 'Sit down!' at people who are standing up.

3 For a longer 'Writing for an audience' task, plan and then write a magazine article (600–900 words) using some of the techniques and approaches of the extract. It should be aimed at a teenage audience, offering advice and guidance about an issue which will be relevant and engaging for readers. For example:
   - How to survive a weekend at a rock or pop festival
   - Making your room at home inviting for your friends to see/visit
   - Buying clothes for a party without spending a fortune
   - Making sure weekends aren't boring by doing something useful or original.

 LINK

Look back to the guidance on generating and planning your ideas on pages 72–75.

87

When planning a response which involves giving advice, remember to:

- Use the planning and generating ideas advice earlier in this unit, for example by dividing the material into clearly defined sections.
- Give reasons why you are offering advice about that particular section.
- Use repeated sentence structures [*You might not like whatever song is playing. You may be bored with the show in general. You may have been dragged here against your will. But …*] followed by a word such as *but* or *however* which then outlines the case against.
- Use imperatives and *if* clauses [*Take five if you want! But please, don't take 77.*]
- At certain points adopt informal language to make a connection with your readers [*Please shut up. Please.*]
- Vary sentence length and structures for effect – almost as if thoughts are popping into your mind, or you are speaking them aloud [*I get it. You want to show all your friends on Facebook and Twitter that you saw a cool concert. Fine. Take a photo.*]
- Insert occasional direct personal opinion [*I can hear them. Maybe go to a coffee shop when the show is done. Lie under an oak tree and talk until the sun comes up. I don't care. Just quiet down so I can enjoy the show.*]

All this suggests that you use a similar tone to the one in the sample passage. You don't have to do this of course, but bearing in mind the audience – teenagers – you will need to make it engaging in some way.

Further practice

You have already written a plan for this question (see page 86) but for more practice in writing for an audience, write the article as instructed. Use your original plan to help you.

A magazine aimed at the over 50s publishes an article called Nothing to Fear. *The article tries to persuade readers that technology (such as computers, tablets and smart phones) and the internet can bring benefits to their lives. Write the article (600–900 words). In your writing, create a sense of enthusiasm and practical advice.*

Reviews and writing to comment

In an exam situation you may be asked to write:

- **either** a section (120–150 words) of a review
- **or** a full review (600–900 words).

Reviews both comment on and describe an event or experience. They are a form of persuasive writing in that the writer's viewpoint/opinion is key to the way the text works.
   Writing an effective review depends on:

- knowing the kind of publication you are writing for and the intended readership
- understanding what the reader wants to know
- knowledge and authority about the subject
- forming an overall opinion which will give the review a framework
- relating any examples to that overall opinion and framework.

Reviews generally:

- provide an overview of the 'key facts' of the experience (e.g. prices, who played what part, name of the restaurant)
- suggest the writer's expertise or knowledge of the field (e.g. theatre, film, food)
- express opinion via loaded language (positive and negative adjectives or vivid imagery)
- use exaggerated or humorous ideas through comparisons
- adopt informal, chatty language designed to make contact with the reader.

Look again at the review of the film on pages 54–55 in **Unit 1**. Here is a possible directed writing task based on this review:

The writer of the review publishes a further article about another film. Basing your answer closely on the style and language of the original extract, write a section (120–150 words) of the review.

SAMPLE RESPONSE

Does Brad Smith really know what he's doing? Not long after his acclaimed performance in *The War Years* he's trying way too hard to pretend he can capture the spirit of President Carter. He's got guts thinking he can put himself in the shoes of 'one of the key figures of the late 20th century', a figure no director would dream of attempting to portray. Yet he's not really that brave. The way of playing Carter totters along, like a young child trying on some high heels before crashing to the floor in disbelief at how much they hurt. The stiff neck, the forced grin, the steely eyes; it's like Smith is being prodded with a needle to get him to show the ways and habits of Carter …

ACTIVITY 2.19

List any *other* elements which show the writer has managed to imitate the style of the original text.

COMMENT

Here are some good points about this response:

■ it offers an apparent compliment using noun phrases (*his acclaimed performance*) followed by instant criticism of the star (*he's trying way too hard*)

■ it employs a harsh direct statement followed by understatement (*He's got guts … Yet he's not really that brave.*]

●●● FURTHER RESEARCH

Search for theatre or musical reviews online. Newspapers or magazines often have them in their Entertainment, Arts or Culture sections. Note how skilful reviewers have to conflate information and opinion into a few lines for the short reviews you often see in listings.

Now look again at the review of the restaurant on page 56 in **Unit 1**. Here is a possible directed writing task for this piece:

The owner of the restaurant remembers the visit of the original reviewer but has a different view of the experience. Basing your answer closely on the material of the original extract, write a section (120–150 words) of the owner's own blog entry.

Draft a quick response to this task. Remember:

■ the key thing here is that the 'material' should be similar, in other words, cover similar ground (arrival of the reviewer, décor, drinks, starter, price/value, etc.)

■ you are not being asked to write a review so you do not need to imitate the style of the original; however, you should think about the conventions of blog entries – the fact that they are a form of public diary.

ACTIVITY 2.20

1 Compare your draft with a friend. Have you both:
   ■ changed the viewpoint?
   ■ used material from the original extract?
   ■ written in a style that matches that of similar reviews?
   Mark up each other's drafts and then rewrite, improving where needed.

2 Now, plan a response to this longer task for a specified audience:

   To celebrate the fact that a local cinema has been open for 25 years, the owners have asked for reviews of any favourite movies which have been released in that time. They will publish the reviews on their website. Write a review of any film you have seen (real or imagined) and create a sense of the emotions it stirs and why it is so enjoyable. You should write between 600 and 900 words.

   For your plan, you could jot down notes using this framework:
   ■ introduction: the name of the film, when it was released, who it starred, etc.
   ■ body of the review: comments on the action/plot; characterisation/cast/acting; locations (if important); cinematography; music and/or special effects; its impact on you as a viewer
   ■ conclusion: what makes the film so special, and why it will endure.

Further practice

Write the full review.

KEY TERMS

voiceover the voice of an unseen narrator, spoken material

KEY TERMS

rhetorical device a particular word, phrase or pattern of language which a writer uses to prompt a particular reaction from a reader, especially one that makes them see the writer as rational or reasonable

LINK

Look again at the key features in some of the speeches in **Unit 1** on pages 58–63.

✓ TIP

Remember that you should focus only on your writing. You don't need to include instructions for sound effects or other technical issues but you may wish to use a few stage directions here and there.

Speeches, voiceover scripts and debates

In an exam situation you may be asked to write:

- **either** a section (120–150 words) of a speech **or** two contrasting speeches which make up a debate of 600–900 words.
- **either** a section (120–150 words) of a script **or** a more developed **voiceover** script of 600–900 words.

Scripted speeches are planned speeches given for a purpose. These may be persuasive, or recount key or interesting events in the speaker's life that make up part of an explanation of the issue they wish to talk about.

Voiceover scripts may be in the form of a script for a voiceover for a promotional film or video, a radio or television programme or a podcast. The focus here is not on references to sound effects, camera angles and so forth but on the text itself. As with website, newspaper and magazine articles and features, you should not be concerned with the layout and design of your text.

The conventions for speeches, scripts and debates will largely depend on the purpose; so for persuasive speeches you would be expected to include **rhetorical devices**; but more explanatory speeches or scripts might not require them.

Regardless of the particular purpose of the text:

- try to give a good sense of the 'voice' of the speaker/s
- remember to write in the first person
- consider how tenses might play a part (i.e. talking about the situation now, or what is to come).

●●● FURTHER RESEARCH

Look at the TED website (**https://www.ted.com/talks**) and select topics that might be of interest to you. Listen to one of the talks and see if you can identify any of the techniques or devices you have learned that good speech-makers use.

Now read the task below and the sample student response that follows it.

Write the script for a voiceover of a radio programme aimed at a teenage audience called Brave New World. *In the programme, a student on the point of leaving school describes her or his thoughts and feelings about moving into a new stage of life. In your writing, create a sense of the hopes and fears that the narrator is experiencing.*

SAMPLE RESPONSE

So, I've just finished the long and really nerve-shattering process of taking my exams and now I'm just waiting for the results, feeling very scared and worried about what's actually going to happen. I've actually read and been told that waiting to see if you've got into Uni and finding out if you have or you haven't is actually really more stressful than being there.

I go round to my friends' houses and we always talk about 'what if he makes it and I don't? What will I do? What will people say? Will we still see each other?' We're all a bit nervous, to say the least. The number of nightmares I've had these last few weeks about results day – they've all had these different kinds of mad monsters. I've just got this image of me waiting for the results at school and there's just the shadow of a monster waiting around the corner ready to get me: I don't get the grades I need and this shadow looms towards me …

Results day is getting really close now and I'm getting more and more tense, not eating properly, not sleeping properly. It's all like some kind of monster reality coming toward me. I'm really scared what my mum's going to say if I don't get the grades I need. 'Why didn't you revise more? Why didn't you listen to what I told you?'…

ACTIVITY 2.21

1 How well does this speech work? Copy and complete this table, which lists some of the key success criteria. Add examples as evidence of the speech's success.

Feature	Example
Inner thoughts and emotions	*feeling very scared and worried …*
Appropriate to audience	
Use of appropriate tenses to convey feelings now and in future	
Use of images or unusual vocabulary to engage listener	

2 Now continue the voiceover. (Your final piece of writing, including the sample section, should be 600–900 words.)

TIP

When planning a response to this question, you should:

- imagine individual scenes the narrator may experience at this point in his or her life
- try to capture some of the style and language used in the sample opening section to the piece (e.g. use of abbreviations like *Uni*)
- express inner thoughts through questions
- refer to the elements, such as friends and parents, that surround the writer
- convey a sense of immediacy by the use of the present tense.

Promotional texts

Promotional texts may include advertisements, material from brochures, leaflets and so on. However, the definition can be expanded to include texts which promote a particular view on a topic, such as two people conveying different opinions about the same event they have attended.

The wide range of skills required to promote a location, or persuade someone to buy something, mean that any list of key features and conventions is reductive. Many of the persuasive features of promotional texts, such as use of images, size and type of font, colours, are not relevant here as the focus is on language. However, it is possible to differentiate between two key techniques, which are relevant to most, if not all, promotional writing. These are the **soft sell** and the **hard sell** approaches.

Soft sell is where more persuasive, gentle methods are used to promote products or ideas and there are appeals to lifestyle, through images or ideas conveyed to the reader. For example:

Imagine the <u>warm air</u>[1] cosseting you as <u>you stroll along</u>[2] <u>stretches of sandy beach</u>.[3]

[1] and [3] are noun phrases which appeal to the senses
[2] is a verb phrase which places the reader in the scene

Hard sell tends to stress essential matters of value and practicality. For example:

<u>Want a Caribbean beach holiday which doesn't cost the earth?</u>[1] Look no further.[2] 7 nights for just £499.[3]

[1] direct appeal to reader's idea of value
[2] fairly blunt short sentence
[3] a minor sentence (no verb) which bluntly states the cost.

ACTIVITY 2.22

On your own, consider these questions:

- Are there any particular products or experiences which lend themselves more to one approach than the other?
- Why?

In order to explore how to apply these techniques in your own work, read these two extracts from promotional material for two different cars.

Car A

It's not just the quality you will appreciate.

While the rugged good looks of the new BMW are everything you would expect from a vehicle, the details are equally impressive. From the highest quality Dakota leather to the finer points of efficient dynamics and the new generation twin-power turbo diesel engine, this is a car at home in crowded cities or the open countryside.

No matter where you decide to drive it, the car was born to perform. Combining impressive efficiency with agile rear-wheel drive characteristics, the BMW makes any destination a pleasure to get to. At this price, the pleasure goes beyond the performance.

Car B

Like attractive design? Need a spacious interior? Want modern technology, but don't want to break the bank? Say hello to Dacia Sandero.

Big car features.
Beneath its svelte form lies ample space for five adults. A split-folding rear seat and 320 litre boot make transporting luggage simple. Electronic Stability Control, anti-lock brakes and four front airbags ensure safety as standard. And, with Sandero Lauréate, air conditioning and cruise control mean maximum comfort on the move.

Small car prices.
At Dacia, we believe in giving you the choice to pay only for what you value. That's why our comprehensive standard 3 year/60,000 mile warranty may be extended up to 7 years/100,000 miles. Our simple range offers three trim levels to suit your individual needs: from the affordable Access to the luxurious Lauréate. And, with prices starting from just £5,995 on-the-road, there really is a Dacia Sandero for everybody.

TIP

Soft sell features tend to focus on lifestyle, rather than using more direct appeals to the buyer such as cost, practicality, etc.

ACTIVITY 2.23

1   Work with a partner. Copy and complete the table, deciding which words, phrases or sentences are hard sell and which are soft sell.

Soft sell	Hard sell
Car A: *rugged good looks*	Car A: *new generation twin-power turbo diesel engine*
Car B: *maximum comfort on the move*	Car B: *And, with prices starting from just £5,995 on-the-road, there really is a Dacia Sandero for everybody …*
…	

2   Practise your writing skills for directed writing tasks by writing two contrasting advertisements for the same everyday object (e.g. a household item), one using a soft-sell technique, and the other a hard-sell technique.

Try painting pictures and suggesting a lifestyle for the first; for the second, focus on value, cost, practicality and use punchy sentences, and questions where appropriate, to appeal to the reader.

••• FURTHER RESEARCH

1   For more information on the use of the hard sell and soft sell techniques and the language of advertising, follow the online links below:
   www.engl.niu.edu/wac/txtanal.html
   www.linguarama.com/ps/marketing-themed-english/the-language-of-advertising.htm
   www.putlearningfirst.com/language/19advert/advert2.html

2   Carry out some research in newspapers, magazines and online for a variety of advertisements which use different approaches. Comment on the techniques and effects they use.

LINK

Look again at the Star Clippers extract on pages 23–24 of **Unit 1**. Would you say this uses a predominantly hard- or soft-sell approach – or a mixture of the two?

Further practice

1   For a more extended piece of writing for a specified audience, reread the promotional text for the trip along Kenya's coastline on pages 14–15 of **Unit 1**. Look over the key features of the text again, and remind yourself of the techniques used to make the location and trip seem appealing.

2   Now, complete this writing task:

   You work for a travel company who offer cruises to Antarctica. Write a promotional text outlining the sort of experience a traveller would have if they came on one of your cruises. Create a sense of wonder and magic. Write 600–900 words.

   You should use the planning process outlined at the start of this Unit.

Campaign literature

Campaign literature on a range of issues (e.g. the protection of the environment and wildlife) shares similarities with other forms of persuasive texts, such as political speeches. Directly appealing to the reader, setting out risks and rewards and so on, all add to the force of the text.

The text opposite is an example of an online campaign.

VIRUNGA: AFRICA'S MOST BEAUTIFUL AND DIVERSE OIL FIELD?

Keep oil exploration out of Africa's oldest national park.

Your support really matters. People-power works. Together we will draw the line.

WHY VIRUNGA?

Heard of Virunga? It's Africa's oldest national park, and a treasured World Heritage Site.

Rainforests, volcanoes, rare and beautiful wildlife – Virunga has it all. People who live and work there know it's a very special place.

But Virunga is at risk of becoming Africa's newest oil field. When we heard UK oil company Soco were exploring for oil inside Virunga, we had to draw the line. Some places are just too precious to exploit. <u>Find out more about Virunga and the oil threat</u>.

VIRUNGA AND OIL

Virunga National Park is the size of a small country, straddling the equator in Democratic Republic of the Congo.

It's got more than its share of wonderful wildlife – not just huge numbers of unique birds, but African icons like lions, elephants, hippos, chimps and the remarkable okapi. And a quarter of the world's critically endangered mountain gorillas.

Soco's exploring for oil isn't the only threat to Virunga – civil unrest and wars have put pressure on local people, wildlife and resources on-and-off for years. But we believe oil exploration would bring a new and unacceptable level of risk for Virunga's environment and communities.

That's why we need to <u>draw the line</u>.

World Wildlife Fund.

ACTIVITY 2.24

1 Reread the text and identify where it demonstrates the following features:

Feature	Quotation
Uses forceful, using direct statements in the present tense	*Virunga is at risk ...*
Employs brief and abrupt phrases as forms of slogans (perhaps using imperative verbs)	
Sets out who the opponent/'villain' is	
Direct appeal to reader as friend/fellow believer	
Emotional appeal	
Vivid images	
Suggests consequences of not acting	
Ends with a 'call to action'	

Share your ideas with another pair and make sure you are clear about the conventions and elements at work. You will be able to make use of them in the next task.

2 For practice of directed writing questions complete the following task:

The same group posts another online campaign about an environmental issue in the country where you live. Basing your answer closely on the style and language of the original extract, write a section (120–150 words) of the introduction.

96

●●● FURTHER RESEARCH

You can find an example of a similar campaign at **http://www.seashepherd.org/cove-guardians/**

TIP

Some writers try to persuade their readers about issues by adopting a **persona**. A similar technique is sometimes used in voiceovers on campaign issues, for example where the Earth 'speaks' to the reader.

KEY TERMS

persona a role or character adopted by a narrator or writer

Further practice

For practice of a more extended response, plan and write a response to this task:

A recycling charity in your area is very concerned about the amount of waste and household rubbish. Write an online campaign text aimed at parents to persuade them to think carefully about what they throw away. In your article, create a sense of optimism and belief in change.

Summary

Remember these key points from this section:

- Practise writing as many text types as you can.
- Remember that different purposes can be present in the same text.
- Differentiate between questions which focus mainly on style/language and those focusing on re-using the material.
- Always keep in mind the voice of the writer and, where stated, the purpose and audience.

Key focus: discursive writing and writing to argue

In this section, you will learn:

- about the key features of discursive writing and writing to argue
- about different ways of structuring discursive and argument texts
- how to plan and write directed and extended responses with these purposes.

This section focuses on these two purposes – discursive writing and writing to argue – as they are often areas that provide the greatest challenges to students, particularly in terms of structure and tone/mood. Many of the other purposes have been adequately covered elsewhere, for example in the **Text types** section above, or will be covered in **Unit 3** (which addresses writing to describe).

Discursive writing is when you consider a particular issue, problem, or situation and outline the arguments on both sides before coming to a reasoned conclusion. The keys to effective discursive writing are:

- to present both, or multiple, points of view
- to write in a detached, objective manner (avoiding first person statements such as *I think* …)
- to move towards a more personal response at the end of the piece, at which point you give your 'verdict' on the issue.

Argumentative writing is very close in style to discursive writing and indeed discursive writing usually sets out or explores key arguments around a specific issue. However, argumentative writing draws more strongly on the writer's sense of voice from the very beginning. You are, to a large extent, trying to persuade or convince the reader of your point of view from the outset rather than offering a more restrained and briefer judgment at the end. Therefore, argumentative writing tends to have a more personal, direct style.

For the purposes of this section, we are going to focus on the core skills for discursive writing, many of which are transferable.

TIP

Make sure you understand the key words and requirements of the task. This allows you to create a framework for your answer and indicate to the reader the areas you are going to consider.

Planning and structuring discursive writing

As you have already learned, it is important, to **make a list of the key terms and requirements** in the task question. Do any words or phrases need defining from the start? What is your interpretation of such key words and phrases?

Remember:

- planning will involve having points **for** and **against**: two or three points for each side of the case
- each of these points will form a paragraph of your answer in between your introduction and conclusion
- you should decide on the order of your paragraphs. In order to keep reader interest and an increasing sense of authority, it is best to begin with minor points before moving on to the stronger ones.

Depending on your viewpoint about the topic, there are options for how you might plan your writing:

- if you are **for** the topic, your plan could be like this: an introduction, points against, points for, a conclusion
- if you are **against** the topic, your plan could be like this: an introduction, points for, points against, a conclusion.

Another approach would be to begin each paragraph with an argument, followed by its counter-argument. Whichever approach you choose, each paragraph should contain the following:

- a topic sentence or an initial question to outline the subject of that paragraph
- a consideration of arguments about that point in the paragraph.
- exemplification – examples to illustrate each argument (e.g. you might refer to surveys or statistics, real or feasible ones)
- evidence of connectives linking sentences.

The use of connectives might include words and phrases which suggest:

- a consequence or result – *because of this, the effect of this, consequently*
- additional and reinforcing points – *furthermore, moreover, in addition, besides this, similarly, in the same way.*

There should also be connectives linking the paragraphs themselves. Such connectives might include words and phrases which suggest:

- organisation and order – *to begin with, firstly, at the same time, ultimately, finally, in conclusion, overall, as a whole*
- contrast – *however, on the one hand … on the other hand, yet, despite this, conversely*

KEY TERMS

topic sentence an initial sentence, question or phrase containing an idea which outlines the main point or idea of the paragraph or section it introduces

exemplification illustrating and supporting by giving examples

connectives words or phrases which link other phrases, sentences or paragraphs

97

TIP

Offering further (or subtly different) evidence, which nevertheless supports the point you are making will demonstrate your ability to develop arguments, or consider them more deeply.

ACTIVITY 2.25

Using one of the planning approaches mentioned above, set out your plan for this task:

A magazine publishes an article called Can You Have Too Much of a Good Thing? *The article looks at the issue of whether the school-leaving age should be lowered or raised in your country. In your writing, create a sense of controlled and balanced viewpoints.*

LINK

Choose any one of the longer texts from Unit 1 and see if you can identify the topic sentence in specific paragraphs. Where the text is more impressionistic, you may find this quite difficult to do and the topic sentence may not be the first sentence of the paragraph.

Introductions in discursive writing

A good introduction can offer focus, structure and direction. You should avoid stating the obvious in a rather generalised way: *In this essay I am going to write about …* or *I am going to look at both sides of the argument for and against …* However, from the beginning, a sense of balance and control needs to be evident for discursive writing.

Here is one possible response to the task which you planned in Activity 2.25:

SAMPLE RESPONSE

Some people believe that education, the learning of skills and knowledge, is one of the most important ingredients in young people's lives, vital for their personal development and the future of the country. However, others believe that the benefits of long-term education are over-stated and that it is far better for young people to experience the world of work early in their lives for the personal development of the individual and the good of the nation.

COMMENT

Here are some good points about this response:

- there is a brief definition of the idea of education (*the learning of skills and knowledge*) to communicate the writer's interpretation of the key idea
- there is a sense of balanced, opposed views in the use of *some people … other people*
- there is no evidence of a personal opinion at this point
- the contrasting arguments are structured around the word *however*
- the division into two opposed viewpoints helps to establish the management of any writing time – roughly, half the time to each side of the argument.

An alternative way of beginning the article might be to introduce the topic by phrasing the arguments as questions, as in the following example:

SAMPLE RESPONSE

Two famous sayings – 'You are never too old to learn' and 'a little knowledge goes a long way' – are often heard in this country. Yet is education (the transfer of knowledge and skills to other people) that important? Does it really matter if you do not achieve a certain number of grades at a certain level by the time you leave school? Could the money spent on education be invested more wisely?

Here are some good points about this response:

- there is a direct start to the question using well-known phrases or sayings
- there is a definition of the topic
- there is no evidence of a personal opinion at this point
- the use of *yet* creates the contrasting points of view
- both sides of the issue are raised as questions which sets out the main section of the article that follows.

ACTIVITY 2.26

Write introductions for discursive writing on two or three of the following topics:

- whether people should be allowed to carry firearms
- the internet does more harm than good
- there is too much money in sport
- marriage is an old-fashioned idea
- animal rights are as important as human rights
- the punishment should fit the crime
- science does more harm than good
- terrorism can never be defeated.

Either use a general introduction which sets out the views as series of statements **or** introduce the topic/issue via questions that represent the opposing viewpoints.

Using evidence in arguments

The development of argument and evidence (such as the use of particular examples) is a technique that you should use in each paragraph of your discursive or argumentative writing.

Certain words and phrases can be employed to assist this process. For instance, **inserted phrases** such as *they add/argue/believe* or *additionally* in a supporting sentence after an initial topic sentence can give further detail about a specific point. For example:

> *Some people believe that education is the most precious gift a young person can receive. It gives, **they argue**, a foundation for personal development and participation in society …*

The use of relevant data, statistics and surveys (real or feasible) can create the impression of expertise, and of the writer's knowledge and authority. The example above could be continued as follows:

> *… for example, a survey carried out by the EEC recently found that most students who received an education up to the age of eighteen felt more adjusted and ready to experience the world at large than those who had left school or college at sixteen.*

KEY TERMS

inserted phrase words placed into part of a sentence

99

Sometimes, it can be effective in a key paragraph to state the counter-argument with relevant evidence before addressing it. A further continuation of the example response might read:

> *According to a recent survey in the US, many college graduates felt that their years of study had not really proved of long-term benefit for their emotional and psychological well-being. Their stress levels, they argued, had been at an all-time high. However, supporters of college education feel that the time invested in acquiring more in-depth skills and knowledge equips graduates with high-level expertise and understanding of not just their own area of study but the society they live and interact with …*

TIP

Note the use of inserted phrases like *they argued* to develop the idea, and the inclusion of *however* to establish the contrasting point of view.

••• FURTHER RESEARCH

Further information about developing ideas and evidence can be found at **http://library.bcu.ac.uk/learner/writingguides/1.15.htm**; **http://www.umuc.edu/writingcenter/onlineguide/chapter8-08.cfm**

Here is a question asking for a piece of discursive writing, followed by an extract from a sample response.

> *A newspaper aimed at parents and families publishes an article called* Should Teachers Be Paid by Results? *The article offers different views about the topic. Write the article. In your answer, create a sense of controlled and balanced arguments.*

ACTIVITY 2.27

How could this part of the response be improved?

SAMPLE RESPONSE

Teachers are people who give us knowledge about education and the world from their own experience and hard working student life. Teachers should be paid for the degree and knowledge they have got. Well they give the education to students in class and well students do nothing and are always daydreaming or texting on their phones or talking in the lectures of teacher's and why should they be the reason for bad grades? They are providing their education and experience. Well it's all the fault of students who aren't interested or working hard at home or even revising after leaving school. Teachers cannot feed you spoon in mouth to get good grades. It's the job of students to earn and acquire good grades.

'Paragraph for, paragraph against' structure

You are going to read four examples of responses to a longer 'Writing for an audience' task, in sections, using the 'paragraph for, paragraph against' structure. Here is the task:

> *An online magazine aimed at teenagers publishes a feature called* Are Beauty Contests a Thing of the Past? *Write the article. In your writing, create a sense of reasoned arguments.*

Introduction

SAMPLE RESPONSE

'Mirror, mirror on the wall: who is the fairest of them all?': this is a well-known line from a fairytale, a myth, from a world in which magic lives and the 'goodies' always come out on top in the end. Yet it can also be seen as a reflection of the world's preoccupation with vanity. So many people want to be beautiful. So many people want to be the fairest in the land. It's an obsession most people seem to possess these days: the need to be admired, even worshipped, and accepted. Is there anything wrong with this? Must the mirror give us a reflection? Does someone really need to be set apart, as the most appealing? Does there need to be a Snow White?

ACTIVITY 2.28

Write an introductory paragraph (120–150 words) for the following article using the techniques highlighted in the sample response above:

A local newspaper publishes an article assessing the case for single sex schools. The article adopts a balanced and controlled tone.

KEY TERMS

cyclical coming full circle, ending where it began

COMMENT

Here are some good points about this introduction:

- the use of a well-known phrase or saying focuses the reader directly on the subject
- the use of *yet* introduces the contrasting points of view
- both sides of the issue are raised using questions, which sets out the main section of the article that follows
- there is no evidence of a personal opinion at this point
- the use of repeated phrases and structures (*So many people want*)
- the **cyclical** nature of the opening and close of the paragraph with the final question echoing the fairytale referred to at the beginning.

101

••• FURTHER RESEARCH

www.debate.org has a topic area on beauty contests. Read some of the entries and see if you agree with the points put forward. How many of them are assertions and how many are supported by reasoned argument and evidence?

Paragraph introducing an argument using examples

SAMPLE RESPONSE

Beauty contests, it can be argued, have long-lasting effects on mostly women and girls. Some people believe that these effects can be positive: image, they believe, is important in the world around us nowadays. For example, job interviews, public presentations and public appearances, all require a certain degree of image-consciousness. Furthermore, a recent survey by the NBC television channel in America showed that many respondents felt that beauty contests teach girls to present themselves effectively, to be polite and ladylike and, to a degree, to take pride in their appearance by caring for their bodies and adopting a healthy lifestyle. There was evidence girls acquired greater confidence and addressed their fears and concerns about mixing with other people and learned to deal with peer pressure. Beauty contests, it revealed, gave girls aspiration, hope and motivation, elements which are very important at any stage in life.

ACTIVITY 2.29

Write a paragraph of 120–150 words introducing an argument for the following task, using the techniques highlighted in the sample response above.

> *A local newspaper publishes an article assessing the case for single sex schools. The article adopts a balanced and controlled tone.*

COMMENT

Here are some good points about this paragraph:

- the use of a topic sentence (*Beauty contests, it can be argued, have long-lasting effects on mostly women and girls*) and a connective to link sentences (*Furthermore*)
- the use of inserted phrases (*it can be argued … they believe … to a degree … it revealed*) to develop and support arguments with further detail
- the use of an example (*a recent survey by the NBC television channel in America*)
- there is no evidence of a personal opinion at this point (*Some people*) – a detached approach introducing one side of the argument
- the use of lists of three (*aspiration, hope and motivation*) to convey depth and range.

Paragraph using counter-argument with examples

Read this example of a different sort of paragraph.

SAMPLE RESPONSE

However, opponents of beauty contests feel that it is also a sad reality that mothers, in particular, often become obsessed with them, insisting that their often very young offspring participate in these shows and processions. A recent film documentary, *A Life in Showbiz*, shows the audience evidence of how young children are forced to wear heavy make-up, have their hair done, and strut down the runway in high heels. Indeed, this is a form of child abuse, some opponents argue, and strict age limits should be applied to all such contests, and restrictions enforced so that the participants can only appear and dress in certain ways.

ACTIVITY 2.30

Write a paragraph of 120–150 words introducing a counter-argument for the following task, using the techniques highlighted in the sample response above.

> *A local newspaper publishes an article assessing the case for single sex schools. The article adopts a balanced and controlled tone.*

COMMENT

Here are some good points about this paragraph:

- the use of a topic sentence (*mothers, in particular, often become obsessed with them*) and a connective to link sentences (*Indeed*)
- the use of an inserted phrase (*some opponents argue*)
- the use of an example (*A recent film documentary,* A Life in Showbiz)
- the use of lists of three (*wear heavy make-up, have their hair done, and strut down the runway in high heels*) to convey depth and range.

Conclusions in discursive writing

Conclusions in discursive writing should continue the measured approach adopted beforehand, yet also indicate the viewpoint of the reader. Read this example:

SAMPLE RESPONSE

One of the major issues associated with beauty contests is the type of negative self-image it can foster in participants. It seems that beauty should not be judged in this way: competitions, after all, are based on opinions not facts. 'Beauty', it is said, 'lies in the eye of the beholder.' Those who lose out in such competitions may lose self-esteem and motivation, developing feelings of inferiority in relation to those around them. It may well be that these contests would provide a more positive and beneficial influence if they were controlled, and embraced all kinds of beauty: physical and spiritual. We should be very, very careful: the mirror on the wall may reflect the kinds of negative things we don't really want to see.

ACTIVITY 2.31

Write the conclusion of 120–150 words for the following task, using the techniques highlighted in the sample response above:

A local newspaper publishes an article assessing the case for single sex schools. The article adopts a balanced and controlled tone.

COMMENT

Here are some good points about this conclusion:

- the personal view comes only at the end and does not rant or preach but takes a careful approach (*It seems*)
- the use of a well-known saying or phrase (*Beauty … lies in the eye of the beholder*) is employed again, as in the introduction
- examples of possible effects are offered (*lose self-esteem and motivation*)
- the use of *we* creates a sense of inclusion compared to the possibly more opinionated use of *I*
- the final words also create a cyclical ending to the whole piece with the final idea echoing the opening.

103

'Argument and counter-argument in each paragraph' structure

The essay below is a response to the following task.

A celebrity magazine aimed at a mainly female readership publishes an article called Is This the Real Deal? *The article explores whether reality television competition shows do more harm than good. Write the article. In your writing, create a sense of balanced and reasoned arguments.*

This response uses a structure in which arguments for and against are combined in each paragraph. Read through it carefully, noting how it differs from the previous structure ('paragraph for, paragraph against'). The words in brackets refer to techniques that you have learned about and practised.

SAMPLE RESPONSE

It is often heard that 'fame and fortune await you' [use of a well-known saying] and in the current world it seems [word suggests detached rather than personal opinion] that in the media landscape reality is everything. The combination of 'ordinary' people and cameras seems [word suggests detached rather than personal opinion] to be a formula for success. One particular area this can be seen in is the talent show. A long-established format of the entertainment world is now a thriving industry worth enormous amounts of money [definition of the issue]. Yet [connective for contrast], are these seemingly innocent shows a positive addition to our lives, instilling ideas of a work ethic and the sense that if you really work hard enough you can achieve any dream you have? Or are they doing more harm than good by promoting the vision of a lifestyle, a hope of fame and riches, of material luxury and wealth, to an audience who will never achieve it? Are they just making money in their advertising profits by cynically exploiting people's feelings and desires? [use of questions to introduce key areas of the essay]

Supporters of these shows believe that they bring the public closer to the world of entertainment than ever [reference to one side of the case in a detached way through a topic sentence]. Such shows, they add [inserted phrase for development], allow the audience to engage in a kind of democratic process, where people power is the fairest form of judgement. These programmes, a recent survey for a national newspaper discovered [example], allow the audience to feel as thought they belong, giving them some sense of purpose and satisfaction. At the same time, it revealed [inserted phrase for development], voting members of the public believe they get a glimpse of the world of celebrity that they would never ordinarily see. When, for example, contestants are mentored by star judges in, say, the *X Factor*, a vision of a lifestyle that is normally concealed behind the scenes is there for all to watch: the rehearsals, the setting, the personalities. However [connective], critics [the other side of the case in a detached way] of such shows highlight the consistent effort to represent any contestants as 'real', as being just like any one of the watching public. They are made to appeal, they believe [inserted phrase for development], to an audience which is apparently fed up with aloof and distant celebrities. This process, critics add [inserted phrase for development], is a cynical exploitation of the audience's emotions, implying that striving for fame is worth all the effort and sacrifice, and, most of all, that it is achievable. It creates the impression that fame is all that counts, they believe [inserted phrase for development], that unless you acquire it, you are a failure in some way. They point to examples of newspaper [example] articles in which young schoolchildren, when interviewed, said their ambition in life was to be famous and rich or to be a particular star; more seemingly mundane careers and aspiration were not mentioned. This kind of effect, it is believed [inserted phrase for development], creates a 'me me me' society, where social bonds, friendship and family all take a second seat. Years ago, children would want to be firemen, nurses, astronauts. Now, for opponents of such programmes [inserted phrase for development], it appears [word suggests detached rather than personal opinion] that even the idea of work is anathema: why work when you can be famous? Why work for anything?

ACTIVITY 2.32

Read, plan and complete the following task, using the counter-argument structure you have just read about. You should write 600–900 words.

A magazine aimed at teenagers publishes an article called Skin Deep, *which assesses the arguments for and against cosmetic surgery. Write the article. In your writing, create a clear sense of both viewpoints.*

Stage 1: Begin by generating 'for' and 'against' ideas on the topic as you learned at the start of the unit. Then organise your ideas into a series of paragraphs.

Stage 2: With reference to the previous sample responses in this section, write your own introduction (first paragraph) for this task.

Stage 3: Write your own version of the next paragraph, bearing in mind the following:

- avoid giving your personal opinion at this point
- begin with an argument created by a topic sentence
- use connectives
- follow the initial point with further development and exemplification using inserted phrases (e.g. *they believe, it revealed*), as well as references to examples such as surveys or statistics
- follow the initial argument with a counter-argument including development and exemplification.

Stage 4: Write your remaining paragraphs with the related counter-arguments, based on your plan.

Stage 5: Write a conclusion to the article, bearing in mind the example we saw in the answer about beauty contests above.

LINK

Reread the article on motherhood on page 62 of **Unit 1**. To what extent does the writer include both arguments for and counter arguments within the same paragraphs?

105

Other kinds of argumentative writing

When responding to the longer 'writing for an audience' task (600–900 words), you may be asked to write two shorter pieces (e.g. letters) offering two contrasting argumentative pieces about the same topic.

ACTIVITY 2.33

The two letters below are sample responses to a newspaper article about the age requirements for elderly drivers. Rewrite the letters so that there is:

- an appropriate and effective layout
- varied use of argumentative strategies and techniques – such as the use of exemplification (surveys, data, other sources) and connectives
- some use of questions to offer counter views
- brief direct statements to express a sense of voice
- appropriate use of language.

The question marks highlight points that you may need to think about when writing your revised text.

SAMPLE RESPONSE

❓

Dear Sir or Madame ❓,

I am writing in about that ❓ article in your paper last week about the age when elderly people are stopped ❓ from driving. I do ❓ believe their age ❓ should be lowered.

Many people of the requirement age ❓ are usually not in great shape. Statistics ❓ show nineteen out of twenty old ❓ people of that age suffer from poor eyesight. ❓ I don't think ❓ they can recognise people and objects or situations any more like younger people do.

There is no doubt ❓ that it is true ❓ that as we get older our reflexes get much more slow and not as good. These old people usually ❓ find themselves unable to react to situations anywhere near quickly enough ❓, putting their lives at risk as well as the people, especially children, around them. I've seen ❓ loads of occasions when children are being chauffeured around by their grandparents. It's just not safe. If some other driver decides to go through the lights a car with children driven by an old ❓ grandparent could run into them: the grandparent and the children will be really badly injured.

It is often said by people ❓ that the older we get the more set in our ways and the more difficult and less active we are. Most old ❓ people, especially old men ❓, take little notice of their doctors and insist on carrying on driving. They are endangering their health ❓ by pushing the limits, and they are putting others at risk. What would happen if they collapsed behind the wheel? Without any doubt ❓, they will cause a serious accident. There is a lot of evidence ❓ showing that old people are likely to suffer from dementia, a stroke or a heart attack when driving. There is a strong chance ❓ they will not survive and this also increases the risk to other people. If they stayed at home, there are more likely to get help and survive ❓.

This kind of thing could all be prevented ❓ if the age at which old ❓ people could drive was lowered. I think ❓ we would all be far more safe. I strongly believe ❓ that old ❓ people should think long and hard about these things and that those who are in power should make these legal changes as soon as possible.

Yours sincerely ❓,
❓

❓

Dear Editor,

I am writing this letter to respond ❓ to the article from your paper about the age requirement for elderly people to be allowed to ❓ drive being reduced. I genuinely and sincerely ❓ believe this would not be a good and practical thing to do.

   I realise that the fitness and alertness is ❓ an important matter. Most elderly members ❓ of society are still fit and healthy even when they reach the required age for driving. They are not ❓ all weak and frail. Most people of advanced years are fit and sound in mind ❓ and do not suffer from major ailments.

   I realise that some old ❓ people cannot always see that well and sometimes their reflexes are slow ❓. Some people ❓ even tell them to stay off the roads and not to drive at all. Rather than banning them from driving why not make them pass regular health and reflex tests in real driving situations? If they are fit they should be able to drive.

   If you stop all old ❓ people driving, this means taking away their freedom, choice and independence. Old ❓ people would need others to drive them around or worse ❓ or rely on their families and children for mobility ❓ for the rest of their lives … They would ❓ no longer be able to travel or visit particular place at times they chose themselves. They would ❓ stay at home relying on relatives or the newspaper, or the television for interaction of some kind. They would ❓ be trapped. It is a well-known fact ❓ that for old ❓ people to stay fit and mentally stimulated they must be active and participating in a range of activities and social situations. Without transport they will become like prisoners and be lazy ❓.

   In fact, old people are full of wisdom ❓. They are very careful drivers ❓ who follow the law of the road and do not pose any risk to pedestrians and other drivers.

   I really believe the authorities should listen to my plea ❓. Strong and mentally active old people should be allowed to drive. Only those who are not fit and healthy should be stopped ❓.

Yours sincerely,
❓

TIP

It is important that your speech shows an awareness that you are addressing an audience and that your language is appropriate for that audience.

LINK

Look again at the section on scripted speeches in **Unit 1** on pages 58–62 and the techniques and effects involved.

●●● FURTHER RESEARCH

What is the voting age in your country? If you don't know, find out. What about other countries? You could support your scripted speech with some factual information, if you wanted.

Other forms of contrasting argumentative pieces about the same topic could be in the form of two speeches (300–450 words each). You may be asked to create a clear sense of opposing attitudes and viewpoints in your writing.

ACTIVITY 2.34

Bearing in mind the techniques used in letter writing that you learned in **Unit 1**, read and complete the following task.

An article has appeared in your local newspaper which argues that the voting age should be substantially lowered. Two readers write letters to the newspaper, one agreeing with the article, the other disagreeing. Write the two letters (between 300–450 words each).

Cambridge International AS and A Level English Language 8693
Paper 2 (October/November 2012), Q6.

Summary

Remember these key points from this section:

- It is particularly important to plan discursive or argumentative writing.
- You can use a variety of structures to develop your argument.

Practice and self-evaluation

In this section, you will:

- read a variety of extended tasks
- select a task, plan and write it.

To practise the skills you have developed in this unit, and bearing in mind the points you have learned, write responses to one or more of the following tasks. (Each of these should be 600–900 words unless otherwise stated.)

1 *A national newspaper aimed at a family audience publishes a feature called* Why Young People Need to Do Military Service. *The article outlines the reasons the country requires 18-year-olds to enlist in the armed forces. Write the article. In your writing, create a sense of convincing and persuasive reasons.*

2 *A travel magazine invites you to contribute an article called* Scenes You Must See *in order to encourage local people to take a greater interest and pride in their environment and its history. Write the article. In your writing, create a sense of enthusiasm and interest.*

3 *The local authority where you live has published plans for the creation of a theme park in your area. Two residents write letters to the authority. Write the letters (300–450 words each). In your writing, create a sense of opposing viewpoints and attitudes.*

4 *Your government has invited two organisations to offer ideas for the regeneration of a run-down site in the centre of a major city. The organisations are invited to present their ideas before the government's planning committee. Write the text for the presentations. In your writing, create a sense of different viewpoints and contrasting approaches to the project.*

5 *A newspaper aimed at a family readership publishes a feature called* The Rise and Rise of Social Media. *The article explores the pros and cons of their use and the effects on those who have access to them. Write the article. In your writing, create a sense of a balanced and even-handed approach to the topic.*

Remember:

- Generate ideas first, based on the key words in the task.
- Make sure you are clear who the writer is, what the task involves, who or what it is for (if stated) and who or what the audience is (if known).
- Think about the style/tone/mood required.
- Plan your response in paragraphs, based on the ideas you generated at the start.
- Write your response.
- Check your work as you progress and at the end.

Unit 3: Imaginative writing

The principal focus of this section will be on **extended imaginative writing**. However, as a way of developing imaginative writing skills, and for examination practice, you will also look at passages of text, comment on them and respond to tasks arising from them. You should also bear in mind that many of the skills you have developed in non-fiction **Units 1** and **2** are equally applicable to this unit.

Exploring imaginative writing tasks

In this section, you will consider:

- what 'imaginative writing' is
- the types of questions you might meet in examinations
- which kinds of questions you need to work most on.

What is 'imaginative writing'?

Read this short text: it is from a traveller's account of walking the Normandy coastline in winter.

ACTIVITY 3.1

Is this an imaginary account or a real one?

Does this text demonstrate any specific descriptive or storytelling skills? If so, what?

> The sea had retreated miles out into the bay, revealing the mussel beds, like charcoal sticks against the greying sky-line. Above me sand-martins swooped furiously, ducked and dived amongst the dunes, and the tufts of marram grass recalled to me childhood games, picking the spiky leaves and sending them spiralling towards my younger sister. Ah, Alice ... I wish you were here now. But you are gone five years, and nothing can bring you back.
>
> From 'Le Bout du Monde' by Mike Gould.

LINK

Look again at the extract from *Lost in London* by J. M. Coetzee on page 46 of **Unit 1**. It is written in the third person and reads like a story, but it is in fact a memoir.

Deciding what is 'imaginative' is difficult. We could say that all writing arises from the imagination because ideas are mediated between the 'real world' and the printed page or screen. The travel writer above might be a real person and his trip to Normandy an actual one. But what about the sister? Perhaps she was invented to create a story we'd want to read? Or maybe she's real too?

What we really mean when we talk about 'imaginative writing' is writing that arises from invented or imagined situations or deals with invented characters, contexts and story-lines. This does not mean that such writing cannot be *inspired by* personal experience or real events; indeed we all draw on what we see in our heads (often from experience) to 'imagine' new ideas or descriptions into being.

The key point is that it doesn't really matter whether the events in the opening passage actually happened or not – the skills demonstrated here are broadly the same whether the piece is fiction or non-fiction. In both cases, the imagination is at work: either to bring back to life a real memory; or to create an invented one that reads like real life.

Types of question

In an examination situation you may be asked to comment on the style and language of a piece of imaginative fiction or a piece of descriptive writing which shares many features with ficiton. You may also be asked to address a directed writing task based on that piece of imaginative writing. **The directed writing task** may ask you to:

- write a similar piece based on the style and language of the original extract but placed in a different context
- continue writing the extract based on the style and language of the original passage
- write a piece in a particular format, such as a letter or diary entry, based on the material of the original extract.

You may also have to address questions which contain **extended imaginative writing tasks**.

You might be asked to write **two contrasting pieces** based on a 'before and after' scenario. For example:

Write two contrasting descriptive pieces (300–450 words each) about a location immediately before the arrival of a storm and some days after it has passed. In your writing, create a sense of setting and atmosphere.

Write two contrasting descriptive pieces (300–450 words each) about two different times of the day and their effect on a particular place. In describing each time, you should create clear contrasts in mood and place.

Imaginative writing tasks may also require you to write a **complete composition** about one particular topic, perhaps focusing on specific qualities such as sounds, colours and textures, or to explore a particular experience or process. For example:

Write a descriptive piece called The Shopping Centre. *In your writing create a detailed sense of people and setting.*

Write a descriptive piece called The Shower, *in which the narrator describes in detail her or his experience of being caught in falling rain. In your writing, focus on colours and sounds to help your reader imagine the scene.*

Other types of question may have a more **narrative** element to them and ask you to compose the opening to a novel, a story or short story for example. The focus in this kind of title is on creating a sense of possibilities for future development at the end of the piece: for example the gradual revelation of a character's motivation; the way in which the narrative may go as it ends on a cliffhanger; or the way the mystery or suspense of the characters and setting may contribute to future events. For example:

Write the opening chapter of a novel entitled The Private Detective. *In your writing, create a sense of mood and place.*

Write the opening to a story called The Cheat. *In your writing, create a sense of character and motivation.*

Write the opening to a short story called When the Evening Comes. *In your writing, create a sense of mood and place.*

Or you may be asked to write a **complete story**. For example, you will choose a title like one of these:

> Write a short story called The Unexpected Guest. *In your writing, create a mood of tension and suspense.*

> Write a short story called Arriving for the First Time. *In your writing, convey the thoughts and feelings of a narrator moving to a new and previously unseen location.*

Other questions may ask you begin to **begin** your composition with **words given in the task**. These types of question usually stress that you do not have to bring the writing to a close or offer a final ending. For example:

> 'The open road stretched ahead of them. There was only one way they could go.' *Continue the opening to this story (although you do not have to write a complete story). In your writing, create a sense of a mysterious future.*

Some titles may require you to **end** your composition with **words given in the task**.

> Write a short story which ends with these words: '… gradually the light grew clearer: it was real.'

TIP

Remember that if you are given the 'end' words for a composition task, you must make sure that these *are* the very last words used in your answer. Plan thoroughly so that you know from the start where your piece is leading.

ACTIVITY 3.2

Re-read the titles for the extended imaginative writing tasks on page 112 and above and make brief notes in response to these questions:

- Which would you feel **most confident** about writing? Why?
- Which would be the **most challenging**? Why?

Keep a note of your initial thoughts and evaluate how far you have been able to address your concerns about certain tasks by the end of this unit.

Summary

Remember these key points from this section:

- Many of the skills you developed in reading and writing non-fiction will also be relevant to this unit – 'imaginative' is a broad and inclusive term.
- Imaginative writing tasks arise either from a set passage or from a more open style of question.
- You may be required to write part of a text or a whole text so having an understanding of structure and sequence is as important in fictional work as for non-fiction texts.

Key reading and writing skills

It is important that you develop a repertoire of key writing skills used by writers of imaginative texts. These will be useful not only in your directed writing work, but also in freer, more extended writing. These include things such as narrative voice and how you position the reader, through to building and developing characterisation, as well as thematic ideas such as how you can make use of recurring motifs and patterns in your descriptive or narrative writing.

Narrative voice

ACTIVITY 3.3

Discuss with a partner:

■ Is there any difference in how we 'read' the story because of the use of the first or third person here?

■ Does one version **foreground** one person's perspective more than the other?

In this section, you will learn:

■ about first, second and third person narration

■ how to use them in your own work.

When we talk about first and third person narration, at a simple level it can just mean the use of *I* or *he/she* to indicate the perspective from which a story is told, or a description given. For example:

> *I waited at the platform wondering if she would come. The clock ticked slowly past the hour. Sol came back from the cafe and we sat on a bench, staring morosely at the arrivals board.*

> *He waited at the platform wondering if she would come. The clock ticked slowly past the hour. Sol came back from the cafe and they sat on a bench, staring morosely at the arrivals board.*

In this extract from Alice Walker's story *The Flowers*, a girl, Myop, is exploring near her house…

> She had explored the woods behind the house many times. Often, in late autumn, her mother took her to gather nuts among the fallen leaves. Today she made her own path, bouncing this way and that way, vaguely keeping an eye out for snakes. She found, in addition to various common but pretty ferns and leaves, an armful of strange blue flowers with velvety ridges and a sweet suds bush full of the brown, fragrant buds.
>
> By twelve o'clock, her arms laden with sprigs of her findings, she was a mile or more from home. She had often been as far before, but the strangeness of the land made it not as pleasant as her usual haunts. It seemed gloomy in the little cove in which she found herself. The air was damp, the silence close and deep.
>
> From *The Flowers* by Alice Walker.

113

We tend to assume that third person narration creates distance. After all, we're not 'inside the head' of a character as we are with first person narration. Yet here the writer uses third person narration (*she*) but whilst we watch her movements, we're also taken into her world. For example:

■ *Today she made her own path* – straightforward physical 'external' description

■ *the strangeness of the land made it not as pleasant as her usual haunts* – the writer allows us access to Myop's inner thoughts.

ACTIVITY 3.4

1 Note down at least one more example of each of these different modes of narration from the extract.

2 Then write your own short paragraph describing a child in an outdoor setting via third person narration. Do it in such a way that we see what they do, where they go, etc. but at the same time are given access to their feelings.

> **TIP**
> Don't ignore seemingly insignificant details, such as characters' names. In *The Flowers*, the name Myop might remind us of *myopia* (short-sightedness) suggesting that this is a child who does not see, or has not seen, the wider world and all its unpleasantness.

3 As a writer, you have the power to direct or position your reader as you choose, from being inside a character's head, or outside. Now, rewrite your paragraph in **first person narration**.

4 Once you have finished, compare your two versions:
  ■ In what way does it change when you move to first person narration? Did it make you want to make any other changes? How did it change the reader's experience?

More on first person narration

We tend to think that first person narration will allow us access to what our narrator thinks and feels, and his or her reasons for acting in a particular way. But writers use the first person perspective in a wide variety of different ways. We may, for example, follow without question our hero's challenges as we experience the story through their eyes. But what if that narration misleads us, or allows us inside someone's head but at the same time denies us complete understanding?

Read this extract.

A chair, a table, a lamp. Above, on the white ceiling, a relief ornament in the shape of a wreath, and in the centre of it a blank space, plastered over, like the place in a face where the eye has been taken out. There must have been a chandelier, once. They've removed anything you could tie a rope to.

A window, two white curtains. Under the window, a window seat with a little cushion. When the window is partly open – it only opens partly – the air can come in and make the curtains move. I can sit in the chair, or on the window seat, hands folded, and watch this. Sunlight comes in through the window too, and falls on the floor, which is made of wood, in narrow strips, highly polished. I can smell the polish. There's a rug on the floor, oval, of braided rags. This is the kind of touch they like: folk art, archaic, made by women, in their spare time, from things that have no further use. A return to traditional values. Waste not want not. I am not being wasted. Why do I want?

On the wall above the chair, a picture, framed but with no glass: a print of flowers, blue irises, watercolour. Flowers are still allowed. Does each of us have the same print, the same chair, the same white curtains, I wonder? Government issue?

Think of it as being in the army, said Aunt Lydia.

A bed. Single, mattress medium-hard, covered with a flocked white spread. Nothing takes place in the bed but sleep; or no sleep. I try not to think too much. Like other things now, thought must be rationed. There's a lot that doesn't bear thinking about. Thinking can hurt your chances, and I intend to last. I know why there is no glass, in front of the watercolour picture of blue irises, and why the window only opens partly and why the glass in it is shatterproof. It isn't running away they're afraid of. We wouldn't get far. It's those other escapes, the ones you can open in yourself, given a cutting edge.

So. Apart from these details, this could be a college guest room, for the less distinguished visitors; or a room in a rooming house, of former times, for ladies in reduced circumstances. That is what we are now. The circumstances have been reduced; for those of us who still have circumstances.

But a chair, sunlight, flowers: these are not to be dismissed. I am alive, I live, I breathe, I put my hand out, unfolded, into the sunlight.

From *The Handmaid's Tale* by Margaret Atwood.

••• FURTHER RESEARCH

You can read much more about Margaret Atwood on her own site **http://margaretatwood.ca/** Are her other books similar to *The Handmaid's Tale*?

ACTIVITY 3.5

Working on your own, make notes on these questions:

- What do we find out about the narrator in this passage?
- What has happened to him/her? Can we be certain or are we just guessing?

Work through Activity 3.5 then read this commentary from one student in response to the text.

COMMENTARY

The writer uses rather limited descriptive language to create an apparently passive tone. The narrator seems to list or catalogue items in an unemotional manner, as if nothing has greater value than anything else (*A chair, a table, a lamp… A window, two white curtains… A bed… Single, mattress medium-hard*). There is emphasis on logical progression, the positioning of objects, as if the eye of the narrator (and therefore the reader) pans around the room like a camera taking in each component (*on the white ceiling … Under the window … When the window is partly open … on the floor … the wall above… in front of*). The actions of the narrator seem to be minimal (*I can sit in the chair, or on the window seat, hands folded, and watch this*), as if the writer is physically trapped in some enclosed world, unable to escape.

ACTIVITY 3.6

1 This is an effective commentary, but it has not addressed all the elements in the passage. In small groups, discuss the following questions in relation to the passage:
  - What indications are there that the traps are not just physical, but psychological too?
  - How does the writer show, through the narrator's other actions and thoughts, that he or she still has some hope and a sense of life?

2 Bearing in mind the skills used in the passage you have just read, write a short passage of your own of 175–200 words in which a character is confined within a place. Try to imitate the style of the piece you have just read.

  Use this grid of success criteria, checking as you go along and again when you have finished.

Feature	Needs work	Under control
Imply or show that the character cannot leave or is in some way a prisoner.		
Focus on objects or decoration in a similar cataloguing manner and drawing some conclusions from them. (Use shorter or minor sentences to achieve a similar effect.)		
Allow the reader some access to the thoughts and reflections of the narrator.		
Use the same main tense throughout.		

Third person narration

Third person narration is using the *he/she/they* form to describe the actions of characters. It gives the writer the chance to 'enter the heads' of more than one character, although in practice they may choose to focus on one main protagonist.

Read the opening to this short story by Anita Desai:

All was prepared for the summer exodus: the trunks packed, the household wound down, wound up, ready to be abandoned to three months of withering heat and engulfing dust while its owners withdrew to their retreat in the mountains. The last few days were a little uncomfortable – so many of their clothes already packed away, so many of their books and papers bundled up and ready for the move. The house looked stark, with the silver put away, the vases emptied of flowers, the rugs and carpets rolled up; it was difficult to get through this stretch, delayed by one thing or another – a final visit to the dentist, last instructions to the stockbrokers, a nephew to be entertained on his way to Oxford. It was only the prospect of escape from the blinding heat that already hammered at the closed doors and windows, poured down on the roof and verandas, and withdrawal to the freshness and cool of the mountains which helped them to bear it. Sinking down on veranda chairs to sip lemonade from tall glasses, they sighed, 'Well, we'll soon be out of it.' In that uncomfortable interlude, a postcard arrived – a cheap, yellow printed postcard that for some reason to do with his age, his generation, Raja still used. Sarla's hands began to tremble: news from Raja. In

a quivering voice she asked for her spectacles. Ravi passed them to her and she peered through them to decipher the words as if they were a flight of migrating birds in the distance: Raja was in India, at his ashram in the south, Raja was going to be in Delhi next week, Raja expected to find her there. She *would* be there, wouldn't she? 'You won't desert me?' After Ravi had made several appeals to her for information, for a sharing of the news, she lifted her face to him, grey and mottled, and said in a broken voice, 'Oh Ravi, Raja has come. He is in the south. He wants to visit us – next week.' It was only to be expected that Ravi's hands would fall upon the table, fall onto china and silverware, with a crash, making all rattle and jar. Raja was coming! Raja was to be amongst them again!

A great shiver ran through the house like a wind blowing that was not a wind so much as a stream of shining light, shimmering and undulating through the still, shadowy house, a radiant serpent, not without menace, some threat of danger. Whether it liked it or not, the house became the one chosen by Raja for a visitation, a house in waiting.

From 'Royalty' by Anita Desai.

Discuss with a partner:

- In what way does the writer hold back information about the owners of the house for the first 9–10 lines or so?
- Who is the first person mentioned by name? Is it one of the people who own the house?
- Although three people are mentioned in the third person, through whose eyes do you think we are *mainly* seeing the story at this point?

The narrative mode is quite complex in terms of revealing information and emotion. Take this section:

> She *would* be there, wouldn't she? 'You won't desert me?' After Ravi made several appeals to her for information, for a sharing of the news, she lifted her face to him, grey and mottled, and said in a broken voice, 'Oh Ravi, Raja has come. He is in the south. He wants to visit us – next week.'

The first question is what Raja has asked in the letter, but these are not the actual words – these are Sarla's thoughts.

The second question is the actual words Raja has written. We are only being allowed glimpses of the 'real' postcard; the rest is mediated through Sarla's thoughts.

This is a report of what Ravi said – not his actual words. Again information is filtered through Sarla's perspective.

Finally, we get Sarla's *actual* spoken words to Ravi.

So although this is a third person narration, the perspective is specifically channelled through Sarla in these four ways.

ACTIVITY 3.7

In the next stage of the story, Sarla and Ravi go to meet Raja at Delhi railway station at dawn.

Write a further 125–150 words in a similar style describing the station and Sarla and Ravi's wait on the platform.

- Make Sarla's thoughts the main focus of your passage but maintain the use of the third person.
- Use indirect or reported speech for anything Ravi says.

Second person narration

There is another form of narration which is used more rarely – second person narration. Read the following text:

Through the gate and up the walk toward the front door. It'll be good to get this gun belt off, the jacket, the boots. You've earned your supper.

Locked, just as you instructed. You jangle the big key ring, searching.

Open the door and the light blinds you. Fresh bread, and the salty crackle of fat. On the floor of the sitting room lies Amelia's stuffed duck, toppled on its side. You undo the gun belt — Marta won't have it around the child — and stow it high in the front closet, thumping the door shut to announce yourself. When no one comes, you make your way to the kitchen.

It's empty, a wisp of steam floating up through a hole in the stove top.

"Marta," you call.

In the dining room the table's set, your milk poured, the high chair between the two seats so you can each minister to her. The tray holds a spray of crumbs, a slug of gravy. Maybe they couldn't wait.

The back of the house is dark.

"Marta?"

You try your room first, peering in the door. She's not on the bed, and immediately you turn to the nursery.

It's black, and you have to leave the hallway before you see Marta sitting in the rocking chair, her hair a bright frame, her face dark, impossible to read.

From *A Prayer for the Dying* by Stewart O'Nan.

117

This passage shares some similarities with the previous passage on page 116 but there are also some significant differences.

ACTIVITY 3.8

1 Discuss this text with a partner, in particular what we learn about the *you* of the narration and the tone/mood created. Think about:
   - the use of the second person – what effect, if any, does it have on the tone or mood of the piece? Think about the fact that the narrator is simultaneously describing a 'character' doing something and using a direct address to the reader.
   - the use of tenses
   - the range and nature of *what* is described and *how* they are presented to the reader
   - the positioning of the reader in terms of how and where the writer *directs our gaze*
   - what is implied and suggested by what we are told – or not told
   - the use of speech or dialogue.
2 Share your ideas with another pair and make notes before writing up your ideas as a brief commentary on the style and language of the extract.

TIP
Practise altering the form of narration between *I*, *he/she* and *you* to see what different effects you can create.

Further practice
Look again at the text you wrote in the first person in Activity 3.6 – about someone confined or imprisoned. Rewrite the text, or part of it, turning it into a second person account (using *you*). Then look at both the original and the new version; which of the two do you prefer? Is there a difference in the mood created?

Unreliable narration
Another type of narrator is the **unreliable narrator** – someone who deliberately or unconsciously misrepresents the reality of events. Narrators can be said to be 'unreliable' for a number of reasons. It may be because:

- they do not understand or have only a partial picture of what is happening
- they deliberately mislead or misrepresent what is happening for their own reasons.

In some cases, narrators are aware of their lack of knowledge and the way they reveal 'the truth' about events can add to the impression of suspense, happiness, sadness, tragedy, joy, etc.

Read the following extract. As you do so, think about the reasons why the narrator of this passage is 'unreliable'. Is the narrator deliberately misleading the reader? Or is it simply that they do not have the full picture? Or both?

I see us from three hundred feet up, through the eyes of the buzzard we had watched earlier, soaring, circling and dipping in the tumult of currents: five men running silently towards the centre of a hundred-acre field. I approached from the south-east, with the wind at my back. About two hundred yards to my left two men ran side by side. They were farm labourers who had been repairing the fence along the field's southern edge where it skirts the road. The same distance beyond them was the motorist, John

Logan, whose car was banked on the grass verge with its door, or doors, wide open. Knowing what I know now, it's odd to evoke the figure of Jed Parry directly ahead of me, emerging from a line of beeches on the far side of the field a quarter of a mile away, running into the wind. To the buzzard Parry and I were tiny forms, our white shirts brilliant against the green, rushing towards each other like lovers, innocent of the grief this entanglement would bring. The encounter that would unhinge us was minutes away, its enormity disguised from us not only by the barrier of time but by the colossus in the centre of the field that drew us in with the power of a terrible ratio that set fabulous magnitude against the puny human distress at its base.

What was Clarissa doing? She said she walked quickly towards the centre of the field. I don't know how she resisted the urge to run. By the time it happened – the event I am about to describe, the fall – she had almost caught us up and was well placed as an observer, unencumbered by participation, by the ropes and the shouting, and by our lack of co-operation. What I describe is shaped by what Clarissa saw too, by what we told each other in the time of obsessive re-examination that followed: the aftermath, an appropriate term for what happened in a field waiting for its early summer mowing. The aftermath, the second crop, the growth promoted by that first cut in May.

From *Enduring Love* by Ian McEwan.

ACTIVITY 3.9

Write answers to these questions:

- What do you think has 'really' happened here?
- Are the events told in retrospect, looking back with hindsight, or are they told as they happened? Can you find evidence of particular phrases that suggest this?
- Why does the writer choose *not* to tell us the facts directly? And how does the decision add to the tone and emotion of the passage?

These are difficult questions and the piece is, perhaps deliberately, challenging.

○○○ FURTHER RESEARCH

Jane Austen uses a type of third person narration called 'free indirect discourse'. Can you find out what this is and how it links to the 'omniscient narrator'?

In third person texts, be careful to distinguish between a narrative voice that is closely linked and tied to the action, and one that is more objective and all-seeing. The latter is often known as an **omniscient narrator**, who judges and observes events. They may or may not be 'reliable'. In *The French Lieutenant's Woman* by John Fowles, the narrator constantly switches between times and offers different narrative paths, even several different endings, to such an extent that trusting what we read becomes quite difficult.

ACTIVITY 3.10

Write the opening two paragraphs of a story called *The Letter*. In it, someone close to the narrator receives a letter which has a big impact. Try to convey the idea that the narrator is unreliable in one of these ways:

- The narrator has a different view of the letter than the reality (e.g. he/she doesn't think it's as serious as it is). You could start: *The letter said her grandmother was sick, which wasn't such a big deal, surely? After all, my wife hadn't seen her for twenty years and …*
- The narrator doesn't know the full story and only reveals what he or she can see at the time. You could start: *By the time, the postman had called, the envelope lay torn on the table, the letter removed. My husband was in the back yard and I got on with things as usual …*

119

LINK

It is often said of Nick Carraway, the narrator of *The Great Gatsby*, that he is unreliable in terms of his perception of events and people, including Gatsby himself. You could look at the extract from the novel on page 000 to see if this is true, but for a proper sense of it read the opening two chapters of the novel yourself.

Summary

Remember these key points from this section:

- Consider carefully the role of the narrator in texts you read and how what they say 'positions' us as readers.
- Explore in your own writing the multiple possibilities of narrative mode, whether first, second or third person, and think about the effect of that choice.
- Think about the effect of different types of unreliable narration and what that might add to your own writing.
- Consider how the balance between inner thought, outer action and speech can be deployed to reveal – or hide – what you want to say.

Characterisation

In this section, you will:

- read a range of texts introducing you to a variety of characters
- learn what characterisation is and how it is created
- create your own characters in preparation for more extended writing.

What is characterisation?

Characterisation is the methods and devices a writer uses in order to build a convincing character. These may include:

- physical appearance and clothing
- behaviour towards others – general attitude and specific acts (these might include anecdotes or examples of the character's past actions)
- what the character says
- what others say about the character
- how others behave towards him/her
- the location he or she is placed in, or which reflects them in some way
- what we know, or are told, about the character's personal circumstances (family, friends, job, history, etc.)
- and, sometimes, the circumstances of his or her first and last appearance in a text.

However, if a writer were merely to follow this list and provide the details in a form of catalogue or list of bullet points, it would mean very little. *How* the writer reveals this information is as important as *what* is revealed.

Read the following extract which gives us some very direct information about the **protagonist**, a tribal leader in Africa.

120

LINK

We tend to assume characterisation is limited to fictional works but it can often be applied to non-fiction texts, too. Look back at the extract from *Touching the Void* on page 21 of **Unit 1**. In what ways could Joe Simpson be said to be using characterisation to paint a picture of himself in terms of his behaviour, thoughts, observations, etc.?

KEY TERMS

protagonist the main character

Okonkwo was well known throughout the nine villages and even beyond. His fame rested on solid personal achievements. As a young man of eighteen he had brought honor to his village by throwing Amalinze the Cat. Amalinze was the great wrestler who for seven years was unbeaten, from Umuofia to Mbaino. He was called the Cat because his back would never touch the earth. It was this man that Okonkwo threw in a fight which the old men agreed was one of the fiercest since the founder of their town engaged a spirit of the wild for seven days and seven nights.

The drums beat and the flutes sang and the spectators held their breath. Amalinze was a wily craftsman, but Okonkwo was as slippery as a fish in water. Every nerve and every muscle stood out on their arms, on their backs and their thighs, and one almost heard them stretching to breaking point. In the end, Okonkwo threw the Cat. That was many years ago, twenty years or more, and during this time Okonkwo's fame had grown like a bush-fire.

From *Things Fall Apart* by Chinua Achebe.

ACTIVITY 3.11

Make your own notes on the following:

- Which of the characterisation devices listed above are included here?
- We are told quite a lot in this passage but there is no 'story' as such. It is simply a description of how a character got to be where he is at this point. What might you expect to happen from this point to make a story?

Showing not telling

One of the key skills writers use is to **show characters in action**, rather than telling us about them. This is effective at all times in stories but at the beginning of the narrative it can also have the effect of raising questions in our mind, and of withholding or implying factual details.

Read the following extract from *Lord of the Flies*. It is in almost direct contrast to the previous extract in that we are *told* almost nothing about the character or the facts of his situation, but *shown* a great deal.

The boy with the fair hair lowered himself down the last few feet of rock and began to pick his way towards the lagoon. Though he had taken off his school sweater and trailed it now from one hand, his grey shirt stuck to him and his hair was plastered to his forehead. All round him the long scar smashed into the jungle was a bath of heat. He was clambering heavily among the creepers when a bird, a vision of red and yellow, flashed upwards with a witch-like cry; and this cry was echoed by another.

From *Lord of the Flies* by William Golding.

ACTIVITY 3.12

1   Discuss with a partner:
    - what do we learn about *the boy*? (Think about his physical appearance and his actions.)
    - what do we learn about the circumstances he is in? (Think about the world around him and how it is described.)

- how would you describe the overall style and language of the passage (Is it largely abstract, full of inner reflection and thought? Active and physical? Or what?)
- does the writer hint at any ideas or suggest the tone or mood of the story to come? (think about the references to nature, the boy's appearance and so on)

2 Read the openings of two short commentaries by students. Which of the two (if either) do you think best sums up the mood and what we learn about the character?

A *Small physical details such as the boy who* lowered himself down the last few feet of rock *hint at an innocence– like a child playing in rock-pools. However, we can detect inner conflict in the fact that although* he had taken off his school sweater, *he hasn't let go of it, implying a sense of him wanting to do the right thing (not lose his sweater) despite the heat.*

B *There is a sense of optimism and hope in the piece, with the vibrant colours of nature, such as the bird which was a* vision of red and yellow. *The boy seems to be enjoying his adventure,* clambering heavily *about the place, as if he is exploring.*

Sentence structure, variety and order

It is important to consider not only the vocabulary or particular phrases a writer might use to convey physical details or description of location, but to look also at the use of specific sentences and *where* key ideas are placed.

| Subject of the sentence foregrounded at the start of the paragraph. |
| Long subordinate clause emphasises the actions taken (without success) against the heat. |
| Past continuous verb form takes the reader with the boy as he is doing something. |
| Past simple verb form *flashed* introduces the sudden act of the bird seeming to respond to his presence. |

The boy with the fair hair lowered himself down the last few feet of rock and began to pick his way towards the lagoon. Though he had taken off his school sweater and trailed it now from one hand, his grey shirt stuck to him and his hair was plastered to his forehead. All round him the long scar smashed into the jungle was a bath of heat. He was clambering heavily among the creepers when a bird, a vision of red and yellow, flashed upwards with a witch-like cry; and this cry was echoed by another.

These structural and grammatical decisions all help to create the picture of the character.

ACTIVITY 3.13

Introduce your own character into an island setting. In this case, make the island a cold, northerly one and the character older. Try to begin in a similar way:

- a compound sentence joined with *and* in which an unnamed character is seen
- a follow-up sentence which begins with *Despite*, *Although*, or *Even though*
- a longer sentence using the past continuous followed by a simple active verb.

Remember to stick to *showing* what the character does or encounters, rather than *telling* the reader factual information about him or her.

TIP

Remember not to 'micro-analyse'. This means take care not to spend too much time commenting on one individual word or phrase at the expense of others, or to give it undue meaning or weight.

122

Character dialogue

Another key element in characterisation is dialogue. Although speech can be used to advance the plot, it is equally important in conveying character traits and moods. This can be done in a range of ways, for example:

- **what** is said (the actual words spoken and the information or ideas they convey)
- the **style** of speech (e.g. short abrupt statements, questions)
- **how** it is said (e.g. tone of voice, manner)
- **inserted description** between spoken words (e.g. the actions of a character, the setting).

> **TIP**
>
> In drama texts, bracketed words often convey how the character speaks, and there are sometimes stage directions to assist the actors in their movements or gestures. However, the dialogue (the actual spoken words) is even more important than in novels; it has to carry much of characters' thoughts as there is no prose description to tell us what is going on in their heads.

For example in this short extract, the narrator has got into Carlos's car, which is full of newspaper.

> "Just throw it in the back" he said.
>
> As there was no room in the back, I simply burrowed my way into the heap.
>
> "Is there a safety belt?"
>
> "You won't need it here," he said airily. "In Paraguay it is the law to put on safety belts but it is only to make sure that the driver stays near the wheel."
>
> By John Gimlette.

Simple statement suggests Carlos's confidence.

Additional description suggests Carlos isn't too concerned about the reality of the situation.

Manner of Carlos's response, suggested by the adverb, confirms this confident, somewhat comical separation from real life (in this case, safety concerns).

A student, writing about the character portrait here, said:

SAMPLE RESPONSE

The relationship between the two is established by the writer asking questions to which Carlos gives definitive answers, expressed as imperatives ('*Just throw it in the back*') or simple statements of fact ('*You won't need it here.*'). Carlos's 'devil-may-care' attitude is exemplified by the adverb *airily* suggesting a confidence at odds with the reality. The narrator's actions, in which she *burrowed into the heap* of newspapers tell us about Carlos's car and, by implication, his possibly messy life.

ACTIVITY 3.14

Write a few more lines of dialogue and description in which Carlos approaches and drives through some red traffic lights. Try to maintain the same style of speech from both characters.

What the student has done very effectively here is to unpack the dialogue and the detail around it to draw conclusions.

123

Developing dialogue

Dialogue between characters can also be used to convey the shifting status or mood of a piece; for example, the power relationships between people, or someone's developing hope or anxiety.

Read this longer passage and then answer the questions that follow it. As you read, try to trace the development in the way we read or interpret the grandmother's character and her position in the household.

The grandmother didn't want to go to Florida. She wanted to visit some of her connections in east Tennessee and she was seizing at every chance to change Bailey's mind. Bailey was the son she lived with, her only boy. He was sitting on the edge of his chair at the table, bent over the orange sports section of the Journal. "Now look here, Bailey," she said, "see here, read this," and she stood with one hand on her thin hip and the other rattling the newspaper at his bald head. "Here this fellow that calls himself The Misfit is aloose from the Federal Pen and headed toward Florida and you read here what it says he did to these people. Just you read it. I wouldn't take my children in any direction with a criminal like that aloose in it. I couldn't answer to my conscience if I did."

Bailey didn't look up from his reading so she wheeled around then and faced the children's mother, a young woman in slacks, whose face was as broad and innocent as a cabbage and was tied around with a green head-kerchief that had two points on the top like rabbit's ears. She was sitting on the sofa, feeding the baby his apricots out of a jar. "The children have been to Florida before," the old lady said. "You all ought to take them somewhere else for a change so they would see different parts of the world and be broad. They never have been to east Tennessee."

The children's mother didn't seem to hear her but the eight-year-old boy, John Wesley, a stocky child with glasses, said, "If you don't want to go to Florida, why dontcha stay at home?" He and the little girl, June Star, were reading the funny papers on the floor.

"She wouldn't stay at home to be queen for a day," June Star said without raising her yellow head.

"Yes and what would you do if this fellow, The Misfit, caught you?" the grandmother asked.

"I'd smack his face," John Wesley said.

"She wouldn't stay at home for a million bucks," June Star said. "Afraid she'd miss something. She has to go everywhere we go."

"All right, Miss," the grandmother said. "Just remember that the next time you want me to curl your hair."

June Star said her hair was naturally curly.

From *A Good Man Is Hard To Find* by Mary Flannery O'Connor.

FURTHER RESEARCH

Actors constantly try out the different statuses in a relationship. Go to **http://www. nationaltheatre.org.uk/discover-more** and watch some of the rehearsal scenes to see how power can shift between one character and another.

ACTIVITY 3.15

1   Work through the text and list key words and phrases related to the characterisation of the grandmother and the other characters.

2   Then, copy and complete the table. You have been given some examples to start you off.

Character	Things said or responses to speech	Effect
Grandmother	Imperative statement: *read this, You all ought to take them somewhere else, etc.* [add more examples]	Shows her trying to assert her authority
Son and daughter-in-law	*Bailey didn't look up from his reading…*	
June Star		
John Wesley		

124

3   Once you have completed the table, write a short commentary on the characterisation of the grandmother. Refer back to the list of characterisation techniques at the start of this section (on page 120) focusing in particular on what characters say, how they behave and how others behave towards them.

If you can, include a comment about the final sentence, which is an example of **indirect speech**. What is the effect of this on our overall understanding of the grandmother's role in the family and how she is viewed?

(Remember: indirect speech is often called 'reported speech' as it represents what someone reports about another person's spoken words. It does not show the words as they were spoken with speech marks around them, but reports them indirectly. For example *Layla told me that she was going to the market* rather than *'I'm going to the market,' said Layla*.)

4   Write 150–175 words of a text called *The Visit* in which a relative from overseas is staying with a small family in a small apartment. Convey the character of the relative and the way others respond to him or her. You could:

- use a typical situation such as breakfast or walking with the children to school
- include at least three different speakers.

LINK

You might want to look back at the Anita Desai text on page 116 to see how she describes the situation *before* an unexpected visit.

Summary

Remember these key points from this section:

- Characterisation is made up of a range of factors, some of which writers prioritise over others.
- It is generally more effective to reveal characters through showing what they do or say rather than telling readers about them.
- Dialogue, and the description around it, is often an effective way to convey developing relationships and power structures.

Setting and location

In this section, you will:

- read a range of texts which introduce or focus on particular locations or settings
- identify key features and devices used by writers and their effects
- apply some of those features in short written texts of your own.

In your study and examination work, you will encounter a range of passages which contain descriptions of settings or locations. In some cases, these will be used to advance plot or to reveal aspects of character. In others, setting is the focus – for example in memoirs or accounts of journeys. The skills demonstrated in these passages are often very similar, whether the text is imaginative fiction, or non-fiction.

Key techniques for describing settings

Whether a writer is mentioning a room, building, outdoor space or landscape in passing in a phrase or sentence, or writing more extensively, many of the techniques he or she deploys remain the same, and have a similar purpose – to convey a vivid and memorable sense of the place and its atmosphere. How is this done?

- by using detailed, specific **adjectives** and <u>nouns</u> describing geographical or other physical features (*a **squat** <u>hut</u> made of **thin** <u>strips of larch</u>; a **snow-capped**, **jagged** <u>peak</u>*)
- through references to the senses (*The **harsh cawing** of crows at the top of the birch trees outside, their bodies **dark shaggy inkstains** against the sky*)
- by using **verbs**, <u>adverbs</u> and *prepositions* that convey movement, stasis and relationships as required by the text (*the winding streets **curve** <u>mysteriously</u> **towards** the old citadel*)
- through **personification** of inanimate objects, buildings or natural phenomena (*The tower **leans down to inspect us** as we climb the steps, **mocking** our tired paces*)

- through other forms of imagery, such as simile or metaphor, either in individual words or phrases, or across whole texts (*The city is a pond seething with danger from* **creatures hidden in the depths** *or* **openly pursuing their prey**)

- through references to weather, nature and other natural phenomena to reflect or create backdrop for events (*She felt the* **sharp needles of rain** *prick her skin and ran for shelter, watching as the* **grey dome of the sky unloaded its force**)

- by using contrast and juxtaposition (***The new town**, all gleaming glass, noise and money;* **the old town***, a quiet sanctuary of museums and galleries*)

- by using compound and complex sentences that develop initial ideas (*The mountain areas have olive groves, apricots, figs but the desert below provides only oil. The gently sloping vineyards dominated the land for miles, although the rain battered on my windscreen, and, at the head of the valley, storm-clouds reared like warriors before battle*)

- through verbal patterning and repetitions creating effects that imitate what is being described, or reflect the experience of the narrator (*We left the café at midnight,* **the lights flickering** *in the street windows,* **the stars shimmering** *across the dark sky,* **our voices echoing** *along the narrow alleys*)

- by using the pen as a camera lens, allowing it to zoom in, zoom out, pan up, down, across and cut from one detail or person to another (*From above, the Hackney marshes looked like a set of dominoes, rectangles with dots on, but ones that moved and swarmed. By one football pitch, a plastic bag of half-eaten oranges lay in the mud*).

The senses

The importance of referring to the senses as a means of conveying ideas about a place, a person or an experience cannot be overstated. There is no obligation to use all the senses, as this would make your writing feel forced, but they can convey powerful and vivid experiences, as shown in this extract:

I am in my bedroom, alone. I have a glass of water. I want to try to gulp it down, like Jimmy does. This word, thirst, thirsty. It is a word full of resolution. It drives a person to quick action. Words, I think, must be concrete things. Surely they cannot be suggestions of things, vague pictures: scattered, shifting sensations?

Sometimes we like to steal Baba's old golf balls and throw them into a fire. First they curl, in a kind of ecstasy, like a cat being stroked, then they arch, start to bubble and bounce, then they shoot out of the fire like bullets, skinned and free. Below the skin are tight wraps of rubber band, and we can now unroll them and watch the balls getting smaller and smaller, and the rubber bands unfold so long it does not seem possible they came out of the small hard ball.

I want to be certainly thirsty, like Jimmy and Ciru.

Water has more shape and presence than air, but it is still colorless. Once you have the shape of water in your mouth, you discover your body. Because water is clear. It lets you taste your mouth, feel the pipe shape of your throat and the growing ball of your stomach as you drink.

I burp. And rub my stomach, which growls. I fiddle with the tap, and notice that when water runs fast from a tap, it becomes white. Water, moving at speed, rushing from a tap, has shape and form and direction. I put my hand under the tap, and feel it solid.

From *One Day I Will Write About This Place* by Binyavanga Wainaina.

ACTIVITY 3.16

Look back at the texts you read in **Units 1 and 2** and see how many of these techniques you can identify.

FURTHER RESEARCH

Create your own journal of favourite examples from these texts and others you have read as a reference source for your own writing. You could also create an online file of atmospheric locations as inspiration for your own creative texts.

127

LINK

You could use this table as a way in to passage-based questions such as the one in the **Practice** section at the end of this unit.

ACTIVITY 3.17

1 On your own, work through the text and identify occasions when particular senses are evoked. Copy and complete the table.

Sight	*they curl*
Sound	*gulp* (and sight? and taste?)
Touch	
Taste	
Smell	

2 Now choose one of these simple actions and write 50–60 words in the present tense to describe it. Try to use at least three of the senses to make the experience come alive.

- making a cup of mint tea
- diving into a swimming pool or the sea
- picking up a broken bird's egg from the ground.

Camera techniques

It can be useful to read and write imaginative texts as if you were holding a camera – the things you choose to describe are what can be seen through the lens at various times. Think about the way film-makers are able to zoom in and out, or pan up and down, track a person's movements, or cut from one scene or action to another. These are all things you are able to do as a writer.

Read this longer passage:

Very early morning. The sun was not yet risen, and the whole of Crescent Bay was hidden under a white sea-mist. The big bush-covered hills at the back were smothered. You could not see where they ended and the paddocks and bungalows began. The sandy road was gone and the paddocks and bungalows the other side of it; there were no white dunes covered with reddish grass beyond them; there was nothing to mark which was beach and where was the sea. A heavy dew had fallen. The grass was blue. Big drops hung on the bushes and just did not fall; the silvery, fluffy toi-toi was limp on its long stalks, and all the marigolds and the pinks in the bungalow gardens were bowed to the earth with wetness. Drenched were the cold fuchsias, round pearls of dew lay on the flat nasturtium leaves. It looked as though the sea had beaten up softly in the darkness, as though one immense wave had come rippling, rippling—how far? Perhaps if you had waked up in the middle of the night you might have seen a big fish flicking in at the window and gone again ...

Ah-Aah! sounded the sleepy sea. And from the bush there came the sound of little streams flowing, quickly, lightly, slipping between the smooth stones, gushing into ferny basins and out again; and there was the splashing of big drops on large leaves, and something else—what was it?—a faint stirring and shaking, the snapping of a twig and then such silence that it seemed some one was listening.

Round the corner of Crescent Bay, between the piled-up masses of broken rock, a flock of sheep came pattering. They were huddled together, a small, tossing, woolly mass, and their thin, stick-like legs trotted along quickly as if the cold and the quiet had frightened them. Behind them an old sheep-dog, his soaking paws covered with sand, ran along with his nose to the ground, but carelessly, as if thinking of something else. And then in the rocky gateway the shepherd himself appeared. He was a lean, upright old man, in a frieze coat that was covered with a web of tiny drops, velvet trousers tied under the knee, and a wide-awake with a folded blue handkerchief round the brim. One hand was crammed into his belt, the other grasped a beautifully smooth yellow stick. And as he walked, taking his time, he kept up a very soft light whistling, an airy, far-away fluting that sounded mournful and tender. The old dog cut an ancient caper or two and then drew up sharp, ashamed of his levity, and walked a few dignified paces by his master's side.

From 'At the Bay' by Katherine Mansfield.

ACTIVITY 3.18

1   Create a table like this on a large sheet of paper.

Close up	Medium shot	Long shot	Wide angle/landscape shot
Big drops hung on the bushes …	*Big fish flicking in at the window…*	*The grass was blue.*	*The whole of Crescent Bay was hidden under a white sea-mist.*

Then, with a partner or in small groups, sketch or write into the table the various objects, natural features and people that are described in the text, as shown in the examples.

It does not matter too much if you cannot distinguish between long shots and wide-angle/landscape shots; the key is to distinguish between the ways the reader is directed to view the scene at various points.

2   Make notes of the way the description is structured and ordered in other ways, for example:

- elements that are still and moving
- the introduction of particular sound effects or other sensory experiences indicated in the description (not sight)
- the types of sentences and how these suggest change or stasis.

3   Now write a full commentary on the passage in relation to its style and language, as you might be asked to do for a commentary-style task in an exam situation.

Location as a reflection of character

Some writers use contrasting descriptive settings to establish ideas about characters and their way of life in the reader's mind. The extract below is taken from *The Great Gatsby*. In it, the narrator, Nick Carraway, informs us about where he lives.

I lived at West Egg, the – well, the less fashionable of the two, though this is a most superficial tag to express the bizarre and not a little sinister contrast between them. My house was at the very tip of the egg, only fifty yards from the Sound, and squeezed between two huge places that rented for twelve or fifteen thousand a season. The one on my right was a colossal affair by any standard – it was a factual imitation of some Hôtel de Ville in Normandy, with a tower on one side, spanking new under a thin beard of raw ivy, and a marble swimming pool and more than forty acres of lawn and garden. It was Gatsby's mansion. Or rather, as I didn't know Mr. Gatsby it was a mansion inhabited by a gentleman of that name. My own house was an eye-sore, but it was a small eye-sore, and it had been overlooked, so I had a view of the water, a partial view of my neighbor's lawn, and the consoling proximity of millionaires – all for eighty dollars a month.

From *The Great Gatsby* by F. Scott Fitzgerald.

● ● ● **FURTHER READING**

Fitzgerald's wonderful short story 'The Ice Palace' uses location to symbolise the dilemma of a southern girl marrying a northern man. Weather, her own home and the eponymous palace become the means by which she questions her relationship and future.

ACTIVITY 3.19

On your own:

■ make brief notes about the general location and then the two buildings described

■ what do these two descriptions suggest about the two characters?

Location as something that signals character, or suggests a way of life, is equally strong in descriptive writing in memoirs.

Read the following passage:

I was not interested in the things which fascinated my schoolmates: sports and spider hunting and fighting crickets for money. And because of my mixed parentage I was never completely accepted by either the Chinese or the English of Penang, each race believing itself to be superior. It had always been so. When I was younger I had tried to explain this to my father, when the boys at school had taunted me. But he had dismissed my words, and said I was being silly and too sensitive. I knew then that I had no choice but to harden myself against the insults and whispered comments, and to find my own place in the scheme of life.

After school I would throw my bag in my room and head for the beach below Istana, climbing down the wooden steps built into the cliff. I spent my afternoons swimming in the sea and reading under the shade of the bowed, rustling coconut trees. I read everything that my father had in his library, even when I did not understand it. When my attention left the pages I would put the book down and catch crabs and dig for clams and crayfish hidden in the sea. The water was warm and clear and the tidal pools were filled with fish and strange marine life. I had a little boat of my own and I was a good sailor. [...]

There was a small island owned by my family about a mile out, thick with trees. It was accessible only from the beach that faced out to the open sea. I spent a lot of my afternoons there imagining I was a castaway, alone in the world. I even used to spend nights on it during those periods when my father was away in Kuala Lumpur.

Early in 1939, when I was sixteen, my father leased out the little island and warned us not to set foot on it as it was now occupied. It frustrated me that my personal retreat had been taken from me and for the next few weeks I spied out the activities that went on there. Judging from the supplies being ferried across by workmen in little boats, a small structure was being built. I contemplated sneaking onto the island but my father's caution deterred me. So I gave up on it, and tried not to think anymore about it.

And halfway across the world, countries that seemed to have little to do with us were preparing to go to war.

From *The Gift of Rain* by Tan Twang Eng.

ACTIVITY 3.20

1 Discuss with a partner:

■ What do we learn about the places the narrator goes to or visits in this passage?

■ Why were these places important to the narrator? What do they tell us about him?

■ In what way do these places have a more symbolic role to play in contrast with what is going on in the wider world?

2 Share your ideas with another pair and then write a short commentary on the importance of place in this passage in revealing the character of the narrator and his situation.

Read the extract below from *Gone With The Wind*, a historical romance. Here, the writer integrates elements of the background and setting with the description of Scarlett. In fact, you can see techniques in the description of Scarlett that are similar to those related to landscape or place.

Vivien Leigh as Scarlett O'Hara in the film of *Gone With The Wind*.

Scarlett O'Hara was not beautiful, but men seldom realized it when caught by her charm as the Tarleton twins were. In her face were too sharply blended the delicate features of her mother, a Coast aristocrat of French descent, and the heavy ones of her florid Irish father. But it was an arresting face, pointed of chin, square of jaw. Her eyes were pale green without a touch of hazel, starred with bristly black lashes and slightly tilted at the ends. Above them, her thick black brows slanted upward, cutting a startling oblique line in her magnolia-white skin – that skin so prized by Southern women and so carefully guarded with bonnets, veils and mittens against hot Georgia suns.

Seated with Stuart and Brent Tarleton in the cool shade of the porch of Tara, her father's plantation, that bright April afternoon of 1861, she made a pretty picture. Her new green flowered-muslin dress spread its twelve yards of billowing material over her hoops and exactly matched the flat-heeled green morocco slippers her father had recently brought her from Atlanta. The dress set off to perfection the seventeen-inch waist, the smallest in three counties, and the tightly fitting basque showed breasts well matured for her sixteen years. But for all the modesty of her spreading skirts, the demureness of hair netted smoothly into a chignon and the quietness of small white hands folded in her lap, her true self was poorly concealed. The green eyes in the carefully sweet face were turbulent, willful, lusty with life, distinctly at variance with her decorous demeanor. Her manners had been imposed upon her by her mother's gentle admonitions ...

Outside, the late afternoon sun slanted down in the yard, throwing into gleaming brightness the dogwood trees that were solid masses of white blossoms against the background of new green ...

From *Gone With The Wind* by Margaret Mitchell.

> **ACTIVITY 3.21**
>
> Look through the text and identify:
>
> - references to the location, Scarlett's background and her family
> - film/camera style techniques as how the writer uses her 'lens' to select and focus on different parts of Scarlett and her clothes
> - how contrasts and juxtapositions work to suggest where the drama of the story might come from.

Further practice

Write a commentary based on these ideas. Make sure you explain the effect on the reader and the style of the passage.

Summary

Remember these key points from this section:

- Writing about setting and location shares many similarities with other forms of descriptive writing, for example character portraits.
- Think in terms of the writer using the pen like a camera to zoom in and out, focus on and cut between things he or she wants to describe.
- Consider how characters can be associated with, or conflict with, particular locations.

Themes, symbols and motifs

In this section, you will:

- consider the role of themes, symbols and motifs in imaginative writing
- apply what you have learned in short writing tasks of your own.

A **theme** is usually taken to mean a key idea, topic or area of interest which a writer explores in his or her work. Themes are sometimes defined in quite general ways using abstract nouns or noun phrases such as *conflict, atonement, hope, unrequited love* but can also be expressed as dualities such as *fathers and sons* or *rich and poor*. Texts can contain many themes and readers may argue over what those themes might be, so interpretation is an important part of the way themes are explored and discussed.

A **symbol** is one way of understanding what a book's themes might be. A symbol can be an object, person, action or experience that represents a bigger idea. In simple terms, we might say that a rose symbolises love or romance, but in literature we may be looking for more subtle symbols.

The play *All My Sons* by Arthur Miller opens in the backyard of an American house. In it there is:

> *a four-foot high stump of a slender apple-tree whose upper trunk and branches lie toppled beside it, fruit still clinging to the branches.*

In the play we learn early on that the elder son of the household was killed flying planes in the Second World War. His body was never found. This event casts a shadow over the story as it progresses.

> **ACTIVITY 3.22**
>
> Think of any recent book you have read, film you have seen, or play you have attended. What would you say its themes were? How did they manifest themselves? (i.e. how did you know this was the theme?)

> **ACTIVITY 3.23**
>
> How do you think the apple-tree might seem to symbolise this event? (Think about what fruit represents and the state of the tree in the yard.)

TIP

Try to find a range of ways of saying *It's about …* It might be better to say *The text **explores the idea** …* or *One theme of the text **might be** …* or *The writer **seems interested** in the issue of …*

● ● ● FURTHER RESEARCH

In *The Great Gatsby* there is a famous description of a huge, dilapidated sign for an oculist featuring spectacles, which stands by the side of a road in a valley of industrial ash. What might this idea represent, given what you can find out about the novel?

ACTIVITY 3.24

Can you think of any other common motifs from traditional tales? Consider how those motifs have been refined or adapted for modern texts, plays or films.

Motifs are similar to symbols but are ideas that re-occur throughout a text or a part of a text. The term is taken from music and relates to a repeated sequence of notes, or tune, which comes back more than once across the piece. Motifs can also refer to common conventions or patterns to stories, so, *the handsome prince who rescues a girl and marries her* could be said to be common motif in fairy tales.

Exploring themes, symbols and motifs in texts

Read this short extract, in which all three elements are combined.

> The baby lay in a basket beside the bed, dressed in a white bonnet and sleeper. The basket had been newly painted and tied with ice blue ribbons and padded with blue quilts. The three little sisters and the mother, who had just gotten out of bed and was still not herself, and the grandmother all stood around the baby, watching it stare and sometimes raise its fist to its mouth. He did not smile or laugh, but now and then he blinked his eyes and flicked his tongue back and forth through his lips when one of the girls rubbed his chin.
>
> The father was in the kitchen and could hear them playing with the baby. He had turned around in his chair and his face was white and without expression.
>
> From 'The Father' by Raymond Carver.

ACTIVITY 3.25

Write answers to these questions:

- Are there any objects, items or people that could be said to symbolise or represent an idea in the opening paragraph?
- In what way does the baby's facial response suggest or imply something about his character or nature (which runs counter to the earlier description)? Think about what the idea of the *flicked* tongue suggests or might symbolise.
- How does the motif of the baby in the basket and his appearance link with, or echo, the end of the extract?
- How is the extract as a whole a reflection of a common literary motif? (Think about myths and fairytales.)
- If you could suggest any themes (on this very limited evidence) for the text as a whole, what might they be?

Sometimes, motifs and symbols enable writers to blend two scenes together. The extract below is an example of a deceptively simple style of writing which conveys, through the young voice of its narrator, a world in which the season and the feelings of the protagonist reflect each other. The scene of the present is interwoven with a scene from the past.

Read the extract and try to work out how the scenes are connected and how this is established.

Mrs Susan looks at me angrily – her eyes are the same as Mama's, but not the same. I am not really scared of her anymore. There is nothing left she can do to me, except do the things she's done already again. She throws some stale biscuit towards me, and storms out of the house. I swallow the biscuit greedily, then pick up my worn jacket. I put it on, and see the scratches still forming on my pale arms. Where did they come from? I step outside gingerly and breathe in the air and surroundings. The cold air is here today, there is ice on the roofs of the houses and buildings nearby. I shiver as the metal wall sends a pulse of cold through my finger. It isn't snowing. I only ever saw snow once before, when Mama took me to the mountains to show me the flowers, the birds and the trees. Mama liked their colours and the patterns of the leaves. She called me Calla, which is a kind of lily. Mrs Susan doesn't call me Calla, she calls me a witch. She tells me that I brought a curse to their land and that is why the wheat won't come this year. Mrs Susan is stupid. Curses aren't real.

I slowly walk to the other side of the wheat field. It's very big. There is an old wooden hut there, and that's where I have to sit, grinding the wheat into fine powder for Mrs Susan to sell ...

The birds circle over the wheat, black and threatening. I don't like birds either. One flies towards the woods. I need to go, to follow its shadow winging across the field. I follow it. I chase it until I reach the big trees. Mrs Susan has told me never to go in there. But I must follow. The trees loom tall and dark; there are no leaves. It is like a big naked forest. They shield me from the harsh, cold wind though. The bird has begun to climb. I look up at it, but am instantly distracted ...

'Snow!' I yell. Pure white flakes are falling on my naked feet. It is cold but I do not care. I hear a rustling sound. I see a figure. It is Mama. 'Mama! You are back!' I cry. I then feel Mrs Susan's cold grasp, as she pulls me out of the forest. Away from the birds, away from the snow.

Anon

Read this opening to a student's commentary on the text:

COMMENTARY

The idea of the *cold* (a word carefully repeated throughout) is ambiguous. The outside world initially seems to reinforce the girl's cold treatment by the adult. However, by association the temperature reminds her of warmer thoughts about her mother in a past happier time (*I only ever saw snow once before, when Mama took me to the mountains to show me the flowers*). This temporary relief is halted by the thought of her current guardian and the mundane work the narrator has to carry out.

ACTIVITY 3.26

Continue the commentary, focusing on the following elements:

- the birds and the forest and what they seem to represent (Is their depiction consistent, or does the writer alter our perspective of them? Think about conventional ways we might view such birds and such a forest.)
- what the motif of the snow seems to signal in terms of the narrator's emotions and character
- how does the text as a whole play on, or allude to, other myths and fairytales? (Think about the role of Mrs Susan, the mother, the child, the forest, etc.)
- how the *cold* as a motif links the text from start to finish.

Further practice

Write a section (50–175 words) of a modern story involving a child in a walled garden.

Think about:

- the story: why the child is there, what he/she has done, or is going to do
- how you can make elements of the scene and situation echo mythical tales or fairy-stories without copying the originals directly
- using objects, clothing, natural features or the weather to represent or symbolise other ideas
- how you might choose a motif to link the various parts of the story (e.g. a key that is found, a particular plant or flower, a bird or insect ...).

Summary

Remember these key points from this section:

- Motifs and symbols can lend richness and texture to your writing, allowing you to create layers of meaning and allusion.
- Use them sparingly.
- Consider how they can reveal or reflect key themes or ideas in yours and others' writing.

Creating your own imaginative and descriptive writing

The final part of this unit deals with the process of planning and writing your own imaginative texts. It addresses the importance of structure and how particular ideas can be developed and expanded. Many of the skills which have been developed in Units 1 and 2 will also be relevant here, especially in relation to organising a longer text around key ideas or points, although this will be applied slightly differently here.

TIP
Be careful when using motifs and symbols that you don't turn your writing into a kind of puzzle to be unlocked. Use these devices sparingly and remember that you must still have an engaging story to tell.

Planning and structuring descriptive texts

In this section, you will:

- learn how to generate ideas for extended descriptive writing
- develop and apply planning and organisational skills.

It is vitally important that when you come to write descriptive pieces you approach them with the same measure of planning as you would other types of writing, such as persuasive articles or reviews. Think carefully about how you can 'position' the reader in the ways that you have explored in this unit to help create an impact and to make your writing vivid and engaging.

Developing ideas for an extended descriptive writing task

There are many ways you can approach a descriptive writing task. You will now look at a sample task and consider how it could be tackled. This is a 'complete composition', but it provides clues as to how to organise your response.

> Write a descriptive piece called The Shower *in which the narrator describes in detail her or his experience of being caught in falling rain. In your writing, focus on colours and sounds to help your reader imagine the scene.*

A student identifies the following key words and phrases from the task:

- *narrator, her or his experience*
- *shower, being caught in falling rain*
- *colours and sounds*

It is a good idea to use either a list or spider-diagram format to put some flesh onto these details. At this stage, do not worry about how you will organise these ideas in your writing. For now, you need to make this 'skeleton' come to life. Here is the same student's first set of ideas:

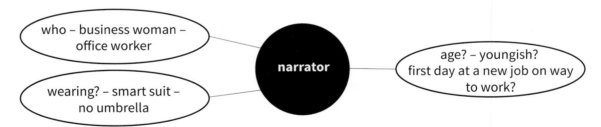

ACTIVITY 3.27

Either use your own ideas to create three spider-diagrams or lists, or use the example above and build on it by adding details for the other two areas (the *shower* – where it happens, when, what impact on narrator – and *colours and sounds*).

Organising and sequencing

Now you have several options in terms of how to organise your ideas into paragraphs. You could:

- Organise it **chronologically** (that is, describe the experience as it happened), for example *Getting off train – walking towards office – sudden rain – trying to find shelter – aftermath as rain stops.*

KEY TERMS

in media res in the middle of the event

ACTIVITY 3.28

Choose one of these approaches and quickly organise the ideas you generated earlier into five or six sections. (These might be paragraphs but see below.) Don't worry if it's not completely precise – this is just a guide for your writing.

ACTIVITY 3.29

Spend two or three minutes looking at the ideas you have organised into sections. Decide on the tense, the person and a draft number of paragraphs. (If you can decide which paragraphs will be short and which long, so much the better.)

- Write it in a more **impressionistic** manner, paying less attention to the time and order and more to the experience. You could begin *in media res* or at the end, looking back, or simply explore the experience in a less 'connected' way. For example *Rain on skin – buildings around me – puddles and images – memories of being a child …*
- Think in terms of the description as a filmed scene, making the reader see things **through a camera lens** (this could be used either with the chronological or more impressionistic approach). For example *Wide angle – me on a street seen from above; long shot; clouds over the buildings; close up – my face, my cheeks; close up; first spots of rain; medium shot; other passers-by …*
- Or any other way you choose to organise your description.

Other structural features

In an examination situation, you may not have time to spend planning in the sort of detail suggested here but if you get used to *thinking* like this, it's likely to improve your work. So here are some other features of form and structure to consider:

- **Tense:** decide which tense you will mostly use: using the present tense means you are less likely to slip into telling a story but make sure you use it consistently.
- **Narrative voice:** the task suggests that the description should be from your perspective (i.e. the first person) but you could consider using the second person (*you*) for a different type of effect.
- **Paragraphs:** these do not have to be uniform in length; might there be a benefit in having a very short paragraph after a much longer one? Could you use this effect for a sudden change in weather or a new description or a change in pace, mood, etc.?

Here is a sample plan completed by a student on a similar task about being caught in a heatwave.

137

SAMPLE RESPONSE

Tense – present; person – first person (*I*)

Para 1: short paragraph: wide-angle, sun appearing after rain over the valley

Para 2: long paragraph: me, working in field picking fruit, the effects of the sun on my neck (close up) and then my arms, body, back and so on

Para 3: long paragraph; the heat's effect on the earth, flowers, crops; a bird flying above me; rocky hills nearby

Para 4: short paragraph; my mouth and tongue, parched

Para 5: long paragraph: mirages in the road and valley; flickering; things blurry

Para 6: sun's abrupt disappearance behind a mountain peak.

ACTIVITY 3.30

1 Once you have finished your plan, share your ideas with a partner.
- Ask them to comment on your plan. Do they have any suggestions to make the description more vivid or detailed?
- Are you happy with what you have planned or could it be amended? Will you be able to write your descriptive piece from this or is more required?

2 If necessary, redraft your plan, adding new elements or cutting others out.

Writing your draft

If you are working in an exam situation, it is likely that your first draft will be your only draft, although you will have the opportunity to proof-read and check it.

ACTIVITY 3.31

With your plan or notes beside you, write your response to *The Shower task*. Before you do so, glance back over the range of language features and devices covered in this unit so far (e.g. symbols, allusions to other stories) to remind yourself of techniques you could use. Try to write about 600 words.

If you prefer to work a different task, use this one:

Write two contrasting descriptive pieces (between 300–450 words each) about a location immediately before the arrival of a storm and some days after it has passed. In your writing, create a sense of setting and atmosphere.

Remember that you will still need to plan, even though the task has already divided the writing into two sections for you. You will need to make the same decisions about how you generate ideas, plan for paragraphs and select tense, voice and style of paragraphs.

Summary

Remember these key points from this section:

- Highlighting or listing the key words and phrases from the task will keep you on track.
- Using these key words to generate ideas will provide a solid base for the plan.
- Consider the range of different ways to organise those ideas (e.g. chronologically).
- Make a conscious decision about the tense, voice and style/length of paragraphs.

Planning and structuring narrative texts

In this section, you will:

- consider how to plan different types of narrative text
- generate ideas about types of narrators you could use.

The planning process for narrative writing is similar to that for descriptive writing, but a number of other issues must also be considered as structure is particularly important when telling stories. The different possible narrative voices, the fact that the text may be sequenced differently from the actual time order of events, all add to the potential richness of the text – but also to its challenges.

Different ways of organising narratives

There are many, many different ways of organising a narrative; the ones mentioned here are perhaps the most obvious you might consider.

Narrative structure	Example	Possible advantages, disadvantages and effects	Questions/ issues
Straightforward chronological account in the first person, past tense	*It was a Tuesday morning when I heard a letter drop on the mat. Opening it, I was astounded to see …*	Usually clear and enables the motives and rationale of the narrator to be explained. Can be predictable, and possibly dull unless very well written.	Can I make the story more interesting by making the narrator unreliable in some way?
Dual or multiple narration	First para: Narrator 1 opens the letter which is from his long-lost father. Second para: Father explains why he is writing.	Gives two perspectives on the same story, but could get confusing and could be boring if it's the same story told twice.	Can I make the two voices sufficiently different? Should I change 'voice' each paragraph, or write half the account from one point of view, then the next half from the other?
Use of flashback (with first, third person, multiple narration, etc.)	*As he sat on the bike at the start of the Tour, it all came back to him – that moment when he was five and rode his first bicycle …*	Need to make sure it isn't confusing. More importantly, there must be a reason for going back in time.	What is the point of the flashback? Is the whole story to be flashback, or just individual moments? How will I get back to the present?
Framed narratives in which stories are contained or revealed through a different context	e.g a series of letters found in a trunk; a woman explaining events in a police interview; a confession to a priest; an old diary discovered by a grandchild.	Can make the main voice (in the framed text) more convincing and real, if found by someone else. Also, can allow the person who found or frames the narrative to comment on or be affected by what he/she reads or hears.	Does the framing have a point? How will I link the framed story to the original context?

Generating ideas and planning your story

The process for this is very similar to that for other forms of writing. Look again at pages 136–137 to remind yourself of the process:

139

ACTIVITY 3.32

A student has come up with the following basic storyline, which fits the first example (simple chronology). For each of the other examples in the table, jot down how the story might be adapted or fitted to the narrative form.

In my story, the narrator is returning home after ten years away, living under an assumed name. He left his family after he lost his job and couldn't bear to tell them. Now he has returned having made his fortune.

KEY TERMS

story arc the overarching curve of a story which sees it begin, build up in strength and drama before descending to a conclusion

- highlighting or listing the key words or phrases from the task
- generating ideas around those key words
- organising those ideas into a narrative structure
- planning for paragraphs, and, if relevant, dialogue.

One key issue to bear in mind when constructing your narrative, regardless of who the narrator is, how many perspectives there are, or whether there is flashback (or flash-forward), is the overall **arc** of a story. We generally talk in terms of a **story arc** having four or five stages:

Stage	Example
Introduction/exposition: the character/ setting, etc.	Woman with children going about her daily life. Very hard as she is on her own.
Complication/problem: something new occurs which changes things	Ex-husband, missing for 10 years, turns up.
Development: life but under new circumstances, situation changing	He explains what happened, tries to start again with her, but she is now dating his brother.
Climax: things come to a head, dramatic moment when events can go one way or another.	Showdown with brother. Husband storms off says he's going forever, won't return.
Conclusion/resolution: events are completed, but not necessarily happily or definitively.	Wife follows him to airport. She tells him she forgives him, but can't change her life. He leaves.

This, of course, is a very simplistic version of a story structure, and many stories have more than one problem or complication. In Hollywood terms, these are often referred to as *reversals* but these could be small problems, which are overcome before the bigger ones occur. Thus, the woman in the story above might not be able to start the car for the school run as it is so old and she is so short of money, so she takes the children by bus. This is not the main 'problem' but it is a symptom.

TIP

Even if you use the five-stage structure which is typical of many stories, bear in mind that if you play around with the time sequence or narration, the order may need to change too.

ACTIVITY 3.33

Take the following title and, using the simple five-part structure above, jot down the outline for a story and the main characters in it.

Write a story called The Cheat.

You might want to jot down some ideas before you try to fit them into the story arc structure.

Unexpected narrators

There is one final aspect to consider: who tells the story? In some cases, an examination task will tell you who the narrator is, but on other occasions, deciding who tells the story is key. We have already considered the use of multiple narrators, but what about **who** those narrators might be?

For example, take this simple story task:

Write a story called Brief Encounter *in which a businessperson on the way home from work on the train gets talking to a complete stranger with surprising consequences.*

The obvious narrators for this story would be the businessperson or the stranger (or both) – but who else could tell the story?

> **ACTIVITY 3.34**
>
> 1 Working on your own, think of **three** further possible narrators.
>   - Which do you think would make the most original storyteller?
>   - Would there be any particular challenges in choosing this other person to narrate the story? Would it create any interesting possibilities (such as misunderstandings)?
> 2 Draft two versions of the opening paragraphs of the *Brief Encounter* story. In the first, use a conventional narrator (the businessperson or stranger); in the second, choose someone more unusual. Which do you prefer?

Further practice

You could write the whole *Brief Encounter* story using an unusual form of narration – either a less obvious narrator or multiple narrators.

Summary

Remember these key points from this section:

- Use a similar planning structure as for other forms of writing.
- Consider a wide range of possibilities for narrative form and voice.
- Be aware of the challenges associated with selecting particular structures.
- Use the five-stage story arc as a basis for your stories, but use it creatively.

Openings and endings in imaginative texts

In this section, you will:

- explore a variety of openings and endings
- consider their effects
- try them out in your own writing.

LINK

This work should be seen in the context of the overall planning and structural help given in the previous section.

Openings and endings do not exist as separate entities within imaginative texts but focusing on them can help identify what it is that makes readers want to read on, and make readers feel that they have had a fulfilling experience by the end. In this section you will encounter a range of different types of openings and endings for imaginative texts along with some elements which can be used to draw texts together.

Different types of openings to stories

What makes a good opening to a story? Story openings are so diverse that it is difficult to identify common features. However, any opening must engage the reader. How this is done varies hugely, but it could be by:

- creating **a particular atmosphere or tone** which fits with the sort of a story we want to read (e.g. a gothic mystery). For example *The candle-light from the old cottage flickered against the window pane as he brushed the branches aside; She could see that the surface of the planet was pockmarked with tiny silver pools as she stepped from the landing craft.*
- offering something **funny, surprising, surreal or shocking**. For example: *It was a bright cold day in April, and the clocks were striking thirteen // I write this sitting in the kitchen sink.*

141

- conveying **a particular memory or occasion** in a way that wants us to find out more about what went on. For example: *It was the day my grandmother exploded // We started dying before the snow, and like the snow, we continued to fall*
- using **a general statement or metaphor** which might thematically 'set up' what is to come. For example: *The past is a foreign country; they do things differently there // It is a truth universally acknowledged that a single man in possession of a good fortune must be in want of a wife.*

In each of these cases, the common factor is that the opening raises questions in the reader's mind. For example *The past is a foreign country; they do things differently there* suggests someone who is looking back, who perhaps questions the actions he or she or others took as a younger person – and we want to know what happened in that *foreign country* of past events.

Holding back information and in media res

> ## ACTIVITY 3.35
>
> Try coming up with four opening sentences for novels by finishing off these prompts. They are similar to the examples given above. If you prefer, write your own opening sentences for each type without using the prompts.
>
> | Type of opening | Prompt |
> |---|---|
> | Atmosphere or tone | *Ahead of me …*
 It was three o'clock in the morning when she … |
> | Funny, surprising or shocking | *It was on a Sunday morning that I woke up and discovered …* |
> | Particular memory or occasion | *It all began when …*
 Ten years ago, to this day … |
> | General statement or metaphor | *Funerals are …*
 Everybody knows that .. |

Sometimes, an opening may not actually reveal very much information. The extract below keeps the reader at a distance, not giving the names of the characters nor any particular location. Only a few snippets of background information are revealed – can you spot them?

Sometimes a piece of imaginative writing opens in the middle of an event or

> A man tells about a letter his wife slipped under his door one night after dinner. He can't find the letter anymore. Their two children are grown and live away. The letter is not in her handwriting, but it says things only she could know, and how she cannot go on with him. He skims different sections of the letter, stopping a few times to go in the hall. The night's unusually foggy. The radio's playing, and the light's on – but he can't bring himself to go into the living room. He prides himself on his memory (he cites a variety of historical facts): that evening he heard someone talking on the phone, muffled, as though they didn't want to be overheard. They hung up the phone. He heard the front door close, and hurried out of the study. They rented this house for the summer (his wife was used to living in the suburbs, not here in the

> country). His wife's suitcase was on the porch, and she was outside. She was with two horses. It seemed like a dream with the fog. Then the sheriff and his assistant pulled up with a pickup for the horses. His wife had spotted the horses loose, and called the police. She tells the sheriff and his assistant that she's leaving, and asks for a ride into town.
>
> From 'Blackbird Pie' by Raymond Carver.

narrative, preventing the reader from knowing exactly what is happening. As you saw earlier, this is known as *in media res*. The extract below is an example of this. You may notice how the writer of this extract also **withholds certain information**,

ACTIVITY 3.36

Discuss with a partner:

- In what way is this passage *in media res*?
- How would the story have been different if it had started earlier? Would it have been more or less interesting?

> The moment that the bus moved on he knew he was in danger, for by the lights of it he saw the figures of the young men waiting under the tree. That was the thing feared by all, to be waited for by the young men. It was a thing he had talked about, now he was to see it for himself.
>
> It was too late to run after the bus; it went down the dark street like an island of safety in a sea of perils. Though he had known of his danger only for a second, his mouth was already dry, his heart was pounding in his breast, something within him was crying out in protest against the coming event.
>
> From 'The Waste Land' by Alan Paton.

143

such as the names of the characters and the exact location. We join the story at a point of suspense. The same technique can also be used to create a mysterious and ghostly atmosphere as we see in this extract from the novella *The Turn of the Screw*:

> The story had held us, round the fire, sufficiently breathless, but except the obvious remark that it was gruesome, as, on Christmas Eve in an old house, a strange tale should essentially be, I remember no comment uttered until somebody happened to say that it was the only case he had met in which such a visitation had fallen on a child.
>
> From *The Turn of the Screw* by Henry James.

There is no 'right' way to write an opening – every imaginative piece will begin differently. However, if you do not immediately engage the reader with something surprising or mysterious, then you will probably need to add a problem or unusual occurrence soon afterwards!

ACTIVITY 3.37

Write the opening (120–150 words) of a different story which also begins in the middle of an unexplained event and location. Base your answer on the style and language of the extract.

Endings

In this final section you will briefly explore different ways of ending pieces of imaginative writing. Some types of endings may leave matters **open** while others will try to draw matters to a **close** or a clear conclusion.

Open endings

Open endings are particularly useful if you are writing the initial chapter or beginning of a novel or story where you are not required to bring your story to a close. There are some very effective ways of using an open ending. For example, you could use a **cliffhanger**, a way of leaving the reader in suspense or wondering how things might develop, perhaps a little bit like leaving an ellipsis (…) at the end of a sentence or paragraph. It is a useful way of engaging readers and encouraging them to do the work. It is another way of showing and not telling, allowing the reader's imagination to come into play.

Read this example of an open ending which occurs at the close of the novel *Gone With The Wind*. It concerns Scarlett and her future.

She had gone back to Tara once in fear and defeat and she had emerged from its sheltering walls strong and armed for victory. What she had done once, somehow – please God, she could do again! How, she did not know. She did not want to think of that now. All she wanted was a breathing space in which to hurt, a quiet place to lick her wounds, a haven in which to plan her campaign. She thought of Tara and it was as if a gentle cool hand were stealing over her heart. She could see the white house gleaming welcome to her through the reddening autumn leaves, feel the quiet hush of the country twilight coming down over her like a benediction, feel the dews falling on the acres of green bushes starred with fleecy white, see the raw color of the red earth and the dismal dark beauty of the pines on the rolling hills.

She felt vaguely comforted, strengthened by the picture, and some of her hurt and frantic regret was pushed from the top of her mind. She stood for a moment remembering small things, the avenue of dark cedars leading to Tara, the banks of cape jessamine bushes, vivid green against the white walls, the fluttering white curtains. And Mammy would be there. Suddenly she wanted Mammy desperately, as she had wanted her when she was a little girl, wanted the broad bosom on which to lay her head, the gnarled black hand on her hair. Mammy, the last link with the old days.

With the spirit of her people who would not know defeat, even when it stared them in the face, she raised her chin. She could get Rhett back. She knew she could. There had never been a man she couldn't get, once she set her mind upon him.

"I'll think of some way to get him back. After all, tomorrow is another day."

From *Gone With The Wind* by Margaret Mitchell.

ACTIVITY 3.38

- In what way is this an 'open' ending?
- How does it also link back to the first description of Scarlett that we get? (See page 131.)

Ambiguous endings

The ending of *Gone With The Wind* is open: we don't know what Scarlett is going to do, but it is not open to interpretation as we broadly know what she means – that she is without Rhett and wants to win him back. However, some endings are even more shrouded in difficulty. An ambiguous ending leaves matters open to interpretation and can be particularly useful if you have chosen to use an unreliable narrator in your piece of imaginative writing.

Henry James's story *The Turn of the Screw* describes how a governess looks after two children, Miles and Flora, in a rather isolated location, after their former governess, Miss Jessel, has died. The new governess imagines that the children are being visited and are in danger of being possessed by the spirits of Miss Jessel and a deceased former valet of the household, Peter Quint. The ambiguity of the story lies in the issue of whether this is the case or whether it is all in the feverish imagination of the nervous, but inexperienced, governess. The tension of this dual perspective runs throughout the narrative and issue of whether the narrator (the governess) is unreliable or not meet reaches its climax at the conclusion of the story. Readers are left to reach their own conclusions about the true source of destruction—the 'spirits' or the pressure exerted by the governess.

My sternness was all for his judge, his executioner; yet it made him avert himself again, and that movement made ME, with a single bound and an irrepressible cry, spring straight upon him. For there again, against the glass, as if to blight his confession and stay his answer, was the hideous author of our woe—the white face of damnation. I felt a sick swim at the drop of my victory and all the return of my battle, so that the wildness of my veritable leap only served as a great betrayal. I saw him, from the midst of my act, meet it with a divination, and on the perception that even now he only guessed, and that the window was still to his own eyes free, I let the impulse flame up to convert the climax of his dismay into the very proof of his liberation. "No more, no more, no more!" I shrieked, as I tried to press him against me, to my visitant.

"Is she HERE?" Miles panted as he caught with his sealed eyes the direction of my words. Then as his strange "she" staggered me and, with a gasp, I echoed it, "Miss Jessel, Miss Jessel!" he with a sudden fury gave me back.

I seized, stupefied, his supposition—some sequel to what we had done to Flora, but this made me only want to show him that it was better still than that. "It's not Miss Jessel! But it's at the window—straight before us. It's THERE—the coward horror, there for the last time!"

At this, after a second in which his head made the movement of a baffled dog's on a scent and then gave a frantic little shake for air and light, he was at me in a white rage, bewildered, glaring vainly over the place and missing wholly, though it now, to my sense, filled the room like the taste of poison, the wide, overwhelming presence. "It's HE?"

I was so determined to have all my proof that I flashed into ice to challenge him. "Whom do you mean by 'he'?"

"Peter Quint—you devil!" His face gave again, round the room, its convulsed supplication. "WHERE?"

They are in my ears still, his supreme surrender of the name and his tribute to my devotion. "What does he matter now, my own?—what will he EVER matter? *I* have you," I launched at the beast, "but he has lost you forever!" Then, for the demonstration of my work, "There, THERE!" I said to Miles.

But he had already jerked straight round, stared, glared again, and seen but the quiet day. With the stroke of the loss I was so proud of he uttered the cry of a creature hurled over an abyss, and the grasp with which I recovered him might have been that of catching him in his fall. I caught him, yes, I held him—it may be imagined with what a passion; but at the end of a minute I began to feel what it truly was that I held. We were alone with the quiet day, and his little heart, dispossessed, had stopped.

From *The Turn of the Screw* by Henry James.

145

Deborah Kerr in *The Innocents*, based on *The Turn of the Screw*.

◦◦◦ FURTHER READING

Read the whole of this story to find out more about Peter Quint and the children. (It is available on various 'free' sites such as **www.gutenberg.org**.)

ACTIVITY 3.39

1 What key elements of ambiguity does the commentary pick up on here?

2 Which of these would you consider using in your own writing?

Much modern writing is deliberately unclear so it can be useful to have a bank of words or phrases at your disposal to describe particular features, such as *ambiguous*, *unreliable*, *uncertain*, *indistinct*, *layered*.

KEY TERMS

closed ending where the reader is informed about the outcome or reasons for the outcome of particular events or the fate of a character

Read this student commentary on the extract.

COMMENTARY

This sense of ambiguity is created in a number of ways. There is some confusion over matters of perception in the story, over who sees what, an idea which is symbolised by the use of a motif of a window throughout the novella. The governess thinks the spirit of Peter Quint is staring through the window whilst Miles believes it that of Miss Jessel, perhaps making the reader wonder about the governess' perception about other events and characters in the story. The metaphors used by the governess also hint at the possibility that she is the one – rather than the spirit – who is trying to possess Miles and the one who causes his death. She refers to herself as *his judge*, *his executioner* and the capitalised *ME* alerts us to the fact that it is she – not any spirit – who *spring(s)* upon the child and *tried to press him against me*. This sense of possession is intensified in the ways that she regards herself as a kind of moral champion, an idea conveyed by a further choice of metaphor: *the drop of my victory and all the return of my battle*. Indeed, she is intent on possessing everything about the child: *I was so determined to have all my proof* … The speech employed in the extract implicitly helps to reinforce this sense of ambiguity. Miles' response to her question is *"Peter Quint—you devil!"*: the final two words could suggest that Miles has seen the spirit of the former valet at the window and has employed those two words to describe what he has seen – or the final two words could be addressed to the governess herself, suggesting that she is the source of any demonic influence in the room. It is interesting to note that when Miles dies, *his little heart (is) dispossessed*: is he no longer possessed by the spirits – or by the forceful pressure placed upon him by his crusading governess?

Closed endings

A **closed ending** brings a degree of completion to the writing. A good example of this is an ending where there is a twist or even a series of twists – an ending the reader does not necessarily expect. This kind of ending might prove effective in tasks where you are required to begin or end your imaginative writing with words quoted in the task.

This kind of ending works well when the planning and writing of the story have included small clues which the reader only realises were there after encountering the surprise at the close. Where a twist or a series of twists are simply added on at the end and bear no relation to the narrative events, characters or implications which have gone before, the writing will be contrived and awkward, an unsatisfying experience for the reader because the unity and cohesion of the piece have been sacrificed.

An example of a series of twists can be found in the short story 'Don't Look Now'. The story describes how Laura and John, a married couple, have gone for a break in Venice after the death of their young daughter. Laura has to return home because their other child is taken ill but John stays in Venice where he is told by a blind clairvoyant that he might be in some kind of danger. He is rather cynical about the prediction. John thinks he sees Laura (even though she is apparently back in England) and the clairvoyant going to a funeral. The idea that he can see things is also suggested at the close of the story when he sees a child who resembles his late daughter. On following the child, he discovers that she is, in fact, a very small, deranged woman responsible for a number of murders in Venice. She stabs him fatally and, as he dies, he comes to a point of realisation:

ACTIVITY 3.40

Discuss with a partner:

- What is the twist here?
- Is there more than one?

And he saw the **vaporetto**[1] with Laura and the two sisters steaming down the Grand Canal, not today, not tomorrow, but the day after that, and he knew that they were together and for what sad purpose they had come. The creature was gibbering in its corner. The hammering and the voices and the barking dog grew fainter, and, 'Oh God,' he thought, 'what a bloody silly way to die ...'

From 'Don't Look Now' by Daphne du Maurier.

[1] **vaporetto** a small passenger boat

●●● FURTHER RESEARCH

A number of famous novels have ambiguous endings, or endings which were changed by the novelist at the request of the publisher. Why did Dickens change the last lines of *Great Expectations*?

147

Summary

Remember this key point from this section:

- Consider a range of openings and endings and the effect they can have on your story, or any story you have read.

Practice and self-evaluation

In this section, you will get the chance to put into practice the skills you have learned over the course of this unit. It is divided into two sections:

- commenting on descriptive texts and writing in response to them
- writing extended imaginative texts.

Commenting on and responding to descriptive texts

In this section, you will:

- read two passages of descriptive/narrative writing
- write commentaries on them
- write in response to the given texts
- evaluate your answers.

ACTIVITY 3.41

The following extract describes an impressive chateau.

A Comment on the style and language of the extract.

B Write a description (120–150 words) of another magical place. Base your answer closely on the style and language of the original extract.

The chinchilla clouds had drifted past now and outside the Montana night was bright as day. The tapestry brick of the road was smooth to the tread of the great tires as they rounded a still, moonlit lake; they passed into darkness for a moment, a pine grove, pungent and cool, then they came out into a broad avenue of lawn and John's exclamation of pleasure was simultaneous with Percy's taciturn "We're home."

Full in the light of the stars, an exquisite chateau rose from the borders of the lake, climbed in marble radiance half the height of an adjoining mountain, then melted in grace, in perfect symmetry, in translucent feminine languor, into the massed darkness of a forest of pine. The many towers, the slender tracery of the sloping parapets, the chiselled wonder of a thousand yellow windows with their oblongs and hectagons and triangles of golden light, the shattered softness of the intersecting planes of star-shine and blue shade, all trembled on John's spirit like a chord of music. On one of the towers, the tallest, the blackest at its base, an arrangement of exterior lights at the top made a sort of floating fairyland—and as John gazed up in warm enchantment the faint acciaccare sound of violins drifted down in a rococo harmony that was like nothing he had ever heard before. Then in a moment the car stopped before wide, high marble steps around which the night air was fragrant with a host of flowers. At the top of the steps two great doors swung silently open and amber light flooded out upon the darkness, silhouetting the figure of an exquisite lady with black, high-piled hair, who held out her arms toward them.

"Mother," Percy was saying, "this is my friend, John Unger, from Hades."

Afterward John remembered that first night as a daze of many colors, of quick sensory impressions, of music soft as a voice in love, and of the beauty of things, lights and shadows, and motions and faces. There was a whitehaired man who stood drinking a many-hued cordial from a crystal thimble set on a golden stem. There was a girl with a flowery face, dressed like Titania with braided sapphires in her hair. There was a room where the solid, soft gold of the walls yielded to the pressure of his hand, and a room that was like a platonic conception of the ultimate prism-ceiling, floor, and all, it was lined with an unbroken mass of diamonds, diamonds of every size and shape, until, lit with tall violet lamps in the corners, it dazzled the eyes with a whiteness that could be compared only with itself, beyond human wish or dream.

Through a maze of these rooms the two boys wandered. Sometimes the floor under their feet would flame in brilliant patterns from lighting below, patterns of barbaric clashing colors, of pastel delicacy, of sheer whiteness, or of subtle and intricate mosaic, surely from some mosque on the Adriatic Sea. Sometimes beneath layers of thick crystal he would see blue or green water swirling, inhabited by vivid fish and growths of rainbow foliage. Then they would be treading on furs of every texture and color or along corridors of palest ivory, unbroken as though carved complete from the gigantic tusks of dinosaurs extinct before the age of man. . . .

From 'The Diamond as Big as the Ritz' by F. Scott Fitzgerald.

ACTIVITY 3.42

The following extract is from a story in which an insurance agent visits a client.

A Comment on the style and language of the extract.

B Continue the extract (120–150 words). You do not have to bring your writing to a conclusion. Base your answer closely on the style and language of the original extract.

I drove out to Glendale to put three new truck drivers on a brewery company bond, and then I remembered this renewal over in Hollywoodland. I decided to run over there. That was how I came to this House of Death, that you've been reading about in the papers. It didn't look like a House of Death when I saw it. It was just a Spanish house, like all the rest of them in California, with white walls, red tile roof, and a patio out to one side. It was built cock-eyed. The garage was under the house, the first floor was over that, and the rest of it was spilled up the hill any way they could get it in. You climbed some stone steps to the front door, so I parked the car and went up there. A servant poked her head out. "Is Mr. Nirdlinger in?"

"I don't know, sir. Who wants to see him?"

"Mr. Huff."

"And what's the business?"

"Personal."

Getting in is the tough part of my job, and you don't tip what you came for till you get where it counts. "I'm sorry, sir, but they won't let me ask anybody in unless they say what they want."

It was one of those spots you get in. If I said some more about "personal" I would be making a mystery of it, and that's bad. If I said what I really wanted, I would be laying myself open for what every insurance agent dreads, that she would come back and say, "Not in." If I said I'd wait, I would be making myself look small, and that never helped a sale yet. To move this stuff, you've got to get in. Once you're in, they've got to listen to you, and you can pretty near rate an agent by how quick he gets to the family sofa, with his hat on one side of him and his dope sheets on the other.

"I see. I told Mr. Nirdlinger I would drop in, but- never mind. I'll see if I can make it some other time."

It was true, in a way. On this automobile stuff, you always make it a point that you'll give a reminder on renewal, but I hadn't seen him for a year. I made it sound like an old friend, though, and an old friend that wasn't any too pleased at the welcome he got. It worked. She got a worried look on her face. "Well- come in, please."

From *Double Indemnity* by James M. Cain.

ACTIVITY 3.43

The extract below is from a story in which a woman's life changes as the result of a shopping trip.

A Comment on the style and language of the extract

B The same writer publishes another short story involving the same central character. Write a section (120–150 words) of the story. You do not have to bring your writing to a conclusion. Base your answer closely on the style and language of the original extract.

It may seem odd to those of you who did not know her but at the time the very simplest of acts became disjointed in her mind. Or so she was told. Her life, something that looked so much like an open book, became complicated. Or so it seemed. It began with such a simple act. The shops. Shopping. An ordinary enough pastime but something that led her into an unfamiliar world. Decisions made without her knowledge. For the best. A phrase that she would hear again and again. She distrusted it. The taste of it. For the best. The sound of it. For her it was the beginning. The beginning of her distrust. The sound of a door slamming shut. Shut against her. Shutting her in.

Spring was early that year. Flower stalls began to sell the sunshine buds. Just looking at the bright array was enough to put a spring in anyone's step. A crisp Spring day. A day similar to many other days in her life. Similar but different. They went to the shops. A journey that was familiar as the parade of shops itself. Usually she only had time for a brief nod or fleeting smile as she hurried on her way past friends and neighbours. Armed with shopping bags and with her head full of worries she would make her way along the invisible path. An invisible string would pull her along the path, that well-worn path that recognised each footstep and guided her to her destination. To places that she recognised and that recognised her. But this time it was different. She had time to browse. She found it difficult not to worry about the mundane things – like the peas defrosting, or what birthday present to buy his sister. She remembered thinking about the peas. Should they try another brand? It was so boring buying the same things every week. Did they buy his sister a photograph frame last year? Or was it someone else? It's strange what passes through your mind on these occasions.

But this visit was hers. All hers. They were going to buy clothes. Just for her. Clothes for the evening and maybe something to wear on the beach. Something light and airy with added layers if it became cooler later. And why not? She deserved a weekend away. It had been a long time since she had done anything for herself, without the added burden of thinking what the family might think or need or want. Working around their lives. Their schedules. Their traumas. But what about her? Didn't she have a life too?

From 'The Visit' by Sue Thakor.

Imaginative writing tasks

In this section, you will:

- write extended responses to a range of imaginative writing tasks.

ACTIVITY 3.44

Choose one of the following tasks. (You should write 600–900 words.)

1 Write the opening to a novel called *The Prisoner* in which a narrator describes his or her experiences of being captured and held captive. In your writing, create a sense of the narrator's outlook and mood.

2 Write two contrasting descriptive pieces (300–450 words each) about a location immediately before the arrival of a storm and some days after it has passed. In your writing, create a sense of setting and atmosphere.

3 Write a descriptive piece called *The Deserted School*. In your writing focus on colours, sounds and textures to help your reader imagine the scene.

Part 2:
A Level

Unit 4: Text and discourse analysis

In this A Level part of your English Language course you will build on the skills which formed the basis of your AS Level programme. During your AS studies you:

■ studied the conventions of a number of different text types as well as analysing how they are constructed

■ practised effective passage-based text analysis and learned how to identify language features using appropriate examples, giving an evaluation of the effects of these features

■ explored examples of English Language material, fiction and non-fiction, from the past and present, and from a range of sources

■ considered the form of a text, its layout as well as the context in which it has been produced, its purpose and style.

You have learned that texts representing scripted speech take on the features of written language. Unscripted speech follows a different set of conventions and you will explore these in this opening unit of Part 2.

Situations where conversational speech may be used.

There is general agreement that speech in communication is what defines us as humans and it is a critically important part of our interaction with others. Consider the following questions:

■ Why do we speak?

■ What do we speak about?

■ We speak differently to different types of people. Why do you think that is?

■ How do you start a conversation? How do you finish it?

■ How do you manage a conversation when several people are talking?

■ What makes a conversation interesting or boring?

You will explore these questions in this unit on spoken language.

TIP

Because conversation is something we do so naturally, it can be very easy to be descriptive rather than analytical when answering questions about spoken language. Here are some tips to help you avoid this:

1 Look at and learn the features of conversation so that they become familiar to you.

2 When answering questions about spoken language, read each piece of discourse to ascertain its purpose then identify the features which will help you support your ideas.

3 Explain the **effects** of the features and give an illustrated example.

ACTIVITY 4.1

1 You need to identify yourself by your voice to someone who is unable to see you. How would you describe your voice? Deep, high-pitched, squeaky, mellow? Is describing a voice an easy thing to do: why or why not?

2 Going by voice recognition only, what clues are there in a person's voice to help us estimate their age and gender?

3 Before referring to a biology textbook, name the parts of your anatomy involved in speech production and the function of each.

KEY TERMS

discourse any spoken or written language that is longer than a sentence

utterance a stretch of spoken language which is often preceded by silence and followed by silence or a change of speaker. It is often used as an alternative to *sentence* in conversation analysis since it is difficult to apply the traditional characteristics of a written sentence to spoken language.

Features of spoken language

153

Whatever your native language(s), you are already an expert in the skill of speech. You may hesitate on occasions while you think of what to say, but most of the time when you engage in conversation, especially with your friends, you are fluent and rarely have to stop to consciously consider what you are going to say and how you are going to say it.

Although we all have distinctive patterns of speech, which we will examine in a later chapter, we conform to certain features of unscripted speech. Discourse (patterns of speech) is not governed by the same rules as writing. Our discourse is in utterances (complete units of speech bounded by silence) and not sentences and these utterances are not transcribed in the same way as written language.

Unlike the majority of what we write, which can be redrafted and polished to achieve the desired effect, most speech is spontaneous and we need strategies to make it flow as smoothly as possible, though there are times when inevitably we say the wrong thing! Public speaking such as speeches, sermons, lectures, commentaries and scripts, shares more common features with written language while text, SMS messages and much other digital communication blurs the boundaries between speech and writing still further.

FURTHER RESEARCH

David Crystal is an acknowledged authority on the English language, including discourse features. There are several clips on YouTube of his lectures about the manner in which, and reasons why, we converse. You may find it interesting and helpful to take a look at these.

The structure of unscripted conversation

Conversations take place between two or more participants. Much unscripted conversation follows recognisable conventions which we develop through early life. By now you have already become a conversational expert!

The following features of discourse are listed separately for clarity but in speaking we often use many of these features at the same time. It is important to look at conversations in context (who is talking and why) rather than just identifying individual features.

- **Opening greetings** Conversation openings are usually formulaic to help ease the participants into the conversations. Greetings such as *g'day, howdy, howzit, hiya, hello, good morning, nice day, how are you?* establish feelings of mutual ease. These formulaic greetings may be accompanied by body language and gestures such as handshakes or kissing and hugging. Participants who are strangers will usually introduce themselves with their full name.

- **Turn-taking** Conversation is usually co-operative with participants taking turns. Quite frequently speakers overlap, though this has to be done with sensitivity as in many cultures interrupting is considered rude. Conversationalists have to make instant, finely discriminating judgements about when to start their turn – this may be done hundreds of times a day in every conversation. When a conversation is not co-operative, for example in an argument, participants adopt very different strategies, often with unpleasant outcomes.

- **Adjacency pairs** 'Statement' and 'response' are the basis of conversation. These often consist of a question/exclamation/declaration from Participant A followed by a response from Participant B and any others. The responses can be of any length and can extend to **three-part exchanges** where the first speaker responds and so the conversation continues. For example:

Teacher:	*What is the capital of New Zealand?*
Pupil:	*Auckland miss*
Teacher:	*No, try again(.) think hard*
Pupil:	*Wellington, miss.*
Teacher:	*Good, that's right*

- **Holding the floor** In discourse, the person speaking is said to be **holding the conversational floor.** When someone is about to finish their turn we use a variety of strategies to determine who will take over:
  - we can name them (e.g. *Hasfah was there, she knows about it*)
  - we can complete what we are saying (e.g. *and so I got thoroughly soaked.*)
  - we can hesitate; it only takes a fractionally longer pause than usual for someone to fill the silence; in fact silences can denote some tension in discourse
  - we can use sound and body language
  - our voice may start to fall and we may look more closely at those who are about to take their conversational turn.

- **Clashing** When two people start to speak at the same time the clash is acknowledged – one participant must stop while the other continues. As in other aspects of conversation, status and context are important here. 'Managing' a conversation is related to the context and to the relative status of the speakers.

LINK

Look at the section on *The language of social groups* later in this unit for more about social language and interaction.

KEY TERMS

turn-taking in conversation, people usually wait their turn to speak. Some may interrupt, out of eagerness or rudeness, but the norm is for one speaker to yield the floor by prolonging a pause or glancing at the elected next speaker who then takes their turn.

adjacency pairs dialogue that follows a set pattern (e.g. when speakers greet each other)

holding the conversational floor speaking until you have finished what you wish to say or until someone interrupts you

154

- **Repairing** During the conversation, participants are constantly monitoring themselves and those to whom they are speaking. A speaker may repair what they say, correcting themselves or using phrases to acknowledge their mistake, for example *I mean, I should have said, no, that's wrong,* or *I wanted to say.* In this way there is instant updating of information and self-correction in conversation. Sometimes another participant will correct the speaker's mistake for them.

- **Topic shift** Conversation is dynamic and spontaneous. We talk about all sorts of things, people and ideas and these topics change frequently. Management of topic shift is most commonly achieved with formulaic expressions, such as *Oh, by the way …* or *… which reminds me …*

- **Conversation endings** Closing a conversation also has formulaic utterances with standard phrases such as *see you later, bye, nice to see you;* or we may make plans to be in contact again with phrases such as *Come round sometime* or *See you next week* which may signal a very vague or more specific intention. As with other forms of conversation, body language reinforces the discourse: we may check the time; start to pack away belongings, stand up or turn away.

KEY TERMS

topic shift the point at which speakers move from one topic to another

LINK

See the first section of **Unit 5** on page 174 for more about the importance of context in discourse.

ACTIVITY 4.2

1 Watch and listen to the conversations around you and gather information on the following:
   - how people open conversations
   - styles of greeting
   - how topic shifts occur
   - how conversations are brought to an end.
2 Cultural differences produce a range of conversational styles in the English-speaking world. Using specific examples, discuss the differences you observe in the conversations around you and try to evaluate why they occur.

Interviews – structured conversations

We talk in a variety of different circumstances. Many public forms of speaking are in the media and although these are unscripted, they take place in a fairly structured environment. The conventions are often clearer to see as an introduction to spoken language.

LINK

To familiarise yourself with the symbols used in transcribed speech, turn to page 169.

ACTIVITY 4.3

Read the following transcript and look carefully at the interaction between the speakers. Note particularly how the conversation moves from one participant to the next.

Consider the differences between this type of conversation and those you hear around you. Why are media texts such as soap operas presented without the non-fluency features of speech?

> **Transcript**
>
> **Context:** *Pearl Nxele interviews Melinda Bam about her entry for the Miss South Africa pageant.*
>
> PEARL   I mean you had a hectic schedule then (.) why (.) what made you think to enter Miss S A even though you had all of that going on (.)
>
> MELINDA   well (.) I was actually scouted back (.) 2009 then (1) erm (.) as I said (.) I didn't have much confidence (.) so I think I decided (.) well (.) um (.) you know what (.) much as I'm not where I want to be (.) or (.) who I want to be at the time (.) I (.) I (.) should enter and (.) um (.) see how it goes
>
> www.youtube.com

Features of unscripted conversation

The following section explains the most significant features of language used in conversation. Although we see a huge number of 'tidied-up' conversations in the media, the conventions listed below are regular features of unscripted language. Because you will use many or even all of these features yourself in your everyday conversations, you should be able to recognise them and give additional examples from your own patterns of speaking.

- **Phatic communion** is the name for the polite 'ice-breakers' we use when greeting people in order to initiate a conversation. We then usually continue with more meaningful topics. Inevitably in English, the weather is often used (e.g. *Nice/awful/freezing/scorching weather we're having*) as well as health, with the general query, *how are you?*, or something more informal. Often both participants will say the same thing and a serious reply is not usually expected. How do you greet people?
- **Adjacency pairs** are the rather standard interactions between people. They are often in the format of question and answer, for example *goodbye, see you soon/ yes you too, take care.*
- **Voiced pauses** are the *ums* and *ers* and *you knows* used when we can't express exactly what we want to say. These non-fluency features or **fillers** give us time to think and/or to announce we are going to say something when the sound is extended (e.g. *mmm*). A **voiceless pause** is when there is a silence; it is interesting that these pauses do not have to be very long before people perceive a break in the conversation. Try a silence of three to four seconds and see how your respondent reacts. There is a lot of non-fluency in unscripted discourse.
- **False starts** are also part of non-fluency features when a speaker realises they have made an error and attempts to repair the error often by use of **meta language** – language which talks about language, for example *I mean to say, I should have mentioned.* Often the utterance is **reformulated** for greater clarity and repairs the conversation.
- **Repetition** in conversation is common for many reasons. We may deliberately repeat for emphasis or unintentionally to gain thinking time in order to continue the conversation.

KEY TERMS

phatic communion the type of exchange which is redundant in terms of meaning but socially significant; it includes 'friendly noises' like *Morning*, *Nice day* and *How's things?*

- **Turn-taking** is how most conversations are managed but by no means always – sometimes participants cut in before their turn.
- **Overlaps and interruptions** are also linked to lack of fluency. How do you know when the other person has finished speaking? When you both start speaking at once, who carries on? Interruptions can sometimes border on rudeness depending on the context. When might this be so?
- **Hedges/vague language** is a strategy used when you want to avoid coming to the point or saying things directly, for example *kind of, you know what I mean, actually, basically*. These soften the force of what is said and are useful strategies when we want to negotiate a point of view. These are often used in conjunction with modality (see below).
- **Modality** is a conversational strategy which allows us to introduce different options and compromises for negotiation between participants. Some of the most common examples are *perhaps, probably, normally, slightly, maybe*. We can also reflect this hesitancy in the verb structure by the use of modal – or 'helper' – verbs, for example *may, might, could, should*.
- **Ellipsis** is the omission or slurring (**eliding**) of syllables, which is also associated with informal English, for example *gonna, don't, wanna*.
- **Transactional language** is discourse to get things done and with a specific purpose. Much of our speech, other than chatting, is transactional, for example *Put the rubbish out, I'd like a Thai curry please, You need to be eighteen to see this film*.

When we are certain about a situation, we tend to be assertive both in our manner and in our speech, using constructions to show that something is definite. This certainty is referred to as **high modality**. Compare *it **will** be necessary to fight* with *it **might** be possible to avoid conflict*, which is much less certain. **Elision** is where the meaning of an utterance is generally understood between the participants and so can be shortened to focus the topic. We omit much in our conversation which is mutually understood; for example in the exchange *Are you coming over this week?/ Might be*, the pronoun *I* and the participle *coming* are omitted which gives a more relaxed and informal tone.

This is an example of a transcript of a very specific context and with a defined purpose.

157

KEY TERMS

modality a conversational strategy which allows us to introduce different options and compromises for negotiation, often using modal verbs (e.g. *will, should, would*)

ACTIVITY 4.4

Give some examples of transactional language.

ACTIVITY 4.5

Read the transcript. Discuss what features this transcript shares with other unscripted conversations and then any features which are context dependent.

Context and participants
*Female 23, hairdresser's receptionist) (**R**), male 25, (client) (**C**), female 30, hairdresser (**H**)*

R   hello sir

C   hiya, I've got an appointment for 2.15 but I'm a bit early

R   that's fine do you want to hang up your jacket and take a seat over there (.) um Tricia will see you (.) 'bout 5 minutes (.) tea (.) coffee

C	thanks, it's cold outside
R	yeah
	[*waits*]
H	morning Neil
C	hi
H	How much do you want off
C	(.) er (.) I like to keep the top long (.) then well (.) maybe side (.) side clipped I mean parting (.) thinned (.) and (2) fringe too
H	yeah
H	I'll clip a bit (.) layers style
C	good (.) been too long (.) am so busy-//
H	//yeah (.) always somethin' to do

COMMENT

This is an everyday activity which shows language in action where the participants are directly involved. They have a purpose in conversing as they have to agree on how the hair will be cut (this is transactional) but they also chat about general topics to be sociable (this is interactional). Most of the transcript is in adjacency pairs.

The different forms of greeting show the conversational conventions of politeness – phatic communion with varying forms of greeting (*hello, hi, hiya*) to reflect the different levels of status between client and service provider as well as familiarity between the participants. The client may have been coming to get his hair cut by this hairdresser for a while so shared knowledge of their requirements can be assumed.

There may be long silences in this type of interaction where actions such as hair washing are taking place.

Many of these utterances are elliptical as the context is understood: *(would you like) tea (or) coffee*; *How much (hair) do you want (cut) off?*

Even though the client is quite specific about the requirements, he still uses hedges and fillers: *maybe side (.) slide clipped*. Perhaps the skills of the hairdresser give her a higher status in this context and the client wants to soften his requests.

••• FURTHER RESEARCH

Conversations like this take place each day in very many different contexts. Listen to conversations in a variety of contexts, then assess their purpose and the language features used to ensure successful communication between the participants.

Compare these with specific TV interviews and chat shows. What key differences are there in the different types of conversations in your case studies?

Characteristics of unscripted conversation

This section introduces the *characteristics* of unscripted conversation. Although these are invariably used with the features already explained, they are more concerned with the interaction between the participants and the establishment of working relationships in the discourse.

KEY TERMS

back-channel a noise, gesture, expression or word used by a listener to indicate that he or she is paying attention to a speaker

- **Back-channel** items are often sounds rather than full words (e.g. *um, yeah, right*) and are used primarily to reassure the speaker (S) that the listener (L) is following the conversation. Sometimes back-channel responses merge with speaking turns, though the respondent may not wish to take a turn as in the following example:

  [S:] I remember how bad it was when I was a kid [L: *oh*] my dad was working away (.) things were awful and my mum (.) it was so hard for her (.) she (.) she had to sell some jewellery belonging to my gran [L: *really*] to pay for my clothes and stuff [L: *mm*] and it was (.) must have been really difficult for her. [L: *awful*] I didn't realise cos' I was only small [L: *mm*]

  Back channelling is particularly important in phone calls. Try not giving any back-channelling in a phone call – the results may be uncomfortable!

- **Discourse markers** are words or phrases which mark boundaries between one bit of conversation and another where the speaker wishes to changes the subject: *so, right, I see, well, then, fine. OK anyway.* These can also be used to signal the conclusion of a conversation, particularly where there are no other cues and they are widely used in phone conversations.

- **Non-standard features and forms** of English are often used where a speaker struggles to phrase utterances clearly. This is very common in speech. Do you know what the end of your utterance will be when you start to speak? Speech is full of constructions considered to be non-standard in writing. A common non-fluency feature is the lack of agreement between subject and verb (e.g. *we was really tired*) or the incorrect use of tenses (e.g. *so I sees him yesterday*). Many utterances are unfinished.

  S: *Are you still playing (.) er*
  L: *guitar*

- **Tag questions** occur at the end of a declarative utterance where the speaker adds on a question to engage and elicit a response from the listener, for example *It's hot in here, isn't it? I'm having a difficult time, aren't I?*

- **Deixis** refers to words which locate the conversation in a particular space or context which a non-participant would not be able to make sense of. *This, that, these those* are important in conversation as they are mutually understood between the participants, for example *we'll move this over here* or *we'll have one of these with our coffee* is only clear to those involved in the conversation at the time.

- **Fixed expressions** You will probably speak to many different people every day and it is very difficult to be creative throughout our conversational lives. Therefore, some of what we say becomes routine and patterned, for example *as a matter of fact, in my opinion, as far as I can see, to be honest*. These expressions are usually known to those to whom we speak and so they have an important function of maintaining a shared understanding of the culture around us. Some of these fixed expressions are colloquial and clichéd (e.g. *driving me mad, at the end of the day, one fell swoop* [from Shakespeare], *an awesome time*) but they have the same function of conversational predictability and security which help when we are faced with conversational overload.

159

- **Vague expressions** can operate to soften authoritative requests and to maintain greater engagement between speakers. Look at the difference between *Can you get me a cheese sandwich…* and *Can you get me a cheese sandwich or something/ anything like that*. Expressions such as *sort of, kind of, around* or *so* allow the speaker some leeway and approximation of arrangements. Vague expressions are not appropriate for travel details and other arrangements where precise information enables cooperation between speakers.
- **Adverbs (adverbial phrases)** are words and phrases which modify – add to – adjectives. Both in written language and in speech, these words and phrases work to convey the attitudes and values of the speaker and so they intensify their feelings and opinions. *Really, absolutely, literally, of course, extremely, basically* are frequently used to add strength and colour to our utterances.

ACTIVITY 4.6

Read the following transcript and then write your own commentary on it, including examples of the features you have identified.

Compare your finished commentary to the one following the transcript. Consider:

- the role of each participant in planning the trip
- the extent to which each participant supports or counteracts the suggestions of the other two
- clues to the relationship/extent of understanding between the participants including their mutual understanding of the topic
- specific discourse features.

Context and participants: Three friends are planning a holiday by rail in Europe
M: male, F1: female, F2: female

M	this website says (.) there's a good rail service to Amsterdam and
F2	really (.) I wanna go (.) heard good stuff
FI	I hear (2) um, nice trains, trains with 2 levels (.) good view
F2	great (.) let's look at the cost for Amsterdam Brussels, (.) try Amsterdam Paris (2) could be better
M	Amsterdam Brussels it cost costs (4) 40 euros
F2	that' quite a lot (.) for each, is it each
M	each, cost 40 euros each we could try another time or maybe weekday (2) could be cheaper
FI	look on another travel site or something (.) we could compare (.) then//
F2	// if we looked at one site each then maybe we could see the going rates for those train routes
M	The only problem is if we do go by train is the hassle of finding the right buses and coaches and//
FI	// nah 'cos the train stations'll be in the city centres won't they
F2	yeah that'll be fine.

When people are planning and discussing informally there is often hesitation and repetition as ideas are developed. Speakers are thinking as they are speaking so may fail to finish their utterances or be interrupted by someone with a more definite point of view. Speakers often soften their utterances by using modal forms of verbs (e.g. *could*, *might*) as well as other words like *maybe* or *quite*, which prevent the speaker from sounding too harsh and dogmatic when the project is a collaborative one.

There is repetition of key lexical words; in the sample above, the places and costs must be emphasised to move the conversation to some sort of resolution so *Amsterdam, Brussels, Paris* as well as the cost must be clarified so that all speakers understand the stage of the planning. It is only when personal experience or some other definite knowledge exists, that the speakers can become more assertive. In the extract above, the speaker knows that the train stations will be located in the city centres but still adds a tag question to soften this declarative utterance.

Other features of conversation are found here. The conversation is amongst friends so the register is informal and colloquial: *hassle* is appropriate to describe the potential problems as is ellipsis *wanna* in this context and the speaker also feels sufficiently secure with her friends to utter the dismissive and slightly scornful *nah* as she seems certain of her facts.

The conversation is primarily transactional with the aim being to book a train trip for the three friends in as economical and trouble-free way as possible. Elision avoids repetition of places and travel, which are understood, however the friends must keep to their equal status by softening assertions and taking account of each others' ideas. Vague expressions soften the imperative (*look on another travel site or something*) while the use of tag questions (*stations'll be in the city centres … won't they?*) gives reassurance for the plans to be adopted.

The planners are all engaged in a collaborative activity with people whom they know well and they are using conversational strategies in order to achieve the most beneficial outcomes for the project and for the maintenance of their friendship.

Further practice

Read the following transcript between students and a teacher in an international school.

- What is the purpose of this discourse?
- What discourse features are present and how to they enable the conversation to proceed?

> **Context:** *a group of Year 11 international students have been reviewing material on racism; they are about to start a short presentation. This transcript is the opening section*
>
> **Participants:** *Teacher, Austin, Ilham, Jaleelah.*

TEACHER	Thanks Ori and your group (.) some interesting points about racism in the 1930s (.) so now um (.) it must be your turn Austin's group (.) yes you were going after Ori and his group (.) so what did you look at from these documents.(.) everyone to say something please.
JALEELAH	we found a picture of some white women with placards (.) protesting in the 1950s (.) they looked like they were going to town (.) all dressed up (.) but they were carrying pla.) cards against integration (.) I think that's amazing (.) you can't tell a book by its cover (.) they were really racist
ILHAM	Then this document about mixed race (.) that's so strange 'cos I'm mixed race..//
JALEELAH	// me too (.) my mum from Jamaica and my dad from Bangladesh
ILHAM	[*laughs*] well I'm mixed mixed race (.) both my parents are mixed race (.) erm (.) my mum's half Saudi and half Egyptian and my dad's parents came from (.) Kuwait and Qatar (.) that would count (.) yes
AUSTIN	I'm not mixed but my mum and dad are from Belize then we lived in the States for a while and now they're teaching in Uganda (.) I'm just mixed
TEACHER	what an amazing mix (.) how much have times changed for the better and you are all together (.) so what else did you find?

Speech strategies

The earlier sections of this unit have outlined the characteristics of **discourse analysis** which are the recognisable ways in which we converse with each other.

What we say is a reflection of how we relate to the people and situations around us and how we feel about ourselves in the dynamic world of social interactions. In doing so, we are engaged both in **semantics**, a study of the meaning of words and sentences and also, very importantly, **pragmatics**, the analysis of the context in which we speak. This will be developed with more examples in **Unit 5: Spoken language and social groups**.

The fact that we all engage in conversation does not necessarily makes us good at it, even though we generally get plenty of practice! And when conversational rules are not followed, comic and often embarrassing situations can occur.

 LINK

You will find out more in **Unit 5** about the part played in spoken language by factors such as politeness, status, naming and gender.

> **TIP**
> You will find it helpful to collect examples of dialogue and of unscripted and scripted speech.
>
> As ethically as possible, try to listen to a variety of conversations between different groups of people then draw some conclusions about the content and style of the dialogue, the tone and speed as well as the body language of the participants.
>
> Make a list of situations for scripted dialogue, perhaps speeches or play scripts, and find some examples. Analyse these to draw conclusions about differences and style.

Conversational maxims

Whenever you speak, you intend to make sense to your listeners according to the rules and conventions of the language and you may have any number of purposes in speaking. You may wish to inform, question, greet, perform, gossip and many more but all of these conditions have conventions to which you should adhere. Underlying all of the various forms is the **cooperative principle**. Hearing may not quite be the same as listening. You have probably experienced a situation where what you said has not been received in quite the way that you intended.

Grice's Maxims (Paul Grice, 1975) are guideline principles which are generally adopted in conversation. These are maxims and not rules since they are broken in almost every conversation but they do provide a general framework for managing conversation.

163

> **KEY TERMS**
>
> **cooperative principle** the principle that speakers usually mean what they say and that hearers accept this in trying to work out the meaning

Maxims of quantity
1 Make your contribution to the conversation as informative as necessary.
2 Do not make your contribution to the conversation more informative than necessary.

Maxim of relation
1 Be relevant.

Grice's maxims

Maxims of quality
1 Do not say what you believe to be false.
2 Do not say that for which you lack adequate evidence.

Maxims of manner
1 Avoid obscurity of expression.
2 Avoid ambiguity.
3 Be brief – don't ramble.
4 Be orderly.

ACTIVITY 4.7

1 Discuss each of Grice's Maxims and how it is used in conversation.

2 Are there other maxims you think should be included? Justify your opinion.

3 Listen to conversations or watch unscripted ones online. Analyse closely where the maxims are followed and where they are not. What are the results when they are not followed?

ACTIVITY 4.8

In a group, select different comedy clips based on conversational dysfunctions. Analyse in what ways the conversation is not working well and why this has come about. To what extent does the confusion and breakdown result from flouting Grice's Maxims?

Note: You may find that some older comedy shows have content that would be considered racist, sexist or politically incorrect today.

Raj and Amy in conversation in *The Big Bang Theory*.

KEY TERMS

conversational face the image that a person has of themselves as a conversationalist

face-threatening acts acts or words which appear to threaten the self-esteem of a speaker in conversation

positive politeness strategies intended to minimise the threat to the hearer's self-esteem

Conversational face

Central to the overarching principle of conversational cooperation is the notion of **conversational face**, which is each speaker's sense of his or her own linguistic image and worth. Potentially every conversation could impose upon and even threaten this sense of face making speakers feel intimidated, ignored or ridiculed rather than supported and included.

Strategies to manage **face-threatening acts** help in all manner of conversational situations. Speakers may use **positive politeness** by being complimentary to the person they are speaking to before starting a potentially face-threatening act. Such strategies are used to make the hearer feel good about himself, his interests or possessions, and are most usually used in situations where the speakers know each other fairly well, for example *You look great/sad, can I help? Would you be so kind* *as to pass me the sugar?* Alternatively **negative politeness** may be used to mitigate a request or situation which they wish to impose, for example *You wouldn't be able to pass me the sugar, would you?* In both of these circumstances the speaker hopes the hearer will comply with their request. Here are some other examples:

- *I'm terribly sorry but …*
- *Would you mind if I asked you to … ?*
- *Could you perhaps … ?*

Disagreements are an inevitable part of discourse and the management of differences of opinion is closely related to face-saving strategies. It is very interesting to observe that when people want to disagree, the word *no* is less often used than *yes but*. Why might that approach be more successful? The **adversative** conjunction *but* qualifies or changes what has just been said in some way; *however* and *not exactly* operate in the same way.

A very important feature in any conversation is the relative **status** of the participants and this topic will be explored further in the next unit. For now, you should be aware that in all manner of formal and informal situations, conversational success is more likely where strategies are employed which take account of the relative status of each participant.

ACTIVITY 4.9

1   Discuss what strategies have been used in the following utterances and consider their likely success in achieving their goal.

- *Excuse me sir, would you mind moving up a little so that I can have a seat?*
- *Could you please shut the window just a fraction? It seems quite chilly in here.*
- *Please may I borrow your pen?*
- *Can you tell me the time?*
- *You haven't got $2 I could borrow have you? I'll pay you back tomorrow.*
- *Please be quiet – the baby has just gone to sleep.*
- *Silence in the library.*
- *The management requires all employees to wear hard hats.*

2   Discuss what positive and negative strategies to save conversational face are used in your own culture. Which do you feel are most effective and why?

3   Read the transcription below and discuss the strategies used. Include a discussion of Grice's maxims and the extent to which they have been followed or broken.

Write a commentary on the conversation, based on your discussion. Then compare your commentary to the one provided below the transcript. Did you pick up on some of the same points, or suggest any different ones?

Context and participants: two women (V and M) on a country walk using a public footpath which crosses a field. They are good friends.

V   there's cattle over there (.) I don't like cattle (3) they're running towards us//

M   // right, right

V   we can't run back (.) it's too far

V, M // what are we gonna do (.) what are we gonna do

V   they're still coming

M   we'll go through there

V   quick quick

M   let's get out their way (.) get over here we've got to get somewhere we they can't get us (.) get in here they can't get us

[*They run to a cattle pen and climb over the metal fencing.*]

V   they're coming through (.) they're still coming after us

M   oh no they're all around us

V   what we gonna do

M   we'll wait til they lose interest

V   we could be here all night

[*At this point the cattle have surrounded the pen and are snorting and pawing the ground.*]

V   (5) we're in their feeding pen they're not going to go away (5)

M   oh no (2) yeah you're right

V   we're going to be in here for hours. what can we do

        [*V looks around and notices portable plastic feeding troughs just outside the pen.*] (5)

V   if we could find some feed (3)

M   yeah yeah (.) brill

        [*V sees covered plastic barrels, they lift the lid and search through plastic bags in the bins.*]

M   oh no they're empty//

V   no no just a minute hang on there's something there's something there's some in this one

M   brill brill I'll get the troughs (4) yuk they're full of water [*empties them*] (3) we'll have to be quick we'll need to fill them and be ready to get out before they've finished

        [*M & V shovel handfuls of feed into two of the troughs.*]

V   [*giggling*] I can't believe we're doing this (.) this is ridiculous

M   we'll need to make it difficult for them (.) we need some time to get out before they've finished eating (2) how much do cattle eat (2) is that enough (.) we need to put a bit more in

COMMENT

- The two women are close friends and are also in a situation that they find threatening so their conversation is unlikely to be carefully thought out. They are responding to the situation with colloquial language (e.g. *hang on*, *yuk*).

- Conversational features include those transmitting the information in the most direct way possible: elision (*you ready*), ellipsis (*gonna*), deixis (*here push it through*), repetition (*right, right*), fixed expressions (*hang on*). Much of the conversation is in the form of adjacency pairs (*Is that right/yeah*) and these adjacency pairs are most frequently in the form of commands and instructions (*push it through*).

- The situation of perceived danger develops rapidly and so the maxim of relevance is paramount. The attempts to get away from the cattle means that the maxims of quantity and relation are followed as the participants assess the situation and make attempts to repair it in a focused and direct way. The maxim of quality is hampered by the uncertainty of the situation and its ramifications so that the speakers do not know whether what they are saying is the truth and this is reflected in different suggestions for escape. The maxim of manner is followed as the situation is alternately a tense yet laughable one requiring swift action to remedy.

- The conversational face of each speaker does not appear to be threatened, most probably because the status of the pair is equal in every way; they are good friends, so an interchange of ideas is perfectly acceptable as both are facing a common problem which neither has faced before. Thus the politeness strategies are much less important than the overriding common need to escape from the cattle pen – a perfect example of the cooperative nature of conversation.

Transcribing speech

By now you will have become aware that speech is not governed by the same rules as writing. This also applies to the transcription or writing down of speech, which 'freezes' the words spoken as well as the pauses. Phonetic transcripts are able to record the sounds of a speaker according to a standard set of **phonemes** (sounds) and some transcripts also record intonation. Phonetic transcripts are a time-consuming but precise method of writing down spoken language.

Transcripts do not follow the normal conventions of writing so few punctuation marks are used: speech marks are never used and other punctuation marks are used only sparingly – primarily where confusion of meaning could occur.

Phonetics

Phonetics is the study of speech sounds. Although language is obviously composed of sound, speech sounds came to be the main focus of linguistic investigation only in the 20th century. Before that, linguists were more interested in written language. Now linguists realise that studying the sounds of language helps to give a much more precise analysis of accents, especially in the way that they change in different conversational contexts. Sounds are also important in the study of child language acquisition.

Symbols used in transcribing speech

The symbols used in speech transcription aim to recreate the manner in which speech is delivered. We pause naturally to take a breath – these are called **micropauses** – between each group of words, known as **tone units**. Transcripts may sometimes indicate rising and falling intonation. In each tone unit, the pitch movement (a rise or fall in tone, or a combination of the two) takes place on the most important syllable known as the tonic-syllable. The **tonic-syllable** is usually a significant word, near the end of the tone unit.

As a general rule, the tone falls when we come to the end of a statement, for example *He left at four o'clock*; and it rises when we are uncertain or are asking a question, for example *Did she really ask for a pay rise?* Antipodean speech patterns generally have a rise in tone at the end of an utterance, not only in questions. This has now spread across the globe, with the influence of the worldwide transmission of Australian and New Zealand TV 'soaps'.

KEY TERMS

transcription/transcript a written record of spoken language which may use symbols and markings to illustrate the distinctive nature of speech

---

LINK

You will find more about the study of speech sounds in child language acquisition in **Unit 7** on page 252.

KEY TERMS

micropause a very short pause to take breath

tone units the natural phrases of speech, usually separated by a micropause

---

TIP

When analysing speech transcripts, it is important to establish the **topic, audience** and **purpose** of the extract, as this will help you understand the tone and the dynamics of the discourse.

LINK

You will be learning more about intonation patterns in the section on *Paralinguistic features* on page 170.

Glossary of speech annotations

Annotation	Indicates ...
//	an overlap of speakers, often an interruption or where two speakers start at the same time
...	an unfinished utterance
(.)	a pause for breath, known as a micropause
(2)	the length of a pause in seconds, for example *She would be about (2) ten I should think*
<u>underlined</u>	may be used to indicate a stressed word or syllable
[ ]	square brackets usually contain information about paralinguistic features, with the feature written in italics, for example [*laughs*]

LINK

You may find it helpful to refer back to this glossary when analysing other examples of transcribed speech in this unit (see pages 156, 162, 166).

ACTIVITY 4.10

Read the following transcript of a short conversation between two coach drivers. This records the actual delivery of words, tone units and pauses. As preparation for the next section on the way in which conversations are spoken, discuss what might be the tone of the two drivers while they are stuck on the road with irritated passengers wanting to get to the airport on time.

Context and participants: two London coach drivers are discussing the traffic congestion on the road ahead and their working conditions. Driver 1 (D1) has just started driving the bus towards one of the London airports. He has taken over from Driver 2 (D2) who is now on his rest break and sitting in a passenger seat alongside his friend – the current driver.

D1 glad you made it now

D2 we was only 3 minutes late (.) two passengers worrying they will miss their flights

D1 depends on this traffic (.) always road works here (.) why do they do it at peak traffic (.) same every day

D2 they've been testing these lights for months (.) dreadful traffic (.) congestion every day (.) been a helluva day(.) you're pushed to get to Heathrow [*London's major airport*] even when there's nothing on the road

D1 I'm on till 11

169

D2	helluva duty (.) long hours
DI	change for me (.) I'm normally on overnights (.) do a fast one
D2	it should have been Terry on this but he's on holiday (.) leaves me doing 5am on the trot for 6 days
DI	I've got 4 overnights and another Monday (.) he's desperate for a driver to do//
D2	// no drivers want to do this trip (1) a nightmare

Paralinguistic features

As an accomplished conversationalist you will know that what you say is only half the story; it is the *way* that you say it which is often key to the effectiveness of your communication with others.

Body language, gestures, facial expressions, tone, speed and pitch of voice are all examples of the **paralinguistic features** which add to the meaning of the total discourse, even if the speakers are not consciously aware of them. When one or more of these features is absent, as in a phone conversation, it is often difficult to interpret the speaker's intentions. The main features of spoken discourse are as follows:

■ **Tone** relates to the emotion associated with the utterance; you can generally tell whether someone is irritated, happy, sad or bored by the expression they use when speaking

■ **Pitch** is a musical term and, in language, relates to the level of voice production, whether it is high or low. We squeal in a high pitch and younger children also have high-pitched voices. Characteristically, when we speak to babies we raise the pitch of our voices. Pitch is closely associated with the sounds we make.

■ **Volume** is the level of voice production, whether loud or soft. Everyone has their own characteristic volume level when they speak, and volume may change according to the circumstances.

■ **Speed** relates to the pace at which someone speaks and again this is related to the circumstances of the social interaction. When excited or frightened, we may speak faster. Conversely, when we are uncertain, or wish to be very careful about what we are saying, we tend to speak more slowly.

LINK

You will learn about individual speaking style in **Unit 5** in the section about **idiolect** on pages 211–218.

ACTIVITY 4.11

1 On what occasions might we speak with a low-pitched voice?

2 Consider the circumstances which make people raise or lower the volume of their voice when they speak. What social signals are sent by the volume of someone's voice?

3 To appreciate the importance of paralinguistic features, try holding a conversation with someone else in your class, **breaking** conversational conventions as follows:

   ■ avoid eye contact with the person you are speaking to

   ■ show no emotion in your facial expressions when you are speaking – no smiles or frowns

   ■ do not change the tone of your voice – speak in a monotone

   ■ do not match the tone of your voice with what you are saying, for example try saying how much you have enjoyed something in a very flat tone

   ■ change the pace at which you speak – faster, slower.

Discuss in a group how you felt about breaking these paralinguistic features of conversation and how your actions affected the hearer's responses. Make an assessment, with evidence, about the importance of paralinguistic features in discourse.

● ● ● FURTHER RESEARCH

Carry out your own observations of paralinguistic features and their importance in everyday conversation.

■ Observe facial expressions which accompany what other people are saying. Look at how your teacher instructs and advises you. How do their facial expressions differ from those of your friends when you are discussing something you plan to do together?

■ Observe body language that people around you use in conversation. Observe people's stance, use and positioning of their hands and arms. How far away do people stand from each other? What is the difference between friendly and threatening body language?

■ Body language, and what it signifies, may vary according to the culture you live in. First of all, analyse the generally understood body language of your own culture, for example handshakes, waving, making a fist. Then, if possible, investigate body language from cultures other than your own and identify any significant differences between them.

■ Listen to the tone, pitch and pace of people speaking and assess how important these features are and what effect they have on what is being said.

■ Watch adverts and assess how paralinguistic features are used to persuade you to buy goods and services.

The importance of paralinguistics

Paralinguistic features are critically important in any conversation, both for the speaker putting across their points and for the hearer interpreting what is being said. The link between the two is assisted by **feedback** – signals that the listener gives to show they are following the conversation. Feedback can be expressed by any of the features shown in the diagram below:

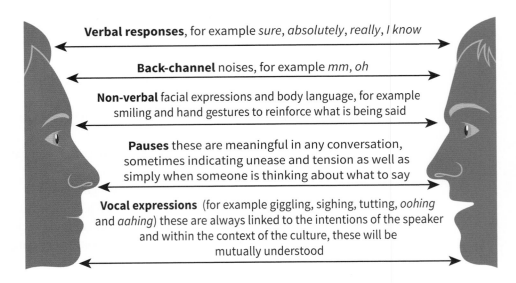

Verbal responses, for example *sure*, *absolutely*, *really*, *I know*

Back-channel noises, for example *mm*, *oh*

Non-verbal facial expressions and body language, for example smiling and hand gestures to reinforce what is being said

Pauses these are meaningful in any conversation, sometimes indicating unease and tension as well as simply when someone is thinking about what to say

Vocal expressions (for example giggling, sighing, tutting, *oohing* and *aahing*) these are always linked to the intentions of the speaker and within the context of the culture, these will be mutually understood

Summary: key points for discourse analysis

At A Level you are required to analyse and comment on an unseen piece of discourse which will show many of the conventions you have explored and discussed during your course.

There is a fundamental difference between the scripted speech of plays, the dialogue in fictional writing, formal speeches, sermons and other texts, where speech is already written and planned, and the unscripted discourse of conversations. The first group have all the characteristics of written texts which you have studied in your AS course. In your A Level course you will also be looking at examples of unscripted spoken language in the form of transcripts.

Remember the following key points and skills when planning and writing your discourse analysis.

Language features

An effective analysis must not only accurately pinpoint a language feature using the correct terminology and giving an example, but it must comment on the meaning and *effects* of the use of that feature. Simply identifying features is insufficient. Remember to use the **point/quotation/comment** technique as the basis for your analysis or commentary.

Context

The context of the utterances – the time, the place and role of the speakers, their relationship and purpose in talking – are fundamental to their choice of language and how they communicate. It is important to establish these elements of context at the outset as this will affect all aspects of the management of the conversation.

You should expect transcripts of conversations from a variety of cultures. It is therefore important to make reference to the possible cultural/societal norms

LINK

For more about using the point/ quotation/comment technique, see pages 17–20.

LINK

For more about the importance of context in discourse, see pages 174–178.

and contexts which may affect the language and management of unscripted conversation.

Register

The register of the discourse should be established; this is seen through the level of formality. You should assess whether the participants use formal Standard English or whether the relationship and purpose ensure that informal varieties of English and slang are used. The register will be evident throughout the conversation through the choice of vocabulary and syntax used for the topic under discussion.

LINK

For more about register, see page 193.

Topic shifts

Once context, register and language features have been considered, the *management of the topic* needs to be analysed. Do the participants talk on one subject only or are there topic shifts where other topics are introduced? If so, how do these enter the conversation? Equally, does the conversation appear to drift or return in a loop to subjects discussed earlier? You will need to look at the strategies the participants adopt in the opening and closing sections of the text. The relationships between the participants including their gender, age and relative status will help to anchor your analysis back to the context and **purpose** (the aim of the conversation).

LINK

For more about topic shifts, see page 155.

Conventions

The body of the transcript will contain linguistic conventions of unscripted conversation which individuals use. The interaction of the participants and their management of the conversation will be evident in the **adjacency pairs** and the extent of equality will be seen in **turn-taking** and interruptions. Your analysis should continue with comments relating to the **maxims of conversation** as well as the politeness strategies which are (or are not) adopted. At all times relate this back to your perceived awareness of the purpose and the context of the conversation.

LINK

For more about the conventions of unscripted conversation, see pages 154–168.

LINK

For more practice and self-evaluation on this unit, see page 286.

173

Unit 5: Spoken language and social groups

The context of spoken language

In the first section of this unit you will explore the ways in which our spoken language is influenced and altered by the people and situations we encounter.

> **TIP**
>
> Because every community has different groups to which individuals can belong, you should always use specific examples from your own country or region.
>
> A huge number of groups exist in any community; many of them may be very ill defined and loosely constituted; they may be permanent or temporary. If you understand the functions of the examples you have selected, it will help you with your language analysis.

When we use language it is invariably for a reason: to greet someone, to pay for items bought in the supermarket, to shout support for a sports team, to worship. The way in which our language is spoken is directly linked to the **context** – the circumstances that form the setting for an event, statement, or idea, and in terms of which it can be fully understood. For example, the context for language used in a school staff meeting is the need to solve common goals and problems related to the school so there will be vocabulary and syntax related to its functioning – such as the curriculum and exams – as well as purposeful discussion about the students' progress. Standard English is likely to be spoken and it is likely that minutes (a written record of subjects discussed and decisions made) will be created. Of course there may be pleasant comments (phatic communion) about topics such as the weather and health, which helps the occasion along, but these are subsidiary to the purpose of the activity.

ACTIVITY 5.1

Try to clarify exactly what is meant by a group. Then discuss with others the different types of groups to which people belong.

ACTIVITY 5.2

Explain how language use may be influenced by the following contexts:

- a visit to the doctor
- advertising a product for sale
- a lesson
- using a social network site
- a visit to an elderly relative
- travelling to a country where you do not speak the language fluently
- talking to a person who is hard of hearing
- talking to a person who has a limited command of your language.

Groups and the context in which they operate provide a complex web of formal and informal interaction within a society. There may be defined rules for belonging, such as enrolment at a college; membership may depend on location such as a neighbourhood; or upon skills achieved (e.g. the Under-14s Auckland Girls' netball squad); or upon preference such as a group of friends.

The language used by group members can also be another form of identification where individuals aim to make their speech more like those of the majority within the group.

Communication accommodation theory

Communication accommodation theory (CAT) is a theory of communication developed by Howard Giles. It argues that *when people interact they adjust their speech, their vocal patterns and their gestures, to accommodate to others.*

The theory explores the idea that as individuals we do not like to appear too different from those with whom we spend time. When using language we try to minimise the differences between us and other people by 'accommodating' or changing our language to become more like theirs. A very obvious example in the United Kingdom and the United States is regional accents where those who do not speak as the majority do, may try to alter their accents. Since speech is a way to express group membership, people adopt convergence or divergence in their communication with those around them. If we wish to create distance between ourselves and other people, we may consciously diverge from the group in the language we adopt, for example by speaking with a different accent or using different forms of address (e.g. first versus family name and title).

As a starting point for studying the language of social groups we can establish the following key ideas:

- At any point in time we function in society as members of many social groups; these develop and change throughout our lives.
- As part of our own identity we want to be similar to – or accommodate to – other members of the groups to which we belong; the CAT theory suggests that changing our language to be more like others in the group is one of the strategies we adopt.
- In our daily lives we adapt and change our styles of language according to the context. As we become more socially competent we accomplish these changes unconsciously and with relative ease.

175

> ### KEY TERMS
>
> **convergence** where we make our language more similar to the speakers around us, often for social reasons or to be part of a group
>
> **divergence** when an individual adjusts his or her speech patterns to be distinct from those of people belonging to another group or social identity; this is usually to indicate greater status (e.g. between an employer and the workers)

ACTIVITY 5.3

Based on your knowledge of social groups and accommodation, what is your response to the following example?

> *Karen is a doctor practising in the city of Bath, in the south of England. She grew up in Barnsley, an industrial town in the north of England where the accent is very different. (You can find examples of these different accents online.)*
>
> **Karen:** When I was ten I moved with my parents and little sister from Barnsley to Oxford as my father had a new job. I didn't realise I had any sort of accent at all until I started school the following week and all my classmates laughed at me. It took me two weeks to learn to talk like they did and in about a month I had lost all traces of my Barnsley accent.

Festivals and ceremonies are an excellent way to see how language changes according to context. Read the following information about the different language contexts used at a recent wedding in Canada.

Before the ceremony
The 'Save the Date' card

Save the date for the wedding of
Ndyana Connage with Niall Daniel Sorour

23rd August

Details to follow later

The Wedding Invitation

Mr and Mrs Donald Connage

*request the pleasure of your company on the occasion of the
marriage of their daughter*
Ndyana *with* **Niall Sorour**

at 1pm on **Saturday 23rd August**
at the **The Lakes Hotel, Squamish, BC**

Followed by a reception at the **Riverside Hotel**

Carriages at midnight

RSVP by June 24th 2014

The wedding invitation is also likely to contain details of the wedding present list, which these days may give information about on line purchases from a particular store. Depending on the location of the wedding and the distances travelled by the guests, details of hotel accommodation may also be included.

The wedding service is a legal ceremony and as such must be accompanied by certain formal statements, for example *Does anyone know of any just cause or impediment why these two people should not be joined together in marriage? I now pronounce you husband and wife.* As well as written documentary proof that the marriage has taken place and has been publicly witnessed the Marriage Certificate is the legal proof.

Formal 'set pieces' of language are also present in the social side of the reception: there are speeches and toasts to the married couple, and the cutting of the cake and the first dance are also accompanied by public announcements to the guests which are often formulaic, for example *Ladies and gentlemen, please join me in raising your glasses to Ndyana and Niall, Mr and Mrs Sorour; the bride and groom are about to cut the cake.*

The social interactions between the guests are naturally varied, light-hearted and often noisy. Because many people will not know each other, formal introductions will take place and some of the conversations will reference the nature of the relationship of the guests to the bride and groom, with many stories and anecdotes about them.

After the wedding the bride and groom will send thank-you cards to those from whom they have received gifts.

Of course, each wedding ceremony is different but the established rituals and legal requirements clearly show the differences of language according to the context of the different elements of the occasion.

ACTIVITY 5.4

Now choose an important celebration where you live and list, with explanations, the variety of language styles used.

ACTIVITY 5.5

Read the following extract about Indian film star Shahrukh Khan, which includes some fan postings. Use this as a starting point to discuss the different language styles which exist around a celebrity. Consider their fans and the critics of their work.

Shahrukh Khan is a highly acclaimed award-winning Indian film actor who works in Bollywood films, as well as a film producer and television host. Khan began his career appearing in several television serials in the late 1980s. He made his film debut with the commercially successful *Deewana* (1992). Since then, he has been part of numerous commercial successes and has delivered a variety of critically acclaimed performances. During his years in the Indian film industry, he has won thirteen Filmfare Awards, seven of which are in the Best Actor category. While some of Khan's best-known films: *Dilwale Dulhaniya Le Jayenge* (1995), *Kuch Kuch Hota Hai* (1998), *Chak De India* (2007) and *Om Shanti Om* (2007), remain some of Bollywood's biggest hits, films like *Kabhi Khushi Kabhie Gham* (2001), *Kal Ho Naa Ho* (2003), *Veer-Zaara* (2004) and *Kabhi Alvida Naa Kehna* (2006) have been top-grossing productions in the overseas market, making Khan one of the most successful actors of Hindi cinema.

The following are comments from Shahrukh Khan's fans:

– *HIiii SRK i'm ur big fan....i like ur dressing, attitude, communications, and ur voice .....these are amazing ...I like u ....best of luck for ur new film "Raees"....I hope that New One record becomes with this film... Take Care*

– *No matters whatever he does, The main thing is - SRK Did.. Thats Enough For Me*

– *Best of luck Shah Rukh!!! Love u soooo much... Hope thisfilm will be a blockbluster like your other films. Love u soooo much..*

– *Hope and prays that Happy New Year Film will be a blockbluster IN india and Overseas like ur other films*

– *big fan of uuu......i like your movies..my favrite is darr and bazigar dewana*

entertainment.oneindia.in

177

> ### ACTIVITY 5.6
>
> For practice with essay writing, attempt one or both of the following suggested titles.
>
> 1 With close reference to specific case studies, explain in what ways features of spoken language can be influenced by context.
> 2 With close reference to specific case studies and your wider knowledge of ways in which language varies according to context, discuss your response to the following extract from the British Library website:
>
> *Language also changes very subtly whenever speakers come into contact with each other. No two individuals speak identically: people from different geographical places clearly speak differently, but even within the same small community there are variations according to a speaker's age, gender, ethnicity and social and educational background. Through our interactions with these different speakers, we encounter new words, expressions and pronunciations and integrate them into our own speech.*
>
> www.bl.uk

Language used to include and exclude

Inclusion and exclusion are very broad terms for the functioning of many groups in society where national, regional, and local neighbourhood groups continue to change. The language of inclusion and exclusion is frequently accompanied by the more sociological concepts relating to ethnicity and the politics of a country. These factors may be very significant in the area where you live and language here becomes one of a number of informal signifiers of the opportunities which are given or denied to particular groups in society.

TIP
- This section covers a broad overview of economic, social and historical ideas linked to language. Make sure you understand these ideas and have appropriate case studies and examples to use when discussing them.
- In an exam, you may be given stimulus material which tests your general understanding as it applies to the exam question. You will be expected to appraise and justify your view using both the exam question and your own resources.
- Discussion and evaluating points with evidence are important skills to practise.

••• FURTHER RESEARCH

The examples chosen in this unit are based on the size of the group and the impact their actions have made on language. However, these case studies should act as signposts for your own individual research; examples from your own region or country will also be useful to you.

Is he one of us? This question was famously asked by Margaret Thatcher, former prime minister of the UK, about any new arrival on the political scene. Jamaican immigrants arriving in Britain in the 1950s often found that their style of spoken English was not readily understood by British people. The difference in spoken English often reinforced differences between the immigrant and resident communities. Studies of young male gang members in New York showed that although they spoke fluently amongst their peers, they often failed at school where a different style of English was spoken.

In this section you will explore situations where language contributes to the inclusion or exclusion of individuals or certain groups in society.

William the Conqueror.

Examples of national and international exclusion

Group inclusion and exclusion has almost always been linked to power wielded by a dominant group. Nations have conquered, invaded, and colonised others and the incoming group often enforces their language on the weaker group. History provides many examples of ethnic exclusion and these are still common today; many have a direct link to language.

Read through these case studies after which there will be activities and further research. Remember, the case studies are only very brief accounts of complex events.

England

When William the Conqueror invaded England in 1066, Norman French became the official language, replacing the language spoken by the defeated Anglo Saxons. For two hundred years, French was the language of the aristocracy and the powerful in England, while the peasants continued with Old English. However, the two languages gradually merged into important components of present-day English.

South America

Under colonial rule, Spanish replaced Quechua and other Amerindian languages in much of South America after conquest by Spain, while Portuguese became the official language of Brazil. While the Indian languages are still spoken today, Spanish and Portuguese are the main languages throughout the continent.

New Zealand

Colonisation wiped out many languages. British colonisation of the Indian sub-continent, parts of South-East Asia, North America and Australasia led to the imposition of English onto the newly colonised populations. Where the minority languages survived, such as Māori in New Zealand, official attitudes and policy discouraged its use, and children were forbidden from speaking it in schools. Māori was seen as irrelevant to economic advancement, with the view that English needed to replace it. Subsequent concern from all groups in New Zealand has reversed this policy and Māori is now one of the official languages of New Zealand. A policy of encouragement and inclusion has transformed what had become a minority native language into a mainstream component of the nation's culture.

North America

Forced transport of groups such as the slave trade between Africa and the United States had a huge impact on language. Africans who were transported to work as slaves on the plantations of the Southern United States spoke a variety of languages and were totally excluded from any rights in their new environment. The slave owners feared rebellion and adopted a policy of mixing different language groups in the same working area. The impact of this deprivation was the emergence of a functional mix of vocabulary and syntax, known as **pidgin**. In time, this basic language developed more complex grammatical structures to form a fully functioning **creole** language. The partial fusion and adaptation of the many languages of New Guinea are a particularly good example of the language process of pidgin and creolisation.

LINK

For more on the impact of colonisation on language, see the section on *Language death* in **Unit 6** on page 254.

KEY TERMS

pidgin a simple but rule-governed language which emerges as the basis for communication between speakers with no common language

creole a pidgin language that has become the native tongue of a speech community and is learned by children as their first language

179

TIP

Writing down the conclusions from your discussions, including discussions of case studies, will provide points of view and relevant material for this topic for future essays and coursework.

ACTIVITY 5.7

1   Discuss in a group why language is so important to the power and control of a country. Think about the motives of those who are in control and the attitudes of those who are denied the freedom to speak their native language.

2   Choose one of the case studies given in this section and carry out some individual or group research on the current situation with regard to the language which was used to exclude sections of the population. What brought about the changes?

3   Discuss the view that it is easier to run a country when all the population speaks the same language and that the use of a different language by certain groups may be divisive.

4   Find out about any instances where language has been used to exclude certain groups in your own part of the world and the responses to this situation.

5   The use of language to exclude is closely linked to the notion of social exclusion – where communities are blocked from opportunities and benefits available to other groups, for example, civil rights, housing and education. Investigate a specific case study of language exclusion and assess the extent to which language and social exclusion are linked.

Language and religion

The violence of the actions taken to exclude some controlling groups, and the significance played by language in this process, should not be underestimated. Religious groups have often experienced this extreme control. For example, the Roman Catholic Church fiercely opposed the first translations of the Bible into English from Latin, which appeared in England in the 1300s. Many people were burned as heretics because of their wish to worship in English. The language elected by a group for their religious worship literally became a matter of life and death.

South Africa

Under the South African Apartheid regime, the controlling white government proposed that Black children should be taught in Afrikaans, one of the native languages. This was unpopular and sparked riots in 1976 as these groups saw education in English as an advantage which was being denied to them.

Language and negative stereotypes

As well as being a factor in direct exclusion as described above, language is an integral part of stereotyping. You may know that a stereotype is a broad generalisation about one group by another, and the judgements and labels associated with stereotyping are frequently negative. In Nazi Germany negative stereotyping of Jewish people was reinforced by official policy, with atrocious consequences.

In South Africa during the era of apartheid, and in the United States before Civil Rights reform, negative stereotyping in society resulted in huge racial inequalities.

The language of the American Civil Rights movement

The power of language to include those suffering exclusion is well exemplified in the 1960s United States Civil Rights movement. Although this was a protracted struggle,

• • • • FURTHER RESEARCH

Research Martin Luther King and his speeches, then analyse: the style he adopted; his use of rhetorical techniques; and the language methods he used to persuade his listeners of the justice of his cause.

it is undeniable that significant advances were made through speeches made by civil rights leaders such as Martin Luther King.

From 1963 to 1964 Nelson Mandela and several other ANC leaders were on trial at Pretoria's Supreme Court (known as the Rivonia Trial; they would later receive life sentences). Below is a short extract from Mandela's statement on 20th April 1964, made at the opening of the case for the defence.

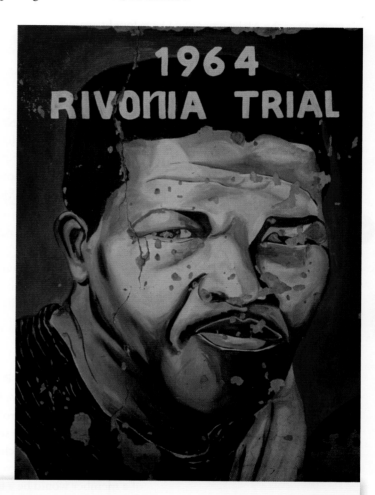

A mural in Soweto depicting Nelson Mandela at the time of his trial.

181

Africans want to be paid a living wage. Africans want to perform work which they are capable of doing, and not work which the government declares them to be capable of. We want to be allowed to live where we obtain work, and not be endorsed out of an area because we were not born there. We want to be allowed to own land in places where we work, and not to be obliged to live in rented houses which we can never call our own. Africans want to be part of the general population, and not confined to living in our ghettoes. African men want to have their wives and children to live with them where they work, and not be forced into an unnatural existence in men's hostels. Our women want to be with their menfolk and not be left permanently widowed in the reserves. We want to be allowed out after eleven o'clock at night and not to be confined to their rooms like little children. We

want to be allowed to travel in our own country and to seek work where we want to and not where the Labour Bureau tells us to. We want a just share in the whole of South Africa; we want security and a stake in society.

Above all, My Lord, we want equal political rights, because without them our disabilities will be permanent. I know this sounds revolutionary to the whites in this country, because the majority of voters will be Africans. This makes the white man fear democracy.

But this fear cannot be allowed to stand in the way of the only solution which will guarantee racial harmony and freedom for all. It is not true that the enfranchisement of all will result in racial domination. Political division, based on colour, is entirely artificial and, when it disappears, so will the domination of one colour group by another. The ANC has spent half a century fighting against racialism. When it triumphs as certainly it must, it will not change that policy. This then is what the ANC is fighting for. Our struggle is a truly national one. It is a struggle of the African people, inspired by our own suffering and our own experience. It is a struggle for the right to live. During my lifetime I have dedicated myself to this struggle of the African people. I have fought against white domination, and I have fought against black domination. I have cherished the ideal of a democratic and free society in which all persons live together in harmony and with equal opportunities. It is an ideal which I hope to live for and to achieve. But if needs be, My Lord, it is an ideal for which I am prepared to die.

From *No easy walk to freedom* by Nelson Mandela.

ACTIVITY 5.8

1   Read the text of Nelson Mandela's speech carefully and analyse the language used. How does the language include the black population of South Africa as equal citizens?

Consider the following:

■   the methods Mandela uses to include all racial groups

■   the effects of imagery and rhetorical techniques to emphasise the importance and urgency of the need for racial equality within South Africa.

2   Find a video clip of Nelson Mandela giving this or another speech. How does his delivery affect the impact? Imagine you were a listener in the crowd while Mandela was speaking; what would your reaction have been?

●●● **FURTHER RESEARCH**

Find out more about the life of Nelson Mandela – this link will get you started:

http://www.telegraph.co.uk/ news/worldnews/ nelson-mandela/

Language groups and social class

Some social groups have formal admission procedures such as subscriptions, or through academic or professional qualification. Other groups do not; membership is informal and may be selectively adopted as part of a lifestyle such as membership of a running or fitness club.

There are very few groups where specific consideration of the language of a member would be a formal condition of entry, perhaps a group such as Toastmasters – an international public-speaking group. As you learned in the previous section, communication accommodation theory suggests that when people wish to share interests, however loosely, their speech patterns tend to converge – that is, they become more alike. The other side of this is that those groups who speak differently may suffer exclusion. Studies have shown that immigrants whose command of English may be limited may suffer discrimination, which results in more limited educational and career prospects.

Not speaking English may mean being trapped in a low-paying job with no obvious means of advancement. A New York Times report of 2006 suggested (and a New Zealand Government paper has made similar assertions) that there is a penalty in being from a non-English speaking background which also relates to ethnicity.

The attitude of many in the USA towards the varied non-English speaking populations is an interesting one because an important attitude in the growth and settlement of the 'melting pot' of the United States was the Latin motto *e pluribus unum* ('one out of many') and this included the speaking of English. Today there are large areas where many languages other than English are spoken and there is much debate about the possible exclusion from opportunities for those non-English-speaking groups.

The language of class in Britain – a case study of exclusion and inclusion

Many societies, probably including yours, have different forms of social stratification. The example of the British class system will be discussed here, as it demonstrates well both group inclusion and exclusion through language.

In Britain, informal judgements and media commentary often generate an understanding of who belongs to which class. Historically, the social classes were defined as the upper class, the middle class and the working class – other groupings are more directly related to employment.

Social class is a subject much discussed in British society: what defines the classes; who belongs to which class; how you move upwards through the class system; and, for an increasing number of people, whether the social classes actually still exist.

LINK

For more about RP (Received Pronunciation) turn to page 231 in **Unit 6**.

What is social class?

The word *class* is derived from the Latin *classis* which was used in the Roman Empire as a measurement of wealth; this meaning still underpins the concept of class. Apart from wealth, class refers to how you display your wealth in your lifestyle both in material and non-material ways. Traditional British values assume a member of the upper class to have a large income, a big house in a desirable area, to spend liberally on expensive consumer goods and also to speak with an RP (Received Pronunciation) accent. In addition, and this is less easy to define, the upper classes are thought to possess a confident approach to life derived from the best of British education and family background.

183

This view is arguably long outdated as industrial economic prosperity generated an influential British middle class in the 19th and 20th centuries. The welfare state with universal health and education provision also helped to blur the earlier sharp divisions. Later on, with the new digital revolution, new technological skills produced a new class of affluent people that cut across traditional class lines. Although Britain in the 21st century is certainly not without social inequalities, the divisions are no longer as clear. However, social anthropologist Kate Fox asserts that class *pervades all aspects of English life and culture* and emphasises the subtle boundaries within people's lives which classify them within the hierarchy.

ACTIVITY 5.9

Read the following account.

> In the late 1960s a large engineering company, famous for making bicycles, needed to employ more factory workers. Their advertisement read Hands wanted. The same company provided food for its workforce: the factory workers ate their midday meal (their) dinner) in the canteen, while the middle

FURTHER RESEARCH

Find out more about the research carried out by Howard Giles on language convergence.

Go to **education.cambridge. org** to download a list of useful websites related to this topic.

managers ate lunch, *and the senior managers ate* luncheon, *in different restaurants. Female managers (there were very few) ate in the senior ladies restaurant.*

1   Organise the following list of employees into their appropriate midday meal arrangements, as they would have been in the 1960s.
    - human resources manager (female)
    - bicycle assembly worker
    - director of factory production
    - bicycle assembly manager
    - children's cycle design manager
    - cycle factory cleaner
    - training officer (female)
    - training director
    - managing director's secretary (female)

    Give reasons for your answers.

2   What links are there between the language of the restaurants and the different classes of workers in the factory?

Language and group identity

Research has shown that individuals accommodate to each other by adopting similar speech patterns for inclusion in the group they wish to be part of, such as a social class. Linguist Howard Giles developed this theory of convergence, which is an important feature of group identity. Conversely an individual may diverge to accentuate differences in speech. TV comedy has often used convergence and divergence to help satirise the class system.

ACTIVITY 5.10

Research a TV or radio comedy show that is concerned with social class – you may find it easier to use a British show, as social class is often present. Consider how standard and non-standard language, and any regional accents and dialects, are used to show differences in social class.

Discuss the extent to which the language used influenced the comedy situations that emerged, and try to analyse how these were created.

Note: You may find that some older comedy shows have content that would be considered racist, sexist or politically incorrect today.

Research studies on language and social class

It will be clear to you from the preceding information that many assertions have been made about social class without being backed up by relevant research. Indeed, it is the case that comments and stereotypes about social class are regularly made without systematic back up from reliable research. It is an area full of unsubstantiated claims because many people feel that they know instinctively to which groups they and others belong. However, there have been significant studies on language and social class from which clear observations and conclusions can be drawn.

FURTHER RESEARCH

Search online to find additional information on the research studies featured here and on other relevant studies.

KEY TERMS

post-vocalic a consonant directly following a noun

schwa a generic vowel sound that is usually pronounced in unstressed syllables, for example the 'e' in system or the 'a' in alone

William Labov

Labov (1966) researched the use of the **post-vocalic** /r/ in New York City. This is where the /r/ is actually pronounced, often at the end of a word such as *car, far*. This type of pronunciation is much more widely used in North American/Scottish English than British English which weakens the sound to pronounce these words as /ca/ or /fa/. The weak pronunciation of the final syllable in this pronunciation of English is a **schwa** where the sound is unstressed.

The postvocalic /r/ in the United States has a prestige similar to the pronunciation of the /h/ at the beginning of a word in British English (i.e. it is considered 'lower class' in Britain to pronounce */house* as *l'ouse* and *happy/* as *'appy*). Labov theorised that as the sound connoted prestige, people would pronounce it and his predictions were largely confirmed in unscripted speech.

Peter Trudgill

Trudgill (1973, revisited 1988) investigated a similar language and social class link but with the dialect features of omitting the third person singular inflection (e.g. *she sleep a lot*; *he do cause trouble*) and found that this construction was a feature of some British working-class speakers (e.g. in the Norfolk region).

Advertising

You have learned that that group membership can both be imposed from outside, such as a professional association, and can also be more complex such as social class. Group membership can sometimes be unclearly defined.

One significant group that we are all allocated to in an increasingly sophisticated way is that of consumers. The language of advertising targets our psychological needs to ensure that we include ourselves in specific categories and buy items which are appropriate for the group to which we feel we belong.

ACTIVITY 5.11

1 You may already be familiar with the following examples of the language of advertising from earlier work. If you are, then remind yourself of their meaning by writing a short definition of each. If not, then carry out some research to find out their meaning.
   - loaded language
   - appeals to basic needs
   - bandwagon
   - testimonial
   - snob appeal
   - connotation

2 Discuss some of the ideas about the language of inclusion and exclusion presented in this section. Investigate a group you are interested in and focus on the use of language associated with that group.

3 Much of the information in this section relates to social class in Britain. Select another country or region and assess its system of social stratification. To what extent do you think that language plays a part in maintaining the hierarchy?

4 Write an extended piece suitable for inclusion in the editorial section of a quality newspaper where you discuss, with evidence, the part that language plays in group identity.

LINK

The language of teenagers is explored further in the section on *Language acquisition* in **Unit 7** and this section relates closely to that. However, this section focuses specifically on this age group in relation to their interaction with other teenagers and with other groups in which inclusion and exclusion can occur.

The language of teenage groups

What would your life be like without your phone? Teenagers are early adopters of technology and use it extensively. They effortlessly tweet, text and communicate through a variety of media. A sample taken of two English classes showed that, although all students used their phones almost all the time, a clear majority did not use text language in any other medium. They gave their English teacher a test on words used commonly in 'text speak' and the teacher knew hardly any of them! So text speak can act in the same way as jargon, to exclude those who are not familiar with the abbreviations and emoticons.

As teenagers are arguably the group who use electronically mediated communication more than any other, concerns are being raised at the extent to which the increasing use of text language is making an impact on Standard English constructions. This is nothing new: generations of older people have complained about a decline in standards of language amongst young people. In 1908, Thomas Lounsbury, a professor of language and literature at Yale University, observed that there has existed *in every period of the past, as there is now, a distinct apprehension in the minds of very many worthy persons that the English tongue is always in the condition of approaching collapse.*

However, with the dramatic increase in electronically mediated communication, perhaps this generation of complainers has a good point. The areas of concern about declining language standards among teenage groups focus on the extensive use of electronically mediated information such as texting and the language of emails and tweets.

Recent research by Naomi S. Baron highlights areas of concerns on the increasing use of abbreviations and emoticons combined with a reduction in the use of standard punctuation and capital letters. Media articles have expressed unease about the increasing reliance on this form of communication. Concerns about how electronic communication will affect the English language include:

- the extent to which these new forms intrude on the traditional areas of writing and speech. For example, is the use of *brb* and *lol* in speech as well as in a text significantly different from the use of acronyms such as *RSVP* and *SOS* which are considered as standard use?
- whether the lack of spaces in web addresses will tip over into general use. This would be an interesting return to medieval language where there were no spaces in the writings of monks in monasteries.

- worries about a lack of standardised spellings and of prescriptive direction as to whether one form of language expression is 'right'
- whether certain groups who do not regularly write or speak in this way will be excluded.

ACTIVITY 5.12

Devise and conduct a questionnaire on text language. Try to get a range of ages amongst your respondents as an interesting variable.

- Ask your respondents whether they think the use of text language is ever appropriate outside texting. If so, in what situations?
- Compile a list of the text abbreviations you use regularly and ask your respondents how many of these they are familiar with. Is age the only reason for a lack of knowledge of this type of language?
- Use the results of your research to write a reasoned blog for an education website on *The role of text language in teenage lives*.

Language in cyberspace

One of the problems associated with the internet is the issue of cyber-bullying, which is defined as a young person tormenting, threatening, harassing, or embarrassing another young person using the internet or other technologies, such as cell phones. This behaviour is now possible because of the internet and the anonymity it provides through the bullies being able to block information. Face-to-face bullying has been in existence wherever inequalities of power or status exist and language is one of the strongest weapons available to the bully.

It is not just text speak which defines teenage groups. Teenagers are able to **code switch** according to their audience, but still present a casual colloquial face to society in general.

> **KEY TERMS**
>
> **code switching** moving backwards and forwards between different registers or levels of formality of language, depending on the audience (e.g. close friend, teacher, employer)

ACTIVITY 5.13

Read the article below in which Oscar-winning actress Emma Thompson reflects on the language of teenagers and the impact she feels it has.

1. Discuss how far you agree with her view that the language people use influences other people's opinions of them.
2. This article gives one clear example of broadly based social groups, in this case teenage girls, using language for group identity in particular circumstances. Discuss whether you feel this type of language has uses for teenage social groups.

That Emma Thompson's, like, well annoyed, innit

The Oxford-educated actress has hit out at slang used by the young, claiming it makes them sound stupid when they're not. The 51-year-old, known for her roles in Shakespeare film adaptations, said the use of sloppy language made her feel "insane".

"I went to give a talk at my old school and the girls were all doing their 'likes' and 'innits?' and 'it ain'ts', which drives me insane," she told the Radio Times.

"I told them 'Just don't do it. Because it makes you sound stupid and you're not stupid. There is the necessity to have two languages – one that you use with your mates and the other that you need in any official capacity."

www.mirror.co.uk

Online social groups—case study of fansites

The origin of *fan* is an abbreviation of the word *fanatic*, which has a very different connotation from the fan as an enthusiastic follower but which does allude to the excesses of some fans' behaviour. The media world of TV and film has always generated fans, from the earliest days of Hollywood where they were initially depicted as hysterical screaming girls. Now though, a fan can be anybody and it can be quite a serious endeavour. Fan clubs and fan magazines have existed for a long time, but the internet has enabled global communities to flourish. Almost all stars and films have some sort of following but it is international sport coverage and large film and TV franchises which have resulted in the largest number of fans forming online groups with communities of interest.

Real Madrid before a Champions' League match in 2012.

••• FURTHER RESEARCH

Examples of online fan communities are varied and represent many interests. Follow the links to some examples of fan sites:

Fan site for the famous and recently retired Indian cricketer Sachin Tendulkar: **http://www.sachintendulkar.in/2008/09/sachin-tendulkars-gallery.html**

The French fan site for the Lebanese-British singer-songwriter Mika: **http://www.mikafanclub.com/**

The Spanish football club Real Madrid's fansite: **www.realmadrid.com/en**

Fan communities of Apple computers: **http://applefansite.com/**

All fan groups have common characteristics. They provide a forum for the sharing of interests and ideas where detailed knowledge gives status to group members. Fans of TV shows and book series, for example, not only know the twists and turns of the stories but may also have extensive background knowledge. Fan sites allow people with a very specific interest to meet like-minded people. The fans share a common language and this jargon gives linguistic cohesion to the group. On a Harry Potter website for example, all fans of the J. K. Rowling books and films would be able to discuss the relative merits of Gryffyndor and Hufflepuff as houses at Hogwarts School. These are lexical items relevant to the books and the films. Non-members of these fan groups are excluded by their ignorance of specific terms and they are often not allowed to post messages on the forums. Membership and language are important discriminators.

Fan groups are bound together by the continuing spin-offs from the books and films; merchandise is available for sale and fan art and fan fiction further reinforce solidarity and group interests. The boundaries between fiction and real life are frequently crossed, such as in fan fiction and fan art where the original narrative is developed by fans or by conventions where actors in role can meet their fans.

English-speaking websites have a global spread and other fan groups develop sites for other regions.

The following quotes are taken from the Harry Potter *SnitchSeeker* fan website.

Notices
Established in 2002, SnitchSeeker is a Harry Potter fansite, forum, and news site with a large member base and an active and welcoming community. Most of our discussions and activities focus on J.K. Rowling's Harry Potter books and movies, and our members are passionate about them. Here on SS there are various places for discussing almost any Harry Potter topic that appeals to our members. Perhaps you want to talk about your all-time favorite Harry Potter character, or share what flavor of Bertie Bott's Every Flavour Beans you would most like to try. You can do that right here on SS.

Welcome to <u>snitchseeker</u>

Yesterday at 3:14pm

You can find me here mostly in the School RPG, the ministry RPG as well as the WWW forums. That however doesn't mean I don't visit other forums. In the School RPG I play a Slytherin girl named Cassia and she's going to be a sixth year soon! Oh and as for the house, I am a Slytherin in pottermore, too! So it's not only an IC thing. Slytherin is my favorite house, next to it comes Gryffindor. Of course I do like all the four houses.

Yesterday at 4:23pm

[*my favourite character?*] Voldemort. Hehe kiiiiidding. =3 You know that's a tough one. As much as I'd like to say George or Fred I couldn't because I'm not like them. xD I'd saaaay Remus Lupin.

Yesterday at 4:45pm

In answer to *What is your favourite Harry Potter film?* I think mine would have to be POA and OOTP, because that's where everything starts falling into place and we really learn some things about our favorite characters.

www.snitchseeker.com

ACTIVITY 5.14

These activities are designed to show you the language of fan sites so that you can assess the extent to which the fans become an exclusive group, defined by the language used amongst its members.

1   Look at the extract above from the *SnitchSeeker* fan site. To what extent do you think the material would be understandable to anyone? Identify any jargon words and phrases which would not make sense and would therefore exclude someone who was not a fan.

2   Research a fan website for a book, TV show or film of your choice. What jargon is used that would be understandable to website members but not outsiders?

3 Explain, with examples that you have researched, how fan sites give status to their members and reinforce the solidarity and mutual support of the fan group.

4 Read the extract from *HPearth*, an Indian-based Harry Potter website, and assess the role of such international sites for fans throughout the world.

It had quite a humble beginning in early months of its formation where it was known by a different name, 'Potter's India: Harry Potter comes to India'. Its foundation was laid by Harsh Sadhvani with a website hosted on geocities and a range of Harry Potter fanmade videos under the section 'Homemade HP'. Meanwhile Suman Barua was running a yahoo group called HPindia sucessfully with a lot of participants grouped into houses conducting HP Web Activities. Both Suman and Harsh were also staff at Harry Potter India (a well established website that time) under Chetan Bansal (now an IITian). It was there that these two guys came in contact, and being in the same city, connected. Both wanted to spread to an international dominion and hence came up with 'HPearth.com' and launched it on 31st October 2005. The duo began adding the bricks to the foundation and now it has grown to the cadres of being an International website, the only Harry Potter fan website with Indian roots which has survived the downfall of many big HPfansites.

www.hpearth.com

Interviews

The relationship between a star and his or her fans is another medium whereby a community of shared values develops and language is a part of this.

The following is an edited version of an interview with the actor Chris Rankin who plays the character Percy Weasley in the Harry Potter films. Interviews like this are supplemented by posts, online forums and tweets, all of which use specific references to the films and books and are of course mutually understood by the fans.

In addition to highlighting some of the mutually understood language of the fan group, this extract will give you more practice with unscripted conversational features. The commentary which follows highlights the ideas of the language of an inclusive group, but you should also be able to analyse this from the point of view of discourse.

Chris Rankin, who played Percy Weasley in the Harry Potter films.

Speakers: Chris Rankin (Chris), interviewer (Int).

CHRIS   I play Percy Weasley (.) in six of eight films (.) and I am a (.) um a regular [*laughs*]

INT   so (.) in the events (.) er do you wanna (.) to talk about these events (.) what makes you want to come back every year

CHRIS   it's a lot of fun (.) um I think the first one y (.) I accidentally went to [*laughs*] that sounds weird but it is (.) 7 is it 7 years ago (2) yes 7 years ago (2) nearly 7 years ago (.) I got asked by Salem town council (.) to be the guest of honour at their Halloween parade (.) which in Salem is quite a big deal/

INT   yeah/

CHRIS   That was awesome (.) I said yes I would love to go (.) so I didn't really know what to expect // … Then I turned up and there were all these people in costume (.) um and (.) er (.) I got arrested by a bunch of Death Eaters (.) and we stage crashed a Harry Potter gig (.) and (.) it was awesome and I bumped into a load of people I had spoken to on line (.) (.) I'd um done podcasts for Leaky Cauldron and I'd spoken to HPNA about stuff (.) and actually met them face to face (.) and really just ended up having a really cool time and //

INT   //so it was (.) like larger than life (.) was it (.) like what you were expecting

CHRIS   it wasn't what I was expecting (2) initially I was really scared of it (.) well because I was like (.) I'm an actor in these films and I'm staying in a hotel full of Harry Potter fanatics and um I'm not entirely sure if I'm safe// [*laughs*]

INT   // [*laughs*]

CHRIS   Then I started speaking to people (.) they were really great (.) they were really nice and friendly and enthusiastic (.) we shared a lot of common interest cos (.) obviously I'm a big Harry Potter fan as well (.) so (1) um kind of rocked up to a couple of events (.) sat in on a couple of screens and things and (.) just had an awesome time. um (.) and then 'cos of filming commitments and stuff (.) I couldn't do any for a while for a while (.) and then I came to Ascatraz which was in San Francisco about three years ago … and I'm here now and (.) it's cos I love them// and they're a lot of fun

www.youtube.com

COMMENTARY

This interview took place at a Harry Potter convention where Chris was being interviewed for both the fans and a wider audience. The purpose was to 'get behind' the character and get to know the actor. Chris is a British actor who was at a fan convention in the United States.

Both Chris and the interviewer are young, and use colloquialisms (*rocked up, awesome*) which are familiar to the audience who, as a social group, are likely to be of a broadly similar age and so would feel some connection with the young actor who carries through his enthusiasm for the world of Harry Potter. In this context, Chris has the higher status but there is an equality between the two, with the interviewer overlapping, with feedback and some supportive comments:

> *… ended up having a really cool time and//*

> *//So it was (.) like larger than life*

The language is a structured conversation with question and answers in adjacency pairs. The expectation of the listener and viewers is that Chris will dominate the conversation and will be informative. The lexical field of Harry Potter and fandom is another shared understanding and there is no need to explain specific language such as *Death Eaters*, *Leaky Cauldron* and *HPNA*.

Chris makes a wary but friendly reference to the possible *fanatic* behaviour of the fans when he wonders about his safely as the character in a hotel full of fans but this is comprehensively mitigated when he enthuses about the fans' friendship and the enjoyable time spent with them. This relationship between a star and fans is usually one-way, so this provided an unexpected chance for the fandom virtual relationship to change to a face-to-face one.

ACTIVITY 5.15

1 Explain the role that language plays in a relationship between a star and their fans.
2 Find an online interview with a popular film star, singer or sports personality and analyse the language. Discuss whether the language has any elements of exclusion for those who are not part of the fan base.

TIP

The terms *Standard* and *non-standard* English are very broad, so it is essential that you have a clear understanding of their meaning and particularly of the connotations attached to the term *non-standard*. This will help you in writing essays as you may be asked to appraise issues relating to these types of English and their acceptability.

KEY TERMS

prescriptivist (prescriptivism)
the view that language should have a strict set of rules that must be obeyed in speech and writing.

descriptivist (descriptivism)
the view that no use of language is incorrect and that variation should be acknowledged and recorded rather than corrected

192

Non-standard features of English

Non-standard speech is a general term for language which differs from the usual, accepted and recognisable speech of native speakers. In this section you will explore slang and non-standard forms of English in the context of language change and current usage.

Standard and non-standard English

The term *non-standard* has a value judgement attached to it. A **prescriptivist** viewpoint would consider non-standard language 'wrong' since this approach evaluates and judges language according to recognised rules of grammar. Prescriptivists talking about language use in Britain often refer to a very general 'Golden Era' where the population was able to read, write and talk 'correctly'. The suggested dates are always rather vague but have been put by some linguists, James Millroy for example, at between 1944–1965, after the introduction of the 1944 Education Act which legislated for universal secondary education in Britain.

This 'Golden Era' of supposedly correct English speaking is sometimes also commented on in other English-speaking areas of the world, such as Singapore where the government promotes the values of English over the Singlish local dialect.

A **descriptivist** viewpoint observes and describes the linguistic world as it is, without preconceived ideas about how it ought to be. In this view, there is no single 'right' standard by which others are judged. Linguist Jean Aitcheson, for example, believes that language is continually developing and is not deteriorating because of generation change.

●●● **FURTHER RESEARCH**

1 The following linguists have researched extensively about language change and many later studies have been based on their work:
- James Millroy
- Peter Trudgill
- Jean Aitchison
- Guy Deutscher
- Harry Harlow.

Find out more about one or more of these and their contribution to the study and understanding of language change.

2 Search online for and read the article 'Children Can't Speak or Write Properly Anymore' by James Millroy (**aggslanguage.wordpress.com**). Examine the claims of prescriptivists that there is a general decline in the standards of written and spoken English.

The idea that the rules of English grammar are laid down and must be followed at all times has given way in recent years to the concept of appropriateness and differing **registers** of language use. (As you know, register is a variety of language appropriate for use in a particular setting.) There are many different contexts for language use, but we can identify the following main categories:

- **formal:** where recognised, Standard English is followed in both speech and writing
- **colloquial (or casual):** the everyday language of discourse; the register used by friends and the more informal media
- **slang and non-standard:** situations which demand that a more basic and very informal variety of language is used; slang is used much more widely in spoken than in written language
- **frozen language:** language which is unchanging and generally full of **archaisms** (words and phrases used in earlier times but no longer in use).

193

ACTIVITY 5.16

Using the four broad divisions given above, consider what type of language register would be most appropriate for the following situations. Give reasons for your opinion.

- the American Declaration of Independence
- two friends meeting in a café
- an English Language text book
- New Zealanders watching their national rugby team, the All Blacks, play Australia
- a recipe
- a music video
- a technical training manual
- a TV game show
- a marriage ceremony
- teenagers on a social networking site
- a Bollywood movie
- a job interview

Language change

The context of any discourse determines the style of language used and therefore it is evident that language must change with society. English is a vibrant and dynamic language which has changed, spread and adapted to cultural variations. However, an apparent deterioration in speech, writing and general literacy, particularly in the digital age, is a cause for concern amongst some groups, including educationalists. Will English break down until it is incomprehensible?

Others are more optimistic and see a language which changes according to the needs of its speakers. This is a more democratic process as language belongs to those who use it and languages die if they fail to serve the needs of those who speak them.

All languages change constantly with a steady stream of new words appearing as others drop out. Pronunciation changes too, so that it is only when we hear a speaker from the past, even the recent past, they strike us as 'old-fashioned'. The *Oxford English Dictionary*'s 2013 Word of the Year was *selfie* which, with the advent of social networking, is now used worldwide. We can look forward to many more new words being added to the dictionary in the future.

In addition to the introduction of new words, the meaning of existing words can change and four major trends have been identified:

- **pejoration**, in which a term acquires a negative association. The word *silly* is a example of pejoration. In early Middle English (around 1200), *sely* (as the word was then spelled) meant 'happy, blissful, blessed, fortunate' as it did in Old English.
- **amelioration**, in which a term acquires a positive association. For example, the word *nice* when it first appeared in Middle English (about 1200) meant 'foolish, silly, simple, ignorant, senseless, absurd'.
- **widening**, in which a term acquires a broader meaning The modern English word *dog* derives from the earlier *dogge*, which was originally a particularly powerful breed of dog.
- **narrowing**, in which a term acquires a narrower meaning. The old English *mete* (meat) originally meant any sort of food, but has now narrowed to refer to food of an animal origin.

Reasons for language change

- **Technology:** new words are coined for new processes and changes. Equally words disappear as the things that they are describing fall out of use.
- **Geography:** landscapes, flora and fauna require naming and these words become part of regional dialect. For example English immigrants to Australia coined *outback* and *bush* as words describing particular features of the landscape in that country.
- **Social conditions:** a whole range of economic, social (including gender), ethnic and age changes require words to support new conditions
- **Increasing specialisation:** requires a body of language to support it – for example in law, medicine and the media
- **International travel and contacts:** mean that vocabulary becomes international; food is a good example here as we are becoming increasingly globalised in our tastes
- **Changing communities:** influence changes in language.

195

ACTIVITY 5.17

1 Select one area of technology and list as many new words and phrases that you can think of that are related to it. Try to establish how these words have developed, for example some may have derived from Latin words such as *video*.

2 The following words were once in common use but have now almost disappeared. Explain the meaning of each:

betwixt	naught	whither	wrought	ye	yore
forsooth	verily				

ACTIVITY 5.18

Read the article on slang.

- What are the functions of slang?
- Why does slang keep changing?
- Give some examples of specific words or phrases to show how slang originates and becomes dated.

Slang

Slang is unusual, direct, sometimes offensive language which is not regarded as standard. It may not be considered polite and may feature words or phrases concerned with sexuality and bodily functions. Slang words are always changing and can become dated very quickly. Slang also acts as an identity marker for groups – as we know, language is used to include and exclude people from different social groups.

The Joy of Slang

Slang such as ain't, innit and coz has been banned from a school in south London. The following paragraph is an extract from author Charles Nevin and emphasises how speedily fashionable slang phrases die out even if they are later reinvented. Please do not misunderstand me. I love modern slang. It's as colourful, clever, and disguised from outsiders as slang ever was and is supposed to be. Take 'bare', for example, one of a number of slang terms recently banned by a London school. It means 'a lot of', as in 'there's bare people here', and is the classic concealing reversal of the accepted meaning that you also find in 'wicked', 'bad' and 'cool'. Victorian criminals did essentially the same with back slang, reversing words so that boy became 'yob' and so on.

www.bbc.co.uk

*Regarding **Australian slang**, a TripAdvisor traveller article says:*

Be prepared and know the slang so you won't look like a drongo.

Colloquial Australian English was once very distinctive, however, in recent times it has adopted many Americanisms and British slang. That said, there are still many phrases and words that are uniquely Aussie. Travellers should note that Australians use many words in day-to-day speech which may be considered profanities in other parts of the world.

Indian slang has caught the attention of the *Indian Times*:

SLANGING CATCH: Mind Your Language

I blurted out an 's' word as an expression of instantaneous disgust after the lights went out one day. To my horror, my little girl picked it up. That made me realise how much care we should take with our language, particularly when speaking in front of children. Having said that, it is difficult to put paid to the use of four-letter words, because slang, curses and obscenities have immense therapeutic value for venting our pent-up rage and disillusionment.

timesofindia.indiatimes.com

TIP
Find examples of Standard and non-standard English from your own region that you can use as examples. This topic benefits from specific case studies rather than broad generalisations.

Teenage language is widely perceived to be full of slang, which changes very rapidly. Teenagers are early adopters of new forms which can become instantly global. However, many slang phrases are local and act as a badge of identity for the group who uses them.

ACTIVITY 5.19

1. Should we be concerned about teenagers' use of slang? Give reasons for your answer.
2. Explain why slang words and phrases are continually changing. Give some examples of your current local slang and try to find the origins of some of the words and phrases used.

"That's like, so random!"

www.CartoonStock.com

TIP

The boundaries between colloquialisms, slang and 'bad language' can be blurred. Make sure that you know the difference between these, but be careful not to offend or shock people when you carry out research on people's views on what constitutes bad language.

⦁⦁⦁ FURTHER RESEARCH

Research other Shakespearean insults and curses. Here are two for you to start with:

Thou art as loathsome as a toad. (Troilus and Cressida)

Thou clay-brained guts, thou knotty-pated fool, [...] obscene, greasy tallow-catch! (Henry IV Part I)

Slang and bad language

What is forbidden can sometimes be tempting and this is the same with language. What is considered 'bad', insulting or forbidden language is purely a guideline adopted by those within a particular group or community.

Here are some points to remember when considering 'bad' language:

- Most cultures have some form of insult; the Romans are said to have had 800!
- Insults and 'bad' language are most often focused on: bodily parts and functions; that which is forbidden; and also the sacred, which refers to the religion of the group.
- Shakespeare used some very interesting-sounding insults. In *Romeo and Juliet* Lord Capulet, in a furious temper that his daughter Juliet is disobeying him, calls her *you green sickness carrion ... you baggage ... you carrion.*
- Slang originating in one area can spread rapidly: the following slang phrases originated in New York City but have spread throughout the United States and beyond: *schlep* (a tedious trip), *bagel and a schmear* (bagel and cream cheese), *uptown* (travelling north in New York City), *wavy* (good), *bananas* (crazy). Here are some more examples of slang words that have come into English from around the world: *chai, hooch, arvo.* Are these words known in your region?

As with slang, insults change with social values. Fifty years ago, Britain was much more sensitive to insults using religious terminology, but used many racial terms which are not tolerated now. Your own society may have experienced similar changes. As we have established, language is closely related to social values.

You are unlikely to be asked to write exclusively about bad language and slang but you need to be able to discuss those areas of language which, for whatever reason, are not considered acceptable. It is worth remembering that most of these words and phrases will slip quietly out of usage, to be studied with interest by future English language students!

Jargon

Jargon is another form of non-standard English because it is often not part of mainstream usage. It relates most frequently to technical words and phrases used by specialist groups, or by professionals such as doctors and lawyers. In some extreme cases it may become almost unintelligible, and examples of wordy government documents often make the headlines. However, jargon can be similar to slang, in that it is restricted to a certain group where its use ensures mutual and precise understanding between group members.

197

ACTIVITY 5.20

1 Select a group, for example doctors, teachers, lawyers or online gamers, and research some terms which they might use when communicating with members of their own group.

2 Select a group to which you belong – either formally or informally – and think of jargon which you share with other members of that group. Evaluate the role of jargon in communication amongst your group members.

3 What might be the impact of hearing jargon on those outside the group?

Speech sounds and accents

The huge number of sounds that you produce during the course of a day are almost all used in the production of speech. You can cough, giggle, snort and laugh but you are constantly re-forming your speech organs to communicate with others through language.

You will know the basic information about the alphabet and the sounds associated with each letter, and this is relevant here as it adds information about the sounds of the **accents** used in our speech.

English is spoken in very many different ways and these variations in speech produce a variety of accents. In many parts of the English-speaking world, the accent spoken is closely associated with social class and prestige. Read the following results from a newspaper survey of the importance of accent to people in Britain:

- one in five people change their accent to sound more posh, to get a job or to chat someone up
- eight per cent of Britons have made themselves sound more posh
- four per cent have tried to make themselves sound less posh
- reasons for changing accent include job interviews or to be understood.

www.dailymail.co.uk

Speech sound production

Speech is the primary medium of language. Speech sounds are produced as we breathe out. The column of air that we exhale is modified as it passes from the lungs, out past the glottis in the throat, through the mouth or nose; it is given voice (noise) by the vocal chords in the glottis; and individual sounds are shaped by the mouth and the tongue.

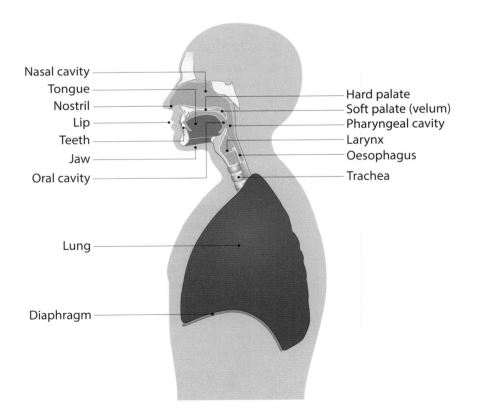

The parts of the human anatomy used for speech production.

- **Vowels** are sounds made with no restriction of air through the mouth; the different sounds are formed by the shape made by the mouth.
- **Consonants** are sounds made with some restriction to the airflow, for example by the tongue, teeth or lips.

There are 21 consonant letters in the written alphabet (B, C, D, F, G, H, J, K, L, M, N, P, Q, R, S, T, V, W, X, Y, Z), and there are 24 consonant sounds in most English accents … Because of the erratic history of English spelling, there is no neat one-to-one correlation between letters and sounds.

From *The Cambridge Encyclopedia of the English Language* by David Crystal.

Our alphabet has no single letter for spelling some consonant sounds, for example *ch* as in *chain* or *th* as in *thin* and *ng* as in *sing*.

The term *alphabet* comes from *alpha* and *beta*, the first two letters of the Greek alphabet.

The International Phonetic Alphabet

The purpose of the International Phonetic Alphabet is to provide a means of accurately transcribing the sounds of speech independent of any language. The IPA is used in some foreign language textbooks and phrase books to transcribe the sounds of languages which are written with non-Latin alphabets. It is also used by non-native speakers of English when learning to speak English. You will see that the symbols are not all recognisable letters, as in the English alphabet, and the symbols created can replicate the sounds which are not accurately represented by single letters.

TIP

The phonetic alphabet is invaluable in helping you to clarify the exact sounds of pronunciation, but you do not need to learn it. It is not examined specifically at A Level but it is important to know that this alphabet provides the definitive description of speech sounds and so is an important reference tool in spoken language.

iː READ	ɪ SIT	ʊ BOOK	uː TOO	ɪə HERE	eɪ DAY	
e MEN	ə AMERICA	ɜː WORD	ɔː SORT	ʊə TOUR	ɔɪ BOY	əʊ GO
æ CAT	ʌ BUT	ɑː PART	ɒ NOT	eə WEAR	aɪ MY	aʊ HOW
p PIG	b BED	t TIME	d DO	tʃ CHURCH	dʒ JUDGE	k KILO	g GO
f FIVE	v VERY	θ THINK	ð THE	s SIX	z ZOO	ʃ SHORT	ʒ CASUAL
m MILK	n NO	ŋ SING	h HELLO	l LIVE	r READ	w WINDOW	j YES

ACTIVITY 5.21

- Investigate the ways in which we produce the different consonant sounds of our voice.
- Select ten words and, with the help of the table above, write them out using the correct phonetic symbols. You could start by writing your name.
- Are there different accents in your class? Ask your fellow students to say the same word and use the IPA to show how it is pronounced Try to represent the sounds as precisely as possible.

199

LINK

Turn to page 166 in **Unit 4** to find out more about the prestige and status of different accents in English.

KEY TERMS

Received Pronunciation (RP) an accent in English which does not indicate a person's geographical location and which is recognised as having a high social status; RP is found throughout the English-speaking world

200

The sounds of speech – our accent

The means of voice production is universal in human beings. It is the sound, stress and intonation which produce the wide variety of accents in the English language.

Accent refers only to the way a word is pronounced and the huge variety in ways of speaking which exist in English. Apart from **Received Pronunciation (RP)**, accents may associate a person with a certain region. Received Pronunciation is a concept which originated in Britain and developed solely through reference to conditions existing in Britain although the accent can be spoken by anyone throughout the English-speaking world. RP itself is an accent with a high social status rather than being linked to a specific geographical location. If an accent is very different from RP it is said to be 'broad' and of a correspondingly lower status.

Accents change far more quickly over time than the spellings of written language, so many English words are not spelled in the way that they are pronounced. Nearly all students of English experience difficulties in spelling correctly as there are many irregularities and inconsistencies, for example:

- words with the same pronunciation are spelled differently, for example *write*, *right*, *rite*
- words with the same spelling are pronounced differently, for example *invalid*, *invalid*; *refuse*, *refuse*
- many words have silent letters, for example *climb*, *knight*, *ballet*
- words may diverge with the English/American system of spelling, for example *plough/plow*, *neighbour/neighbor*, *programme/program*.

Social accents

> *It is impossible for an Englishman to open his mouth without making some other Englishman hate or despise him.*

> English playwright George Bernard Shaw in the preface to his play *Pygmalion*.

Traditionally, in the UK, broader regional accents have been associated with lower socio- economic groups who have fewer formal qualifications. In previous generations, many people did not travel extensively and were therefore heavily influenced by their local culture and speech. Today globalisation has changed this situation as, throughout the world, higher socio- economic groups have professional jobs as a result of higher qualifications and are more mobile both geographically and socially. This generalisation is true for all areas of the world including English-speaking ones.

There is some debate about how far this situation has changed in recent generations but with a far greater ethnic mix and much wider travel for work and leisure, a greater mix of accents can now be heard in urban areas. In the English-speaking world there may still be perceived advantages in speaking RP and some people will consciously modify their accents to speak in this way for professional or social reasons. However, some have moved away from RP for a non-standard accent such as **Estuary English**, which has become widely established in the UK from its origins around the London area. A former British Prime Minister, Tony Blair, modified his accent in this way, possibly to make himself sound 'less posh' and to speak more like many of the electorate.

Research studies have shown that women are more likely to use standard pronunciation rather than their local accent. This is thought to be because in the past women's status was lower than men's and so speaking in Standard English

KEY TERMS

Estuary English a 20th century English accent which originated in the areas around the River Thames in London. It is a mixture of Received Pronunciation and London speech and is now found in many areas of the English-speaking world and is often spoken by younger people

helped them. With recent greater gender equality, this reason may not now be so valid. Educationalists in England have placed higher priority on speaking (and listening) in national English exams in an effort to make students aware of the situations when Standard English is appropriate.

The United States is said to have no prestige dialect though, in practice, the General American accent is more widely spoken in public forums than pronounced regional accents.

A recent phenomenon has been the association of certain accents with particular personal qualities. Business communication over the telephone from global call centres, for example, has given rise to stereotypes of the speakers with particular accents. For example the completely unfounded assumption that accents from rural areas indicate that the speaker is of low intelligence.

It is a particular feature of British English that status and accent are closely linked. The following article comments on the different perceptions of accents within Britain, based on recent research in the UK. Yorkshire is a large county in northern England, while *Brummie* is a slang term for a person from Birmingham, the UK's second largest city, in the midlands.

Yorkshire named top twang as Brummie brogue comes bottom

Silence could well be golden for ambitious Brummies after research found people with the distinctive nasal Birmingham accent were seen as stupid while those with a Yorkshire twang were considered clever.

The study into dialect and perceived intelligence found that people who said nothing at all were regarded as more intelligent than those with a Brummie accent.

This is despite a general trend in which regional dialects have become more respectable. The Yorkshire accent is rated as the most intelligent-sounding, beating Received Pronunciation, the accent of royalty and public school alumni, for the first time. [...] Times have changed since the days when received pronunciation, also known as the Queen's English, was seen as the language of the elite.

"Thirty years ago 10% of the population went to university," said Dr Workman who led the study. "If someone had RP you'd probably think they had gone to university. Today, 44% of young people go to university. I think there's been a shift in what we expect from somebody who is educated. There's been this change from elite education to mass education."

Workman added that while RP was once ubiquitous on the BBC, nowadays many broadcasters have regional accents. RP was now widely regarded as "dull and boring", he added.

www.theguardian.com

ACTIVITY 5.22

1 To what extent are you influenced in a positive or negative way by different accents? Can you explain why?

2 Discuss why different accents may have stereotypes attached to them.

3 A variety of English accents are now heard throughout English-speaking areas. Do you feel that there are differences in status amongst these accents? If so, what do you think has been the reason for these differences?

4 Read the following article and explain the reasons why Indian call centre workers are changing their accent. Do you agree with what they are being asked to do? Give reasons for your answer.

Accent neutralisation and a crisis of identity in India's call centres

The demand for a neutral global accent in the call centre industry is seeing Indian workers stripped of their mother tongue.

Initially, workers in the Indian call centre industry were trained in specifically American and British accents, but the preference is increasingly toward a "neutral" global accent, as it allows workers to be shifted around to serve various markets without additional training.

The demand for globalised speech has led to the creation of specialised institutes for accent neutralisation. "Those with extremely good skills don't want to [work in call centres]," says Kiran Desai, a veteran accent trainer. "What you get is a lot of people who don't speak very well and aren't from the best schools" she adds, in a crisp British-Indian accent.

Schools do not concentrate on phonetics enough "and so they pick up sounds from their mother tongue. We teach them to get rid of mother-tongue influence [...]". The complete programme, Desai says, takes three to four weeks to take hold in places such as Bombay and Pune, but can last up to two to three months in the south.

For Desai, these are purely technical issues; she is adamant that these practices do not lead to a "loss of culture." [...] Yet Desai says, uncomprehendingly, that there is sometimes resistance to training: "They say, 'I'm an Indian and I speak fairly well. Why do I need to change?' I don't know why [they object]."

www.theguardian.com

Towards the middle of the 19th century, many members of the newly emergent middle class felt the need to shore up their status by taking elocution lessons, learning to speak in RP, to establish their position of respectability. Voice coaches still exist but are unlikely to instil the 'cut glass' tones of years ago.

The accents of English are changing, through the voices of the millions worldwide who speak the language with varying degrees of fluency. It is therefore likely that the status of these accents will vary and will affect the social fabric of the English-speaking community.

••• FURTHER RESEARCH

- What variety of English accents exists in your own region?
- Are there differences in status associated with these accents? Investigate how these differences have occurred.
- Are the accents in your region changing? Discuss whether you think they are influenced by global media?
- Find out more about 'accent neutralisation'. Where is it taking place and what reasons are suggested for it?

Theories and studies of social variation in language

This section further demonstrates the close relationship between ideas and language. Recent social changes have changed our attitudes towards different social groups. This has brought about a general tendency towards equality for all, irrespective of gender, ethnicity, age, sexual orientation and disability. This helps to ensure social progress and eliminate discriminatory treatment of people according to preconceived stereotypes. The use of language to avoid discrimination is often known as **political correctness**.

> **●●● FURTHER RESEARCH**
>
> Investigate ideas about political correctness. Identify specific examples in your own society and region.
>
> You may find the following link helpful:
> **http://aggslanguage.wordpress.com/the-impact-of-political-correctness-on-language-change/**

Political correctness and language links: the Sapir-Whorf hypothesis

An important link with language and political correctness is the idea that language can, in some way, affect the way we view the world and the people in it. Edward Sapir and Benjamin Lee Whorf developed their own hypothesis about this. They combined two related ideas:

- Language determines the way we think. The words we use, directly frame our thoughts. This is known as **linguistic determinism**.
- A weaker form of language determinism is that language is only a contributory influence on what we think. This is known as **linguistic relativism**.

One way of understanding this is to ask yourself whether you can only express your thoughts with the vocabulary you know; to what extent are you limited by it? For example, if you are prevented from using a word to describe someone in a particular way, then, according to the stronger theory, you will also change your thoughts about them. If the connection between language and thought is weak, then you will still find words to think about the person – you will not be directly limited.

If people believe members of other social groups to be inferior then they may use inappropriate or abusive language to express these thoughts.

Here are some recent examples of language changes which have reinforced greater social equality for various groups.

- **Gender** Traditional words for employment imply that only men can do certain jobs, for example *policeman*, *fireman*. These words have been neutralised to make them applicable to all – *police officer*, *firefighter*.
- **Comedy** Certain types of comedy are now not acceptable such as personal or derogatory comments at the expense of people's physical appearance, for example size and shape.

A female firefighter.

203

LINK

See opposite for more about the issues related to language and gender.

- **Ethnicity** Politically correct language combats many unpleasant racist slurs and insults. In the UK it is illegal to use racist language, gestures and acts.
- **Workplace changes** The increasing number of women in senior roles in workplaces throughout the world break down the assumption that the boss will always be a *he* and that the secretary or personal assistant will be a *she*.
- **Age** In Britain, it is illegal to discriminate in terms of age; this is usually taken to mean older people. There is anecdotal evidence that older women in particular are subject to discrimination in a broader context. Changing attitudes about ageing have made people aware of words that reinforce stereotypes (*decrepit*, *senile*) and the need to avoid mentioning age unless it is actually relevant. Terms like *elderly*, *aged*, *old* and *geriatric* are increasingly replaced by *older person*, *senior citizens* or *seniors*.
- **Disability** Laws against disability discrimination aim to remove the belief that people are defined by their disability. The term *handicapped* has generally been replaced by the term *disabled*. A United States Government Paper states that the term *disabled* is less desirable than *people with disabilities* because the former implies that a person's disability is the whole person rather than just one of many personal characteristics. In Australia, the government-led National Disability Strategy has as one of its core principles the inclusion and participation in everyday life for people living with a disability.
- **Religious beliefs** are respected in language usage. In a multi-faith society for example the term *Christian name* does not apply to all religions and so would be replaced by *first name* or *personal name*.

Political correctness has worthy intentions but some PC language has been subjected to ridicule for its excess and exceptionally sensitive phrasing. The term itself now has negative connotations. Many extreme examples appear to attempt to allow for all group sensitivities. For example, it has been suggested that the city Manchester should change its name to 'Personchester', while a person without hair should be referred to as 'follicly challenged'.

There are concerns that policing and controlling language brings the denial of some freedoms of speech and the accusation that certain powerful groups are adopting dictatorial methods. However, if people are brought up to treat others respectfully, then hopefully this will bring about a more tolerant society.

ACTIVITY 5.23

1 Assess the extent of political correctness in the country where you live. Which groups benefit?
2 Discuss the criticism that overuse of politically correct language threatens freedom of speech.
3 Give a politically correct alternative for each of the following and explain why the original word may be considered unacceptable:
   - lady doctor
   - air hostess
   - one-man show
   - a short fat man
   - man-made.

4 *The struggle to be 'politically correct' has made people impatient and oversensitive to what they and others say. It has created a society that walks on eggshells and that has problems talking to each other for fear of causing offence.*

How far do you agree or disagree with this statement?

Language and gender

Gender and language is a complex subject which covers a range of issues concerning the language referring to males and females as well as perceived differences in the language used by each gender.

As in other areas of language study, gender issues are part of the cultural fabric. In 1963 a United States Federal Law enshrined the rule of equal pay for equal work. Other societies have followed suit. Before that, women were automatically paid less and for long periods in history, girls grew up with many more restrictions on their educational and career prospects than boys. In many societies today, equal opportunities are enshrined in law.

There are very specific and traditional contrasts of language used to describe male and female and the lack of parity between them. Examples include *master* and *mistress*, *hen* and *rooster*, *actor* and *actress*. Associated with this use of language has been the grammatical maxim that males dominate in writing thus always the reference to *he* before *she*; the male gender name being used as the norm (as in *mankind*); and the pronoun *he* being applied to both genders.

ACTIVITY 5.24

Interview a woman from an older generation, perhaps a relative or friend or a member of your local community. Ask them about their memories of language specific to females and to what extent they feel this has changed.

Differences in the language used by males and females

Traditionally there has been an assumption that males and females hold different types of conversation. There has been a stereotype that women are passive listeners whose lightweight discourse is described as mere *gossip*, while men have been thought to deal with more weighty and serious matters in debate and discussion.

There is also a contrast of input from males and females. Men are seen to interrupt and to 'hold the conversational' floor more than women and this perception has led to some interesting experiments in measuring the extent of equality in conversation between the genders.

The assumptions of this theory are largely taken from a mid 1970s study of a small sample of conversations, recorded by Don Zimmerman and Candace West at the Santa Barbara campus of the University of California. The subjects of the recording were white, middle-class and under 35. Zimmerman and West produce 31 segments of conversation in evidence. They report that in 11 conversations between men and women, men used 46 interruptions, but women only 2.

Changes over time as well as cultural changes would suggest a different outcome in the early part of the 21st century.

The perceived dominance of males in mixed communities has been of great concern in many educational institutions. There is a the continuing debate about the benefits of single-sex education and, even where the genders are mixed, high schools have experimented in separating some curriculum subjects, particularly the sciences, by gender. Increasingly, in societies where the genders and ethnic groups are approaching equality, the stereotype of male dominance can be seen as outdated.

Differences in language and gender in the globalised world of computer-mediated communication (CMC) have produced research to claim that women use an online language style typified by friendliness and a lack of hostility; this contrasts with the men who use an online language style typified by hostility and sarcasm. Other studies however, claim that women use the hostile language typically associated with the male online language style and that women are more aggressive users of language than men in CMC.

●●● FURTHER RESEARCH

The following is a link to research on females and computer-mediated communication:

http://www.academia.edu/3756954/The_Language_Style_of_Women_in_ Computer-Mediated_Communication_A_Content_Analysis_of_Gendered_ Language_in_Facebook

This is only one of a number of studies which you may wish to investigate where increasingly fluid gender roles are breaking down the traditional stereotypes described in this section. This study reflects a contemporary pattern of gendered communication styles.

Male and female conversation

Consider some of the vocabulary used to describe the ways in which people speak: *debate, chat, gossip, discuss, converse, communicate*. Sometimes different vocabulary has been stereotypically applied to the conversational styles of men and women. You may be familiar with anecdotal stereotypes about the quality and quantity of female language. In this section you will focus on the contrasts in language and information which studies have revealed.

One of the more extreme and unpleasant historical images of gossiping women is that of the *tricoteuses* – the French market women who sat knitting and gossiping around the guillotine as members of the French aristocracy were being executed during the French Revolution. Social Psychologists suggest that gossip is an evolutionary strategy to forge friendships and also to keep abreast of observed activities which may have provided an advantage in an uncertain world. As such gossip would be of equal advantage to both men and women.

Researchers have found that men gossip just as much as women and men were found to be no more likely than women to discuss 'weighty' and important matters such as the state of the economy and the meaning of life, except when women are present. Gossip in single-sex conversations takes up roughly the same amount of time with one very interesting difference – that men talk about themselves a lot more than women do!

Research studies have shown the following characteristics of male and female language:

- Men are less likely to give supportive feedback such as *really*, *yeah* and *mm*, and are less likely to cooperate in turn-taking.
- Women's conversation is the reverse: in summary, they tend to be conversationally more cooperative, giving feedback, using tag questions, and using modal verbs more frequently to suggest possibilities or alternatives for discussion, whereas men tend to use assertions and commands.
- Women tend to do the 'hard work' in keeping a conversation going by asking questions and continuing conversations. Robin Lakoff (1975) identified the 'politeness principle' in women's conversation: women use politeness strategies more frequently, such as *please* and *thanks*.
- There is evidence that the vocabulary choices of women tend to be more evaluative and descriptive (e.g. *lovely*, *wonderful*, *delightful*) as well as showing increased use of adverbs of degree to embellish what is being said (e.g. *very*, *really*).
- Traditionally men's language has been considered coarser than women's. Women consistently use more standard forms of language while men are more likely to use grammatically incorrect forms.

Deborah Tannen's research

Deborah Tannen is a distinguished American academic of in the field of language. She has written extensively on the gender differences in the conversational style of men and women. Her findings are closely linked to the status and roles of the participants in the Western societies where she has carried out her research. Tannen's work was a development of earlier studies by John Gumperz who examined differences of speech styles in different cultures. Tannen considered gender differences in a similar light.

Tannen contrasts the discourse style of men and women in Western societies using the following styles. She attributes the first characteristic in each pair as male and the second as female:

- status vs support
- independence vs intimacy
- advice vs understanding
- information vs feelings
- orders vs proposals
- conflict vs compromise.

ACTIVITY 5.25

1   Look at Deborah Tannen's list of contrasting discourse styles and think of specific examples to match each descriptor.
2   You may live in a very different society to that researched by Tannen. Using the descriptors given above, discuss, with evidence, how far these labels apply in the region where you live. Investigate whether any research

has been done to answer this. You might want to set up a controlled experiment of your own.

3 Take extracts from social media sites to test to what extent the claims of contrasting language styles of the assumed gender of the participants conforms to Tannen's research findings listed above.

4 Do you recognise these gender distinctions in conversation from your own experience? Discuss with other members of the class. If you perceive big differences, can you explain why?

5 Listen to unscripted and scripted conversations and assess to what extent you observe the patterns from Tannen's research results.

6 Listen and watch a range of radio and TV shows including the relatively unscripted talk shows. In what ways do these conversations follow a similar pattern?

• • • FURTHER RESEARCH

Results from research studies have been briefly outlined in this section. Investigate more closely an area of research which interests you and report on your findings.

Traditionally, girls have been brought up to be much more compliant than boys; in the past, a girl who engaged in a great deal of physical activity was labelled a *tomboy* and this more conformist attitude extended to speech. Females are almost universally responsible for childrearing and are expected to display a model of correct behaviour to their children; this includes speech and conversational patterns.

All of the above paints rather a dismal picture of inarticulate male speech, which is clearly not the case. In fact, more recent studies have not shown the expected degree of difference between men and women, with many adolescent girls using non-standard language as well as a level of assertiveness traditionally associated with male language. Men too may not need to display such domineering conversational practice as the changing gender roles in society lead to greater equality in language.

ACTIVITY 5.26

Social changes are taking place for males and females in all parts of the world. Discuss how far these changes might affect male and female language.

ACTIVITY 5.27

Analyse the transcript below with particular reference to features of discourse. Can you observe any characteristics relevant to gender?

Context and participants: Madeline (M) and Alastair (A) are an engaged couple in their late 20s. This is an extract from their conversation with Madeline's cousin, Freya (F). They have not seen Freya for nearly two years, and they are chatting to her about the details of how they met and their wedding plans.

F   it's so good to see you two (.) you both look so happy (.) well (1) really happy and I'm so glad we have finally got to meet up before the wedding (.) how long till you get married (.) I'm so pleased to be coming//

M   // well not long really is it Al (.) three months (.) and five days(.) er (.) four days actually (.) it's on Jan 26th (.) am so excited (.) can't wait-//

A   is it that close (.) well yes um (.) should be great fun in.. (.) a winter wedding in Wales (.) we could get snowed in//

M	// us and all our guests (.) that would make for a different wedding (laughs) but (.)//
A	// we love the country house where we're having the ceremony (.) the people are fab (.) really helpful and there will be big fires burning so we'll be cosy if it snows (.) a real white wedding and//
F	// Why January (.) it could be freezing (.) you could be snowed in (.) well (worse.) nobody could get there (.) sorry to sound a bit negative (.) but//
M	// well (.) you know (.) I thought that a winter wedding would be good because nobody will expect good weather and (.) so if it's a sunny day that's a bonus but (.) you know (.) it could rain even in summer (.) so it's going to be awesome and I'm so glad you'll be there with Auntie Debra (.) I can't imagine why we haven't seen each other for ages (.) I think I'd only just met Al hadn't I (.) I mean when I last saw you (.) yes because you were going travelling around India with your two friends from uni (.) Auntie Debra told me you had an awesome time with only a few adventures and problems (.) what was it like (.) did you want to stay longer (.) I heard you cut it short//
F	that's a long story (.) I'll tell you about that later (.) but you tell me about how you guys met (.) well I sort of know but fill me in (.) I did meet you at mum's fiftieth party Al (.) but I was in charge of food and (.) do you remember I had to make a speech (.) scary that (.) so we didn't get to talk or anything so I don't know all the details (.) it was when you were both working in the theatre (.) right
M	You've got a good memory (.) yes it was so funny because I was stage managing the show (.) and Al and I used to talk back stage and then he asked me out for dinner (.) and it was so nice 'cos we had a lot in common- well the theatre and performing for a start(.)//
A	(*laughs*) // yes well (.) she was a bit bossy back stage (.) she even made a point about me on a show report that I had missed an entrance (.) in Act II one evening but I've forgiven her (1) I think (.) *laughs*(.) so let's say (.) it went on from there and we've been (.) um sorta (.) able to get jobs together and now I'm in TV production (.) so we're in one place and//
M	// and I've been able to get a job in the Arts Centre (.) which I'm so pleased about (.) and then (.) well we both knew we wanted to be together and (.) Al asked me to marry him
F	Aah (.) that's so cool (.) I'm so pleased for you both and I'm even more pleased to be coming to the wedding (.) will it be a big wedding (.) will all the family be coming(.)
A	Think everyone we've asked has said yes (.) so it'll be a great big get together (.) friends and family (.) Anne and Charlie are coming across from Canada (.) and my godmother, Carol, is aiming to get here from Sydney
M	it will be such a fantastic time and (.) special (.) really special.

209

Further practice

For essay writing practice, attempt one or both of the following suggested titles.

1 With reference to specific examples explain how political correctness in the treatment of specific groups has affected language.

2 With reference to specific examples from your broader knowledge of all areas covering the language of political correctness, discuss your response to the extract below.

> 'Ladies' and 'gentlemen.' Please avoid such words. Heavens, don't call her a lady. And forget about 'gentleman,' 'history,' 'chairman,' 'manmade,' 'Mrs.,' 'normal couple' and 'postman' – along with 32 other terms. They have all been deemed 'unacceptable language' by the exquisitely sensitive folks at Stockport College in northwestern England and banned from the campus.

> http://www.lawandliberty.org/eng_spch.htm

Dialect, sociolect and idiolect

These three terms relate to the sub-divisions of a language according to the different groups who speak it.

- **Dialect** is a particular form of language which is peculiar to a specific region.
- **Sociolect** is the dialect of a particular class or group.
- **Idiolect** is the speech habit of an individual; the words and phrases they choose.

Dialect

Most importantly in English, however broad the dialect, it is comprehensible to other English speakers; all dialects are generally understandable but the accent in which they are spoken may limit some understanding for those who are unfamiliar with the speech style.

It is very easy to confuse the meaning of **accent** and **dialect**. Accent refers only to the *pronunciation* of speech while the meaning of dialect broadens to include specific words and phrases and the order in which they are spoken. Standard English is a form of dialect which has no regional connection. It originated as the recognised form of English and quickly became associated with status and education, the prestige variety of English which is also discussed in the Global English section.

Unless there is a physical boundary such as a range of mountains, the boundaries between different dialects and accents can be blurred. Linguists use language maps with lines known as **isogloss** to locate the general boundaries between one type of accent or dialect and another. An example of accent differences in the United States appears below.

Since dialects and accents are closely linked, the same questions of status operate. The more geographically remote the dialect group, the less that community will be influenced by incomers. Melvin Bragg, a British writer and broadcaster, describes the local dialect of Cumbria, in the north-west of England, where he grew up many years ago, as using *thee* and *thou*; a horse was a *grey* and a good horse was a *baary grey*. The pronunciation was also distinctive: *rrreet* for *right* in an accent which Bragg feels was broad and 'could appear coarse'. Bragg comments directly on the level of prestige given to this dialect.

KEY TERMS

isogloss a geographic boundary delimiting the use of a local term

TIP

Make sure you do not confuse **dialect** with **accent**. Although they are often used together, accent refers to the *sound* of the language – the way it is pronounced.

A *scorrie* is a Scottish term for a seagull.

ACTIVITY 5.28

The following are dialect words and phrases which may be spoken by people from the following countries. You may be familiar with some of them! Try to match each word or phrase to the correct country.

- South Africa
- Australia
- India
- the United States
- New Zealand
- Scotland

anti	billy	wee	brumby	biltong yabber
crib/bach	scorrie	half pie	dorpie	threads
dandle	goof around	hokey pokey	lekker	Bollywood
chota	chai	billfold	boomer	

British dialects

Many dialects exist throughout the English-speaking world but this section focuses on British English dialect characteristics.

The United Kingdom is well known for its many local dialects; someone from the city of Nottingham, in the English Midlands, will have a slightly different dialect to someone from Derby, another city just twelve miles away. The main dialects in England are spoken in the following regions:

- the South-West
- Wales
- the Midlands
- the South
- the East
- the North
- Scotland.

Those of you who live in Britain will be aware that there are many different dialects within each region. Whatever differences exist within a region, these are not as great as the dialect differences between regions. For example, a Northern dialect is significantly different from a Welsh dialect.

Dialect in the USA

Look at the map of the dialect regions of the USA, where similar regional variation exists to that in Britain, although the area covered by each dialect is more extensive than in Britain.

Even with a relatively simplified map, you can see that there is a greater diversity of accents along the eastern seaboard and within these accents there exist more localised dialects; one of the most notable is the dialect spoken in New York City. The same historical processes are at work in the USA as elsewhere in the English-speaking world. Settlers from Britain were concerned to imitate speech that was then considered to be of high prestige. These accents subsequently changed. Settlers arrived later in the west and were not as closely connected to England and generally did not imitate English speech patterns to the same degree.

General American (GA) is a major accent in American English, also known as Standard American English (SAE) and is often the preferred way of speaking in films, on TV. It is the accent most commonly used by politicians. Like the use of Standard English in Britain, GA is not spoken by everyone in the United States, but it is a widely taught form of English in other parts of the world. **African American Vernacular English** (AAVE) within the USA contains many distinctive forms, but there are also many regional variations within this dialect.

● ● ● **FURTHER RESEARCH**

Carry out your own research to find out more about the regional variations in **African American Vernacular English** within the United States. Consider differences in pronunciation and grammatical construction.

212

Map of USA dialects.

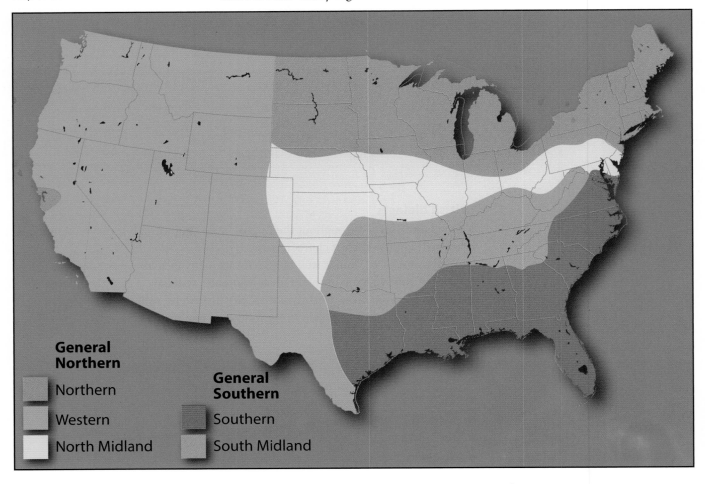

General Northern

- Northern
- Western
- North Midland

General Southern

- Southern
- South Midland

Here are some examples of USA regional dialect words:

- *faucet* (northern), *spigot* (southern)
- *frying pan* (Northern and Southern, but not Midland), *skillet* (Midland, Gulf States)
- *clapboard* (chiefly North-east) and *weatherboard* (Midland and Southern)
- *gutter* (North-east, Southern), *eaves trough* (inland Northern, Western), *rainspouting* (chiefly Maryland and Pennsylvania)
- *teeter-totter* (widespread), *seesaw* (Southern and Midland), *dandle* (Rhode Island)
- *pail* (Northern, North midland), *bucket* (Midland and Southern).

And from New York City:

- *punchball* – a baseball-like game suitable for smaller areas, in which a fist substitutes for the bat and the ball is a *spaldeen*
- *scallion* – spring onion
- *stoop* – a small porch or steps in front of a building, originally from Dutch

ACTIVITY 5.29

Try to work out from the context what the following British English dialect phrases mean.

- [*Mother to child aged two*] Are you sad? Come and *cwtch* with mummy. [Wales]
- He's delayed, he won't be here *while* tea time [Yorkshire/Northern]
- He *do go* there tomorrow; he has to clear out the weeds in the *dyke*. [Norfolk, Eastern]
- She's just a *bairn* – she didn't mean to break the teapot. [Scottish]
- I'm so thirsty I just fancy a nice cup of *Rosie-Lee* [London Cockney]/*cup o' char* [Liverpool]
- *Eyup m'duck*, how are you this morning? [Derbyshire/Northern]
- Take that scowl off your face, you *mardy* child. [Midlands]
- Don't eat that raw lemon it'll *make your tabs laugh*. [Midlands]
- Light that fire, I'm *starved* in this temperature. [Northern]
- You've won the lottery? *Away on!* Northern Ireland]

Eye dialect

In order to give **verisimilitude** to conversations in literature, writers sometimes use **eye dialect** in speech and dialogue.

 KEY TERMS

verisimilitude the appearance of reality

eye dialect the deliberate use of misspellings to identify a speaker who is using a regional form of colloquial English

The following poem, by Jamaican poet Louise Bennett, is about Miss Mattie's strong desire to return to Africa and to her roots. It is written in eye dialect so you may not understand all of it. Read the poem carefully and then answer the questions.

Back to Africa

Back to Africa, Miss Mattie?
You no know wha you dah seh?
You haf fe come from somewhe fus
Before you go back deh!

Me know say dat you great great great
Granma was African,
But Mattie, doan you great great great
Granpa was Englishman?

Den you great granmader fader
By you fader side was Jew?
An you granpa by you mader side
Was Frenchie parlez-vous?

But de balance a you family,
You whole generation,
Oonoo all barn dung a Bun Grung-
Oonoo all is Jamaican!

Den is weh you gwine, Miss Mattie?
Oh, you view de countenance,
An between you an de Africans
Is great resemblance!

Ascorden to dat, all dem blue-yeye
White American
Who-fa great granpa was Englishman
Mus go back a Englan!

What a debil of a bump-an-bore,
Rig-jig an palam-pam
Ef de whole worl start fe go back
Whe dem great granpa come from!

Ef a hard time you dah run from
Tek you chance! But Mattie, do
Sure a whe you come from so you got
Somewhe fe come back to!

Go a foreign, seek you fortune,
But no tell nobody say
You dah go fe seek you homelan,
For a right deh so you deh!

Louise Bennett

ACTIVITY 5.30

1 The poem 'Back to Africa' is about the search for identity as a Jamaican. Discuss the importance of the eye dialect to the poem's themes.

2 Select four dialect words or phrases from the poem and describe the ways in which they differ from their Standard English equivalent.

3 What do you think is achieved by the poet by choosing to write in eye dialect?

4 Find examples of texts from your own region which are written in eye dialect and assess the extent to which they reflect the shades of the local dialect.

5 Many poems and novels use the eye dialect method. Select an extract from a poem or novel of your choice and then from that, select five eye dialect words or phrases. With the help of a dictionary of etymology, trace their meaning and origins.

> **TIP**
>
> **Etymology** is the study of the origin of words and the way in which their meanings have changed throughout history. There are online and hard copy dictionaries of etymology which can help you see how a word has arrived at its modern usage.

Read the following extract and discuss the likely future of regional dialects when influenced by the social media. Do regional dialects matter?

How regional dialects are spreading around the UK thanks to Facebook and Twitter

Age-old regional dialects from around the country are undergoing a resurgence and spreading like wildfire thanks to the likes of Twitter and Facebook. Language experts have found the increased speed at which people communicate on social networking sites means they are more likely to lapse into colloquialisms. And the rapid rise of social media and instant messaging in recent years has seen such regional phrases spread swiftly from one end of Britain to the other.

Now social media is having the same effect TV campaigns had in encouraging the spread of regional phrases

'But social changes such as the speed of modern communication mean they are spreading much faster than they would have.

'Twitter, Facebook and texting all encourage speed and immediacy of understanding, meaning users type as they speak, using slang, dialect respellings and colloquialisms.

'The result is we are all becoming exposed to words we may not have otherwise encountered, while absorbing them into everyday speech.'

Dr Eric Schleef, lecturer in English Sociolinguistics at The University of Manchester, said the UK's rich landscape of regional accents and dialects is evidence of society's continuity and change, local history and day-to-day lives.

As a result, the English language continues to evolve as a colourful and expressive language.

Norfolk – 'bootiful' (beautiful/great), 'bishey-barnee-bee' (ladybird), 'mardle' (talk), 'putting on parts' (misbehaving), 'squit' (rubbish)

Cornwall – 'andsome' (lovely/good - handsome without the 'h'), 'dreckly' as in 'directly' (I'll do it dreckly)

Liverpool – 'boss' (good), 'scran' (food), 'busies' (police)

Aberdeen – 'ken' (know), 'bairns' (babies)

Newcastle – 'canny/mint' (good), 'ket' (sweets), 'raggies' (chavs)

Manchester – 'mint' (v good), 'mardy' (moody)

Midlands – 'cob' (bread roll), 'pikelets' (crumpets), 'gitty' (alley)

Leeds – 'in a boo' (in a mood)

Hull – 'tret' (treat)

Southampton – 'nipper' (affectionate term, for anyone aged 0 to 100).

Glasgow – 'wean' (child), 'awayyego' (no way!), 'geeze' (give)

Wales – 'lush', 'tidy' (very nice, attractive)

London – 'pukka' , 'sick', 'bangin' (v good), 'wack' (rubbish), 'butters' (ugly)

Birmingham – 'taraabit' (goodbye), 'babby' (baby), 'donnies' (hands)

Bristol – 'gert lush' (very nice), 'keener' (someone who works too hard), 'mind' (do you know what I mean?)

Nottingham – 'gizza glegg/gizza gozz' (may I see that?), 'twitchell' (alleyway)

●●● **FURTHER RESEARCH**

Listening to the dialect(s) of your own region, and to speakers who use different dialects, will be of huge benefit to you in terms of collecting good case studies to reference in your work and in your exams.

ACTIVITY 5.31

Investigate how social media are changing the language of your region. Ask older members of your family or community about the language they used when they were younger and how they think it has changed.

Sociolect

Sociolect is a variety of language used by a particular social group which usually refers to age, occupation, gender, or ethnicity. Sociolect is easily confused with dialect but remember that dialect has a geographical basis whereas sociolect is socioeconomic.

The loose composition of sociolect groups means that they will naturally come into contact with other members of the community and so the practice of **code switching** occurs where people switch back and forth between two different styles of language.

The Tamil caste system in Sri Lanka have scholarly Brahmin members who use different vocabulary amongst themselves but switch codes when they speak to the non-Brahmin people. In the United States, African Americans may use African American Vernacular English also known as *Ebonics* amongst themselves (e.g. *If I don't get out my sister room I get in trouble*) but code switch to standard American English in different circumstances.

Code switching of sociolect groups is closely linked to language **registers**, where an appropriate style of English is needed to match the context. Sociolects are also linked with different social classes in many societies.

These have been discussed in previous sections and the following activities will help you to review what you have learned.

ACTIVITY 5.32

1   In British English the word *dinner* is often seen as part of a sociolect vocabulary depending on the time when the meal is eaten. Research this word and explain its links with social class.

2   In British English the descriptors for the sweet course at the end of a meal are variously known as *pudding, sweet, dessert, afters*. Linguists use this vocabulary choice as a sociolect variable. If you have access to various British English speakers, ask them which word they use and why.

3   Age groups may share a core of common vocabulary. Select a teenage interest group and compile a list of current words and phrases that they use regularly. Identify words and phrases now considered outdated. Do these words have more recent replacements?

4   Explain why occupational groups have a set of specific vocabulary and technical terms. Select an occupation group such as lawyers, or heavy metal music enthusiasts and list words and phrases they may use along with non-technical equivalents. Give the list to a non-specialist to test their understanding. Which terms did they find difficult, and why?

5   Gender groups may be included here. List five features often present in conversation between females. Explain why these may be absent when men are conversing.

6   Investigate the sociolect of a group you are familiar with. Assess the distinctiveness of their language. To what extent do members of other groups use the same sociolect?

Idiolect

Each of us has an **idiolect** which is our own personal language. This is made up of the words we choose and extends to our patterns of conversation – what we say and how we speak, for example our tone, speed and pitch. This springs from our own life experiences.

We alter our style of speech whenever we perceive it to be appropriate. You may have the benefits of speaking more than one language and be able to change between these languages according to circumstances, adding to the sophistication with which you use language on a daily basis.

ACTIVITY 5.33

Select a close friend and family member.

1. Listen to them speak as naturally as possible and try to describe the features that make their speech patterns unique.
2. Note their conversational style and their paralinguistic features. What additional descriptions have you added?
3. Now think about your own idiolect. Use the same analysis for your own style of speech as for your observations on other people. Compare your own perception of your idiolect with those that a friend has made about you.

LINK

For more practice and self-evaluation on this unit, see page 289.

Unit 6: English as a global language

Stop for a moment to think about what makes us human.

Language must be one of the most important factors, as everything we have ever achieved springs from us being able to communicate our wants and needs. In this unit we shall look at English as a global language which plays a significant role in the world communication necessary in the 21st century.

English and other languages

Many of us live in societies where English is either the native language or a second language. English has spread around the world to become a global language. It is the world's second largest language and the official language in about 70 countries.)

There are roughly 7000 languages spoken in the world, but 90% of these are spoken by fewer than 100,00 people. There are claims that 46 languages have only a single speaker! So where does English fit in? It is eclipsed only by Mandarin Chinese in terms of the actual number of speakers but English is spoken more widely round the planet than any other language.

English is spoken as a first or native language by around 375 million speakers in the world but speakers of English as a second language outnumber those who speak it as a first language. So English as a first *or* second language is spoken by approximately two billion people throughout the world. One in four of the world's population speaks English with some level of competence and the demand to learn English from the other three quarters is increasing.

ACTIVITY 6.1

In this set of activities you will learn about the geographical spread of widely spoken languages and also reflect on your use of English.

The world's most widely-spoken languages in order of the number of speakers are:

1 Mandarin Chinese
2 English
3 Spanish
4 Hindi
5 Arabic
6 Bengali
7 Russian
8 Portuguese
9 Japanese
10 German
11 French

1 Use an atlas to map the countries where the population speaks these languages, either as native (first) or second-language speakers.

2 Research the numbers of native and non-native speakers for the top five languages and any other languages in which you have a special interest. How do the numbers of native and non-native speakers for these languages compare?

3 List the languages you know of. How does this number compare with the estimate of the total global languages?

4 Which languages have you learned? Why? Which languages would you like to learn? What use might you make of new languages?

5 Are there any advantages in speaking more than one language?

6 Do you feel any differently towards people who speak the same language as you and those who speak another language? Give reasons for your answer.

The world's languages

If you have ever been a tourist visiting a country where you do not know the language, you will appreciate that, at the very least, the difficulties of communication between people who speak different languages can be very frustrating! On the other hand it is immensely rewarding to appreciate a society's way of life other than your own, by speaking their language fluently.

Language does not exist in a vacuum; the growth of different global languages often reflects both the geography and history of different speaking groups.

There have been many attempts to create a single worldwide language. The best known of these is Esperanto, with a current estimate of about 3 million speakers but it has failed to make a significant difference to the national languages of the world. Indeed it might be argued that the language spoken is part of a person's national identity. Many cultures have myths concerning the reason for the diversity of languages, for example the Tower of Babel.

KEY TERMS

Esperanto an artificial universal language

The Tower of Babel

This story is found in the Christian Bible, in the Book of Genesis, and gives one explanation for the many languages spoken across the globe. According to this story, the people of Shinar (Babylonia) decided to build a giant tower that would reach into heaven. It was an enormous enterprise, taking a long time and lots of cooperation among people who all spoke the same language. After a while, God disrupted the project. To make it impossible for the workers to communicate, he forced everyone to speak a different language.

LINK

For more about the different varieties of English, see page 235.

KEY TERMS

lingua franca a common language or form of communication which is used over and above local languages or dialects in order to allow communication between groups of people who speak different languages

ACTIVITY 6.2

Fewer than 100 languages are spoken in all of Europe west of Russia, but Africa and India have over 1000 native languages each; the small Pacific island nation of Vanuatu, with an area of less than 5000sq miles has 110 languages!

1 Would a universal language such as Esperanto put an end to these language variations? Explain the reasons for your answer.

2 Would you like to learn an artificial global language such as Esperanto? Why or why not?

3 Do you know of another myth explaining the diversity of languages in the world?

4 What reasons can you suggest for the existence of so many languages around the world? Why do you think the different languages are distributed in the way they are?

5 Should we aim for all people to have a common language? Would this help communication between different groups? Explain your point of view.

Language takeovers

Why does one language grow and another decline or even die out?

We have already established that the world spread of languages is dominated by relatively few languages which have a very large number of speakers. Many languages have already become extinct and languages are continuing to die as their last remaining native speakers die. It matters whether a language dies out because of the spoken traditions which may disappear along with it. As many (but not all) languages die out, their place is often taken by English. This takeover process is not a recent situation.

Throughout history there are examples of languages that have been widely spoken beyond their borders, becoming the *lingua franca*, particularly for the purposes of government. For example, Latin was used throughout the Roman Empire, and Spanish became the language of many Spanish colonies in Central and South America. It is not unusual for a language to spread beyond its native region, but what makes English unique is the many distinctive varieties that have developed from it.

In his book *The World Until Yesterday*, scientist Jared Diamond explains that world regions have repeatedly been swept by what he terms *language steamrollers*. This is a situation where one group which has some advantage of population, food supply or technology, uses that advantage to impose its language on the regions it takes over and exploits. It is a question of power. The language of the more powerful group replaces the local language(s) by driving out or killing its speakers or by forcing them to speak the incomer's language.

In the case of English, for example, the growth of its worldwide status is linked to Britain's naval and trading power which was so important in the growth of the British Empire and the colonisation of places like the Indian subcontinent, Southern Africa and Australasia. In the military and commercial activities that followed, native languages were often suppressed by British rulers. The arrival of British settlers in North America in the early 17th century was another significant stage in the development of English as a global language and by the end of the 18th century, English was the dominant language in North America.

ACTIVITY 6.3

1 Investigate the ways in which one or more of the following languages have 'steamrollered' others into minority language status or even extinction.
- Latin and the Roman Empire
- Norman French and the Norman conquest of England in 1066
- Spanish conquests of Central and South America in the 16th and 17th centuries
- French conquests in Asia, Africa and the Americas in the 17th and 18th centuries

2 Investigate the ways in which English displaced native languages in the countries which it colonised, for example New Zealand, the Indian subcontinent, Australia, Singapore, Southern Africa.

Like all living languages, English is changing all the time. The only languages that do not change are 'dead' ones such as Latin or Sanskrit. The English you speak is different from that of previous generations and English will continue to change in your lifetime. How? Some linguists predict that English will change in the same way as Latin, which evolved in different regions to become the core of the three distinct languages of French, Spanish and Italian. So if English followed this pattern, it would break up into related but separate languages.

Others predict that as we now live in a 'global village' with a constant flow of personal and media-generated English, the different varieties of English will converge and a common language will evolve. The following sections of this chapter will continue to investigate the issues surrounding the status of and changes to English as a global language.

ACTIVITY 6.4

These activities ask you to think about yourself as an English speaker in the world today.

1 What is your language status? Are you a native English-speaker or do you speak it as a second or third language? Describe the circumstances in which you use English.

2 How widely is English spoken where you live? What other languages co-exist with it?

3 What form of English do you speak? Do you think it is significantly different from Standard British English? If so, in what ways?

4 If many languages are spoken where you live, what is the function of English? For example is it used for official documents and occasions? Do you use English online? Do you hear it on TV, in films and in songs?

5 Are there languages which used to be spoken in your area but which are now spoken by fewer people? If so, why do you think this has happened? Do you think this language loss is important?

6 How important is it to you to speak English? Explain your reasons to others in a group debate.

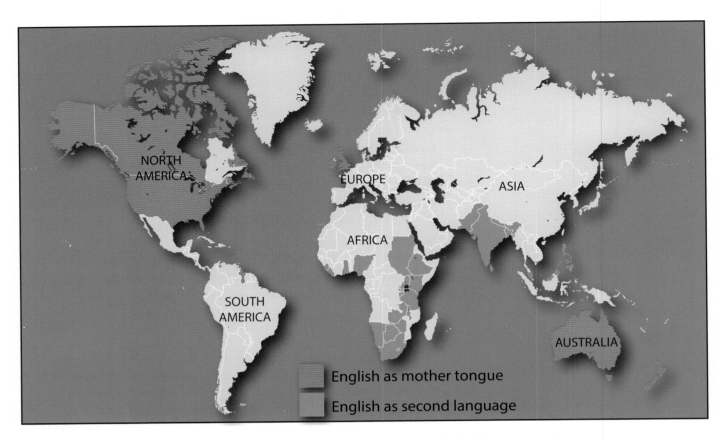

A map showing English-speaking regions of the world.

How did English become a global language?

This section summarises the evolution of the English language from its origins as a language spoken by Angles and Saxons, tribes in northern Germany, to a language which is spoken throughout the world. Your own country or region will be a good case study for the various issues to be discussed.

In its early history, English was not considered to have any status at all and was considered unworthy of use in any official capacity. The early development of British English was quite a struggle with little evidence of its worldwide importance today. 1500 years ago English did not exist. It was brought across to England as Anglo-Saxon by tribes from Northern Germany in a series of invasions after the Romans left Britain in 400 CE. The fledgling language came under further threat from repeated Viking invasions along the east coast of Scotland and England between 800 and 1000 CE. The Vikings did not speak Anglo-Saxon but a language called Old Norse. They gained power in the eastern areas of England and were spreading westwards until a victory by Alfred the Great in 878 saved the Anglo-Saxon language (which is also referred to as Old English).

After 1066, English disappeared as an official language for two hundred years as a result of the Norman Invasion of England led by William the Conqueror (William I). Norman French became the language of government while Anglo-Saxon was spoken by the peasant class. English re-emerged three hundred years later as a combination of the English and French spoken at the time.

Later, bitter battles were fought between the Church who wished to preserve Latin as the language of church services and the Bible, and those who wished to change to English. The latter group eventually won and the English language of the time became dominant in England. However, in the 16th century there were fewer than five million English speakers in the world.

As we have already seen, military and commercial power then launched English beyond its national borders. The British Empire's role in the spread of English was critically important for over 200 years. The international role of Britain declined during the 20th century but by then the language was sustained by the global spread of the predominantly English-speaking United States' economic, political and military influence, as well as the influence of the American media. More recently, with the dominance of English as the language of the internet, English continues to be at the forefront of significant global developments.

Linguist David Crystal believes that the reason why a language is widely used is because of the power of the people who speak it. He believes that *It's English turning up at the right time during these last four hundred years or so which has produced the enormous cultural status that it has.*

223

ACTIVITY 6.5

Read the extract and, as preparation for the next section, research the different varieties of English spoken throughout the world.

English is the dominant language of the internet.

The following is a light-hearted and very speedy summary of the development of English and raises the issues of the many varieties of English which are spoken. This leads us to consider the current status and power of English.

Global English – or whose language is it anyway?

In the 1500 years since the Romans left Britain the English language has shown a unique ability to absorb, evolve, invade and if we're honest, steal.

After foreign settlers got it started, it grew into a fully fledged language all of its own before leaving home and travelling the world, first by the high seas then via the high speed broadband connection pilfering words from over 350 languages and establishing itself as a global institution.

All this despite a written alphabet that bears no correlation to how it sounds and a highly irregular system of spelling.

Right now, about 1.5 billion people speak English: of these about a quarter are native speakers a quarter speak it as their second language and half are able to ask for directions to a local swimming pool.

There's Hinglish, Chinglish, Singlish ... so in conclusion the language has got so little to do with England these days it may well be time to stop calling it English and if someone does think up a new name for it, it should probably be in Chinese.

www.youtube.com

The status of English as a global language

This section provides some of the evidence for giving English the status of a language spoken throughout the world. Your own country or region will be a good case study to compare with the world statistics given here.

How can we assess the status of English as a global language?

Here are some key indicators:

- **the number of first language speakers must be high:** English is spoken as a first language by around 375 million and as a second language by around 750 million speakers in the world (*British Council figures*).
- **users must be spread over a wide geographical area:** English is spoken on all five continents.
- **political and economic affairs must be stable so that the language can spread without large-scale opposition:** English is the recognised language of trade, scientific research and international affairs. It is used by international organisations like the United Nations, by pilots and by air traffic controllers, by international traders and by international police agencies.

A further investigation of the importance of English throws up more evidence for its status as a global language. English can be understood almost everywhere as it is the predominant language of the world's media, and the language of cinema, TV, pop music and computer technology. All over the world, people know and use many words derived from English.

English is used for:

- three-quarters of the world's mail
- half of the world's technical and scientific journals
- half of all newspapers
- 80% of all information stored in computers
- all communications for international air and sea traffic
- many movies and songs
- half of European business deals
- seven of the largest TV broadcasters (CBS, NBC, ABC, BBC, CBC, CNN, C-Span).

Additionally there are many countries where English is an official second language and where it operates as the language of government, higher education, international communication, science, technology and the media.

English appears to have dominance as the international language but as we have seen, times change. At the end of the 20th century *The Economist* magazine described English as *impregnable, established as the world's standard language; an intrinsic part of the global communications revolution.* More recently however, it has been predicted that economic growth in the next 50 years is likely to come from non-English speaking countries in Asia, South America and the Pacific. These areas will start to generate wealth and ideas and these ideas will not necessarily be communicated in English. Education trends in many countries suggest that languages other than English are providing competition in the school curriculum.

Even at a local level, in Britain, the balance may be shifting. According to a recent report, there are 240 schools in England where over 90% of students do not speak English as a first language. In the academic year 2012–13, UK Department of Education figures revealed that five primary schools in England (out of a total of

ACTIVITY 6.6

1 Summarise the benefits outlined in the article of speaking English in a globalised world. Then discuss your views on the role of local languages in a globalised world.

2 Investigate the importance of English in the area where you live, and then evaluate the role of other local languages.

nearly 17,000) had no native English speakers, with 100% of their pupils speaking English as a second language.

The current status of English in the world is as a native language and also as a second language suitable for official functions where it is neutral and avoids favouring a particular regional dialect. Where English is used in conjunction with other languages, its use may indicate officialdom whereas the local languages function for friendship and informal communication. In countries where English is used as an official second language, the majority of the population is able to code switch when circumstances require it.

Global English

In the following sections you will explore the status of British English and the ways in which it has been transformed into many different varieties of English, each with its own particular characteristics.

Everyone talks about how English is the global language, but that means more than hearing occasional American pop songs on your local radio. English has become the global language because it has become a vital part of international society, culture and the economy. Whether you're aiming to be a professor or a reporter, a doctor or a banker, knowing English can give you what it takes to succeed.

It's become almost a cliché that speaking English well is a huge help in the business world, and it's increasingly true as international trade expands every year, bringing new countries into contact. Many of the best MBA programs are taught in English, so speaking it well can put you in a position to get the best training and credentials. With more and more companies being bought or merging with foreign firms, you never know if one day you might need to speak English to your new boss!

If your ambitions lie in science or medicine, you can't neglect English either. Much of the technical terminology is based on English words, and if you want to learn about the latest developments and discoveries from around the world, you'll read about them in journals and research reports published in English, no matter whether the scientists who wrote them are from China or Norway. And, of course, with good conversational English, you'll be able to mix at conferences and seminars.

English also opens doors in the academic world. Of course, if the best program in your field is in England or America, English will give you the opportunity to study with the top scholars. Many Western universities are becoming highly international, with visiting scholars, students and professors from all around the world, and their common working language is English. Attending international conferences and publishing in foreign journals are some of the key steps to success in academia.

Journalists and writers around the world are finding a good command of English to be an increasingly useful skill. Even if you're writing your articles and doing interviews in your own language, with good English you can get background material from international wire services and papers and magazines from around the world. You can interview foreign businessmen, diplomats and maybe even get sent to cover overseas stories.

www.englishtown.com

TIP

You need to be very clear about the significance of English amongst the world's languages, with evidence to support your statements.

When writing essays it is important to be able to summarise complex ideas and processes. The way in which English has become a global language is complex so try to select important reasons with evidence.

225

ACTIVITY 6.7

1 Research details of military, industrial, financial and cultural events where the English language has assumed an important role.

2 English and the internet: discuss with your fellow students the language(s) you use on the internet. Try to assess the types of websites which are in English and whether websites in other languages provide translation facilities.

3 Given that the internet is likely to remain the main means of global communication, assess the relative importance of English for you alongside any other languages you may use.

Whose English is it? Kachru's Circles model

Following the development of English from its British origins to its current status as a global language, we need to examine its spread and the different ways in which it is used. From there we can compare some issues and also some of the characteristics of Standard and Non-Standard English throughout the world.

An important point raised in the previous section is that the number of people learning and speaking English as a foreign language is now much larger than the number of native speakers. Should those who speak English as a foreign language therefore set the standard? Although change is happening, all varieties of English do not yet have equal status. A key issue is whether there is, or should be, one 'correct' form of English which all others should be measured by or whether all varieties have equal merit.

This issue goes further than simply the level of competence in speaking and writing the language; it is central to the relative status of the different forms of English, where they are spoken and the status of local varieties in relation to what is perceived to be correct form of the language. Linguist David Crystal feels that by weight of numbers alone, the language produced by non-native speakers is bound to have an effect on the way in which the language will evolve since contact is fundamental to the way in which a language is spoken. If we get along with people, we want to sound like them (this is the process of **accommodation**) and so a common form of pronunciation and syntax develops within a community. Within the UK and in different areas of the English-speaking world, local accents and dialects have developed.

A classification about the origins and usage of English will help us to look at the way in which the English language has spread and is continuing to spread across the globe.

FURTHER RESEARCH

To hear Professpr David Crystal talking about English as a global language, search on *YouTube* for 'David Crystal', 'Global English', and select the clip 'Global English with David Crystal' (Macmillan Education).

You can find out more about David Crystal's theories by reading his book *English as a Global Language* (Cambridge University Press, 2003) .

ACTIVITY 6.8

■ Discuss the variety of English which you and those around you speak. Is it a local variety or part of a country or region-wide style? Give reasons for your answer.

■ Can you assess the status of the English you speak in relation to other Englishes? If it is possible to do so, on what basis have you made this judgement?

The spread of English: Kachru's Circles

The rapid spread of English has given rise to models which classify the ways English is used throughout the world. One of the most influential models was developed by the linguist Braj Kachru in 1985. **Kachru's Circles** is a model used to describe the circumstances in which English is spoken.

Kachru's model consists of three circles:

The Inner Circle

English is the native language or mother tongue of most people in these countries. The total number of English speakers in the inner circle is approximately 380 million. Other languages are spoken in these regions but English dominates communication here. English is used for all administrative and social purposes. The Inner Circle represents the traditional bases of English in regions where it is now used as a primary language: the United Kingdom, the United States, Australia, New Zealand, Ireland, English-speaking Canada and South Africa, and some of Caribbean territories.

The Outer Circle

In these regions, English is regarded as a second language, where much of the administration is through the medium of English, mainly as a colonial legacy, as in Asia and Africa. In these areas, English is not the native tongue, but serves as a useful common language – the *lingua franca* – between ethnic and language groups. Higher education, the legislature and judiciary, national commerce and ceremonial functions are carried out predominantly in English. This circle includes India, Nigeria, Bangladesh, Pakistan, Malaysia, Tanzania, Singapore, Kenya, and non-English speaking South Africa.

227

The Expanding Circle

These are countries where English plays no historical or governmental role, but where it is nevertheless widely used as a medium of international communication. English may be employed for specific, limited purposes, usually business English and the internet. This includes much of the rest of the world's population, particularly China, Russia, Japan, most of Europe, Korea, Egypt, and Indonesia.

These circles are interesting both historically and geographically but are also central to the standards or 'norms' of English. But how and from where do these norms of the language come? Most people have an idea of how the language should be spoken, especially in the rapidly changing modern world. The issue here is whether, with English as a global language, ideas of correctness come from one source such as Standard British English or whether any group speaking English across the globe can set the standards.

The most generally held view is that the Inner Circle (e.g. UK, US) is **norm-providing**; this means that English language norms are developed in these countries and spread outwards. The Outer Circle (mainly New Commonwealth countries) is **norm-developing**, easily adopting and perhaps developing its own norms. The Expanding Circle (which includes much of the rest of the world) is **norm-dependent**, because it relies on the standards set by native speakers in the Inner Circle. This is a one directional flow and learners of English as a foreign language in the Expanding Circle look to the standards set in the Inner and Outer Circles.

This model may seem very theoretical and yet it goes to the core of the dynamics of the spread and the usage of English.

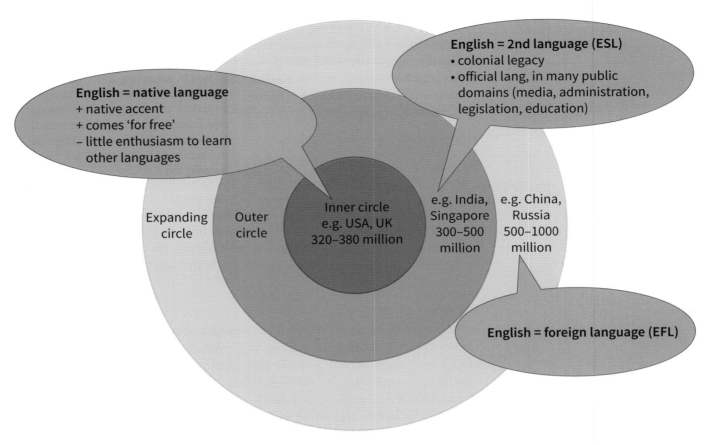

English = native language
+ native accent
+ comes 'for free'
– little enthusiasm to learn other languages

English = 2nd language (ESL)
• colonial legacy
• official lang, in many public domains (media, administration, legislation, education)

Expanding circle

Outer circle

Inner circle
e.g. USA, UK
320–380 million

e.g. India, Singapore
300–500 million

e.g. China, Russia
500–1000 million

English = foreign language (EFL)

Kachru's Circles of English.

ACTIVITY 6.9

1 Discuss the variety of English you speak and decide which of the circles it belongs in. Do you think that the variety of English you use has been influenced by contact with other countries and their English speech? Give reasons for your answer.

2 Kachru's Circles model assumes that the spread of English is one way, from the Inner Circle outwards. How is language spread? Consider your contact with other speakers of English through the internet and media and discuss whether you think the spread is one way only.

3 If you are a non-native speaker of English, in what situations do you use your native tongue and what situations do you use English? Explain why.

4 Do you think Kachru's Circles model is a useful classification? Give reasons for your views.

••• FURTHER RESEARCH

Gorlach's Circle model of English and Modiano's model of English are other ways of trying to classify varieties of English across the world. Investigate these models and assess their strengths and weaknesses in categorising the different types of English.

There are other theories which you may also wish to investigate and evaluate.

Attempt these essay questions.

1 Describe a model which explains the spread of English throughout the world. Explain the reasoning of the model and evaluate its usefulness in showing different varieties of Englishes.

2 'English spreads out from a core area of native speakers.' Describe a theory which supports this statement and, using specific case studies, evaluate ways in which different types of English are found worldwide.

Standard English a dialect of English considered 'correct' and 'normal', because it has distinctive and standardised features of spelling, vocabulary and syntax. It is the form of English usually used in formal writing.

TIP

The term *Standard English* is critical to your understanding of different styles of English. Make sure you understand the status of Standard English and when it is used. Specific case studies of different English styles will be valuable to back up your opinions with evidence.

FURTHER RESEARCH

You can read Paul Kerswill's article 'Standard English, RP and the standard – non-standard relationship' by going to **www.ling.lancs.ac.uk** and searching on 'Kerswill'.

From British to Global English

In this section you will assess some generally accepted terms associated with English language study. Standard English is often discussed with reference to British English because of the way in which the language was traditionally seen as 'correct' or not. Also the many local dialects of British English have in the past been regarded as non-standard. This British classification is not as evident when global varieties of English are described.

A trawl around dictionaries, websites and English Language textbooks reveals that a definition of Standard English is often very general and stated in comparative terms. Standard English is a form of English which has been accepted as the norm and the variety with which other forms are compared. Language researcher Paul Kerswill states that he has actively been trying to avoid a definition of Standard English because the idea of it as correct or good English is *closely related to the perspective of the particular language user*.

So what is the generally accepted understanding of Standard English? It originated in the UK as the variety of English spoken in the politically and economically powerful triangle between Oxford, Cambridge and London and over the last 200 years it has come to represent the norm of spoken and written English. It is often referred to as **BBC English**, as it is associated with a distinctive form of media communication. Because Standard English follows the accepted constructions of the language, it is the form of English most often learned by non-native speakers. It is generally perceived as the variety of English spoken by educated people.

Change the following examples into Standard English form. Consider which grammatical rules have been broken in each case.

■ I ain't done nothing.
■ She come here tomorrow.
■ I dunno.
■ It was him what did it.
■ Yup.
■ Did you do it? No I never.

Received Pronunciation (RP)

Standard English is usually associated with an accent known as **Received Pronunciation**, which for many people is perceived as 'proper' English. While it is estimated that only 3% of the British population use RP, it has always been disproportionately influential, spoken by upper-class people, academics, actors, TV personalities, politicians and teachers.

Received Pronunciation (RP) is sometimes referred to as 'The Queen's English'. The monarch speaks in an advanced form of this accent.

RP is a recent development relative to the length of time that English has been spoken. It emerged in the British public schools where the middle and upper classes educated their children, who often became influential members of British society. It is generally the case that people who mix in the same circles tend to, consciously or unconsciously, converge in their speech patterns. RP, with its perceived high status, established itself as the prestige accent. It was also neutral – free from any regional associations – so that it was not possible to tell the geographic or social origins of the speaker.

Standard English and RP spread quickly with the arrival of BBC radio in 1922 and television in 1936. RP was adopted by the BBC and for sixty years was the only accent heard on television and radio. It became 'the voice of Britain' and the establishment. Today, a much wider range of British regional accents and dialects can be heard on the BBC.

Language and social change go hand in hand. In post-war Britain, greater educational opportunity began to break down the social class barriers into which British society had largely been organised. The lower-middle and working classes become more socially mobile and more affluent. Standard English and RP became associated with the middle classes, their success and their growing prosperity, to which many now aspired. Looking outwards, RP became the recognisable and 'proper' voice of Britain for speakers of English in other countries.

RP is an accent, but all who speak in this way also use Standard English Grammar with its recognised standard grammatical constructions. With only 3% of British English speakers actually using RP it is not the most widely used accent, but it is the most widely recognised.

TIP

To make sure you understand and recognise the sounds and grammatical constructions of RP, try to watch or listen to television, radio and online recordings which use this form of English. You are most likely to find RP in more serious documentary and news broadcasts on national channels.

ACTIVITY 6.12

'The Queen's English' is a particularly advanced form of English pronunciation which, like all language, has changed over time. Search online for both early and recent recordings of Queen Elizabeth II. How is her pronunciation different from that of other RP speakers? How has her own pronunciation changed during her lifetime?

Read the following extract carefully. It is from the novel *The Adventures of Huckleberry Finn* by the American writer Mark Twain and was published in 1884. It is the story of a young boy and his struggles to fit into society. The novel contains much non-Standard English. Look particularly at the following:

- vocabulary
- syntax (the way the sentences are put together).

I see Jim before me, all the time; in the day, and in the night-time, sometimes moonlight, sometimes storms, and we a-floating along, talking, and singing, and laughing. But somehow I couldn't seem to strike no places to harden me against him, but only the other kind. I'd see him standing my watch on top of his'n, 'stead of calling me, so I could go on sleeping; and see him how glad he was when I come back out of the fog; and when I come to him again in the swamp, up there where the feud was; and such-like times; and would always call me honey, and pet me, and do everything he could think of for me, and how good he always was.

And at last I struck the time I saved him by telling the men we had small-pox aboard, and he was so grateful, and said I was the best friend old Jim ever had in the world, and the only one he's got now; and then I happened to look around, and see that paper.

It was a close place. I took it up, and held it in my hand. I was a-trembling, because I'd got to decide, forever, betwixt two things, and I knowed it. I studied a minute, sort of holding my breath, and then says to myself:

'All right, then, I'll go to hell' – and tore it up.

From *The Adventures of Huckleberry Finn* by Mark Twain.

ACTIVITY 6.13

1 What are the main differences between the language used in this extract and Standard English? Why do you think the novel was written in this way?
2 Standard English and RP are usually the dominant forms taught to non-native speakers. What do you consider to be the main reasons for teaching this variety of English over any other?

People using Standard English dialect and an RP accent are likely to be perceived as educated, professional and possibly in some position of authority and trust. However, responses to this style of English, both in Britain and elsewhere, vary from admiration to ridicule. In the recent past, some high-profile people who once spoke with a regional British accent – such as Margaret Thatcher, a famous British Prime Minister – have changed to using Standard English. Others, who perceive this style of speech to be élitist – including another recent British Prime Minister, Tony Blair – have consciously adopted styles of speech perceived to be more 'of the people'.

RP is perceived as an accent spoken by those in authority so people who deliver news bulletins often use it, because they are likely to be trusted and what they are saying is assumed to be true. During the Second World War, a popular British radio presenter, Wilfred Pickles, occasionally broadcast the news. This was the first time that anyone who spoke with a regional accent had broadcast serious news material rather than light-entertainment programmes and it was considered quite revolutionary.

The poem extract which follows is on the same subject of accents and trust, and satirises people who do not want to hear serious news items from people speaking with a regional accent. The poem is written in eye-dialect which replicates the sound of someone speaking with a Glaswegian accent. (Glasgow is a large city in Scotland where the accent is perceived to be very broad.)

LINK

Look back at page 215 in **Unit 5** for more about eye dialect.

this is thi

six a clock

news thi

man said n

thi reason

a talk wia

BBC accent

iz coz yi

widny wahnt

mi ti talk

aboot thi

trooth wia

voice lik

wanna yoo

scruff. if

a toktaboot

thi trooth

lik wanna yoo

scruff yi

widny thingk

it wuz troo.

From 'Unrelated Incidents - No.3' by Tom Leonard.

canny	cannot
six a'clock news	six o'clock – a traditional time for a UK national news bulletin
scruff(s)	uneducated person/people
thirza	there's a
tok	talk
widny	would not

ACTIVITY 6.14

1 Explain what point the poet is making about the use of Received Pronunciation to communicate important matters in British English. To what extent do you agree with the poet? How do people today respond differently to accents which are used in media broadcasts in your region? Suggest reasons for your answer.

2 Discuss the view that Received Pronunciation is the most suitable English accent to use for nationwide communication in the media.

3 There are many debates about speaking the Standard English dialect with a Received Pronunciation accent. What perceptions would you have about someone who used RP?

4 Do you trust the RP accent over others? There are now many other forms of English, some of which you will learn about in this course. Are these as well regarded as Standard English? Give reasons for your answer.

FURTHER RESEARCH

You may find it helpful to listen to examples of Standard English spoken with an RP accent. You will be able to find many useful examples on websites such as YouTube that explore where and how RP is used, and comment on the way it is changing. The online British Library Sound Archives have a section devoted to 'Accents and dialects', with thousands of audio examples of variations in spoken English across the UK. A section on 'Changing Language' includes a timeline explaining how English has developed and changed over hundreds of years.

New forms of non-standard English

New forms of non-standard English are constantly evolving. **Estuary English** (EE) is quickly spreading in the UK from its origins along the Thames Estuary outwards from London. There is general agreement that it is being adopted by many, including TV and film personalities who would previously have spoken RP. There is some debate about whether the current pronunciation of RP will die out – it will certainly change!

The word **Mockney** is a word combining *mock* (in the sense of *fake* or *unreal*) with *Cockney*. It is a 'portmanteau' word – one which combines two words to describe something. Cockney is the traditional accent of working-class people in the East End of London and Mockney is sometimes used inaccurately in the media to describe Estuary English. But it is distinct from EE, referring to a deliberate and often temporary accent. It originated in the 1990s and describes middle class people who usually speak with an RP accent altering the way they speak to sound 'more Cockney'. This is an interesting change where people perceive the non-standard accent to be more up-to-date than the traditionally 'correct' RP.

The rise of Estuary English

The past 25 years has seen the rise of a style of speech with an accent known as Estuary English. It has spread far beyond its original location on the Thames Estuary and is now sufficiently widespread to raise important issues about the changes to different varieties of British English because it is spoken by people from such a wide cross-section of society. A dictionary of phonetics and phonology describes EE as an accent *falling somewhere between broad Cockney at one extreme and unmistakable RP (received pronunciation) at the other.*

In the Cambridge Encyclopaedia of the English Language (Cambridge University Press, 2005), David Crystal comments:

> *There's a phenomenon which seems to be spreading throughout Britain which is called 'l vocalisation' and that's where the 'l' sound gets replaced with something that's more like a vowel.*

> *The glottal stop is used where the vocal cords are momentarily closed to stop the air flow and no sound is made. A very recognisable result is the non-pronunciation of the 't' so that 'part'y becomes 'par'y.'*

Estuary English may therefore be the result of a confluence of two social trends: an up-market movement of originally Cockney speakers, and a down-market trend towards 'ordinary' (as opposed to 'posh') speech by the middle class. There is certainly plenty of anecdotal evidence that many people these days wish to avoid the 'establishment' connotations of Received Pronunciation, and try to speak in a way which they perceive to be more down-to-earth.

233

●●● FURTHER RESEARCH

Investigate the changes taking place in standard and non-standard English. Look for articles online suggesting that people from all sections of British society speak Estuary English.

The British royal family has traditionally spoken in Standard English with a definite RP accent. Search for online articles and video clips to show that the younger generation of royals have different styles of speaking from their parents and grandparents.

Changes to Standard English and Received Pronunciation

It is important to remember that there is nothing specific about Received Pronunciation which makes it superior to other accents; it is only the attitudes of English speakers which linked this way of speaking with power and influence in society. However, since the 1960s, there has been a much greater acceptance of regional accents. They are now heard widely in the media in Britain so that in some circumstances Received Pronunciation is seen as old-fashioned and rather pompous.

The British newspaper, *The Guardian*, reported as far back as 1994, that *the cut-glass* [very upper class] *accent of home counties Britain is to be banished from the air waves by the BBC in favour of more energetic and vigorous voices from the regions.*

However, as regional accents have become more acceptable, there has actually been a decline in these distinctive forms of speech. People travel widely and no longer spend their lives in the same area, as was the case in previous generations. Certainly the accents of English will continue to change and develop and the vast numbers of non-native speakers of English will contribute to this process.

> ### ACTIVITY 6.15
>
> 1 Using examples from specific regions, discuss the idea that it is important to teach native English speakers and non-native English students the standard form of English.
> 2 Using examples from specific regions show in what ways non-standard forms of English differ from Standard English.
> 3 Discuss, with specific examples, the idea that any English speaker who uses non-standard forms of English may be socially disadvantaged.

English: standard and non-standard

Here are some summary points to reinforce the most important issues surrounding Standard and Non-Standard English.

- Although Standard English is widely known, it is spoken by a only a minority of English speakers both in Britain and worldwide.
- Many other dialects of English are spoken.
- Language changes through time and with the changes come differences in attitudes towards what is acceptable usage.
- Different registers or levels of formality are regularly used in English according to the situations the speakers are in. Most speakers are able to unconsciously adjust their register of language according to the linguistic demands of the situation; this is known as code switching.
- Slang is a rapidly changing feature of non-standard English.
- The position of English as a global language means that many global varieties of English are emerging.
- Is there a 'right' form of English or are all varieties equally important? Whose view counts?

LINK

For more on Standard English and the English of social groups, turn to pages 192, 200 and 229–231.

In this section you will be exploring current attitudes and values related to non-standard varieties of English, but it can be interesting to find out some past views on these issues too. Linguist David Crystal asserts that in earlier English language study, dialects of English have been consciously neglected. He references an English language textbook published in the 20th century (H. C. Wilde's *A Short History of English*) which informed its readers that English dialects were *of very little importance* and even called them *quaint and eccentric* – in other words they were not worth bothering with even as a language study. This has completely changed in recent years but the belief that one form of English was superior led to the notion of non-Standard English as we shall see in this section.

It follows that if Standard English was seen as the prestige form, that non-standard dialects were considered to be inferior and deficient in some way. This attitude underpins earlier linguistic beliefs that there is only one correct form and all the others are less worthy. In Britain, when the BBC (the British Broadcasting Company, now Corporation) was formed under Lord Reith he specifically instructed that that the English style spoken on BBC radio and television was to be Standard English. This form of 'BBC English' has been widely parodied for being so artificial that it can seem comical.

Varieties of English

We will now move on to consider varieties of English spoken throughout the world. You should be able to recognise the areas where the following are spoken: Japlish, Russlish, Spanglish, Deutschlish. These and other forms are offshoots of English where the standard form of the language has merged with elements of the local language to give a new form; so Deutschlish for example is a mix of English and German vocabulary and syntax. There is some debate as to whether these varieties can be considered a new language or an evolving dialect of English.

Because English is learned around the world, it is spoken in a variety of ways. People in different regions of the world are creating new varieties of English which are distinctive and of equal value to British English. There are hundreds of these varieties of non-standard English.

In this section you will consider three examples of these:

- Singapore English
- South African English
- Australian English.

Singapore English ('Singlish')

'Singlish' is the variety of English spoken in Singapore, which is included in the Outer Circle of Kachru's Circles of English. British rule in this geographically small but economically influential island was established in 1819 by Stamford Raffles on behalf of the British East India Company. The English language has been used in government and many other areas of life since British colonial rule began in 1824. Singapore and Malaysia are more than 10,000 kms from Britain and include many ethnic groups principally Malays, Chinese and Indians. It is therefore not surprising that the form of English spoken in this region changed.

Singapore and Malaysia (previously the Federation of Malaya) were colonies of the British Empire. Whereas Malaya soon became a commodity producer (rubber, tin), Singapore was a trading post and administrative centre so a single language for communication was essential. Standard English was used by the British, with the assistance of English-educated Straits-born Chinese, to control this region

ACTIVITY 6.16

Find out more about the local variety of non-standard English spoken where you live. Look for examples of the language used and comment on the attitudes towards its usage in your area and in the wider English-speaking world

TIP

You need to have a good understanding of the historical and social factors which have contributed to the development of different varieties of English. It will be helpful to know two or three case studies in detail.

Use the examples which follow as a pattern for your own research. You will then have a range of information and examples about the ways in which different varieties of English developed.

LINK

Look back at page 228 to remind yourself of Kachru's Circles model.

The port of Singapore, 1830.

 LINK

For more about creolisation, look back to page 179 in **Unit 5**.

which was, and still is, a hub of world trade. There was much money to be made in trading and effective communication between the many different ethnic groups was essential for business to run smoothly.

In British Malaya, English was the language of the British administration whilst Malay was spoken on the street, to avoid alienating the indigenous Malays.

Languages evolve wherever there is a mix of speakers, and in Malaya Standard English soon moved out into the streets to be used and changed by non-English speakers. It evolved in a pidgin form mixed with vocabulary from Malay and Indian English, along with some Chinese dialects, and eventually came to be spoken as a language in its own right. This merging of languages, to produce a new and distinctive one, is called **creolisation**. This process happened in Singapore and 'Singlish' is now a fully formed variety of English.

The English taught in Singapore was British English and it was often taught through missionary societies as well as schools to perpetuate the style of the English spoken for government. It therefore closely resembled British English. Words describing anti-social people, for example, named them as *rascals*, *scallywags* and *mischief-makers* long after such terms had disappeared from mainstream English vocabulary. This old-fashioned style became a distinctive feature of Singapore English.

Political changes in the mid 1960s lessened the status of Standard British English taught in Singapore schools. This was also accompanied by Britain's decline as a world power, while the influence of the USA grew and American English became the form to aspire to.

Characteristic features of 'Singlish'

- reduplication (exact repetition) of verbs: *I cough, cough*
- reduplication of adjectives to intensify meaning: *this curry is hot hot*
- a variety of phrases adopted from Malay or from Chinese dialects, depending on the ethnic identity of the speakers: *chop chop* = hurry up
- marking of plurals and past tenses is optional: *what happen last week?*

KEY TERMS

particle a short word which only has a function when used with another; its structure does not change; e.g. *the, a*.

FURTHER RESEARCH

Improve your understanding of Singlish by listening to audio clips. The British Library Sound Archives and Youtube are excellent places to start your search for good examples.

- complex verb groups are often substituted by more description within the sentence: *my mother talk already* (I have already spoken to my mother)
- it is often optional to use the verb *to be*: *he so angry*
- use of **particles**, mostly borrowed from Hokkien or Cantonese, to indicate an attitude towards what is being said; they work rather like *you know* and *you see*. The three most common particles are *ah* (usually expects agreement), *lah* (strong assertion) and *what* (usually corrects something): *I want to leave, lah.*
- the subject of the sentence can be omitted: *gone already* (he has already gone)
- syntax is often abbreviated, as in the conditional tense: *you do that I go away* (if you do that I'll go away).

The Status of English in Singapore

The Singapore government recognises the importance of competence in English in order to sustain economic competitiveness and has recently promoted campaigns such as the Speak Good English Movement to emphasise the importance of Standard English.

Singlish is widely used and can be heard in some TV shows. Many young people in Singapore code switch easily and maintain competence in this local form of English as well as in Standard English. Singlish appears to be a permanent form of the language in an ethnically mixed society and coexists with the Standard English promoted by the government.

South African English

The provinces which make up South Africa have two major divisions of language and culture – English and Afrikaans. South African English (SAE) is the dialect of English spoken by South Africans, with the English varieties spoken by Zimbabweans, Zambians and Namibians being recognised as offshoots.

The English language in South Africa (SAE) dates from the arrival of the British at the Cape of Good Hope in 1795. Like other areas which became English colonies, English was introduced into South Africa by soldiers and administrators, then by missionaries, settlers, and fortune-seekers. English became more established during the 19th century as a southern African language, as a result of the British settlements of 1820 (in the Eastern Cape), 1848–51 (in Natal), and the subsequent rushes to the diamond mines of Kimberley and the gold mines of the Witwatersrand.

A power struggle developed between the English-speaking settlers and those of Dutch descent, which eventually resulted in the Boer War of 1899–1901 and the two languages coexisted throughout the 20th century. Afrikaans replaced English as the language of government, administration, the police, and the armed forces, and was the language closely associated with the repressive system of apartheid. Afrikaans is a language which emerged from the Dutch language spoken by the early settlers in South Africa. However, the English language remained a major influence in business and higher education. It was also the language used by the African National Congress and other liberation movements, as it enabled communication between speakers of the country's many other languages and with the outside world. South African English was a powerful political tool. When the South African Nationalist Government tried to make Afrikaans a teaching language in black schools in 1976, it triggered an uprising in Soweto (an abbreviation of <u>So</u>uth <u>We</u>st <u>To</u>wnship.

237

The ANC used English to enable effective communication between different language speakers in Africa, and with the rest of the world.

This situation continues today, with many ethnic groups within South Africa seeing English as a means of advancement in society. As in many other multi-lingual communities, English is considered to be neutral since it ensures that no local dialect is viewed as more influential than any other.

Characteristics of South African English

- Settlers adopted words to describe landscape and social features unique to their new environment: *donga, impala, kraal* (although some were derived from Afrikaans).
- The Afrikaans language has had an enormous influence on vocabulary and syntax in SAE; a very widespread example is the use of *ja* (yes)
- Many SAE words have also been borrowed from the African languages of the region: *tsetse, tsotsi, kgotla, marula*. As well as vocabulary, intonation also reflects these languages.
- Vocabulary also came from other settlers. Malay words such as *atchar, bobotie, sosatie, kaparrang,* and *kramat* came into SAE during the 19th century (via Afrikaans). These originated in the community of slaves and political exiles at the Cape, who were sent from what are now Indonesia and Malaysia during the 17th and 18th centuries.
- Some vocabulary current at the time of British settlement in South Africa is still maintained: *geyser* (a boiler), *robot* (traffic light).
- Different levels of SAE exist in the same way as Standard English and are an indicator of social class.

Australian English

Australian English differs from other varieties primarily in its accent and vocabulary. The major features of the accent were established by the 1830s. In the period between colonial settlement in 1788 and the 1830s, when the foundation accent was established, new vocabulary to describe the new environment, especially its flora and fauna, was developed either from aboriginal languages (e.g. *coolibah,*

••• FURTHER RESEARCH

There are many sources of information about South African English including some where you can listen to the accent and style of speech. The websites of *The Guardian* newspaper, *The Economist* magazine and the Oxford English Dictionary are particularly useful.

wombat, wallaby, waratah) or from English vocabulary (e.g. *native bear, wild cherry*). Many more vocabulary items were later added during the 19th-century process of settlement and expansion. This was the usual process by which a colonial society imposed its linguistic footprint on a subjected land.

At the end of the 19th century, something curious and largely unpredictable happened to Australian English. Some Australian speakers modified their **vowels** and **diphthongs** to make them closer to the British way of speaking. From the 1890s until the 1950s, elocution teachers in Australia found that many people wanted to 'sound British'. These were Australians who wanted to be viewed as upper class. This modified form of Australian speech came to be called **Cultivated Australian**.

In response to this new British-based Cultivated Australian, another form of Australian English developed in the first part of the 20th century. This accent developed as **Australian English** which is most distinctive in its pronunciation of the vowel sounds so that to many non-Australians, the pronunciation of words such as *mate* or *race* sounds much like *mite* or *rice*. Unlike the Englishes developing in African nations, English in Australia has always been more widely used than the indigenous languages so that the characteristics of Australian English has dominated both official and informal communication in the country.

239

> ### KEY TERMS
>
> **vowels** the basic sounds of pronunciation, where there is a relatively free passage of air in the vocal chords; the sounds of *a, e, i, o, u* (and sometimes *y*) are the core vowel sounds in English
>
> **diphthong** combination of two vowel sounds where the tongue glides from one position to another to make a slight change in the syllable produced (e.g. *tie, boil*)

Waltzing Matilda

Once a jolly swagman camped by a billabong,
Under the shade of a coolibah tree,
And he sang as he watched and waited till his billy boiled,
'Who'll come a-waltzing, Matilda, with me?' 'Waltzing Matilda, Waltzing Matilda
Who'll come a-waltzing, Matilda, with me?'
And he sang as he watched and waited till his billy boiled,
'Who'll come a-waltzing, Matilda, with me?'

Traditional Australian folk song.

---

swagman	an itinerant bush traveller who carried all his belongings wrapped up in a blanket or cloth called a 'swag'.
billabong	a waterhole near a river. It is an aboriginal word that originally meant *little or no water*.
coolibah tree	a eucalyptus tree. It may be from the aboriginal name *gulabaa*. Since it was commonly found near water, the white settlers may have changed its pronunciation to reflect where it was found and the shade it provided.
billy	a tin can with a wire handle, used to boil water.

ACTIVITY 6.16

1   Remind yourself of what you consider to be written Standard English. Match your ideas with the verse of *Waltzing Matilda* and say to what extent it conforms to Standard English. Explain any differences using lexical and syntactical points, with examples from the article.

2   Compare the language in the song to the variety of English with which you are familiar. What are the similarities and differences?

3   Is the language used in this song recognisable as English? What are its strengths as a regional variety of English?

The characteristics of Australian English

- Informality with many abbreviations: *Put on your **lippie** before you go to the **barbie*** (put on your lipstick before you go to the barbecue).
- Many sounds and syllables are left out; this is known as **elision**: *g'day* (good day, hello).
- British or American English vocabulary may be followed: *cell phone* rather than *mobile*.
- The rising intonation at the end of any statement, not just for a question, is characteristic though it has travelled globally, probably through media influence.
- Australia is a huge country and there is a surprising amount of similarity in accents between places which are hundreds of miles apart.
- Today there are many languages competing with English particularly in urban areas where sizeable immigrant groups have settled.
- Individualised vocabulary which relates primarily, though not exclusively, to the Australian environment (see below).

KEY TERMS

elision when sounds or syllables are left out in speech to make the pronunciation easier and quicker; words sound like they are slurred together, e.g. *d'ya* instead of *do you*.

The majority of Australians continued to speak with the accent that had been established in the first 50 years of settlement and this form of speech came to be known as **General Australian**. This widely spoken form of English coexists with Cultivated Australian and Broad Australian. These three forms of Australian English came to carry with them very different sets of values. Cultivated Australian, for example, was seen to express a longing for British values and nostalgia for a country that was still regarded by many as 'home'. Broad Australian was strongly nationalistic and carried with it notions of an equal society without out the rigid social class structures which Britain was thought to have.

Read this article, taken from the Australian government website, about how the history of Australia has affected the development of its language.

Australia's everyday language is rich with slang that reflects experiences from the country's history. From borrowings of Aboriginal language words, through convict sources, the gold rushes and bushranging, to the First World War, words have emerged to describe essential aspects of the Australian character and identity.

Kangaroo was borrowed even prior to colonisation. The convicts gave us 'muster', 'bolter', 'rollup' and 'servants of the crown'. Bush rangers gave us the 'bush telegraph'. A key part of the Australian psyche, 'the digger', came out of the First World War – the term adapted from its use in the gold rushes.

Australian slang utilised humour, wit, rhymes, flash language, the bizarre experiences of the bush and the beach, the familiar and the personal, to realise terms that could describe experiences that were often new or transforming. For example, 'having a bash' at something is similar to 'giving it a burl', and both phrases reflect a history of Australian improvisation and hard work as part of working in the bush.

http://australia.gov.au/about-australia/australian-story/austn-slang

ACTIVITY 6.17

Using specific examples, discuss the view that regional varieties of English reflect the culture and history of the area in which they are spoken.

All three forms of Australian English included most of the vocabulary items that had developed in the second half of the 19th century, for example *billy* and *swag* (see definitions earlier in this section), but also:

fossick	to search for gold (perhaps a variant of the midland and southern English *fussock* – to bustle about)
the outback, the never-never	wild country, far from urban areas
brumby	a wild horse
larrikin	an urban hooligan

●●● FURTHER RESEARCH

There are a great many varieties of English, each of which has an individual history and set of circumstances surrounding its development. Carry out an investigation to utilise your skills as an independent learner.

- Choose a variety of English and trace its development and changes in the way that it has become distinctive.
- Assess the extent of adaptation and incorporation of vocabulary from the local area and its status as a formal or informal form of communication. You should include specific examples to accompany any general points you make.
- Search for examples of the spoken form of your chosen language variety. (Try starting with an online search of the British Library Sound Archives, or on YouTube.)
- You have seen how languages constantly change and develop. If possible you should try to research and suggest ideas about current influences on the English language variety you are investigating, and likely future developments.

241

British vs American English

It is sometimes said that the United Kingdom and the United States are two nations separated by a common language. This seems to make no sense until we look at some of the differences of vocabulary and expressions between the two nations.

The Emergence of American English

The first European settlers in what became the United States were members of a religious sect known as Puritans, who brought their English language with them. They landed on Plymouth Rock, New England in 1620 and, over the years, were followed by many thousands more migrants who travelled across the Atlantic for a new life, often to escape religious intolerance.

Like settlers and colonists in other parts of the world, the settlers adapted and changed the variety of English they spoke, discarding words which were no longer useful or relevant to their new lifestyle and rapidly adding a store of words that were. Different landscapes, animals and food sources were a rich source of new vocabulary and expressions as the settlers spread out across the continent. Words like *racoon*, *squash* (for pumpkin) and *moose* were borrowed from the many languages of the Native Americans.

There was a great deal of land on which to settle though large parts of it were occupied by Native American tribes who all spoke separate languages. Apart from words describing the natural habitat, very few Native American words entered American English and references by the Europeans to describe the life of the Native Americans were largely phrased in English such as *pale face*, *war path* and *Big Chief*. However American English did adopt vast numbers of new words from Europe and beyond. The Dutch came and shared *coleslaw* and *cookies*; the Germans bought *pretzels* from *delicatessens* and the Italians arrived with their *pizza*, *pasta*, *pepperoni* and many more.

Once independence had been gained from Britain and as a growing powerful economic dominance in the western world, Americans developed their own vocabulary to meet the needs of large-scale *capitalism*. Businesses become concerned about *breakeven* and their *bottom line*, and whether they were *blue chip* or *white collar*. The *commuter* needed a whole new system of *freeways*, *subways* and *parking lots* before new systems of *merger* and *downsizing* could be invented. America became a global superpower and confidently sent some of its own English back across the Atlantic so that the British in turn referred to *cool movies* and *groovy jazz*.

This borrowing of vocabulary has continued with more recent waves of immigrants from all parts of Asia and the Pacific. As the United States continues to dominate globally, American English has become the standard means of communication throughout the world. Individuals and groups who wish to be a part of this economic success do so through the medium of English.

American and British English vocabulary, phrasing and pronunciation remain very different from each other, although they are largely mutually understandable. You have seen that language is constantly changing and these two distinctive forms of English are evolving too. While America remains a superpower with global influence, Britain's place on the world stage is no longer as influential. From these two relative positions, it should follow that American English should be the one setting the standards for the English language. This issue is discussed in the following article, with some surprising findings.

How is your English? Research shows Americanisms AREN'T taking over the British language

Anyone who has ever taken a ride in an elevator or ordered a regular coffee in a fast food restaurant would be forgiven for thinking that Americanisms are taking over the English language.

But new research by linguistic experts at the British Library has found that British English is alive and well and is holding its own against its American rival.

The study has found that many British English speakers are refusing to use American pronunciations for everyday words such as schedule, patriot and advertisement.

It also discovered that British English is evolving at a faster rate than its transatlantic counterpart, meaning that in many instances it is the American speakers who are sticking to more 'traditional' speech patterns.

Jonnie Robinson, curator of sociolinguists at the British Library, said: 'British English and American English continue to be very distinct entities and the way both sets of speakers pronounce words continues to differ.

'But that doesn't mean that British English speakers are sticking with traditional pronunciations while American English speakers come up with their own alternatives.

'In fact, in some cases it is the other way around. British English, for whatever reason, is innovating and changing while American English remains very conservative and traditional in its speech patterns.'

As part of the study, researchers at the British Library recorded the voices of more than 10,000 English speakers from home and abroad.

The volunteers were asked to read extracts from Mr Tickle, one of the series of Mr Men books by Roger Hargreaves.

They were also asked to pronounce a set of six different words which included 'controversy', 'garage', 'scone', 'neither', 'attitude' and 'schedule'.

Linguists then examined the recordings made by 60 of the British and Irish participants and 60 of their counterparts from the U.S. and Canada.

When it came to the word attitude, more than three-quarters of the British and Irish contingent preferred 'atti-chewed' while every single participant from the U.S. opted for 'atti-tood.'

Tim Charrington, a dialect coach who has worked with actors on the West End stage, said it was true that American speech patterns could be more traditional.

www.dailymail.co.uk

American English within the United States

The history of North American settlement is very complex; it is a continent traditionally described as a 'melting pot' of peoples and their languages. Spanish is spoken by a large minority and more recent waves of immigration from Asia and the Pacific have resulted in the languages and culture of these regions being spoken in many major cities and large urban areas. However, in the United States, American English is the *lingua franca* form of communication which ensures a common understanding; all official government work is carried out through the medium of American English.

American English has a variety of pronunciation and dialect forms and the North American Accent is said to be a legacy of the sounds of English used in 17th-century England. It is suggested that the distinctive Southern Drawl comes closest to the manner of speech in England at the time of the first migration. American English also uses significantly different constructions from British English. An example of this is the American use of the simple past tense, for example *She ate too much* when a British English speaker would naturally use the *have/had* + past participle – *She has eaten too much.*

ACTIVITY 6.18

1 List as many American words, phrases and constructions that you can think of that differ from Standard British English. Try to discover their origins and whether any changes in spelling and/or meaning have taken

place. Here are some examples to start you off: *girl, cop, hood, trunk, thumb tacks, apartment, elevator, truck, buddy, diaper, gas, stroller, candy, flashlight, long-distance call.*

2 Make a list of words and phrases in American English which have passed into British English and are now used in the other English-speaking regions, for example *cool, to go, apartment, elevator.*

3 From what you have learned in this section about the spread of dominant languages, explain why American English is now a global language.

4 Look at the following constructions and discuss whether they are more likely to be British or American English. Explain the reasons for your answers.

- Is Sean here? No, he's just left./Is Sean here? No, he just left.
- I didn't read the book yet./I haven't read the book yet.
- May I take a shower?/May I have a shower?
- It's a quarter past four./It's a quarter after four.

5 Read the article above about British and American English. Using the information in the article and your knowledge of the differences between these two varieties of English, assess which you think is more influential in the world today.

6 Using case studies, evaluate to what extent you believe the idea that 'Britain and America are two nations separated by a common language'.

●●● FURTHER RESEARCH

The very obvious differences between British and American English have been extensively investigated and presented, often in a very-light hearted way. This is an ideal topic for independent research followed by collaborative presentations.

Possible areas of research could include:
- early North American English vocabulary adopted from Native American peoples
- vocabulary adopted from the waves of non-English-speaking migrants such as the Germans, Italians and Dutch
- different regional accents within the United States and theories about their origin.
- British English vocabulary rarely used in the United States and American English rarely used in Britain: some British celebrities appear on clips trying to guess what a *shawty* (young girl) or *flossing* (showing off) is while American participants do the same for *chin wag* (a long chat) and *chuffed to bits* (very pleased about something); there are many clips about American English vocabulary
- differences in some grammatical constructions
- the history of Canadian English and the dominance of French-speakers in Quebec province.

Language death

In this section you will explore the ways in which languages spread and decline and how the spread of English may have contributed to the death of other languages over the last 150 years. What is lost when a language dies? The number of language spoken worldwide is expected to shrink rapidly in the coming decades. In 1992 a prominent US linguist, Claude Hagège, predicted that by the year 2100, 90% of the world's languages will have ceased to exist.

> ## Language death: some statistics
> - 6% of the world's languages are spoken by 94% of the world's population.
> - It is well documented that languages are vanishing at an accelerating rate. Since 1500 CE, the world has lost about 15% of the more than 7000 languages we think were spoken then.
> - In just the last few decades dozens of Native American languages have died and the same is happening in Australia, South America, New Guinea, and Africa.

Language decline, endangerment and death

A language dies when the people who speak it die out, taking their language with them. The circumstances in which this happens are relevant to the continuing growth and dominance of English as a global language.

Language death can be sudden and violent. Of approximately 200 languages spoken by aboriginal Australians when the Europeans arrived in the late 18th century, between 50 and 70 disappeared as a direct result of the killing of aboriginal people or their death from diseases introduced by Europeans. On the island of Tasmania, the aboriginal population of between 3000 and 4000 was hunted and wiped out within 75 years. Their languages died with them and are no longer spoken anywhere.

Other examples of language death are more gradual as speakers of a language drift into the use of another more dominant language and begin to use the latter more often in their daily lives. This has frequently happened with colonial expansion and the increasing economic importance of a dominant nation.

National Geographic magazine recently stated that half the languages spoken in the world today are not being taught to children; when the next generation shifts to another language, these languages will die out with the last native speakers.

UNESCO (the United Nations Education, Scientific and Cultural Organization) distinguishes five levels of language endangerment, based on the extent to which language is passed on from one generation to the next:

- *vulnerable*: most children speak the language, but it may be restricted to certain domains (e.g. home)
- *definitely endangered*: children no longer learn the language as mother tongue in the home
- *severely endangered*: language is spoken by grandparents and older generations; while the parent generation may understand it, they do not speak it to children or among themselves
- *critically endangered*: the youngest speakers are grandparents and older and they speak the language only partially and infrequently
- *extinct*: the language is no longer spoken.

www.unesco.org

245

ACTIVITY 6.19

1. Latin is widely known as a 'dead' language. Is this true? If so, why does it continue to be taught in some schools?
2. What other languages do you know which might be considered to be dead? Are there any languages in this category in the country or region where you live?
3. UNESCO states that *Language diversity is essential to the human heritage.* What do you understand by this?
4. Does it matter if a language dies? Consider what benefits a language gives to the community who speak it. Give reasons for your answers.

• • • FURTHER RESEARCH

UNESCO publishes a huge amount of interesting material about endangered languages. The UNESCO report on 'Language Vitality and Endangerment' and the 'Ethnologue' web-based materials include statistics about endangered languages and there are also helpful individual case studies.

- Choose a region near you and carry out your own investigation into languages which are currently spoken there, as well as those which may have died out in the last 200 years or so.
- Research possible reasons for the decline or death of any languages that have disappeared.
- Investigate whether there has been a spread of English in the region.
- If there have been any examples of language decline or even language death in your chosen region, examine whether there have been any changes in a minority language (e.g. Māori in New Zealand) and the reasons for these changes.

Language shift

Language death is far more likely to occur when the language of one group is seen as less important than that of a more dominant language spoken in the same region. For example, the Breton language in Brittany was perceived to be inferior to French and until the 1950s children speaking Breton in the classroom and even in the playground were forced to wear a clog (a very heavy wooden shoe, symbolic of their lack of education) around their necks as punishment. Similar attitudes prevailed in Wales for native Welsh speakers and in New Zealand for Māoris.

Where people believe that one language offers greater advantages for employment and general advancement, that language will be promoted and spoken. There may be no incentive to maintain the minority language, so it is unlikely to be taught to children and the use of the language in the community is reduced until it may only be spoken in the home and by older generations.

A minority language suffers when it is not taught in schools, used in the media or in formal administrative situations such as courts. The language becomes restricted to the home and in this way language shift, leading eventually to language death, can happen over the course of only a few generations.

There are variations in this process according to attitudes of the speakers and also in the extent of contact with other speakers of the minority language. For example, younger people will often want to 'get ahead' especially where they see that knowledge of the dominant language gives them an economic or social advantage; conversely, people in rural areas may have less exposure to the dominant language and can therefore use the minority language more freely. The Māori language in New Zealand was the dominant language in more inaccessible areas for many years after Māoris in the cities were using English. This was especially important before the arrival of English-language TV.

Global English and language death

A national language must be recognised as a 'real' language, have a high status and should enable and facilitate its speakers in their daily lives. We have seen that English in all its many forms is spoken both as a native language and also as a second language across the globe. Is it also a 'killer language'? Is it a chief cause of the death of minority languages?

Is English a killer language?	
FOR	AGAINST
Papua New Guinea	**Germany**
Colonisation by Britain and later Australia led to the development of a creole language (standard *Tok Pisin*) essential for native people's improved economic well-being. There was no official written language and local languages were not seen to offer any advantage so they ceased to be spoken. *Tok Pisin* and English became the *lingua franca* for both official and unofficial communication in the country.	Elements of English absorbed into another language, for example German. German is an established written and spoken language and Germany is part of the European Union where much administrative business and many technological advances are conducted in English. Many Germans speak English fluently so that the two languages coexist. English words appear in the German media and in music and are used quite widely, especially by the young.

New Guinea

New Guinea is a particularly good example of a country where hundreds of languages were spoken rather than written down. The ruling elite felt that multilingualism was bad for economic progress so schooling took place through the medium of English. The pidgin language *Tok Pisin* was used in schools and this new language form helped to unify the people of New Guinea.

The linguist Suzanne Romaine reflected in 1992 on the past status of the different languages in the late 19th and early 20th centuries. She said that *To speak English was good; to speak Tok Pisin was bad, but to speak Tok Ples [the local language] was worst*. The people of New Guinea were therefore made to feel that they and their language were inferior to the dominant language, English.

Is English under threat?

It is difficult to believe that English itself maybe under threat, but you have learned that different forms of English are evolving all the time. In the USA for example, large numbers of Hispanic immigrants continue to speak their native Spanish and this has led to a movement seeking to ensure that all Americans speak American English, as this is seen to be beneficial to the nation.

English as it is currently spoken and written must continue to change but the nature of these changes has caused some alarm about the status of the language. So how might English be under threat?

ACTIVITY 6.20

1 Discuss the arguments to suggest that English itself is under threat. Can you construct an argument, using relevant examples, to support or refute the idea of the decline of English?

2 What, if any, educational and media channels exist to support a minority language in your region? Should there be more provision for this and by whom? Give reasons for your ideas.

- The internationalisation of digital forms: texting, emails and emoticons may produce a language form that is international rather than English-based.
- The illiteracy of its speakers and writers. There are frequent news items about graduates who are unable to use English – their native language – fluently.
- With the greater acceptance of the idea that all forms of English have equal validity, these forms may continue to develop as separate languages.
- Mass migration of non-English-speaking populations to cities may create large areas where English is not spoken.
- The focus for technological and economic growth may pass from the US–Western Europe axis to Asia, especially China and the Pacific.

Can Language death be prevented?
Case study: Scottish Gaelic

Gaelic (pronounced Ga-lek, not Gay-lik) is a Celtic language that was at one point the predominant language in Scotland, but today is only really spoken in remote areas of the northern and western Highlands. There are 20,000–30,000 native Gaelic speakers worldwide, while more than 50,000 others claim to understand the language. Some children learn the language, but there are serious problems in language maintenance even in the core areas.

The General Register for Scotland in 2005 gave the following information: where both parents in a family were Gaelic speakers, 70 per cent of the children also spoke Gaelic; where only one parent spoke Gaelic, just 23 per cent of the children spoke the language.

The Gaelic Language (Scotland) Act 2005 gave official recognition to the language but it is not an official language within the United Kingdom. Scottish Gaelic is spoken:

- in Scotland, including rural areas of the Western Isles and Skye, and a few locations in the rest of the Inner Isles and the Highland mainland
- by some speakers in immigrant communities in Nova Scotia and Prince Edward Island in Canada.

There was a time when Gaelic appeared to be heading towards extinction, with few schools teaching it and little interest in learning it and with English having become the *lingua franca* of Great Britain. In the past 50 years or so however there has been a huge resurgence in interest in the language. In 2006 a school that taught solely in Gaelic opened in Glasgow, and in 2009 the Scottish government pledged to double the number of schools teaching Gaelic. Alongside this increase in teaching, there has been a large boost in spending for BBC Gaelic language broadcasting services such as BBC Alba and BBC Radio nan Gaidheal. All this has had a huge impact on the number of Gaelic speakers.

Language is not just a collection of words and grammar: it is a fundamental part of the life of a people. When a language dies, a whole culture, a whole set of songs, stories, legends and sayings die with it. As the French linguist Charles Hagège writes: *What we lose is essentially an enormous cultural heritage, the way of expressing the relationship with nature, with the world, between themselves in the framework of their families, their kin people* … If Gaelic was allowed to die out, to give way to English, then in many ways the Gaelic culture would die with it. The British Isles was once a place of multiple languages and cultural diversity, and in order to preserve that diversity, many people believe that Gaelic should be revitalised.

ACTIVITY 6.21

1 Discuss the following questions and give reasons for your points of view.
 - Should we try to revive Gaelic, a language spoken only in small parts of the Scottish Highlands and hardly anywhere else in the world?
 - Why should the British government invest money in producing Gaelic radio and TV programs? Why should schools start offering it alongside French or German?
 - Why should we put time, money and effort into breathing new life into a language that some might say has reached a natural end?
 - Do you believe that the fewer languages there are in the world, the easier and more efficient communication and interaction will become? Give reasons for your point of view.

2 Governments in Wales and in New Zealand have been very proactive in trying to revitalise their minority languages. The Welsh Government's pledge is to *strengthen the place of Welsh in everyday life*. The New Zealand Government is *committed to supporting the regeneration of te reo Māori* and has developed a Māori Language Strategy.

 Investigate in detail the measures these governments have taken and what effect these have had on the number of minority language speakers in these countries.

3 Using the case study material above and/or from your own region, list the benefits of speaking minority languages even where English has become the *lingua franca*. For example, should official and public notices and documents be published in all the languages spoken in the region? Give reasons for your answers.

4 Using specific examples, discuss whether the death of a language should be allowed to take place in a country or region and possible actions which could prevent this happening. The following articles will provide you with some useful case study material.

Here are two extracts from news articles about languages in various parts of the world which are dying or dead. With the exception of the Andes region, where Spanish dominates, English will replace the local languages.

In Australia, where nearly all of the 231 spoken aboriginal tongues are endangered, researchers came upon such tiny language communities as the three known speakers of Magati Ke, in the Northern Territory, and the three Yawuru speakers, in Western Australia. In July, they met the sole living speaker of Amurdag, a language in the Northern Territory that had already been declared extinct.

"This is probably one language that cannot be brought back, but at least we made a record of it," linguist researcher, Dr. Anderson said, noting that the Amurdag speaker strained to recall words he had last heard from his late father.

Many of the 113 languages spoken in the Andes Mountains and Amazon basin are poorly known and are rapidly giving way to Spanish or Portuguese, or in a few cases, to a more dominant indigenous language. In this region, for example, a group known as the Kallawaya use Spanish or Quechua in daily life, but also have their own secret tongue, used mainly for preserving knowledge of medicinal plants, some of which were previously unknown to science.

The dominance of English threatens the survival of the 54 indigenous languages of the Northwest Pacific plateau of North America, a region including British Columbia, Oregon and Washington. Only one person remains who speaks Siletz Dee-ni, the last of many languages once spoken on a reservation in Oregon.

www.nytimes.com

ACTIVITY 6.22

Read the article (right) about language death in a small community in Cromarty, a remote region in the Scottish Highlands. What are the processes which might have led to the death of this local language?

LINK

For more practice and self-evaluation on this unit, see page 291.

Final word from Cromarty:
Scottish Black Isle dialect silenced forever as last native speaker dies aged 92

Bobby Hogg was the last person still fluent in the fisherfolk dialect. It was a traditional dialect used for centuries by fisherfolk. But it emerged that the language of Cromarty had finally died with the passing of its last speaker.

Bobby Hogg was the only person still fluent in the age-old tongue of the Black Isle and his death at the age of 92 means it will now exist only in audio recordings.

But the Hoggs were from the fishing community. In 2007, the brothers were recorded by Am Baile, the project that has created a digital archive of the history and culture of the Highlands and Islands.

Mr Hogg said: 'Our father was a fisherman and all his folk had been fishermen stretching way back. It was the same on our mother's side too. When we were young, we talked differently in the fishertown to the rest of Cromarty. 'It wasn't written down. It was an oral culture. We had this sort of patois, which I think had both Doric and Gaelic in it. There were words, a lot to do with the fishing, which nobody else could understand. It is dying out. You hear a smattering in some things people from Cromarty say, but nobody speaks it fluently but for us.'

www.dailymail.co.uk

Unit 7: Child language acquisition

TIP

As you work through this unit you will find it helpful to talk to infants and children that you know wherever possible. Adjust your language and speaking style to the level of conversational competence of the child and you will observe how even a very young child can take part in a conversation.

The main stages of early development

In this unit you will explore the journey of infant and childhood language acquisition. You will gather information, ideas and theories about the stages that babies, infants and young children pass through in order to become proficient in the language(s) spoken around them. You will also be made aware of the critical importance of the family and community with whom they come into contact. You may also be amazed at the speed at which young children learn language and become confident conversationalists. This unit also examines teenage language use.

It must be emphasised that children do not all go through these stages at the same age, so some degree of approximation is essential. However, all children do go through the stages in the same sequence, so although each child will learn language at his or her own pace, the stages they go through can be predicted.

Before birth

The acquisition of language skills is an extraordinarily complex process which most linguists believe starts before birth. Research in France (Mehler *et al.*, 1988) found that French babies as young as four days old were able to distinguish French from other languages. When they were exposed to French being spoken, the babies sucked more vigorously (suggesting increased interest) than when they heard English or Italian. This has led to speculation that even before birth babies become attuned to the rhythm and intonations of the language around them.

The first year

The similar pattern of language development across cultures suggests a universal sequence of events in the process of language acquisition. All new parents quickly become aware of the sounds made by their newborn infants and can begin to distinguish the reasons for different sorts of cries, for example hunger or distress. It would appear that these cries are not language-specific. A newborn baby's cry in Nigeria is the same as that of a newborn in India; language differences are not yet apparent.

251

LINK

For more about turn-taking, look back at page 154 in **Unit 4**.

The baby's first smile at around six weeks is accompanied by 'cooing' and repetitive sounds. The baby starts to make these repeated sounds – **reduplication** – such as *baba*, *gaga* as the vocal chords develop the motor skills needed for the eventual production of speech. This is followed at about six months by more sustained 'babbling' where the child's sounds more closely resemble those of the language they will speak.

At this and every stage, parents and family will help the child's development by speaking to them. Even though the baby does not understand the specific meaning, learning about conversational skills is already taking place at this stage. This **caretaker** language of the parent initiates and teaches **turn-taking**. The style of caretaker language is very distinctive. It is the language used by family and friends who speak to the baby in a higher and lighter tone than normal speech and with frequent repetition of words which are important in the infant's world (e.g. *lovely boy*; *happy baby*; *who's mummy's favourite girl?*). In reply, the baby can make all manner of noises including spluttering, blowing bubbles and 'raspberries' with the lips together; the baby is exploring its vocal repertoire. Babbling to its parents or carers enables the baby to develop its organs of speech production.

PARENT	hello Maya (.) hello (.) who's a lovely girl (.) aah (.)
BABY	[*gurgles*]
PARENT	yes she is (.) she's mummy's best girl
BABY	[*smiles*]

The infant smiles, coos and burbles, while the parent or caregiver replies with a range of words and smiles, and often with hugs, cuddles and close contact. These 'conversations' teach the conventions of turn-taking and the repetition of key words leads in time to an understanding of vocabulary and syntax.

Even babies aged between 0–3 months can differentiate between voices and will turn in response to a familiar one. They are likely to quieten if they are crying as human voices appear to be comforting from the earliest age.

In the early months of a baby's life, the individual sounds or **phonemes** they produce are not culturally specific. At around ten months, these sounds develop into those that the child will use as a native speaker so that noises made by babies from different cultures are now significantly different. At around this time the baby may also start to point, wave and babble in a way that more closely resembles speech. The baby comes to recognise simple and often repeated phrases such as *bye bye* or *night night* along with the names of family members and favourite toys.

KEY TERMS

phoneme the smallest individual unit of sound in a language which conveys a meaning, for example in *fell* and *well*, the *f* and *w* sounds are phonemes

ACTIVITY 7.1

1 Carry out an individual investigation of a parent and infant under one year old. If possible, try to observe the baby's progress over a period of a month, as you should see significant developments during that time. Interview parents or caregivers about the ways in which they talk to their baby: what phrases do they remember using? When do they talk to their baby?

Compare your results with others to see if there seem to be any ages for milestones in speech development.

2 Read the extract of caretaker speech. Explain how you think this way of speaking is helping the baby's speech development.

Participants and context: *Kiri is talking to her baby girl, Charlotte, aged 9 months. She is putting Charlotte into her high chair.*

KIRI	into the chair we go (.) yes there we are (.) in the chair (.) who's a good girl (.) a very good girl
CHARLOTTE	uumm (.) [waves arms]
KIRI	Here's some banana (.) banana for Charlotte (.) to eat all up (1) good girl, yes some nice banana
	[*Charlotte grabs a piece of banana, squashes it in her hand and puts it and her fist into her mouth.*]
KIRI	Is that nice Charlie (.) do you like that (.) good girl (.) mummy's good girl
CHARLOTTE	[*squeals and bangs the highchair table*]
KIRI	Ah good girl (.) here's teddy (.) shall we give teddy some banana Charlie (.) oh good boy teddy eat up your banana
	[*Charlotte looks at Kiri pretending to feed the teddy with banana and laughs and bangs the table again.*]

From one to two years – the holophrastic stage

This is the stage of rapid vocabulary acquisition and basic syntax. A child's first words are usually spoken at about twelve months and, on average, he/she will have gained a vocabulary of about 200 words before their second birthday.

The term **holophrastic** refers to the first grammar, where the meaning of a word may have many possibilities: *milk*, for example, may mean *I've spilled the milk*, *I want some milk*, *you have the milk* or something similar. The familiarity of the parent with the child combined with gestures – waving arms or crying for example – facilitates understanding.

The following are key features of language acquisition between the ages of one and two years.

Many of the lexical items learned are **nouns** referring to people and items in the infant's world (e.g. *mummy, ball, juice, milk, doll, train, book*) as well as family names and pets. Vocabulary items relate to personal interactions (e.g. *bye bye, thank you, no, hello*), simple verbs (e.g. *kiss, sit, drink, walk*) as well as general conditions in their environment (e.g. *hot, all gone, more*). The young child is now much more aware of the world around them so their speech at this stage (as with subsequent ones) links with their wants and needs as well as expressing emotions and naming people and things in their world. Naturally at this stage, children's vocabulary is limited – one word such as *car* may refer to anything with wheels.

KEY TERMS

holophrastic in language acquisition, a single word that expresses a complete idea (e.g. *ball* – could mean the child wants it, has found it, likes it, etc.); caregivers need contextual clues to interpret holophrases

It is perhaps at this stage more than any other that the language used by young children depends on how much they have been spoken to by the family around them.

The child's rate of learning is phenomenal and the **two-word stage** emerges roughly halfway through this period as the child's mastery of their language broadens and their range of expression becomes more complex. They start to use two words together, for example *more milk, daddy juice, mummy sock, train go.* These sentences are not usually **inflected** – there are no indications of tense or person – but there is the emergence of a sequence and order of meaning.

The child is able to use a wider range of initial consonant sounds in the words. Consonant sounds are produced at different times; the earliest consonants pronounced in English are *m, h* and *b.* Certain sounds (**phonemes**) arrive before others. Sounds in the earliest vocabulary include **plosive** sounds (which require a small explosion in production – put your fingers close to your lips to say them and you will feel a small puff of air) *b* and *p*; and **nasal** sounds (produced in the nasal area) *m* and *n.* The words spoken may be only partially formed or pronounced. Many of the sounds produced by very young children seem to have no meaning; they seem to babble for the pleasure of it. Their own language is limited but they have a wider understanding of what is said to them.

The basic conversational pattern of discourse is established as the child begins to chatter, often to himself as well as to others. By the age of two the child has a working vocabulary and is poised for much greater conversational interaction with those around him.

Read the following exchange which takes place outside a shop. Ben, 17 months old, has been walking behind his father and has just fallen over:

BEN	OW OW OW OW
FATHER	[*still walking ahead*] ow ow ow ow
BEN	OOW OW OW OW
FATHER	ow ow ow ow [*turns, goes back and picks up Ben*]

Ben is clearly upset from falling over and is shouting to gain attention with natural expressions of pain. He does not have sufficient vocabulary to express his injuries in any more specific way and as he is shouting loudly and still walking, he is unlikely to be badly hurt. He is more concerned to alert his father to gain comfort and reassurance.

His father is still walking ahead and repeating Ben's sounds, which he may see as showing sympathy; these sounds are immediately repeated by Ben. Now that both child and adult are saying the same sounds, there is a distinct pattern of turn-taking which has changed the distress resulting from the fall into a pattern of mutually repeated vowel sounds, strong and monosyllabic. The language is part of the care giving.

ACTIVITY 7.2

Using the exchange between Ben and his father and its context as evidence, evaluate Ben's stage of language acquisition.

Ages two to three – including the telegraphic stage

During this period and thereafter there is a huge increase in the vocabulary actively used by the child, often by as many as ten words per week. Rough estimates give a vocabulary of about 2000 words by the age of five and many of these words are acquired between the ages of two and three.

> The name of this stage of language development is taken from telegrams, which were printed out from a telegraph machine from the late 19th to the mid-20th centuries. Telegrams were used to deliver urgent messages and, because they were paid for according to number of words, they were usually very brief and only key information was included, for example *Arriving Kuala Lumpur 9pm*.

KEY TERMS

overextension a process used by young children to extend the meaning of a word (e.g. using *dada* as a reference to all men); also called **over-generalisation**

underextension the use of a word in a limited way which does not recognise its full meaning (e.g. young children may use *ball* to describe their own ball but not other balls)

Children have to learn to express their meaning using their limited vocabulary. This often causes **overextension**, when a word is used more broadly than it should be. This occurs at a very early stage of language acquisition. For example, the word *daddy* might be applied to all men; a sibling's name may be used for other children; and words for items with distinctive properties, such as *plate*, may be used for a other things sharing those properties (e.g. a full moon). This is quite a common feature of language acquisition at this age as the child begins to notice more of the world around them.

Overextension sometimes gives way to **underextension**, where a word is used in a very narrow context. For example, a child may use *shoes* to mean his or her shoes but no one else's.

The telegraphic stage follows on from the two-word stage, where a child's utterances become longer and more grammatically complex, and complete utterances emerge although some parts may be missing. The words now have a greater purpose than simply identification of people and objects, but are they still condensed. Look at the following examples:

> *food all gone*
> *mummy come home*
> *we going now?*
> *dada get juice*
> *Asma not sharing ball*

The child is now much more linguistically coherent. The word order is usually straightforward with subject (*food*) and verb (*gone*) though often omitting the auxiliary words (*is*). Additional information such as prepositions (*to, from, under, by*), determiners (*the, a*) and inflections/suffixes to show tense and person (*-ed, -ing, -s*) are omitted in the early telegraphic stage but appear over time.

Pronunciation difficulties still continue. The child is able to produce a wider range of consonants: *p, t, d, n, w, f, v, a*, with *k, g,* and *ng* following later. Other more difficult sound combinations are *sh, ch, j* and *th*, the latter being one of the more difficult sounds to say. Where children cannot say **polysyllabic** words, they abbreviate, for example *banana* becomes *nana*. Interaction with adults shows the child the correct form of the utterances spoken by the adult who is conversing with them.

255

CHILD	[at a station] *train (.) train (.) big train*
FATHER	*Yes (.) up we go into this train (.) careful now (.) it will be going soon (.) see the guard is blowing his whistle*

Even when children are unable to pronounce a word correctly, they recognise the correct pronunciation from adults. Interesting research from Berko and Brown (1960) involved a child who called his plastic fish *fis*. When the adult imitated the child's pronunciation and asked *Is this your fis?*, the child replied *No my fis*. After this the adult said *Is this your fish?* and the child answered *Yes my fis*.

The child's language production – what is *said* – goes hand-in-hand with rapid progress of language reception – what is *understood*. They can now understand two-clause commands such as *pick up teddy and bring him here please* and contrasting concepts such as *hot* and *cold*. They are much more engaged in the language and activities of the household, such as meeting a visitor.

Types of child language

Monologues

From the age of about two, children will often provide a running commentary about what they are doing, as they are doing it. This may extend into their imaginative play.

Mehdi, aged two and a half, is playing with his trains:

Train here (.) [*makes train noises*] no train, yes more train (.) come [*drives toy train and carriages quickly along the tracks and they fall off*] train – train over (.) train back (.) oh dear all fall over (.) train here (.) Thomas train (.) Gordon train (.) vroom [*more train noise*] go in your house trains

As the child becomes older, these short monologues become more like narratives particularly when accompanying imaginative play:

Willow, nearly four, is playing with her dolls:

Now time for bed (.) time to go to bed (.) come on babies time for bed (.) let's put you in the cot (.) do you want your milk now (.) that's nice drink it up (.) now to bed (.) you have to go to bed' cos mummy said (.) mummy said bed (.) night night (.) sleep tight (.) night night

Dialogues

We have seen how important the interaction is between the infant and members of their family, particularly the caregiver. This develops from day one and is helped by the attention of the adult or older sibling to the sounds that the baby makes.

TIP

As you are conversing with a young child, be conscious of the topics that interest them and the type of vocabulary and syntax they use.

Although young children can engage in a dialogue they cannot easily continue a conversation without the input of the parent. Additionally, for the majority of their pre-school years, and even for sometime afterwards, young children talk almost exclusively about their immediate environment and activities.

ACTIVITY 7.3

Reading with young children provides enormous benefits for their development and the impact of reading on their language development is immense.

1   Find a variety of picture and early reading books in your native language at a level suitable for children under three years old. Describe the language and layout of the pictures. In your opinion, how do they help maintain the interest of the young child?

2   The child cannot yet read and must have someone to read to them. Analyse the language used, for example the topics covered, the nouns, adjectives and verb tenses used.

3   Carry out an analysis of the cultural context of the books you are reading and the values which are being promoted.

4   Based on your research, try to produce a rough draft of the first few pages of an early reading book. You could do simple sketches to show how each page would look, for example how you would position the text and pictures.

Three to five years – continuing development

Language development continues rapidly during this stage along with cognitive and social development as the young child's interactions with others in their world continue to broaden.

The following features of language develop at great speed:

- connecting words (e.g. *because, and, if*)
- number words
- words connected with emotions
- family terms (e.g. *auntie, brother*)
- colours
- contrasting concepts (e.g. *longer, bigger*).

This broadening of vocabulary includes distinguishing **hypernyms** (words for categories of things, e.g. *animals*; *vegetables*) and **hyponyms** (words within those categories, e.g. cat, hamster; carrot, cabbage).

Young children learn thousands of new words by listening to parents, siblings and other family members and guessing meaning from context. With a wider social network, including attending play group and listening to stories, children of this age understand many more words than they say. They begin to use longer words at this stage, often words of three or more syllables (e.g. *elephant* and *helicopter*). They often take great delight in saying new and complicated words.

Between the ages of three and five, children become increasingly competent in their communication. Their increasing knowledge of syntax and vocabulary seems to be accompanied by an understanding of the principles of inflection as past tenses

> **KEY TERMS**
>
> **virtuous error** when children make a mistake by over-generalising or over-applying a grammatical rule to an unknown word, for example *I runned, he swimmed*

are added as well as plurals. Children make **virtuous errors**, applying regular grammatical endings to words with irregular forms, for example *runned, mouses, goed, swimmed, wented*.

The Berko *wug* test

A famous experiment was carried out by Jean Berko (1958) to show the application of grammatical rules by children. Young children were shown a picture of an imaginary creature which Berko called a *wug*. Clearly the children had not heard this name before. When they were shown a picture of two of the creatures, children were asked to complete the sentence *There are two ___*. They applied the grammatical principle of adding *s* for plurals and replied *wugs*.

Children between three and five become more fluent, can handle greater vocabulary requirements and are increasingly able to talk appropriately in different situations, such as family and play group. By this stage they are using question forms (*Can I have one?*) and negation (*He doesn't want one*). They are now able to use auxiliary verbs: *do* is the first to appear, followed by *can* and *will*. Children may duplicate modal verbs (*Please may can I … ?*), which might reflect an understanding that *may* is required for manners, while *can* indicates the fact of being able to do something.

By this stage, children can handle more complex utterances with two or more parts. By the age of three, children understand that words often have more than one meaning and although they inevitably mix things up, their fluency is increasing.

Oscar (aged three) and his mother have been playing a game; this is the conversation that followed:

OSCAR	mummy I winned
MOTHER	No, you won
OSCAR	I winned mummy
MOTHER	No Oscar, you won
OSCAR	I not one I three

This mix-up of **homophones** – words which sound the same – show Oscar's understanding of words which sound the same (*one/won*) but he does not grasp that they have different meanings.

Children start to understand **idioms** – expressions with non-literal meanings. For example, in English, the idiomatic phrase *you're pulling my leg* has nothing to do with legs but means *you're teasing me*. This understanding of idiomatic aspects of language starts at around three years but is not fully learned until much later in the child's life.

By now you will be aware that the period from three to five is a time of massive learning and consolidation for young children. They delight in chatter, ask lots of questions, and outsiders can follow what they are saying as their conversation is generally clear in spite of errors with more complex structures.

At any time from infancy onwards, young children are likely to experience the wider world in the form of pre-school or nursery education. As well as meeting a range of new children and adults to communicate with, they will be exposed to an extraordinary breadth of new language and conversations. Pre-school children rarely play together in the style of primary children (they play alongside each other) but language is still exchanged and so their language world is broadened.

As emphasised earlier, exact ages vary from child to child, but in general, by the age of five, children can do the following:

- converse effortlessly in the majority of situations
- understand and articulate complex language structures and tenses
- use the conditional tense: this requires the understanding of an element of possibility or uncertainty (e.g. *If it stops raining we could go to the park.*)
- understand abstract ideas as well as idioms
- take part in conversations – though they may still only be interested in conversations about themselves!

They have come a long way from their early babbles and coos, and are set to become full linguistic participants in their world.

259

> **TIP**
> The greater your awareness of language acquisition by babies and young children, the more confident you will become at recognising stages and assessing the strength of theories.

ACTIVITY 7.4

What linguistic features are evident in the following brief conversation?
Six-year-old Eesha is cross with her father.

EESHA   dad you are so immature

DAD   me

EESHA   I'm mature; I'm six

Read the transcriptions of two conversations and the commentary, which provides a brief overview of both. Choose one of the conversations and analyse closely the language skills of the child.

The children in these two conversations are both four years old.

Conversation 1

ILHAM   I made this picture for you (1)

MOTHER   what is it

ILHAM   it's a tiger

MOTHER   it's a tiger

ILHAM   I thought you liked tigers

MOTHER   I love tigers

ILHAM   that's why I made you one

MOTHER   it looks like a tiger too

| ILHAM | you can put it anywhere in your room |
| MOTHER | I'll put it on the wall, thanks for drawing me this lovely picture Ilham |

Conversation 2

MALAKAI	can I buy those cars that are on TV
GRANDMA	yes with your own money you can buy whatever you want
MALAKAI	but I don't have any money
GRANDMA	well I suppose that means that you can't buy those cars
MALAKAI	well then you buy them for me
GRANDMA	but I don't have much money or a job
MALAKAI	I know I'll give you a job
GRANDMA	what's my job
MALAKAI	a driver (.) driving toys and cars

COMMENTARY

In both of the conversations the four-year-olds are entirely comfortable with the conventions of turn-taking and are able to introduce and change topics. They are talking to family members whom they know well and the topics relate to the children's areas of interest – painting a tiger and wanting more toys. The children are focused in their own world and interests. They are able to move from concrete issues of drawing and buying toys to more imaginative areas such as the mother's interest in monsters or the grandmother's new job of driving toys and cars (the latter proposition is a little unclear!).

Both children are fluent and articulate; they are able to pronounce words clearly and are using questions and statements with adverbials (*well*) as well as appropriate tenses (*I thought you liked*) and ellipsis (*I'll give you*).

Both four-year-olds are able to sustain the conversations. They have no difficulty in responding and are well on the way to conversational competence.

TIP

Within clear ethical limits, try to observe babies with their caregivers (often, but by no means exclusively, the mother) and the ways in which they communicate. Remember this will not only be by the spoken word but by smiles, cuddles and other body language.

ACTIVITY 7.5

Read the following extract and the accompanying commentary which will help you to analyse some features of language acquisition for children of this age. Then, after seeking permission, transcribe a short conversation between a caregiver and child. Analyse the language used by the child and note the types of errors they make.

Joelle, aged 27 months, is having a conversation with her mother while they look at a book together.

JOELLE	look (.) sheeps in field (.) two sheep and big sheep
MOTHER	yes Joelle (.) look there in the field (.) there's two lambs (.) one (.) and two (.) The mother sheep is with them and they're eating grass for their supper.
JOELLE	eat grass (.) sheep eat (.)
MOTHER	look Joelle (.) on this page(.) here is the farmer with his tractor
JOELLE	a tractor (.) a tractor (.) brm brm (.) big tractor in the field with sheeps (.) over the grass (.) big tractor (.) green tractor (.)
MOTHER	that's right Joelle, the farmer is driving the tractor (.) but it's a big red tractor (.) and the sheep are in the field. Let's turn the page and see what else the farmer has on his farm (.) what can you see there (.) look
JOELLE	[*shouting*] ducks ducks on pond (.) ducks on pond swim ducks
MOTHER	You and I fed the ducks on the pond last week didn't we (.) we gave them bread (.) you gave them bread and they were hungry (.) they ate it all up and said 'quack quack' thank you Joelle
JOELLE	ducks quack quack (.) on pond big ducks on pond (.) no bread
MOTHER	you're right Joelle, the ducks in the story don't have any bread (.) do you think the farmer will give them any

Joelle and her mother are sharing a book about a farm. In their conversation, the mother is building on Joelle's limited vocabulary and syntax by using more complex utterances which Joelle can understand even though her own speech is more limited.

Joelle is able to recognise animals which may or may not be present in her own environment. If they are not, then she is able to understand and maybe imagine a little about the animals; they are in a field, they eat grass and are on a farm. Joelle knows the appropriate nouns even though she is making virtuous errors (*sheeps*). Her language is moving though the telegraphic stage as she is phrasing utterances in the simple way of subject/verb (*sheep eat*) and is also using modifiers for extra description (*big, green*). Interestingly she has an understanding of linking words and some determiners (*a, the*). However, she is not using them all the time showing that they have not yet been assimilated as the appropriate forms to use. She is not yet secure with her colours.

Through talking with her mother, Joelle has a clear understanding of the conventions of turn-taking conversation and adds her comments to the more extensive ones which her mother is making. Joelle understands a lot more than she is able to say.

Language acquisition by children and teenagers

The speed of language acquisition in the pre-school child makes it an exciting area to observe and analyse. By the time a child with no significant development problems is in full-time school at around the age of five, they are able to function as independent conversationalists with others in their world.

Your own language will have developed along with all your other cognitive abilities during your time in school. In addition to speech development, you will have become skilled in reading and writing. Unlike speech, these skills are not instinctive and have to be taught. They are however, central to our measurement of an educated society.

ACTIVITY 7.6

1   How did you learn to read and write?
2   What early children's books did you enjoy? How important were books and shared reading while you were learning to read and in your early days as an independent reader?
3   Which particular elements of learning to read and write in your native language were challenging? Which did you enjoy most?
4   Do you feel you have more to learn with regard to reading, writing and speaking? If so, in which particular ways? A discussion of your ideas with other members of your class would be useful here.

Language development from five to eleven years

You may find occasional overlaps between the information in this and earlier sections of this unit. This is because the stages at which language development takes place, although sequential, are approximate and may cut across different age groups.

LINK

For more about **register** turn to page 193 of **Unit 5**.

When children go to school, they broaden their experience from familiar family routines and have to learn about what happens in the outside world, especially at school. They must develop the ability to speak appropriately to a range of people with whom they have different relationships, for example the head teacher, classroom teacher, classroom assistants, bus drivers, dinner ladies, classmates, older and younger pupils. They learn that these different relationships are reflected in the different **register** or level of formality they must use in their speech.

Reading and writing skills assume more importance at this stage of development. There have been many research studies about the influence of language skills on pupils' progress across the curriculum. In Britain, language skills are often linked to lifestyle and social class and it is widely documented that children from economically deprived backgrounds achieve less academic success than their wealthier counterparts. One theory which linked language with achievement was developed in Britain in the 1960s by Basil Bernstein. Bernstein asserted that there are two patterns of language used by school children – a **restricted code** and an **elaborated code**.

The restricted code is associated with lower socio-economic groups. The elaborated code is usually associated with higher socio-economic groups. The codes are not dialects and both are found within Standard English.

According to Bernstein's theory, the restricted code is briefer and more condensed and is very context-bound, so that only the immediate group would be able to understand it. He linked the theory of the different codes and educational success with the assertion that schools use the elaborated code of communication

Restricted code

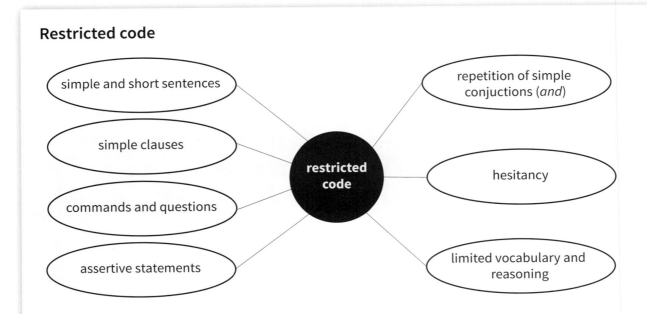

Examples of restricted code: *Don't do that 'cos I said not to; Get your lunch box and get ready and we'll get to school; Shut that door; Right, keep the noise down, I said keep it down, OK; Come on get a move on, you'll be late for school, and make sure you get home quickly we're off down the road, now get moving!*

Elaborated code

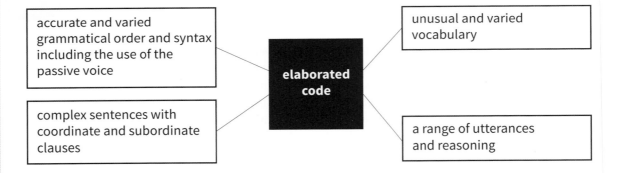

Examples of elaborated code: *Please don't keep banging the door, it's noisy and we'll all develop a nasty headache; After I meet you from school today we'll go on the bus into the city where we'll meet Granny so please try to leave school as quickly as possible.*

with their pupils. Middle-class children arrive at school familiar with this style of language and therefore have an advantage. Working-class children, with their restricted code, are not so familiar with the elaborated code and so struggle to make sense of the communication of information in the curriculum.

Social conditions have changed since Bernstein's theory was first proposed and the sharp divisions between the working and middle classes in Britain and other parts of the world have become blurred. However, regular reports about the lack of educational attainment in areas of deprivation may suggest that the language codes outlined by Bernstein could be a contributory factor.

●●● FURTHER RESEARCH

Bernstein's theory of codes is relevant to the language skills of children aged 5–11. Carry out your own research to find out more about Bernstein's theory.

For very clear review of Bernstein's theories go to **www.youtube.com** and search on 'introduction to Basil Bernstein'.

1 Discuss the strengths and weaknesses of Bernstein's theory of codes.

2 Investigate and discuss some strategies and programmes for primary education which could help children who are only familiar with a restricted code of language. Consider reading, writing and literacy activities.

3 Apply Bernstein's restricted and elaborated codes to the area where you live. Are you inclined to accept or reject his theory? Give reasons.

Language skills of children aged five to seven

■ At this stage, children are good at speaking and expressing requests and ideas using **connectives** (words which join clauses giving additional information and reasons, e.g. *because, as*); these words give the linguistic freedom to express opinions and ideas.

■ The beginnings of reading and writing broaden the exposure to language so that children understand the different meanings of a word and the context in which each meaning is used.

■ Vocabulary extension includes the understanding that different words can have similar meanings (e.g. *unhappy/sad*).

■ Children begin to understand that words can be used both literally and in more imaginative ways; the child's imagination is developing with story reading and creative writing.

■ Children are able to use language for different purposes as they begin to speak more fluently; it is possible to have a sustained conversation with a five-year-old though most of it may relate to themselves and their own world.

ACTIVITY 7.7

1 Read the extract of a conversation in which five-year-old Ethan talks about what he will let his own children do. Use this as a template to assess conversational features of children of this age. If possible, use an example of your own or from your own region.

2 Transcribe an extract from a conversation with a child aged between five and seven. You could search for an example online, or provide your own example. Write an accompanying commentary, using the example provided as a model.

MOTHER	Ethan (.) what did you just tell me you were going to do when you grow up and have your own children
ETHAN	I would let (.) whenever they want to do a paint craft (.) they could paint on the walls
MOTHER	the walls of your house

ETHAN	aha
MOTHER	any craft they want
ETHAN	yep
MOTHER	what else could they do to the walls if they want to
ETHAN	(1) errm (.) they can write words for me (.)
MOTHER	that wouldn't bother you (.) any wall in the house (.) not just the basement …
ETHAN	that would be fine
MOTHER	and in your bedroom
ETHAN	no I wouldn't allow them in my bedroom (.) but downstairs in the basement (.) or in their room (.) they could do it in their room (.) if they wanted
MOTHER	what kind of food would you feed your children
ETHAN	(3) every child could have a different meal (.) I would let them pick out whatever they want to (.) and I would [… *unclear*] let it cook its own dinner …
MOTHER	when would be their own bedtime
ETHAN	(4) probably about ten o'clock
MOTHER	don't you think that's a little late
ETHAN	(2) no (.) cos I'd let 'em play (.) cos they would probably want to play (.) at night time (.) so I would let 'em (.) if they play (.) towards 10 o'clock

COMMENT

This is only part of an extended conversation that Ethan is having at home and where he is being asked to think hypothetically about his own future. He is confident in his answers which, although clearly unrealistic, are nonetheless clearly expressed and in some detail as when he is talking about allowing his children to draw on the walls. He is expressing his views in full utterances (*that would be fine*).

He gives reasons for his decisions (*I'd let 'em play (.) cos they would **probably** want to play*) and here too he is able to consider likelihood or possibilities shown in the use of the conditional tense (*they could paint on the walls*).

Ethan's vocabulary is varied and he is able to embellish ideas with examples such as the different rooms of the house to be used (*room, bedroom and basement*). He uses a modifying adjective to explain his points (*different meal*) and an adverb of time to add detail (*whenever they want*).

He is competent with the rather tricky practice in English of changing the singular *every child* into the plural pronoun *their* although interestingly he makes the **virtuous error** of changing the child into the neuter *it*.

Ethan is at ease with the conversational conventions of turn-taking and is direct in disagreeing about the lateness of bedtime; he does not attempt to use any face-saving strategy. He is dealing with a projected future very much in terms of his own life now.

Language skills of children aged seven to eleven

A whole set of development milestones occur around the age of seven and this applies to language too.

Children of this age speak fluently with a wide vocabulary of several thousand words. Their language efforts at this time are mainly directed towards reading and writing, which unlike speaking, are usually taught in formal education. There are a number of theories about the most effective way of teaching these skills.

Speaking skills continue to develop with a mastery of humour and play on words, which are specific to the native language(s). The child will almost inevitably be involved in arguments and must develop language strategies to manage these, difficult though this is.

Children are still very self-oriented but increasingly look outwards; they are becoming aware that different styles of language are used according to the people and situations they encounter. Their grasp of abstract issues (ideas about what is good and bad and other ethical issues) must all be expressed through their language. Their spoken language may be guided at school and they will have lessons to gain more competence in their native language(s).

Many children are brought up to be bilingual; you may be one of them. This includes children of parents who speak different native languages and transmit this to their children, as well as children who speak one language in the home and another outside. The value of speaking more than one language is becoming more widely recognised in our globalised society.

● ● ● FURTHER RESEARCH

Investigate current theories on the advantages of being brought up to speak more than one language.

267

ACTIVITY 7.8

The following are all major tasks. If possible, and where agreed with your teacher, you may prefer to work with a classmate or in a group.

1 Construct a questionnaire and then interview a range of children and teenagers. If possible, interview a mixture of monolingual and bilingual speakers to assess their views on the advantages and disadvantages of bilingual speaking.

2 Access a reading scheme and evaluate the sequence of language used for learning to read. If possible, speak to someone who teaches children to read and write to find out their views on the most effective strategies for learning these skills.

3 Where ethically possible, obtain examples of children's early writing to see the content and structure of the work. Examine spelling patterns, including any words which emergent writers find difficult.

4 Where ethically possible, listen to emergent readers in your native language. Examine the way they approach unfamiliar words and whether there is a consistent pattern in the difficulties they experience.

Teenage language

As teenagers you may think you receive a very bad press! The media seem happy to represent teenagers as an inarticulate group who express themselves largely through Facebook and who are chained to their cell phones using 'text speak'. This section offers a more balanced approach to the ways in which teenagers use language.

Teenagers are often early adopters of popular culture; style, fashion, music, new technology and language. Older people often criticise the language they hear teenagers using but words they may have used themselves such as *OK*, *blast* and *groovy* once raised eyebrows in the 1950s and 1960s for the same reason! Teenagers are innovators of language and this is an important feature of their conversational styles.

Teenagers are fluent conversationalists. Having learned the conventions from their earliest years, they are now able to bend and break these established patterns, especially in conversation with their peers. Teenagers talk a lot! Their world is bursting with activity which needs to be communicated and, in the digital age, instantaneous transfer of this information is critical to them. Skype, Facebook, FaceTime, phone, twitter, bbm, Snapchat, Whatsapp and Instagram are just some of the methods of social networking which increasingly redefine the boundaries between written and spoken language. These forms of communication generate language which may be unclear or even incomprehensible to those outside the teenage circle.

A criticism of teenagers and their language use is that they may actually reduce their lexical base from a vocabulary of several thousand words acquired in childhood. Teenage language has often been associated with lowered standards, as defined by older generations who often fail to understand teenage use of **patois**. Additionally, there is now the medium of the internet on which teenagers may share different language styles which were not available to their parents and grandparents.

Teenage language acquisition is clearly not about *learning* language, but it is about learning to adapt and use language in situations where they are beginning to play adult roles in society and for which clear communication is essential. Teenagers, more than adults, may live in contrasting language worlds. Online digital communication and behaviour is immediate; it is generated by the user themselves, for example videos posted on YouTube. Teenagers can create their own virtual lives with games and activities that they themselves choose and control. These online activities invariably have their own vocabulary which is understood by the participants. Online teenage gaming advertisements encourage teenagers to *create your own avatar* or *build your own medieval kingdom while you chat and hang out with friends*. Investigation into such games shows that there is a lot of jargon and colloquial phrasing, sometimes leading to bad or abusive language.

By contrast, the style of traditional education, which takes up more and more of the teenage years, may demand more standard English usage. Successful students have to demonstrate that they are able to write and express themselves appropriately. The majority of teenagers successfully code switch between different language styles, but it is those who cannot switch, and are therefore perceived as inarticulate, who become the object of negative media attention.

LINK

For more about language and social groups, turn to page 174 in **Unit 5**.

KEY TERMS

patois the dialect of a particular group, especially one with low status in relation to the standard language

LINK

For more about code switching, turn to page 187 in **Unit 5**.

268

ACTIVITY 7.9

1   Think about your own personal communications. What digital forms of communication do you use? With whom do you communicate and how frequently?

2   To what extent do you code switch when you move from digital conversations with your peer group to communication with the broader community, such as older family members, teachers and employers? Analyse the type of vocabulary and syntactical changes you make, and the reasons why.

3   One online blogger has said that:

Daily, teens confront the challenges and opportunities of code switching in digital spaces, at home and at school. Code switching is not easy to do and can bring coping fatigue, confusion, missteps and distractions.

afsusa via flickr

Discuss this statement with classmates and consider whether it is a fair assertion of the difficulties teenagers face today.

4   Analyse a range of magazines aimed at both male and female teenagers, and TV programmes and films where teenagers are featured, both from your local area and from other countries. What forms of language are prominent? Is the language used in the magazines similar to your own style of speaking? To what extent do teenagers code switch from standard forms of English to teenage colloquial language?

Here are four transcripts of conversations demonstrating teenagers using both appropriate and inappropriate forms of language in order to speak in public.

Transcript 1
Teenagers in a classroom are discussing the ethics of animal testing as part of an exam assessment.

TOM	We're goin' to start to discuss animal testing
PETE	um (.) I reckon that animal testing is wrong (.) because (.) it only harms a few animals but it um (.) saves a large percentage of humans
LEILA	I'd like to argue against that because it doesn't always save humans lives (.) because some products that are tested on animals are in the name of vanity because (.) they're like beauty products which are unnecessary really so (.) would you really kill an anim-/ an animal for a beauty product 'cos I wouldn't (.)
TOM	um (.) we also think it's important to do animal testing because (1) there's been instances in the past where large numbers of humans were about to die from an illness or a disease (.) and some animals have been harmed in animal testing but it's resulted in hundreds and thousands of people being saved from that particular disease

SHANNON	but who says (.) um that they can test a product on an animal an' it's fine on them and then (.) then (.) they test it on a human and it kills them or (.) //
LEILA	// yeah because they've got different DNA so (1) if it's ok with an animal (.) it might not always be all right on a human//
TOM	well life's about survival of the fittest (.) and it's in the best interest to test it on an animal not knowing if it's the right thing to do

www.youtube.com

Transcript 2

The following conversation involves a teenage girl and her maths teacher in a classroom in Essex, near London.

STUDENT	What is pi (.) where did it come from (.) sir who made up pi
MATHS TEACHER	I told you last lesson where it came from
STUDENT	I don't really pay attention [*snaps pen*]
MATHS TEACHER	you were going to do some practice questions on area of a sector
STUDENT	Fun fun fun [*hums and laughs*]
MATHS TEACHER	it's not funny … you're here to work, you're here to learn maths yeah
STUDENT	[*… unclear*]
MATHS TEACHER	I don't care
STUDENT	ooh err
MATHS TEACHER	it's taken you nearly five minutes to open a book (.) come on
STUDENT	[*makes face at teacher*]
STUDENT	[**voiceover**] When I'm messing around I don't really know I'm messing around till I get into an argument with a teacher or somethin' like that but I do actually wanna get good grades and that and listen
MATHS TEACHER	how many questions of those four have you tried
STUDENT	the date
MATHS TEACHER	none. my (1) problem with some people in the class is that they don't seem to remember stuff (.) so you need to remember the area of the circle formula and the circumference of the circle formula

Educating Essex, TV programme

Transcript 3

An extract from Malala Yousafzai's speech at the United Nations. Malala was shot in the head by the Taliban in Pakistan for championing girls' rights to education.

Dear Friends, on the 9th of October 2012, the Taliban shot me on the left side of my forehead. They shot my friends too. They thought that the bullets would silence us. But they failed. And then, out of that silence, came thousands of voices. The terrorists thought that they would change our aims and stop our ambitions but nothing changed in my life except this: weakness, fear and hopelessness died. Strength, power and courage was born. I am the same Malala. My ambitions are the same. My hopes are the same. My dreams are the same.

Dear sisters and brothers, I am not against anyone. Neither am I here to speak in terms of personal revenge against the Taliban or any other terrorist group. I am here to speak up for the right of education of every child. I want education for the sons and the daughters of all the extremists especially the Taliban.

I do not even hate the Talib who shot me. Even if there is a gun in my hand and he stands in front of me. I would not shoot him. This is the compassion that I have learnt from Muhammad – the prophet of mercy, Jesus Christ and Lord Buddha. This is the legacy of change that I have inherited from Martin Luther King, Nelson Mandela and Muhammad Ali Jinnah. This is the philosophy of non-violence that I have learnt from Gandhi Jee, Bacha Khan and Mother Teresa. And this is the forgiveness that I have learnt from my mother and father. This is what my soul is telling me, be peaceful and love everyone.

Dear sisters and brothers, we realise the importance of light when we see darkness. We realise the importance of our voice when we are silenced. In the same way, when we were in Swat, the north of Pakistan, we realised the importance of pens and books when we saw the guns.

271

Transcript 4

An interview with an American teenage competition finalist.

| INTERVIEWER | Recent polls have shown a fifth of Americans can't locate the United States on a world map. Why do you think this is? |
| TEENAGER | I personally believe the U.S. Americans are unable to do so because, uh, some, uh (.) people out there in our nation don't have maps, and, uh, I believe that our education like such as South Africa and, uh, the Iraq everywhere like, such as and ... I believe that they should, our education over here in the U.S. should help the U.S., err, uh, should help South Africa and should help the Iraq and the Asian countries, so we will be able to build up our future. |

www.youtube.com

LINK

For more about slang, turn to page 195 in **Unit 5**.

ACTIVITY 7.10

1 Read the transcripts and evaluate, with evidence, the extent to which the teenagers are able to use an appropriate register of language for the situation.

2 Source your own examples of teenage speech from your local area and, using the same criterion, assess whether teenagers have the ability to code switch.

How is teenage slang developing?

In **Unit 5** you learned about slang and how this form of language is undergoing constant and rapid change with new forms emerging and words appearing and falling out of use. Particular forms of slang are used by teenagers and teenage slang can be a very lively form of expression!

Read this news article about recent developments in new forms of slang used amongst multi-ethnic teenagers in London.

From the mouths of teens

A 'perfect storm' of conditions has seen teen slang from inner-city London spread across the country. But where does this new language originate from? And, if you can't stop kids from speaking it, is there any way to decipher what the words mean?

At the back of a London bus, two teenagers are engaged in animated conversation. "Safe, man," says one. "Dis my yard. It's, laak, nang, innit?

What endz you from? You're looking buff in them low batties."

"Check the creps," says the other. "My bluds say the girls round here are nuff deep."

"Wasteman," responds the first, with alacrity. "You just begging now." The pair exit the vehicle, to blank stares of incomprehension. Later, this dialogue is related to Gus, a 13-year-old who attends an inner London

comprehensive; he wastes no time in decoding it.

''Safe just means hi,'' he says briskly. "Your yard is like your home, where you're from. Nang just means good. Your endz is your neighbourhood. Buff is, like, attractive. Low batties are trousers that hang really low on your waist. Creps are trainers. Bluds are your mates. Nuff means very. Deep is the same as harsh or out of order.

Wasteman is what you say to someone when you're fed up with them. And begging," he concludes, with a flourish, "means chatting rubbish."

There's more: butters means ugly, hype is excitement, bare is a lot, cotching is hanging around, and allow it is a plea to leave something or someone alone. "Everyone in my school speaks like this," says Gus, a little wearily. "It's because you hear the cool kids saying these words and then you have to do it too. You've got to know them all and you've got to keep up. Nobody wants to be uncool," he adds, with a shudder. "That's, like ..."

Sick?

"No, sick is good," he says patiently. "I guess it would just be, you know, deep."

Gus and his ilk have been caught up in an emerging linguistic phenomenon. Researchers have found that, while most traditional cockney speech patterns have followed traditional cockneys as they've migrated out of London, teenagers in inner London, one of the world's most ethnically diverse areas, are forging a separate multi-ethnic youth-speak based on common culture rather than ethnic or social background.

"It is likely that young people have been growing up in London exposed to a mixture of second-language English and varieties of English from other parts of the world, as well as local London English, and that this new variety has emerged from that mix," says Sue Fox, a language expert from London University's Queen Mary College, who's in the middle of a three-year project called Linguistics Innovators: The Language of Adolescents in London. "One of our most interesting findings," she says, "was that we'd have groups of students from white Anglo-Saxon backgrounds, along with those of Arab, South American, Ghanaian and Portuguese descent, and they all spoke with the same dialect. But those who use it most strongly are those of second or third generation immigrant background, followed by white boys of London origin and then white girls of London origin."

"The message is that people are beginning to sound the same regardless of their colour or ethnic background. So we prefer to use the term Multicultural London English (MLE). It's perhaps not as catchy," she says, "but it comes closer to what we're trying to describe."

"Adolescence is the life stage at which people most willingly take on new visible or audible symbols of group identification," says US Essayist, Logan Pearsall Smith. " Thus, fashions specific to this age group change rapidly. Fashion and music often go together, and these in turn are often associated with social class and ethnicity. The same is true of language. It's most obviously observable in terms of slang and new ways of expressing themselves, such as the substitute of 'I'm, like' for 'I said' or 'I thought' a few years ago "What we're seeing with MLE is qualitatively different," continues Professor Paul Kerswill, who is leading the study. "It's a real dialect rather than simply a mode of speech, and there's already evidence that it's spreading to other multicultural cities like Birmingham, Bristol and Manchester. It'll become more mainstream through force of numbers and continued migration, and because it's considered cool."

The last word goes to Gus: "Words change all the time," he says wearily. "It's, like," (even in his out-of-school Standard English, he pronounces this "laaahhkk") "you have to learn a whole new vocabulary every few months just to keep on top of it. It's like, just recently, swag now means bad."

And that's not nang?

"Allow it," he proclaims, switching effortlessly into standard MLE. "It's all getting bare swag."

www.independent.com

ACTIVITY 7.11

1 Read the article and describe how teenage slang is developing and changing in multicultural London.

2 Using the article as a case study, explain how code switching operates for adolescents.

3 Research the extent to which teenage slang is developing in the area where you live.

The functions of young people's language

So far in this unit you have learned about the stages of language development of babies, children and teenagers. These underpin all spoken and written skills throughout life.

However, we all need more than these technical skills in order to engage with those around us and to interpret and manage our lives effectively. This is where **pragmatics** is essential. This concerns the context and reasons for speech, and the ways in which these factors affect the way we speak.

KEY TERMS

pragmatics the study of language as it is used in a social context

We learn many of these conventions unconsciously, for example the most appropriate ways of speaking to different individuals in our lives such as a grandparent or a respected member of the community. However, we may also be taught these codes. For example, many children are taught to say *please* and *thank you* as infants whereas other parents may not emphasise this convention so much.

Pragmatics is a very broad topic and is bound up with other features of a society's accepted ways of communication. As with all forms of communication, what is acceptable changes between places and over time. Traditionally, students addressed their teachers either as Mr, Mrs or Miss and their family name: in many institutions teachers and students are now on first name terms.

In the 19th century children were largely expected to be 'seen and not heard' whereas now much greater self-expression is encouraged for children. In a stereotypical view held by some older British English speakers, American English speakers are thought to have a much greater level of friendship intimacy such as being on first name terms after a very brief acquaintance. English speakers do not have the tu/vous disctinction of address which French speakers use in their personal communications.

In the section about discourse analysis in **Unit 4** you learned that there are times in conversation where we say the wrong thing, resulting in discomfort or even disagreements. Throughout our lives, we continue to adapt, develop and change our pragmatic skills in order to avoid such situations.

ACTIVITY 7.12

The following would not generally be considered appropriate in the context of British English pragmatics:

- Hiya, nice to meet you. How much do you earn?
- You look so much older and more wrinkled since the last time we met.
- This is such a boring conversation, I'm off to find someone much more interesting.
- [*having dinner at someone's home*] This food is disgusting – only fit for the bin.
- Come on then, tell me how old you are. You look about 100.

Think of similar examples of inappropriate communications for the region in which you live.

Halliday's functions of language

The linguist Michael Halliday has described language as *the creature and creator of human society*. This sums up the pivotal importance of language particularly in the development of young children as they acquire skills they will continue to use throughout their lives.

Halliday identified seven functions of language that children need in their early years:

- **instrumental:** language used to fulfil a need – obtaining food, drink and comfort

- **regulatory:** language used to influence the behaviour of others – concerned with persuading, commanding or requesting other people to do things you want (*Mummy get Alex juice*; *play with me*)
- **interactional:** language that develops social relationships and ease the process of interaction – concerned with the phatic dimension of talk (*you're my friend*; *here's my teddy*; *shall we play pirates? Love you mummy*)
- **personal:** language that expresses the personal opinions, feelings and identity of the speaker – sometimes referred to as the 'Here I am!' function, announcing oneself to the world (*me good girl*; *best stripey socks*; *tired boy*)
- **representational:** language used to exchange information – concerned with relaying or requesting information (*need to see Granny*; *finished tea all gone*)
- **heuristic:** language used to explore the world and to learn and discover – children use language to learn; this may be questions and answers, or the kind of running commentary that frequently accompanies children's play (*why is that bird singing? why is the sun yellow? where does the sea go?*; *the dollies are having tea in the doll's house*; *Suki is building trains*; *Ted needs hat for Tigger*)
- **Imaginative:** language used to explore the imagination – may also accompany play as children create imaginary worlds, or may arise from storytelling (*teddy's going to school*; *farmer in his tractor driving brum brum*)

Actions and events in a child's life, however routine, are often accompanied by utterances from adults and other children around them. From about three onwards, young children often live in a constant world of language; this is much more effective if they are active speakers and hearers in their world, rather than passive receivers of language.

The influence of TV on children's language development

Many studies have been carried out to assess the influence of television on children's development. The results of this research are briefly summarised here:

- TV appears to provide no educational benefits for a child under two and the time spent watching TV is time that could be spent more productively interacting with family and other people.
- Passive TV viewing does not develop cognitive language skills which develop in the context of real life and interaction with others.

- The pictures presented on TV may numb a child's imagination.
- Children who watch cartoons and entertainment television during pre-school years have poorer pre-reading skills at age 5 (Macbeth, 1996). Children who watch entertainment TV are also less likely to read books and other print media (Wright & Huston, 1995).

There are many other studies which show that the passive nature of watching TV, even educational TV, may have negative effects on young children's language development. However, this is an area of intense debate. Many claim that pictures on TV may spark some children's imagination for example and new studies emerge regularly.

ACTIVITY 7.13

1 Watch and listen to a young child speaking. Record some of their utterances, then try to categorise them using Halliday's functions of language. These functions were drawn from English-speaking children. If you do not live in a native English-speaking culture, try to apply these functions to your own language: to what extent does the study work as a cross-culturally?

2 What is your opinion of the influence of TV and videos on young children's language development? Investigate research studies and their conclusions.

3 What are the opposing arguments on the benefits of selective TV viewing by young children?

4 Ella, aged four, is talking to her aunt. They are looking at the fish in the pond in her aunt's garden. Ella asks:

- *Why do fish live in water?*
- *Is the water dirty?*
- *Why is the water dirty?*
- *Where does the dirt come from in the pond?*
- *Is the water dirty for the fish?*

Describe the ways in which Ella is using language.

Theories of language acquisition

Language enables us to express a limitless number of ideas and utterances using a limited range of sounds. Language acquisition is a complex process and one for which there are a number of explanations. We have already examined observable events in babies, young children and teenagers, but in this section you will investigate theories about the processes which are thought to take place when children learn language. Many children learn only one native language but in some families and communities, children grow up speaking two languages (bilingual) and sometimes even more.

You will be introduced to key theories which help explain children's ability to learn language. The debate continues about the relative importance of 'nature and nurture' in language development. Another important link is between a child's language and thought. Does thinking come before the production of language? Or can we only think if we have the words to do so?

TIP

The section below explores theories about how language is acquired. You will find it helpful to gather supporting evidence and criticisms from practical observation and research to use when evaluating theories in an essay. By now you will have probably collected some of your own examples of children speaking. You may find these helpful when exploring the theories discussed in the section.

276

KEY TERMS

nature in this context, the inherited genetic and physical make up of a person, for example gender and ethnicity are inherited and almost always fixed

nurture the sum total of all the environmental influences a person experiences – things like schooling and the family environment are important features in nurture

KEY TERMS

conditioning a process whereby behaviour is changed or modified due to the repeated presence of a stimulus; repetition of the stimulus over time triggers a specific form of behaviour (e.g. words of praise are a stimulus to learning language)

Imitation and reinforcement

According to the psychologist B. F. Skinner (1957), language is acquired by **conditioning**. This is process whereby the child imitates the sounds around them, receives praise and approval (*good girl*; *that's a clever boy*) which encourages them to repeat and develop language. The reinforcement of treats, praise and an expanding world enables the child to acquire competence in language.

B. F. Skinner (1904–1990)

B. F. Skinner was an American psychologist who was very influential in developing psychology as a discipline in the mid 20th century. Skinner followed the theories of the Russian scientist Ivan Pavlov, who had worked with dogs to develop the stimulus–response mechanism to influence behaviour. The basis of this idea is that all human and animal behaviours are learned responses, which occur as a result of reinforcement; this is achieved through rewards. These rewards, in the case of children learning language, are given through praise, as well as the desired object such as food or treats or whatever the child wants. Conversely, unwanted or bad behaviour can be extinguished by punishment according to the behaviourist theories proposed by Skinner.

●●● FURTHER RESEARCH

The behaviourist school of psychology was extremely influential in the early days of psychology.

Research the work of Pavlov, particularly his experiments with dogs relating to their learned conditioned response.

Research the work of Skinner, who developed Pavlov's investigations; his research led to his theories on how children acquire language.

Support for this behaviourist theory is evident in that we learn to speak the language we grow up with and adopt the accent of those around us. It is therefore clear that there is a strong environmental influence in the language that we speak.

An important strength of Skinner's work is that he generated early ideas about the process of language development from which other theorists developed further ideas, including those outlined below.

However, there are arguments which suggest that behaviourist theory is unlikely to account entirely for language acquisition:

- Each child produces an infinite number of utterances, many of which they will never have heard before, so they do not imitate exactly.
- Children make virtuous errors of grammar and language which adults do not generally do (*I rided my bike; me want that*). This shows that they are applying rules which they understand such as the *-ed* inflection of many verbs in the past form.
- Babies and children seem to pass through the same stages of language development; if this were entirely dependent on the people around them, there would probably be much more variation.

- Children correct their own language to a standard form even when adults do not correct them.
- Children can understand a lot more language than they are able to speak. A mother may tell her 14-month old toddler to put her toys away; the child will understand but will not be able to answer in the same way.

ACTIVITY 7.14

1 Discuss the ways in which you may have imitated your family and friends as you were acquiring language.
2 Ask your family or caregivers how they helped you to learn to speak when you were a child. What encouragement did you receive?
3 Review Skinner's theory of conditioning and evaluate its contribution towards our understanding of language acquisition.

KEY TERMS

Language Acquisition Device an innate system in the brain which allows the spontaneous development of language in a child from birth, according to Chomsky (1965). This is in contrast to the learning of a second or subsequent language later in life

278

Innate language competence – the Language Acquisition Device

The inadequacies of the imitation and reinforcement theory were criticised by the eminent linguist Noam Chomsky (1965). He disagreed that all behaviour, including that of learning language, was learned and put forward an opposing theory. He suggested that the human brain has an innate ability to learn language – a **Language Acquisition Device (LAD)** – which allows children to develop language skills. The theory suggests that this device enables children to be receptive to language development and that they are able to acquire the language(s) around them.

According to this view, all children are born with an instinct for a universal grammar, which makes them receptive to the common features of all languages. Because they possess an instinctive capacity to learn grammatical structures, young children easily pick up a language when they are exposed to its particular form.

Chomsky's initial theory was supplemented and popularised by linguist Eric Lenneberg (1967), who stated that the LAD must be activated at a **critical period** for native language acquisition to take place. The time of this period was broad, but early and mid-childhood are variously proposed. There has been a further development to broaden this to a **sensitive period** when language learning might be more successful. Again, the suggested age-range is broad but from birth to puberty is considered a sensitive time for language acquisition of a native language.

Evidence for an innate human capacity to acquire language skills comes from the following observations:

- The stages of language development occur at about the same ages in most children, even though different children experience very different environments.
- Children's language development follows a similar pattern across cultures.
- Children generally acquire language skills quickly and effortlessly.
- Deaf children who have not been exposed to a language may make up their own language. These new languages resemble existing languages in sentence structure, even when they are found in different cultures.

Language Acquisition Device (LAD): key points
- Children learn to speak very rapidly and an innate capacity for language explains this.
- Children make virtuous errors of tenses and syntax by applying deep language structures before they are aware of the correct forms.
- The subject–verb form of grammar is common to all languages and children seem to be aware of this structure even when they make up their own languages.

However, the LAD may not be sufficient to explain language development. Linguistics author Harry Ritchie argues against Chomsky's Language Acquisition Device and is of the opinion that Chomsky was *brilliant but wrong.* He cites recent evidence from neurology, genetics and linguistics, which all point to there being no innate programming. Ritchie appears to veer towards a more Skinner-like view when he states that *Children learn language just as they learn all their other skills, by experience.*

The following studies show some of the limitations of the theory of the Language Acquisition Device.

Study 1: Jim

Bard and Sachs (1977) studied Jim, a child of deaf parents. His parents wanted Jim to speak normally so they did not use sign language to him and he spent much time watching TV. In this way he heard a lot of language but did not produce any himself and became very retarded in his speech development until he was placed with a speech therapist. According to Chomsky's theory, the LAD would have enabled Jim to speak but he failed to do so, suggesting that the LAD itself was not enough for Jim to learn to speak.

Study 2: Genie

Genie was an infamous case of parental neglect. She was discovered in Los Angeles in California in 1970 at the age of 13, tied to a chair in a small room in the family home where she had been confined throughout her life. She had no language and could only grunt. She was taken into care and her parents prosecuted. Genie posed an ethical dilemma for researchers: humans can never be subjected to this sort of deprivation for the sake of an experiment, so Genie's situation was used for psychology development studies as well as studies on language acquisition.

Genie soon began to make rapid progression in specific areas such as learning to use the toilet and dress herself. In her initial assessment, Genie scored only at the level of a one-year-old but she quickly began adding new words to her vocabulary. She started by learning single words and eventually began putting two and, later, three words together in sequence as in typical infant language acquisition. However, the rapid language development which would have been expected thereafter never materialised. Importantly, Genie never appeared able to sequence words which Chomsky felt was critical in the Language Acquisition Device.

Genie's unfortunate situation did prove interesting for testing theories and it would seem to support the idea of a critical period for native language acquisition. However, there are many other variables here including the innate ability of Genie as well as the severe nature of the abuse she had received. Her case could not definitively prove or disprove the theories of Chomsky and Lenneberg.

●●● FURTHER RESEARCH

Find out more about Jim and Genie in relation to the extent of their ability to acquire language.

There have been other studies of **feral children** – that is, children who have lived isolated from other humans for an extended period. Some of these children may have been reared by animals. You may wish to learn more about them. There are many books and online resources.

The Language Acquisition Support System (LASS)

Chomsky's Language Acquisition Device has limitations which were addressed by linguist Jerome Bruner (1983) with the **Language Acquisition Support System (LASS)**. The limitations cited for the LAD were as follows:

KEY TERMS

Language Acquisition Support System (LASS) a system of support from caregivers to children that helps them to acquire language and become sociable, according to Bruner (1983)

- The theory takes no account of any interaction of the child with those around him. The LAD is assumed to be innate and so will develop automatically into the native language spoken around the child.
- There is no evidence of a grammar structure or language device in the brain.
- Studies of deprived and feral children have shown that language does not develop automatically in the absence of language stimulation around the child.
- The LAD implies that children play no active role in their language acquisition but observation shows that children are active learners.
- The LAD takes no real account of the child's social world.

According to Bruner, the innate abilities of the child (the Language Acquisition Device) are supported and brought out by parents, family and educators.

Language Acquisition Support System (LASS): key points

- Parents and carers regularly interact with the child and give help in naming while they talk to him or her. This includes caretaker language, singing songs, reading and playing games with the child. The family surrounding the child will often repeat the same words and phrases. The child is actively interacting with the caregiver.
- The Language Acquisition Support System is particularly important between the ages of two and five when the child's language learning is most intense. This links with the idea that there is a critical period for native language learning to flourish.
- Pre-school education provides a scaffold of support for the child's language development by extensive interaction with adults and other children in a variety of situations as well as broadening the child's horizons.

LINK

To find out more about virtuous errors, look back at page 258 in this unit.

ACTIVITY 7.15

Read the transcript of Alex, aged two years and ten months, talking to his mother.

1 Analyse the transcript and look at the **virtuous error**s Alex makes.
2 What observations can you make about Alex's developing language and the role his mother is playing in the conversation?
3 What evidence for the LAD and the LASS can you find here?

ALEX	I tired (.) very tired (.) Teddy tired
MOTHER	are you tired (.) you've been a busy boy; teddy must be tired too
ALEX	I runned fast (.) very fast (.) teddy runned with me (.) fast (.)
MOTHER	You ran so fast(.) you must be tired (.) you ran to the park and then mummy pushed you on the swing (.) you liked that swing didn't you (.)
ALEX	teddy had a swing too (.) wheee [*runs around the room swinging teddy round and round*] Alex push teddy on big swing (.) nana mummy
MOTHER	Say please Alex. Say please may I have a banana
ALEX	pease nana mummy

KEY TERMS

cognition the mental processes involved in gaining knowledge and abilities through thought, experience, and the senses

Cognitive development

In both the LAD and LASS theories, humans have a capacity for language development that is separate from **cognitive development**; one is not dependent on the other.

However, cognitive theories link the child's language with their cognitive development. The originator and most important cognitive theorist, Jean Piaget (1896–1980), revolutionised child development ideas with the assertion that a child was not a miniature adult in their thinking, but went through stages of increasingly complex mental development alongside their language development. Piaget believed that children are born with cognitive ability which develops along with the child and upon which all subsequent learning and knowledge is based. For Piaget, language development goes hand in hand with cognitive development. In each of the stages of the child's development, a greater level of mental ability brings about a greater understanding of language and communication. For Piaget, language does not stand alone; it develops alongside the child's understanding of their world.

Piaget believed that children construct an understanding of the world around them and this understanding develops in specific stages of their thinking:

■ the **sensorimotor stage**: babies acquire their earliest knowledge through their physical actions and the sensations they experience. This stage lasts until about the age of two. An important feature of this stage is the development of **object permanence** for the child where they realise that things apart from themselves have an independent existence and so have names (e.g. *ball*, *mummy*, *juice*).

In this way language begins and develops quickly with the infant's increasing engagement with the environment.

- the **pre-operational stage**: between the ages of two and five, young children are able to think in more definite terms and this is when language develops quickly although the child only thinks of the world in relation to themselves (an **egocentric** perception – everything is about *me*).
- the **concrete operational stage**: between the ages of five and eleven or twelve, the child is able to use language for situations outside their immediate experience and is able to think more logically about specific 'concrete' or observable situations. One important element of this stage of cognitive development is **conservation** where the child understands that something stays the same in quantity even if its appearance changes (e.g. transferring water between different-sized beakers).
- the **formal operational stage**: the final childhood stage in cognitive theory where, from the age of about twelve, adolescents are able to understand abstract ideas and the language associated with them.

Notice that there is an integration of psychology and language in this summary of Piaget's work. Educationalists have developed school curricula and styles of learning based on his work. Piaget was the first in his field so his work has been extensively reworked and developed, but essentially his theory – that children's thinking is **different** from that of adults – revolutionised the field of child development throughout the world.

Piaget's stages of development: key points

- Cognition theories form an important branch of psychology and branch out from language development. While there is almost certainly a close link between the development of cognitive understanding and language, there are other influences too.
- More recent studies have highlighted that children progress through the cognitive stages more quickly than Piaget stated and this is also reflected in their language development.
- Piaget's theories have had an enormous influence in the development of the curriculum for primary education.
- Lev Vygotsky is another cognitive theorist who took Piaget's ideas of child development stages further. He particularly emphasised the value of language in developing thought and the fact that adult interaction with children was vital in their development.

ACTIVITY 7.16

1 Many countries now show TV documentaries about child development, for example *Child of our Time* presented by Professor Robert Winston, is a good British example. Try to find studies of child development from your own region.

2 Play *Peepo* with a baby and watch their response. Why is a young baby always really pleased to see you again when you disappear behind a cushion and re-emerge? How is this explained by Piaget's development stages?

3 Arrange some different shaped containers in front of a two-year-old. Pour liquid from a short, fat container into a taller, narrow one. Ask the child if there is the same amount of liquid in the second container. Try to link their responses to Piaget's stages of development.

1   Research Piaget's theories of cognition in more detail and read about the practical ways in which he measured cognitive development in children. There are many books and online resources including some of the fascinating studies Piaget carried out to show the patterns of children's thought.

2   Vygotsky was another giant of the cognitive development school of thought. Research his views on how language development affects the stages of child development.

Evaluation of the theories of language acquisition

The number and complexity of language acquisition theories means that this section is merely an outline of some of the more significant ideas. All children who have the physical capability of voice production will learn to speak their native language. It is a huge achievement, as impressive as it is effortless.

You probably feel that the different theories of language acquisition are complex and that there is no easy way to assess their relative strengths and weaknesses. The explanation of the theories in this section has provided some general principles to consider for the kind of discussion which you might undertake in critical essays where you are asked to compare and evaluate theories of language acquisition.

Since child language acquisition is a universal feature it should be possible to apply the theories cross-culturally. Much language acquisition research has been carried out in the USA and Europe. It would be useful for you to investigate what language acquisition studies have been carried out in your part of the world and the extent to which these support or modify the theories discussed above.

Give me a child for the first seven years and I will give you the man is a quotation from St Ignatius Loyola. This might have been quite difficult to understand previously, but you will now have come to appreciate that all of the theories discussed in this section emphasise to some degree the fundamental importance of the family and wider circle in the young child's environment.

Summary of language acquisition theories

The main language development theorists stress different elements in the acquisition of language:

- **Skinner** believed learning took place in the environment with constant rewards.
- **Chomsky** put forward the existence of an innate skill in language learning. His Language Acquisition Device (LAD) has been modified by later studies to include support and interaction from people in the child's world – the Language Acquisition Support System (LASS).
- **Piaget** and other cognitive development theorists saw language acquisition and development going hand in hand with the maturing child and their understanding.

The theories and discussions continue!

How would you approach an essay asking you to 'critically evaluate'?

A Level essay questions, particularly those at A2, require candidates to write a critical essay on topics from the specification. You will know that this form of answer is an extended piece of reasoned writing where you will explore issues in an informed way, combining your knowledge with independent research on the topics you have covered.

Essay questions at A Level will always ask you to *evaluate*, *appraise* or *discuss* the topics and theories rather than simply state facts about them. You must not only learn and understand the theories, but be able to comment on their strengths and weaknesses using research evidence or case studies. You should be positively and negatively critical of an idea, but always with supporting evidence.

Any evaluation of a theory must be prefaced with a succinct account of its key points. The majority of your answer should focus on a discussion of the extent to which the ideas strengthen general principles. Inevitably research will have been carried out with some statistical levels of proof for the theory. You will need to quote the main points of this research and consider both the **reliability** and the **validity** of the results. You will have studied supporting evidence and weaknesses in your preparation for this exam. Make your views clear by using clear connectives – words and phrases which signpost the building of your argument.

Of course, researchers have invested considerable time and energy into their work and you may feel that your own voice is insignificant – but your informed voice should be heard. If you live in a region significantly different from the culture in which the theory has been tested or you know of such differences, it is important that you add your evaluative comments which could be very useful as part of a conclusion.

A critical approach is not only useful for evaluating research-based ideas but can be also applied to any essay where you are asked to assess the strength or weakness of a point of view. Phrases like *to what extent …* or *How far do you agree that …* are signposts that you should evaluate your material and then give your own substantiated conclusions.

Scientific studies are always developing so it is important to assess the extent of useful research which has taken place since the theory was put forward, to strengthen or perhaps weaken its original premise. Cross-cultural validity is an important factor so if you are able to cite studies carried out in a different part of the world and compare results, you will strengthen your argument.

Make sure you get plenty of practice with writing introductions because this is where you set out your plans for your writing. There is no template for writing an effective introduction, but some helpful strategies include:

- providing an explanation to your reader about your interpretation of key words or phrases
- giving an evaluative overview
- avoiding weak phrases which state the obvious. Avoid sentences like *In this essay I am going to write about …* This is pedestrian and will fail to set you and your reader off on an interesting exploration of ideas.

In an exam, spend a few minutes planning the structure of your essay. Time management is crucial. You should know the allocation of time for each question – make sure you stick to it! You stand a better chance of success with two reasonable essays than one very long essay followed by a much briefer and rushed one.

KEY TERMS

reliability the extent to which an experiment gives the same results on repeated trials

validity the degree to which a study accurately reflects or assesses the principle that is being measured

Your essay plan should always include the sequence of the argument. Topic sentences for each paragraph should explain the content which follows. The topic sentence can then be followed by further specific details, research and theory. Connectives are hugely helpful for foregrounding your pattern of thought. *Firstly, secondly* can help to set you off. Then use pointers which build and reinforce what you have already said: *Additionally, Therefore, In consequence* flag up additional support while *however, nevertheless, although* and *whereas* will introduce material to modify or refute the case you have been building up. Your examiner is looking for clearly explained points which focus on the question so avoid 'empty' words such as *cleverly, basically* or *of course* which do not demonstrate your learning.

Avoid asking too many questions in your answer: remember that you are supposed to be answering the question! You might, however, question the topic quotation and its slant.

There will be extract-based questions which ask you to discuss characteristics evident in the extract. Invariably these will also ask you to use your broader knowledge of the topic. Credit will be given for this so try to range more widely than the given extract.

There is no need to repeat information in an essay though you may summarise key points supporting or refuting your argument in your conclusion.

These are very general guidelines, appropriate for all work at A Level. Remember, when writing essays your engagement with the topic should reflect the interest, enthusiasm and hard work with which you have undertaken your programme of study.

LINK

For more practice and self-evaluation on this unit, see page 292.

285

Part 2: Practice and self-evaluation

Unit 4: Practice and self-evaluation

In this section you will:

- have the opportunity to apply and practise independently the skills and knowledge you have gained in Unit 4
- evaluate what you have learned and what you need to improve.

Ask your teacher or refer to the exam information in your syllabus to set an appropriate time limit to complete the reading and the tasks below. Once you have completed the tasks, it is important that you think about what you have done effectively, and what you need to improve. If you need to revisit key skills, re-read the relevant sections of Unit 4.

> **ACTIVITY 4.12**
>
> The following extract is from an online newspaper article about how children's development may be affected by concerns for their health and safety.
>
> 1 Imagine you are a consultant in the children's unit of a large hospital, and you have seen many injuries from childhood accidents. Write the beginning of a letter to the online newspaper giving your views on the need for safety in children's lives. Write your response in 120–150 words.
> 2 Compare the style and language of your response with the style and language of the original article.

When we stop children taking risks, do we stunt their emotional growth?

Playgrounds are closing down. Parents rarely let their kids out of sight. Society is hamstrung by 'health and safety', says Susie Mesure

A small face looms out of the gloom, bringing his red scooter to a halt just before the road. The boy, five, is on his own. Seconds later, he's off again, calling over his shoulder, 'I'll meet you after the bike tunnel.' I find him, breathing heavily, by the school gate, beaming with pride not at beating me but making the journey (more or less) alone. But his bubble is soon pricked: his face crumples after a classmate calls his exploits 'naughty'. And heaven knows what his grandma would say!

For parents, this is the dilemma of everyday life in the urban jungle: do we keep our children on a metaphorical umbilical cord or cut them free? It's little wonder that kids are growing up afraid to take risks when we're so scared of letting them live for themselves. And admit it, if you're a parent, you are scared, your heart beating a little faster at every headline of woe or tree they climb. Even, or perhaps especially, when we're paying someone else to look after them. Thus a working mum grabbing lunch in a café calls to check up on her child. First eavesdropped question, "Is the playground nice?" Then, "Is it soft underneath?"

We like our playgrounds cushioned and our children accounted for: they're signed up to music lessons, drama classes and organised sports as soon as they can walk and talk – the latest being mini rugby clubs for tots as young as two. "The dominant parental norm is that being a good parent is being a controlling parent," says Tim Gill, author of No Fear, which critiques our risk-averse society. But at what cost? And what's the alternative? And most importantly, when are we letting them play?

A Danish conference hall gently buzzes with grown men and women trying to replicate the exact pattern of six coloured plastic bricks being held up on stage. About 150 people have gathered in Billund, Lego's HQ, at the invitation of the brickmaker's philanthropic arm, the Lego Foundation, because they are worried that children are being short-changed when it comes to that "p" word, the right to which is enshrined in a UN declaration no less. They range from Harvard professors to ambitious entrepreneurs; all are united in their concern that children are paying the price for our parental panicking. In other words, playtime is over.

The upshot, warns Peter Gray, a psychologist at Boston College and author of Free to Learn, is anxiety and depression; even suicide is increasing. And it's all because children feel "their sense of control over their lives has decreased". He should know: now 70,

he recalls growing up in the US in the 1950s. "By the time I was five, I could go anywhere in town on my bike. I could go out of town as long as I was with my six-year-old friend." His research links the rise of emotional and social disorders with the decline of play: "If we deprive children of play they can't learn how to negotiate, control their own lives, see things from others' points of view, and compromise. Play is the place where children learn they are not the centre of the universe." And in case you're not sure: "When there's an adult there directing things, that is not play."

From an article by Susie Mesure in *The Independent online*, Sunday May 25th 2014 at http://www.independent.co.uk/life-style/health-and-families/features/when-we-stop-children-taking-risks-do-we-stunt-their-emotional-growth-9422057.html

---

ACTIVITY 4.13

Texts A and B both relate to the American writer James Ellroy.

Text A contains extracts from a transcription of a radio interview with him. Text B is an extract from a magazine article about Ellroy, also featuring part of an interview. In both texts, Ellroy describes his relationship with his parents and his experience of growing up.

Compare the language and style of Text A and Text B.

Cambridge International AS and A Level English Language 9093 Specimen Paper 3 (2014), Q2.

Text A
Key: E = James Ellroy; I = Interviewer (.) = pause

I as a little boy did you have many friends (.) did you have people over to play (.) did you go and play in other peoples gardens

E very (.) rarely (.) i talked to animals (.) a lot (.)

I and were you aware of the rumbling unhappiness between your parents was it something that was lived out in front of   5

E profoundly aware

I right

E yes (.) they were (.) an acrimonious (.) couple they had each others number (.) she knew that (.) he was weak slothful fanciful duplicitous (.) they couldnt quite let each other go (.) then she got tired of their (.) antics 'n pulled the plug first   10

I james (.) how old were you when you first thought of writing

E (.) eight (.) or (.) nine years old i knew my destiny was to become a novelist (.) it took me (.) twenty one years (.) to get around to it (.)

| I | when you were eight or nine (.) i have a picture of (.) someone (.) who was living quite a (.) solitary life (.) a life in his head (.) did (.) did you (.) was it where you retreated to inside your head and thought of writing books | 15 |

| E | (.) yes (.) i wanted to (.) to (.) do (.) well (.) surpassingly well (.) at what (.) i most loved to enjoy (.) | |

| I | and did your mother (.) and your (.) father encourage you to read | |

| E | they were both big readers my father taught me to read when i was three | 20 |

| I | okay (.) oh (.) so you were a very smart little boy | |

| E | it wasnt that i was smart (.) it was that i could read damn young (.) i was a great big kid with poor social skills (.) a very dim social sense (.) very little awareness of (.) the world (.) around me (.) but i was a disciplined thinker (.) and it is something that has (.) aided me immeasurably (.) in my life as a writer (.) i can sustain concentration (.) i can lay in a dark room (.) and think | 25 |

| I | is it right you dont own a computer you dont own a cell phone | |

| E: | no (.) no cell phone no computer | |

| I | why | |

| E | (.) i deliberately isolate myself from the culture (.) so that i might more efficaciously live in my head (.) past periods of american history (.) in order to recreate them better for my readers (.) i dont go to the store (.) i dont go to the dry cleaners (.) i dont go to movies (.) or watch television | 30 |

| I | do you like feeling different (.) i mean most of these things are the tentpegs that support peoples lives these days doing all those things | 35 |

| E | i like to brood (.) i like to think (.) i like to lie in the dark and do absolutely nothing | |

Text B

His apartment could double as a film-noir set: dark red walls, heavy shades, dim yellow lights, plush leather furniture. There are posters for the movie adaptations of L.A. Confidential and The Black Dahlia. Two massive dark mahogany bookshelves frame the entrance to his living room. The bookshelves are full. Every single book is by James Ellroy.

Ellroy is a hulking presence. He is six foot three, with strong eyes and a tall, gruff face that reflexively composes itself into a frown. He does not walk so much as stomp. During rare pauses in conversation he makes deep guttural noises to fill the silence. His tone is relentlessly jocular, conspiratorial, wisecracking. He screams with laughter…   5

We spoke for several hours each afternoon, the sunlight disrupting the darkness of the living room in thin horizontal bars. Ellroy usually nursed his trademark drink, a quadruple espresso on the rocks, and when he got particularly animated he would pitch his torso forward, as if he were about to jump across the table; at other times he'd stand up to full height, blocking out the sun.   10

ELLROY   I was hatched in the film-noir epicenter, at the height of the film-noir era. My parents and I lived near Hollywood. My father and mother had a tenuous connection to the film business. They were both uncommonly good-looking…   15

I grew up in a different world, a different America. You didn't have to make a lot of dough to keep a roof over your head. There was a

	calmness that I recall too. I learned to amuse myself. I liked to read. I liked to look out the window.	20
INTERVIEWER	What did your parents do?	
ELLROY	My mother was a registered nurse. She worked a lot. At one point she had a job at a nursing home where movie stars brought their aging parents. She was fluent in German... She was a big reader of historical novels, and she was always listening to one specific Brahms piano concerto—I remember a blue RCA Victor record...	25
INTERVIEWER	What was your childhood like before your mother's death?	
ELLROY	I don't remember a single amicable moment between my parents other than this: my mother passing steaks out the kitchen window to my father so that he could put them on a barbecue.	30
	I had my mother's number. I understood that she was maudlin, effusive, and enraged. I also understood that she had my father's number—that he was lazy and cowardly.	
	There was always something incongruous about them. Early on, I was aware of the seventeen-year age gap. When I knew her, my mother was a very good-looking redhead in her early forties. My father was a sun-ravaged, hard-smoking, hard-living guy. He looked significantly older at sixty than I do now. Everybody thought he was my granddad. He wore clothes that were thirty years out of style. I remember that he had a gold Omega wristwatch that he loved. We were broke, and then all of a sudden, one day, the watch wasn't there. That broke my heart.	35 40

Text A © transcribed from Desert Island Discs, Sunday January 17th 2010, http://www.bbc.co.uk/iplayer/console/b00psp99.
Text B © Nathaniel Rich; James Ellory; The Art of Fiction No. 201,
http://www.theparisreview.org/interviews/5948/the-art-offiction-no-201-james- The Paris Review 2011.

Unit 5: Practice and self-evaluation

In this section you will:

- have the opportunity to apply and practise independently the skills and knowledge you have gained in Unit 5
- evaluate what you have learned and what you need to improve.

Ask your teacher or refer to the exam information in your syllabus to set an appropriate time limit to complete the reading and the task below. Once you have completed the task, it is important that you think about what you have done effectively, and what you need to improve. If you need to revisit key skills, re-read the relevant sections of Unit 5.

ACTIVITY 5.34

Spoken language and social groups
The following text is a transcription of part of a conversation between some teenagers (two boys Amrik and Zack, and two girls Bina and Yasmin) talking about some of the part-time jobs they have had.

Discuss ways in which the speakers are using language here to communicate as a group. You should refer to specific details from the transcription, relating your observations to ideas from your wider study.

Cambridge International AS and A Level English Language 9093
Specimen Paper 4 (2014), Q1.

290

AMRIK	so (.) after that job (.) after the
	//
BINA	after the one where
	//
AMRIK	then it was removals (.) you know [*laughs*]
	//
YASMIN	you mean like
	FURNITURE removals	5
	//
ZACK	i can just see you amrik (.) like (.) you know (.) like the chuckle brothers[1]
	[*imitates comic voices*] TO ME (.) TO YOU
	//
BINA	[*laughs*] yeah i can just see him too
	//
AMRIK	i
	sort of (.) i still (.) sort of do that in the summer now (.) like (.) every so often 10
	(.) like (.) cause its
	//
YASMIN	yeah its (.) like
AMRIK	so its like (.) so i've signed on with this (.) this agency
BINA	its its (.) good money
	//
AMRIK	so they get me (.) like (.) its all like (.) MANUAL labour (.) so 15
	its like (.), erm (.) what do you call (.) like the (.) you know
	//
BINA	its good money for that (.) cause
	i've done that before
	//
AMRIK	its not
	GREAT money (.) its like four pounds fifty an hour 20
YASMIN/	
ZACK	[*both laugh*]
BINA	i did this (.) this thing (.) where i worked like three (.) three days and i got
	three hundred pounds for it
	//
YASMIN	REALLY

	//	
ZACK	thats a lot for	25
	//	
AMRIK	sometimes you get	
	//	
YASMIN	mm hmm	
AMRIK	you get (.) like (.) you know (.) TIPS and stuff (.) like (.) if youre doing	
	//	
YASMIN	yeah (.) like if youre	
	//	
AMRIK	if youre	30
	doing (.) like a house move (.) then some people (.) like (.) i got	
	//	
BINA	yeah	
	//	
AMRIK	i got twenty quid[2]	
	one time	

[1] *chuckle brothers* a comedy series involving two clumsy furniture removal men, shown on children's television
[2] *twenty quid* slang for twenty pounds (money)

TRANSCRIPTION KEY
(1) = pause in seconds (.) = micro-pause // = speech overlap
[italics] = paralinguistic features [UPPER CASE] = increased volume

291

Unit 6: Practice and self-evaluation

In this section you will:

- have the opportunity to apply and practise independently the knowledge and understanding you have gained in Unit 6
- evaluate what you have learned and what you need to improve.

Ask your teacher or refer to the exam information in your syllabus to set an appropriate time limit to complete the reading and the task below. Once you have completed the task, it is important that you think about what you have done effectively, and what you need to improve. If you need to revisit key areas, re-read the relevant sections of Unit 6.

ACTIVITY 6.23

Below are two passages dealing with the concept of English as an international or global language.

Discuss what you judge to be the key issues raised in these texts about the emergence of English as a global language. You should make reference to specific details from the two passages, as well as including ideas and examples from your wider study.

Passage A is an extract from a case study called *Minority Ethnic English*.

An international language

English is hugely important as an international language and plays an important part even in countries where the UK has historically had little influence. It is learnt as the principal foreign language in most schools in Western Europe. It is also an essential part of the curriculum in far-flung places like Japan and South Korea, and is increasingly seen as desirable by millions of speakers in China. Prior to WWII, most teaching of English as a foreign language used British English as its model, and textbooks and other educational resources were produced here in the UK for use overseas. This reflected the UK's cultural dominance and its perceived 'ownership' of the English Language. Since 1945, however, the increasing economic power of the USA and its unrivalled influence in popular culture has meant that American English has become the reference point for learners of English in places like Japan and even to a certain extent in some European countries. British English remains the model in most Commonwealth countries where English is learnt as a second language. However, as the history of English has shown, this situation may not last indefinitely. The increasing commercial and economic power of countries like India, for instance, might mean that Indian English will one day begin to have an impact beyond its own borders.

From a case study produced by the British Library, London, UK, at http://www.bl.uk/learning/langlit/sounds/case-studies/minority-ethnic/

Passage B is an extract from an article called *English as a Global Language*.

Since English is so widely spoken, many non-native speakers have found that they've been required to learn it to stay in business. English has approximately 375 million native speakers, born in the United Kingdom, the United States, Canada, Australia and other countries. However, it has been estimated that there are over a billion non-native speakers of English. Some people mistakenly think that English is a Romance language. It is rather a Germanic language which was heavily influenced by the Normans upon their conquest of England in 1066. The Normans eventually went on to become the French. The early Britons adopted many of the Norman word roots, which has resulted in many similarities between French and English today. Today, English is widespread largely due to the fact that it is used so heavily in television, film and music. Hollywood's global spread has contributed strongly to the international popularity of English. It is also the predominant language on the Internet. Web pages in other languages often tend to have an English translation. The British Empire and the dominant nature of American popular culture have contributed overall to the spread of English across the planet.

From an article by Parimal P Gohil in the International Journal for Research in Education, February 2013, at http://raijmr.com/wp-content/uploads/2013/02/2_7-13-Parimal-P.-Gohil.pdf

Unit 7: Practice and self-evaluation

In this section you will:

- have the opportunity to apply and practise independently the skills and knowledge you have gained in Unit 7
- evaluate what you have learned and what you need to improve.

Ask your teacher or refer to the exam information in your syllabus to set an appropriate time limit to complete the reading and the tasks below. Once you have completed the task, it is important that you think about what you have done effectively, and what you need to improve. If you need to revisit key skills, reread the relevant sections of Unit 7.

293

ACTIVITY 7.17

Language acquisition by children and teenagers

The following text is a transcription of conversation between a four-year-old boy (Tom) and his teacher. They are looking at some drawings which Tom has done.

Discuss ways in which Tom and his teacher are using language here. You should refer to specific details from the transcription, relating your observations to ideas from your studies of language acquisition.

Cambridge International AS and A Level English Language 9093
Specimen Paper 4 (2014), Q3.

TEACHER	do you want to put a picture in for me today?	
TOM	i will if you want me to	
TEACHER	NO (.) do YOU want to do one?	
TOM	yeah then (.) okay	
TEACHER	i'll see what I can find to draw with (1) do you want a pencil (.) or what else have i got (.) a biro (.) which do you like better? YOU choose	5
TOM	THAT one	
TEACHER	right (.) are you going to do it on that picture there? (1) THAT would be nice	
TOM	i am going to think (2) i am good at (.) if you show me how to draw a house i will draw one	10
TEACHER	i bet you can do one on your own now	
TOM	i can't	
TEACHER	well (.) do something you can do without any help (.) because then it will be a REAL TOM PICTURE (.) i will close my eyes and you can have a draw and then you can tell me what it is	15
TOM	i can build a dinosaur.	
TEACHER	are you drawing a dinosaur?	
TOM	can't (2) close your eyes	
TEACHER	have i not to look? i will turn this way	
TOM	you can open them that way	20
TEACHER	are you going to tell me when you have finished?	
TOM	BUT no peeking	
TEACHER	i'm not peeking	
TOM	i'm watching you (.) i can see you	

TRANSCRIPTION KEY
(1) = pause in seconds (.) = micro-pause underlined = stressed sound/syllable(s)
[italics] = paralinguistic features // = speech overlap UPPER CASE = increased volume

Index

Acknowledgements

The authors and publishers acknowledge the following sources of copyright material and are grateful for the permissions granted. While every effort has been made, it has not always been possible to identify the sources of all the material used, or to trace all copyright holders. If any omissions are brought to our notice, we will be happy to include the appropriate acknowledgements on reprinting.

p. 7 excerpt from *Rescue at 21.00 Hours* by Tom Trumble, published by Penguin, used with permission of The Random House Group; p. 9 excerpt from CIE paper 8693_s09_qp_1, © Cambridge International Examinations; p. 9 excerpt from *Shooting an Elephant* by George Orwell, © 1948 by Sonia Brownwell Orwell, renewed 1962, 1989 and used with permission of A. M. Heath and Co, London. Also used by permission of the publishers, Harcourt Brace and Penguin Ltd; p. 14 excerpt from Kenya Tourist Board website © 2013 Kenya Tourist Board. All Rights Reserved; p. 19 excerpt from 'Bolivia Carnival: Wet and Wild' by Gemma Bowes, *The Guardian*, 21/09/2012, © Guardian News & Media Ltd 2012, used with permission; p. 21 excerpt from *Touching the void* by Joe Simpson, © 1989 Joe Simpson, The Random House Group. Reprinted by permission of HarperCollins Publishers; p. 23 excerpt from Star Clippers website, © 2012 Star Clippers; p. 26 'Shaaaping in God's Own Land' from *Following Fish: Travels Around the Indian Coast* by Samanth Subramanian, published by Penguin India and used with permission of Atlantic Books; p. 28 excerpt from *The Road from Coorain* by Jill Kerr Conway, published by Random House LLC with permission of The Random House Group; p. 30 excerpt from *Down The Mine (The Road to Wigan Pier)*, by George Orwell, © 1948 by Sonia Brownwell Orwell, renewed 1962, 1989 and used by permission of the publishers, Harcourt Brace and Penguin Ltd; p. 31 'Burning Lights' from *Nothing Like the Sun*, © Bella Chagall, Hodder and Stoughton; 1990 Random House, Inc., with permission; p. 34 excerpt from *A Letter To My Mother* by Chenjerai Hove, © 2007 Chenjerai Hove; p. 39 excerpt from *The Journals of Denton Welch*, edited by Michael De-la-Noy, Allison and Busby, 1984, reprinted in *The Penguin Book of Diaries* selected by Ronald Blythe, Penguin 1991, first published Viking 1989, © Ronald Blythe 1989, 0140122311, David Higham Associates Ltd on behalf of the University of Texas Press; p. 44 excerpt from *Stella in Bombay* by Kirin Naravan, with permission from

Kirin Narayan; p. 45 excerpt from *A Map to the Door of No Return*, © 2002 by Dionne Brand, Vintage Canada, a division of Random House LLC and The Wylie Agency; p. 46 excerpt from *Lost in London* by J. M. Coetzee, published by Vintage (a division of The Random House Group), David Higham Associates; p. 47 excerpt from *My Sister's Perfect Life* by Tobin Levy, 4/07/2012, © 2013 Salon Media Group, Inc., used with permission; p. 49 excerpt from *Loud Dad* by Tom Cox, 25/07/2012, Johnson & Alcock Ltd, with permission; p. 52 excerpt from 'Do Cry for Argentina' by Michael Giltz, *The Huffington Post*, 04/11/2012, used with permission from Michael Giltz; p. 54 excerpt from 'Naomi Watts' Diane is very blond very bland' by Stella Papamichael, *Radio Times*, 19/09/2013, © Immediate Media Company Limited; p. 56 excerpt from 'Restaurant review: 20 St John's' by Jay Rayner, *The Observer*, 29/01/2012, © Guardian News & Media Ltd 2012, used with permission; p. 59 'The Objectives', from *Freedom from Fear and other Writings* by Aung San Suu Kyi, edited by Michael Aris, © 1991, 1995 by Aung San Suu Kyi. Used by permission of Viking Penguin, a division of Penguin Group (USA) LLC; p. 62 excerpt from 'Mothers, stop moaning!' by Bibi Lynch, *The Guardian*, 31/03/ 2012, © Guardian News & Media Ltd 2012, used with permission; p. 64 excerpt from 'Solitude, Serenity and Salt' by Andres Schipani, *The Financial Times*, 17/08/2012, © The Financial Times Limited 2012, used with permission; p. 67 excerpt from CIE paper 8693_s11_qp_11, © Cambridge International Examinations; p. 78 excerpt from *Antartica, A Voyage into Unknown Climes*, by Nikki Gemmell, News limited, 11/11/2012, © News Limited 2013; p. 81 excerpt from *A Fragile Gaijin in Japan*, by Philip Blazdell, all rights reserved. © Roadjunky.com © 2004–2012 with permission from Philip Blazdell; p. 86 excerpt from 'The 10 most annoying concert behaviors' by Andy Greene, *Rolling Stone*, 14/02/2013, with permission from Wenner Media; p. 93 excerpt from BMW leaflet 2013, with permission from BMW Group; p. 93 excerpt from Dacia marketing brochure, © Dacia, with permission; p. 95 excerpt from *About Virunga*, http://www.wwf.org.uk/how_you_can_help/virunga/#why-virunga WWF Free GNU Free Documentation License Version 1.3, 3 November 2008; p. 108 excerpt from CIE paper 157596-november-2012-question-paper-23, © Cambridge International Examinations; p. 113 excerpt from 'The Flowers', from *The Complete Stories* by Alice Walker, The Women's Press, reprinted by permission of David Higham Associates Ltd; p. 114 excerpt from *The Handmaid's Tale* by Margaret Atwood, published by and used with permission of Vintage (a division of The Random House Group) and David Higham Associates Ltd; p. 116 'Royalty' from *Diamond Dust and Other Stories* by Anita Desai, published by Vintage (a division of The Random House Group), with permission from Rogers Coleridge and White; p. 117 excerpt from *A Prayer for the Dying* by Stewart O'Nan, published by Henry Holt and Company, Inc., with permission from The Gernert Company; p. 118 excerpt from *Enduring Love* by Ian McEwan, published by The Random House Group, © 1997 by Ian McEwan. Used by permission of Doubleday, an imprint of the Knopf Doubleday Publishing Group, a division of Random House LLC and Random House of Canada Ltd. All rights reserved; p. 121 excerpt from *Things Fall Apart* by Chinua Achebe, published by and with permission from Penguin Ltd and The Wylie Agency on behalf of the Achebe Estate; p. 121 'The Sound of the Shell', from *Lord of the Flies* by William Golding, © 1954, renewed 1982 by William Gerald Golding, Faber and Faber, and used by permission of G. P. Putnam's Sons, a division of Penguin Group (USA) LLC; p. 123 excerpt from *At the Tomb of the Inflatable Pig* by John Gimlette, published by and with permission from The Random House Group; p. 124 excerpt from *A Good Man is Hard to Find and Other Stories* by Mary Flannery O'Connor, Rutgers University Press; p. 127 excerpt from *One Day I Will Write About This Place: A Memoir*, © 2011 by Binyavanga Wainaina. Reprinted with the permission of The Permissions Company, Inc. on behalf of Graywolf Press, Minneapolis, Minnesota, www.graywolfpress.org; p. 129 excerpt from *The Great Gatsby* by F. Scott Fitzgerald, reprinted with the permission of Scribner Publishing Group, a division of Simon & Schuster, Inc. © 1925 by Charles Scribner's Sons. Copyright renewed 1953 by Frances Scott Fitzgerald Lanahan. All rights reserved; p. 130 excerpt from *The Gift of Rain* by Tan Twang Eng, Myrmidon with permission; p. 131 excerpt from *Gone With the Wind* by Margaret Mitchell, reprinted with the permission of Scribner Publishing Group, a division of Simon & Schuster, Inc. © 1936 by Macmillan Publishing Company, a division of Macmillan, Inc. Copyright renewed 1964 by Stephens Mitchell and Trust Company of Georgia as Executors of Margaret Mitchell Marsh. All rights reserved; p. 132 stage directions for opening of *All My Sons* by Arthur Miller, Penguin Classics edition; p. 133 excerpt from 'The Father' from *Will You Please Be Quiet, Please?* by Raymond Carver, The Wylie Agency and The Random House Group, © Tess Gallagher 1993, with permission; p. 141 excerpt from *1984* by George Orwell, Penguin Ltd; p. 141 excerpt from *Capture the Castle* by Dodie Smith, published by Vintage; p. 142 excerpt from *The Crow Road* by Ian Banks, published by Abacus; p. 142 excerpt from *Tracks* by Louise Erdrich, published by Flamingo; p. 142 excerpt from *The Go-Between* by L. P. Hartley, published by Penguin Ltd; p. 142 excerpt from *Pride and Prejudice* by Jane Austen; p. 142 excerpt from *Blackbird Pie* by Raymond Carver, with permission from The Wylie Agency; p. 143 excerpt from 'The Waste Land' from *Tales from a Troubled Land* by Alan Paton, Ewing Trust Company Ltd on behalf of The Estate of Alan Paton and with permission from Simon and Schuster; p. 143 excerpt from *The Turn of the Screw, and Other Short Novels* by Henry James, with permission from W.W Norton & Company Inc.; p. 144 excerpt from *Gone With the Wind* by Margaret Mitchell, reprinted with the permission of Scribner Publishing Group, a division of Simon & Schuster, Inc. © 1936 by Macmillan Publishing Company, a division of Macmillan, Inc. Copyright renewed 1964 by Stephens Mitchell and Trust Company of Georgia as Executors of Margaret Mitchell Marsh. All rights reserved; p. 145 excerpt from *The Turn of the Screw, and Other Short Novels* by Henry James, with permission from W.W Norton & Company Inc.; p. 147 excerpt from *Don't Look Now* by Daphne du Maurier, published by Penguin Ltd; p. 148 Reprinted with the permission of Scribner Publishing Group, a division of Simon & Schuster, Inc. from *The Diamond as Big as the Ritz* by F. Scott Fitzgerald. Copyright © by Charles Scribner's Sons. Copyright renewed © by Frances Scott Fitzgerald Lanahan. All rights reserved; p. 149 excerpt(s) from *Double Indemnity* by James M. Cain, © 1936 by James M.Cain. Copyright renewed 1964 by James M. Cain. Used by permission of Alfred A. Knopf, an imprint of the Knopf Doubleday Publishing Group, a division of Random House LLC. All rights reserved; p. 150 'The Visit' from *Flaming Spirit* by Sue Thakor, published by Virago; p. 156 transcript from interview by Sun International; pp. 157–8, 160 transcripts: adaptations based on the original corpus transcripts in *Exploring Spoken English* by Ronald Carter and Michael McCarthy; p. 175 excerpt from *Explaining Communication: Contemporary Theories and Exemplars* by Bryan B. Whaley and Wendy Samter, published by Taylor & Francis; p. 177 excerpt from 'Biography of Shahrukh Khan with comments from fans', http://www.oneindiamovies.com/ Greynium Information Technologies/OneIndia, with permission; p. 178 quote about language variety © The British Library Board, with permission; p. 181 From 'No easy walk to freedom' by Nelson Mandela, with kind permission from the Nelson Mandela Foundation; p. 186 excerpt from 'Are

297

Digital Media Changing Language?' by Naomi S. Baron, *Educational Leadership*, March 2009, Volume 66, Number 6, Literacy 2.0, pp. 42–46; p. 187 excerpt from 'Emma Thompson has blasted the sloppy way youngsters speak… but is she right?', *The Mirror*, 29/09/2010, Mirrorpix, used with permission; p. 189 quote from Harry Potter fan website, Snitchsseeker.com ; p. 190 excerpt from HPearth, with permission from HPearth.com; p. 190 transcript of interview with Chris Rankin, with permission from Marlowes on behalf of Chris Rankin; p. 195 excerpt from 'The Joy of Slang', with permission from BBC News; p. 195 excerpt from 'Australia: Australian Slang', with permission from TripAdvisor; p. 196 excerpt from 'Slanging Catch: Mind Your Language', 27/09/2008, *Times of India*; p. 198 excerpt from 'One in five people change their accent to sound more posh to get a job or chat someone up, survey finds', *The Daily Mail*, 02/04/2013, © Daily Mail 2013, used with permission; p. 199 excerpt from *The Cambridge Encyclopedia of the English Language* by David Crystal, published by and with permission from Cambridge University Press and David Crystal; p. 200 excerpt from the preface of *Pygmalion* by George Bernard Shaw; p. 201 excerpt from 'Yorkshire named top twang' by David Batty, *The Guardian*, 02/04/2008, © Guardian News & Media Ltd 2008, used with permission; p. 202 excerpt from 'Accent neutralisation in India', *The Guardian*, 09/02/2011, © Guardian News & Media Ltd 2011, used with permission; p. 214 'Back to Africa' from *Jamaican Labrish* by Louise Bennett, used with permission from The Estate of Louise Bennett; p. 215 excerpt from 'How regional dialects are spreading around the UK thanks to Facebook and Twitter', *The Daily Mail*, 03/09/2010, © Daily Mail 2010, used with permission; p. 223 transcript from *Global English – The History of English* with permission from The Open University; p. 225 excerpt from 'How English became the global language', Education First, with permission; p. 231 excerpt from *The Adventures of Huckleberry Finn* by Mark Twain; p. 232 excerpt from *Unrelated incidents No 3* by Tom Leonard, used with permission of Tom Leonard; p.233 excerpt from *The Cambridge Encyclopedia of the English Language* by David Crystal, published by and with permission from Cambridge University Press and David Crystal; p. 240 excerpt from 'Australian slang – a story of Australian English', © Kathryn Wells, 13 April 2010, http://australia.gov.au/about-australia/australian-story/austn-slang; p. 242 excerpt from 'How is your English? Research shows Americanisms AREN'T taking over the British language' by Chris Hastings, *The Daily Mail*, 13/03/2011, © Daily Mail 2011, used with permission; p. 245 excerpt from *Language Vitality and Endangerment*, Ad Hoc Expert Group on Endangered Languages (2003), UNESCO; p. 247 excerpt from *Is English a 'Killer Language'? The Globalisation of a Code*, Tanja Eckert, Andrea Johann, Anna Känzig, Melanie Küng, Bianca Müller, Cornelia Schwald, Laura Walder; p. 248 excerpt from 'MIT-led team finds language without numbers Amazonian tribe has no word to express "one"', Anne Trafton 24/06/2008, *MIT News*; p. 248 excerpt from 'Preventing the death of a language' by Catherine Dekeizer, *The Elephant*, St Andrews University Modern Languages Magazine; p. 248 excerpt from *Scotland's Census 2001 – Gaelic Report*, © Crown copyright 2014; p. 250 excerpt from 'World's languages dying off rapidly' by John Noble Wilford, *New York Times*, 18/09/2007, © New York Times 2007, used with permission; p. 250 excerpt from 'Final word from Cromarty: Scottish Black Isle dialect silenced forever as last native speaker dies aged 92' by Jane Borland, *The Daily Mail*, 03/10/2012, © Daily Mail 2012, used with permission; p. 269 transcript of teenagers discussing animal testing, Oxford, Cambridge and RSA Examinations, OCR with permission; p. 270 transcript of teenagers in a maths lesson, *Educating Essex*, Twofour Studios; p. 271 excerpt from Malala Yousafzai's speech at the United Nations, reproduced with permission of Curtis Brown Group Ltd, on behalf of Malala Yousafza; p. 271 excerpt from interview with American beauty queen, © NBC; p. 272 excerpt from 'From the mouths of teens', *The Independent*, 05/11/2006, © Independent 2006, used with permission; p. 279 excerpt from *English for the Natives: Discover the Grammar You Don't Know You Know* by Harry Ritchie, published by John Murray; p. 286 excerpt from 'When we stop children taking risks, do we stunt their emotional growth?' by Susie Mesure, *The Independent*, 25/05/2014, © Independent 2014, used with permission; p. 287 excerpt from CIE 129299-9093-specimen-paper-3-2014, © Cambridge International Examinations; p. 287 Text A transcribed from *Desert Island Discs*, Sunday 17 January 2010, BBC; p. 288 Text B from 'The Art of Fiction No. 201' by Nathaniel Rich and James Ellory, *The Paris Review*, 2011; p. 289 excerpt from 129301-9093-specimen-paper-4-2014, © Cambridge International Examinations; p. 292 excerpt from British Library case study *Minority Ethnic English*, © The British Library Board, with permission; p. 292 excerpt from 'English as a Global Language' by Parimal-P.-Gohil, *International Journal for Research in Education*, RET Academy for International Journals of Multidisciplinary Research, with permission; p. 293 excerpt from CIE paper 129301-9093-specimen-paper-4-2014, © Cambridge International Examinations.

Photographs: p. 1 Kathy deWitt/Alamy; p. 10 Royal Geographical Society/Alamy; p. 14 Images of Africa Photobank/Alamy; p. 21 Craig Lovell/Eagle Visions Photography/Alamy; p. 24 Hemis/Alamy; p. 28 John White Photos/Alamy; p. 37 The Keasbury-Gordon Photograph Archive/Alamy; p. 41 GL Archive/Alamy; pp. 46, 202 david pearson/Alamy; p. 56 Directphoto Collection/Alamy; p. 69 Jake Lyell/Alamy; p. 75 Katharine Andriotis/Alamy; p. 81 Ei Katsumata/Alamy; p. 86 James Davies/Alamy; p. 91 Andrew Fox/Alamy; p. 93 RENAULT MARKETING 3DCOMMERCE; p. 95 imageBROKER/Alamy; p. 100 Gallo Images/Alamy; p. 103 moodboard/SuperStock; p. 116 Ladi Kirn/Alamy; p. 125 Exactostock/SuperStock; p. 126 Enigma/Alamy; p. 129 Randy Duchaine/Alamy; p. 131 Granamour Weems Collection/Alamy; p. 135 Supated/Alamy; p. 145 ClassicStock/Alamy; p. 148 John Barger/Alamy; p. 151 Grant Rooney/Alamy; p. 152L Rebecca Erol/Alamy; p. 152M Andy Chadwick/Alamy; p. 152R Neil McAllister/Alamy; p. 164 NASA Collection/Alamy; p. 170 MARC ROMANELLI/Alamy; p. 177 Dinodia Photos/Alamy; p. 179 GL Archive/Alamy; p. 181 epa european pressphoto agency b.v./Alamy; p. 186 Nigel Noyes/Alamy; p. 188 kolvenbach/Alamy; p. 190 Harry Page/Alamy; p. 196 Rob Murray/CartoonStock; p. 203 Blend Images/Alamy; p. 211 Arterra Picture Library/Alamy; p. 219 Masterpics/Alamy; p. 223 Robin Beckham/BEEPstock/Alamy; p. 230 ZUMA Press, Inc./Alamy; p. 236 The Art Archive/Alamy; p. 238 Africa Media Online/Alamy; p. 248 Tim Graham/Alamy; p. 251 TongRo Images/Alamy; p. 261 jacky chapman/Alamy; p. 263 Finnbarr Webster/Alamy; p. 272 Janine Wiedel Photolibrary/Alamy; p. 275 Graham Light/Alamy.

Illustrations: pp. 166, 172, 198, 212, 222 Peter Bull Art Studio; p. 212 Dr. Bruce Weems, Oklahoma Atlas Institute, East Central University Department of Cartography and Geography.